CHOICE OF LAW

CASES AND MATERIALS FOR A CONCISE COURSE ON CONFLICT OF LAWS

■ ■ ■

by

Aaron D. Twerski
Irwin & Jill Cohen Professor of Law
Brooklyn Law School

Neil B. Cohen
Jeffrey D. Forchelli Professor of Law
Brooklyn Law School

AMERICAN CASEBOOK SERIES®

WEST ACADEMIC PUBLISHING

Mat #41655776

American Casebook Series is a trademark registered in the U.S. Patent and Trademark Office.

© 2015 LEG, Inc. d/b/a West Academic
    444 Cedar Street, Suite 700
    St. Paul, MN 55101
    1-877-888-1330

West, West Academic Publishing, and West Academic are trademarks of West Publishing Corporation, used under license.

Printed in the United States of America

ISBN: 978-1-62810-131-7

*To my wife, Kreindel, my children, grandchildren,
and great-grandchildren*

ADT

To Amy, Emily, Liz, and Claudia

NBC

*We also express our gratitude to the Deans of Brooklyn
Law School, Joan G. Wexler and Nick Allard,
who supported this work.*

PREFACE

We prepared these materials for two reasons. First, we were appalled by the large number of students who leave law school without having been exposed to choice-of-law concepts. This is not an esoteric topic with marginal relevance to the everyday practice of law. Rather, there are few lawyers who do not need to address matters with multi-state connections (whether in tort, contract, family law, or another subject) with considerable frequency. With heavy competing curriculum demands, students often do not feel able to devote three or four credits to a comprehensive course in conflict of laws. To address that situation, these materials are tailored to a two-credit course that focuses on choice of law. This narrower focus enables us to keep the length of the materials manageable while exploring choice of law theories in considerable depth.

Second, we were struck by the reliance in many of the existing casebooks on cases that are decades old and that address issues in the context of antiquated laws with little relevance to today's problems. Some of those old chestnuts provide important background for the more modern cases, but others are simply anachronistic. In the area of tort law, one of the prime focuses of these materials, we have largely replaced the old chestnuts with cases arising from modern tort reform, which has brought about significant differences in both statutory and common law doctrines among the states. Similarly, the contracts materials emphasize the increasing frequency with which transactions cross state and national borders and address the increasing role of the autonomy of parties to choose the law governing their contract.

The authors have twice co-taught Conflict of Laws using these materials. We had a blast teaching the course and students tell us that they loved the materials. If you enjoy this book as much as we enjoyed writing it, we will count this endeavor as a huge success.

AARON D. TWERSKI
NEIL B. COHEN

December 1, 2014

v

NOTES AND ACKNOWLEDGMENTS

In presenting the materials in this book, the authors have used the following conventions:

Cases. Some opinions are abridged (without indication of the omitted portions) or presented with adjustments in format and style. Descriptions and restatements of the facts of a case or of omitted portions of a case, if prepared by the authors, are enclosed in brackets. Statutory references in an opinion are as stated by the court.

Citations. In general, parallel citations to cases have been omitted. A citation to a decision does not normally include an indication of subsequent case history having no effect on the merit or authority of the decision cited.

The authors acknowledge the permission granted by the University of Chicago Law School to reprint an excerpt from Brainerd Currie, Married Women's Contracts: A Study in Conflict-of-Laws Method, 25 U. Chi. L. Rev. 227 (1958), and by Gale, a part of Cengage Learning, Inc., to reprint an excerpt from West's Encyclopedia of American Law.

SUMMARY OF CONTENTS

TABLE OF CONTENTS

TABLE OF CASES

The principal cases are in bold type.

CHOICE OF LAW

CASES AND MATERIALS FOR A CONCISE COURSE ON CONFLICT OF LAWS

INTRODUCTION

■ ■ ■

Hang on to your hat. We give you fair warning that a course in Conflict of Laws is a roller-coaster ride. The United States of America is comprised of fifty sovereign states. In many areas common law doctrine is close to identical. But in many areas both common law and statutory law are very, very different. We live our lives basically oblivious to state lines. One does not need a passport or a visa to travel from New York to Jersey or from Illinois to California. Thus, when we cross state lines we pay little attention to the fact that we may be moving into a jurisdiction that has a radically different way of resolving tort, contract or property disputes. Or if we act in our own home state and deal with domiciliaries of other states bringing about repercussions in another state we don't consider the possibility that the law of the other state may govern. As you shall see, the possibilities for conflict are endless. One state may allow unlimited damages for pain and suffering in a tort action. Another state may limit recover for pain and suffering to $250, 000. One state may find a rate of interest usurious and not recoverable. Another state may find it acceptable. One state may give the property of someone who dies intestate to the decedent's spouse. Another may split the proceeds between the sibling and wife.

Hundreds of millions, if not billions of dollars in dispute are resolved one way or another depending on the choice-of-law rules of a given jurisdiction. You might think that all this would, after more than two hundred years of federalism, have been worked out by the courts. The very opposite is true. The choice-of-law rules (if you can call them that) of the fifty states differ substantially from state to state. Even when states appear to apply the same choice-of-law approach, the differences in interpretation and application may lead to surprisingly differing results.

The role of legal scholarship has had a remarkable influence on the courts. The materials will include excerpts from the leading law review articles and books on the subject. Conflict of Laws has been blessed with the writings of brilliant scholars. The debate among them represents some of the very best in legal scholarship. You will find reference to these writings throughout this book. It will be impossible, however, to cover the full panoply of scholarly output in a course of short duration.

The authors have twice co-taught Conflicts of Laws. In preparing for class, they would spend hours talking about the cases in Professor Twerski's office. In this book, we share some of our discussions with you. Hence, you will find "Office Talk" memoranda sprinkled throughout this book. They were fun to record and should be fun to read.

1

These materials are fashioned for a two-hour course that focuses primarily on choice of law problems in torts, contracts and property. We will briefly cover such issues as domestic relations, and estates and trusts. We will cover very briefly some aspects of full faith and credit jurisdiction, but hopefully, these issues have been covered in your first year civil procedure course. When it comes to choice of law in the modern era, we will present cases on the same issue that reach opposite results. You will come to see that there is a great diversity in the opinions and that it is very hard to predict results. When you decide where to file suit, you will have to consider not only which state has the better substantive law, but also the state's choice of law rules.

Thus, rather than attempting to be encyclopedic, this book is focused on the various choice of law approaches as they play out in specific areas of litigation. When you have run the gamut, you should get a good sense of the complexity of the field. If you will be frustrated by the lack of predictability, we can only tell you that we share your frustration.

CHAPTER 1

TRADITIONAL APPROACHES TO CHOICE OF LAW—THE FIRST RESTATEMENT OF CONFLICT OF LAWS

∎ ∎ ∎

A. TORTS

Almost every conflict of laws casebook begins its discussion of traditional approaches to conflict of laws with *Alabama Great Southern R.R. Co. v. Carroll.* It is a classic application of the traditional approach applied to torts and some would say that it is the poster child case for what was wrong with that approach. As you read this case, ask yourself whether it makes sense? How would *you* have decided the case?

ALABAMA GREAT SOUTHERN R.R. CO. V. CARROLL
11 So. 803 (Ala. 1892)

McCLELLAN, J.

The plaintiff, W. D. Carroll, is, and was at the time of entering into the service of the defendant, the Alabama Great Southern Railroad Company, and at the time of being injured in that service, a citizen of Alabama. The defendant is an Alabama corporation, operating a railroad extending from Chattanooga, in the state of Tennessee, through Alabama to Meridian, in the state of Mississippi. At the time of the casualty complained of plaintiff was in the service of the defendant in the capacity of brakeman on freight trains running from Birmingham, Ala., to Meridian, Miss., under a contract which was made in the state of Alabama. The injury was caused by the breaking of a link between two cars in a freight train which was proceeding from Birmingham to Meridian. The point at which the link broke and the injury was suffered was in the state of Mississippi. The evidence tended to show that the link which broke was a defective link, and that it was in a defective condition when the train left Birmingham. . . . The evidence went also to show that the defect in this link consisted in or resulted from its having been bent while cold; that this tended to weaken the iron, and in this instance had cracked the link somewhat on the outer curve of the bend, and that the link broke at the point of this crack. It was shown to be the duty of certain employees of defendant stationed along its line to inspect the links attached to cars to be put in trains, or forming the

3

couplings between cars in trains at Chattanooga, Birmingham, and some points between Birmingham and the place where this link broke, and also that it was the duty of the conductor of freight trains, and the other train men, to maintain such inspection as occasion afforded throughout the runs or trips of such trains; and the evidence affords ground for inference that there was a negligent omission on the part of such employees to perform this duty, or, if performed, the failure to discover the defect in, and to remove, this link was the result of negligence. . . .

[T]he use of that link in coupling the foreign car to the defendant's train, and also in its use throughout the voyage from Chattanooga into Mississippi, was due to the negligence of employees of the defendant. . . . and also of the train men charged with the duty of inspection as the train was *en route*. There is no pretense that the defendant had not been sufficiently careful in the selection of these inspectors, or that they were incompetent. It is not pretended that they were insufficient in number, or stationed at points too widely separated along the line. There is no such idea advanced as that the defendant was negligent in the purchasing of links of adequate strength, and supplying them to these inspectors and to trains generally, or that there was any necessity for the continued use of this link upon a discovery of its defective condition; but, to the contrary, it is affirmatively shown that the defendant purchased and supplied its trains and employees with all necessary links of good quality and perfect condition to be used in its trains, to supply the places of links which became defective from use, and to substitute for defective links coming to this road with foreign cars. The only negligence, in other words and in short, which finds support, by direction or inference, in any tendency of the evidence, is that of persons whose duty it was to inspect the links of the train, and remove such as were defective, and replace them with others which were not defective. This was the negligence, not of the master, the defendant, but of fellow servants of the plaintiff, for which at common law the defendant is not liable. Thus it is said in McKinney on Fellow Servants, § 127: "It is a very common thing for train hands to receive injury through the negligence of persons employed by the company to inspect their cars to discover defects and repair them. The weight of authority, perhaps, is to the effect that the negligence of such employees in the performance of such duties cannot be attributed to the company, and it is consequently not liable for it."

Proceeding, therefore, on the presumptions we are authorized to indulge, and also on the evidence adduced in this case as to the law of Mississippi in this connection, and upon the testimony most favorable to the plaintiff as to the cause of his injuries, we feel entirely safe in declaring that plaintiff has shown no cause of action under the common law as it is understood and applied both here and in the state of Mississippi.

It is, however, further contended that the plaintiff, if his evidence be believed, has made out a case for the recovery sought under the employers' liability act of Alabama, it being clearly shown that there is no such or similar law of force in the state of Mississippi. Considering this position in the abstract,-that is, dissociated from the facts of this particular case, which are supposed to exert an important influence upon it,-there cannot be two opinions as to its being unsound and untenable. So looked at, we do not understand appellee's counsel even to deny either the proposition or its application to this case,-that there can be no recovery in one state for injuries to the person sustained in another, unless the infliction of the injuries is actionable under the law of the state in which they were received. Certainly this is the well-established rule of law, subject, in some jurisdictions, to the qualification that the infliction of the injuries would also support an action in the state where the suit is brought had they been received within that state.

But it is claimed that the facts of this case take it out of the general rule which the authorities cited above abundantly support, and authorize the courts of Alabama to subject the defendant to the payment of damages under § 2590 of the Code, although the injuries counted on were sustained in Mississippi under circumstances which involved no liability on the defendant by the laws of that state. This insistence is, in the first instance, based on that aspect of the evidence which goes to show that the negligence which produced the casualty transpired in Alabama, and the theory that, wherever the consequences of that negligence manifested itself, a recovery can be had in Alabama. We are referred to no authority in support of this proposition, and exhaustive investigation on our part has failed to disclose any. There are at least two well-considered cases against it. . . .

It is admitted, or at least cannot be denied, that negligence of duty unproductive of damnifying results will not authorize or support a recovery. Up to the time this train passed out of Alabama no injury had resulted. For all that occurred in Alabama, therefore, no cause of action whatever arose. The fact which created the right to sue,-the injury,-without which confessedly no action would lie anywhere, transpired in the state of Mississippi. It was in that state, therefore, necessarily that the cause of action, if any, arose; and whether a cause of action arose and existed at all, or not, must in all reason be determined by the law which obtained at the time and place when and where the fact which is relied on to justify a recovery transpired. § 2590 of the Code of Alabama had no efficacy beyond the lines of Alabama. It cannot be allowed to operate upon facts occurring in another state, so as to evolve out of them rights and liabilities which do not exist under the law of that state, which is of course paramount in the premises. Where the facts occur in Alabama, and a liability becomes fixed in Alabama, it may be enforced in another state having like enactments, or whose policy is not opposed to the spirit of such enactments; but this is quite a different matter. This is but enforcing the statute upon facts to which it is applicable, all of which occurred within the territory for the government of which it was enacted. § 2590 of the Code, in other words, is to be interpreted in the light of universally recognized principles of private, international, or interstate law, as if its operation had been expressly limited to this state, and as if its first line read as follows: "When a personal injury is received in Alabama by a servant or employee," etc. The negligent infliction of an injury here, under statutory circumstances, creates a right of action here, which, being transitory, may be enforced in any other state or country the comity of which admits of it; but for an injury inflicted elsewhere than in Alabama our statute gives no right of recovery, and the aggrieved party must look to the local law to ascertain what his rights are. Under that law this plaintiff had no cause of action, as we have seen, and hence he has no rights which our courts can enforce, unless it be upon a consideration to be presently adverted to. We have not been inattentive to the suggestions of counsel in this connection, which are based upon that rule of the statutory and common criminal law under which a murderer is punishable where the fatal blow is delivered, regardless of the place where death ensues Green v. State, 66 Ala. 40. This principle is patently without application here. There would be some analogy if the plaintiff had been stricken in Alabama, and suffered in Mississippi, which is not the fact. There is however, an analogy which is afforded by the criminal law, but which points away from the conclusion appellee's counsel desire us to reach. This is found in that well-established doctrine of criminal law that where the unlawful act is committed in one jurisdiction or state, and takes effect-produces the result which it is the purpose of the law to prevent, or, it having ensued, punish for-in another jurisdiction or state, the crime is deemed to have been committed and is punished in that jurisdiction or state in which the result is manifested, and not where the act was committed. 1 Bish. Crim. Law, § 110 et seq.; 1 Bish. Crim. Proc. § 53 et seq.

Another consideration,-that referred to above,-it is insisted, entitles this plaintiff to recover here under the employers' liability act for an injury inflicted beyond the territorial operation of that act. This is claimed upon the fact that at the time plaintiff was injured he was in the discharge of duties which rested on him by the terms of a contract between him and the defendant, which had been entered into in Alabama, and hence was an Alabama contract, in connection with the facts that plaintiff was and is a citizen of this state, and the defendant is an Alabama corporation. These latter facts-of citizenship and domicile, respectively, of plaintiff and defendant-are of no importance in this connection, it seems to us, further than this: they may tend to show that the contract was made here, which is not controverted and, if the plaintiff has a cause of action at all, he, by reason of them, may prosecute it in our courts. They have no bearing on the primary question of the existence of a cause of action, and, as that is the question before us, we need not further advert to the fact of plaintiff's citizenship or defendant's domicile.

The contract was that plaintiff should serve the defendant in the capacity of a brakeman on its freight trains between Birmingham, Ala., and Meridian, Miss., and should receive as compensation a stipulated sum for each trip from Birmingham to Meridian and return. The theory is that the employers' liability act became a part of this contract, that the duties and liabilities which it prescribes became contractual duties and liabilities, or duties and liabilities springing out of the contract, and that these duties attended upon the execution whenever its performance was required, in Mississippi as well as in Alabama, and that the liability prescribed for a failure to perform any of such duties attached upon such failure and consequent injury wherever it occurred, and was enforceable here, because imposed by an Alabama contract, notwithstanding the remission of duty and the resulting injury occurred in Mississippi, under whose laws no liability was incurred by such remission. The argument is that a contract for service is a condition precedent to the application of the statute, and that, "as soon as the contract is made, the rights and obligations of the parties under the employers' act "became vested and fixed," so that "no subsequent repeal of the law could deprive the injured party of his rights, nor discharge the master from his liabilities," etc. If this argument is sound, and it is sound if the duties and liabilities prescribed by the act can be said to be contractual duties and obligations at all, it would lead to conclusions, the possibility of which has not hitherto been suggested by any court or law writer, and which, to say the least, would be astounding to the profession. . . .

[T]he duties and liabilities incident to the relation between the plaintiff and the defendant, which are involved in this case, are not imposed by, and do not rest in our spring from, the contract between the parties. The only office of the contract, under § 2590 of the Code, is the establishment of a relation between them,-that of master and servant; and it is upon that relation, that incident or consequence of the contract, and not upon the rights of the parties under the contract, that our statute operates. The law is not concerned with the contractual stipulations, except in so far as to determine from them that the relation upon which it is to operate exists. Finding this relation, the statute imposes certain duties and liabilities on the parties to it, wholly regardless of the stipulations of the contract as to the rights of the parties under it, and, it may be, in the teeth of such stipulations. It is the purpose of the statute, and must be the limit of its operation, to govern persons standing in the relation of master and servants to each other, in respect of their conduct in certain particulars within the state of Alabama. Mississippi has the same right to establish governmental rules for such persons within her borders as Alabama, and she has established rules which are different from those of our law; and the conduct of such persons towards each other is, when its legality is brought in question, to be adjudged by the rules of the one or the other state, as it falls territorially within the one or the other. . . .

The foregoing views will suffice to indicate the grounds of our opinion that the rights of this plaintiff are determinable solely by the law of the state of Mississippi, and of our conclusion that upon no aspect or tendency of the evidence as to the circumstances under which the injury was sustained, and as to the laws of Mississippi obtaining in the premises, was the plaintiff entitled to recover. . . . For the error in refusing to instruct the jury to find for the defendant,. . . . the judgment is reversed, and the cause will be remanded.

The fellow servant rule appears Draconian viewed with twenty-first century eyes, but historically it drew support from respected jurists. Consider the following:

> The fellow-servant rule first appeared in 1837, in Great Britain, in *Priestly v. Fowler* (150 Eng. Rep. 1030 [1837]). In that case, an over-loaded delivery van driven by one employee overturned and fractured the leg of another employee. The injured employee's lawsuit against their common employer succeeded, but it was overturned by the Court of Exchequer. The magistrate, Lord Abinger, scoldingly held that the injured employee "must have known as well as his master, and probably better" about the risks he undertook in van delivery. Moreover, concerns about the public good steeled the magistrate against the plaintiff. If suits such as Fowler were permitted against employers, workers would soon forget about their duty not to hurt themselves.

> U.S. law was quick to learn this lesson in employers' immunity to liability. Only five years later, in 1842, the Supreme Judicial Court of Massachusetts announced it in the landmark case *Farwell v. Boston & Worcester R.R.*, 45 Mass. (4 Met.) 49. The case came during the nation's greatest burst of industrial development, as it transformed from an agrarian society to an industrial society. Few state judges appreciated this shift as keenly as the Massachusetts court's chief justice, Lemuel Shaw (1781–1861). Nearing the end of a remarkable life in law, Shaw grasped economic considerations better than social ones, and his plainspoken opinions were tremendously influential.

> Chief Justice Shaw's decision in *Farwell* had blunt logic. Although a railroad employee had lost his hand through the negligence of a fellow worker, Shaw looked beyond the loss of limb to the dangerous precedent that a finding of employer liability would

pose to growing industries at a crucial moment in history. He wanted to encourage this growth. So he imported the fellow-servant rule, justifying it in purely economic terms. Whereas Lord Abinger had reminded employees of their duty to be cautious, Shaw observed that employee alertness was also compensated: workers in more dangerous jobs would be taken care of by the market, through higher wages. Furthermore, employees entered such jobs voluntarily and therefore chose to put themselves at risk. Thus, a contract of employment existed, and it could not place liability on the employer's shoulders except when the employer was personally responsible—and certainly not when a fellow employee was clearly to blame for the injury.

The reverberations of this decision were felt throughout the rest of the nineteenth century. Shaw was not the only judge whose sympathies lay with industry. As more courts adopted the fellow-servant rule, the doctrine had a drastic effect on workers. An 1858 Illinois Supreme Court decision succinctly echoed Shaw's reasoning: "[E]ach servant, when he engages in a particular service, calculates the hazards incident to it, and contracts accordingly. This we see every day—dangerous service generally receiving higher compensation than a service unattended with danger or any considerable risk of life or limb" (*Illinois Central R.R. v. Cox*, 21 Ill. 20).

West's Encyclopedia of American Law 12 Vols., 1E. © 1997 Gale, a part of Cengage Learning, Inc. Reproduced by permission. www.cengage.com/permissions.

———————

1.   Why should a court ever pay attention to the law of another jurisdiction? If a court has jurisdiction over the parties, why not simply apply its own law? This question is essentially the basis for this entire course.

2.   Where did the negligence take place in *Alabama Great Southern R.R.*?

3.   The Restatement (First) of Conflict of Laws (1934), for which Professor Joseph H. Beale was the Reporter, provides that the law of "the place of the wrong" governs most issues with respect to an alleged tort. See, *e.g.*, Restatement (First), §§ 378 *et seq.* According to Section 377 of that Restatement:

The place of the wrong is in the state where the last event necessary to make an actor liable for an alleged tort takes place.

Why the "last event" and not the "first event"? For Beale, the answer lay in the view that in a conflicts case a "right" is vested at the time it matures into a tort and that a foreign court merely enforces that vested right. Beale was in good company. Such icons of the law as Justices Story and Holmes concurred. For example in *Slater v. Mexican Nat'l R.R.*, 194 U.S. 120 (1904), Justice Holmes said "the theory of the foreign suit is that, although the act complained of was subject to no law having force in the forum, it gave rise to an obligation, an *obligatio*, which like other obligations, follows the person, and may be enforced wherever the person may be found."

4. Many current scholars think that this theory is fundamentally flawed. Do you agree? What are the flaws?

5. There are good policy reasons for an Alabama court to apply Alabama law here. Other than mechanical application of *lex loci delicti* (a Latin maxim for the place-of-injury rule for determining the governing law in tort cases), are there good policy reasons to apply Mississippi law? For early commentary on vested rights, see Cavers, A Critique of the Choice-of-Law Problem, 47 Harv. L. Rev. 173 (1933); Cook, The Logical and Legal Bases of the Conflict of Laws 20–21 (1942) (arguing that rights are not vested but that "a state when confronted by a case involving foreign elements always applies its law but in doing so adopts . . . a rule of decision identical . . . to a rule of decision found in the system of law . . . in force in another state."); Rheinstein, The Place of the Wrong: A Study in the Method of Case Law, 19 Tulane L. Rev. 4. (1944) (place of wrong conforms to the reasonable expectations of the parties). For a very different "rights based" view of choice of law, see Brilmayer, Rights, Fairness, and Choice of Law, 98 Yale L. J. 1277 (1989).

B. CONTRACTS

MILLIKEN V. PRATT
125 Mass. 374 (1878)

The validity of a contract, even as regards the capacity of the parties, is generally to be determined by the law of the state in which it is made.

If an inhabitant of this Commonwealth buys goods personally in another state, or orders them by letter mailed here, and they are delivered to a carrier for him there, the contract is made in that state.

A contract of guaranty, signed in this Commonwealth and sent by mail to another state, and assented to and acted on there, for the price of goods sold there, is made in that state.

A contract, made in another state by a married woman domiciled here, which a married woman was not at the time capable of making under the law of this Commonwealth, but was then allowed by the law of that state to make, and which she could now lawfully make in this Commonwealth, will sustain an action against her in our courts, although the contract was made by letter sent from her here to the other party there.

CONTRACT to recover $500 and interest from January 6, 1872. Writ dated June 30, 1875. The case was submitted to the Superior Court on agreed facts, in substance as follows:

The plaintiffs are partners doing business in Portland, Maine, under the firm name of Deering, Milliken & Co. The defendant is and has been since 1850, the wife of Daniel Pratt, and both have always resided in Massachusetts. In 1870, Daniel, who was then doing business in Massachusetts, applied to the plaintiffs at Portland for credit, and they required of him, as a condition of granting the same, a guaranty from the defendant to the amount of five hundred dollars, and accordingly he procured from his wife the following instrument:

"Portland, January 29, 1870. In consideration of one dollar paid by Deering, Milliken & Co., receipt of which is hereby acknowledged, I guarantee the payment to them by Daniel Pratt of the sum of five hundred dollars, from time to time as he may want—this to be a continuing guaranty. Sarah A. Pratt."

This instrument was executed by the defendant two or three days after its date, at her home in Massachusetts, and there delivered by her to her husband, who sent it by mail from Massachusetts to the plaintiffs in Portland; and the plaintiffs received it from the post office in Portland early in February, 1870.

The plaintiffs subsequently sold and delivered goods to Daniel from time to time until October 7, 1871, and charged the same to him, and, if competent, it may be taken to be true, that in so doing they relied upon the guaranty. Between February, 1870, and September 1, 1871, they sold and delivered goods to him on credit to an amount largely exceeding $500, which were fully settled and paid for by him. This action is brought for goods sold from September 1, 1871, to October 7, 1871, inclusive, amounting to $860.12, upon which he paid $300, leaving a balance due of $560.12. The one dollar mentioned in the guaranty was not paid, and the only consideration moving to the defendant therefor was the giving of credit by the plaintiffs to her husband. Some of the goods were selected personally by Daniel at the plaintiffs' store in Portland, others were ordered by letters mailed by Daniel from Massachusetts to the plaintiffs at Portland, and all were sent by the plaintiffs by express from Portland to Daniel in Massachusetts, who paid all express charges. The parties were cognizant of the facts. . . .

GRAY, C. J.

The general rule is that the validity of a contract is to be determined by the law of the state in which it is made; if it is valid there, it is deemed valid everywhere, and will sustain an action in the courts of a state whose laws do not permit such a contract. . . . Even a contract expressly prohibited by the statutes of the state in which the suit is brought, if not in itself immoral, is not necessarily nor usually deemed so invalid that the comity of the state, as administered by its courts, will refuse to entertain an action on such a contract made by one of its own citizens abroad in a state the laws of which permit it. . . .

If the contract is completed in another state, it makes no difference in principle whether the citizen of this state goes in person, or sends an agent, or writes a letter, across the boundary line between the two states. . . . So if a person residing in this state signs and transmits, either by a messenger or through the post-office, to a person in another state, a written contract, which requires no special forms or solemnities in its execution, and no signature of the person to whom it is addressed, and is assented to and acted on by him there, the contract is made there, just as if the writer personally took the executed contract into the other state, or wrote and signed it there; and it is no objection to the maintenance of an action thereon here, that such a contract is prohibited by the law of this Commonwealth. . . .

The guaranty, bearing date of Portland, in the State of Maine, was executed by the defendant, a married woman, having her home in this Commonwealth, as collateral security for the liability of her husband for goods sold by the plaintiffs to him, and was sent by her through him by mail to the plaintiffs at Portland. The sales of the goods ordered by him from the plaintiffs at Portland, and there delivered by them to him in person, or to a carrier for him, were made in the State of Maine. . . . The contract between the defendant and the plaintiffs was complete when the guaranty had been received and acted on by them at Portland, and not before. . . . It must therefore be treated as made and to be performed in the State of Maine.

The law of Maine authorized a married woman to bind herself by any contract as if she were unmarried. St. of Maine of 1866, c. 52. (Citation omitted). The law of Massachusetts, as then existing, did not allow her to enter into a contract as surety or for the accommodation of her husband . . . any third person. Gen. Sts. c. 108, § 3. Since the making of the contract sued on, and before the bringing of this action, the law of this Commonwealth has been changed, so as to enable married women to make such contracts. St. 1874, c. 184. *Major v. Holmes*, 124 Mass. 108. *Kenworthy v. Sawyer*, 125 Mass. 28.

The question therefore is, whether a contract made in another state by a married woman domiciled here, which a married woman was not at the time capable of making under the law of this Commonwealth, but was then allowed by the law of that state to make, and which she could now lawfully make in this Commonwealth, will sustain an action against her in our courts.

It has been often stated by commentators that the law of the domicil, regulating the capacity of a person, accompanies and governs the person everywhere. But this statement, in modern times at least, is subject to many qualifications; and the opinions of foreign jurists upon the subject, the principal of which are collected in the treatises of Mr. Justice Story and of Dr. Francis Wharton on the Conflict of Laws, are too varying and contradictory to control the general current of the English and American authorities in favor of holding that a contract, which by the law of the place is recognized as lawfully made by a capable person, is valid everywhere, although the person would not, under the law of his domicil, be deemed capable of making it. . . .

Mr. Justice Story, in his Commentaries on the Conflict of Laws, after elaborate consideration of the authorities, arrives at the conclusion that "in regard to questions of minority or majority, competency or incompetency to marry, incapacities incident to coverture, guardianship, emancipation, and other personal qualities and disabilities, the law of the domicil of birth, or the law of any other acquired and fixed domicil, is not generally to govern, but the *lex loci contractûs aut actûs*, the law of the place where the contract is made, or the act done;" or as he elsewhere sums it up, "although foreign jurists generally hold that the law of the domicil ought to govern in regard to the capacity of persons to contract; yet the common law holds a different doctrine, namely, that the *lex loci contractûs* is to govern." Story Confl. §§ 103, 241. So Chancellor Kent, although in some passages of the text of his Commentaries he seems to incline to the doctrine of the civilians, yet in the notes afterwards added unequivocally concurs in the conclusion of Mr. Justice Story. 2 Kent Com. 233 note, 458, 459 & note.

In *Pearl v. Hansborough*, 9 Humph. 426, the rule was carried so far as to hold that where a married woman domiciled with her husband in the State of Mississippi, by the law of which a purchase by a married woman was valid and the property purchased went to her separate use, bought personal property in Tennessee, by the law of which married women were incapable of contracting, the contract of purchase was void and could not be enforced in Tennessee. Some authorities, on the other hand, would uphold a contract made by a party capable by the law of his domicil, though incapable by the law of the place of the contract. . . .

The principal reasons on which continental jurists have maintained that personal laws of the domicil, affecting the status and capacity of all inhabitants of a particular class, bind them wherever they may go, appear to have been that each state has the rightful power of regulating the status and condition of its subjects, and, being best acquainted with the circumstances of climate, race, character, manners and customs, can best judge at what age young persons may begin to act for themselves, and whether and how far married women may act independently of their husbands; that laws limiting the capacity of infants. . . . of married women are intended for their protection, and cannot therefore be dispensed with by their agreement; that all civilized states recognize the incapacity of infants and married women; and that a person, dealing with either, ordinarily has notice, by the apparent age or sex, that the person is likely to be of a class whom the laws protect, and is thus put upon inquiry how far, by the law of the domicil of the person, the protection extends.

On the other hand, it is only by the comity of other states that laws can operate beyond the limit of the state that makes them. In the great majority of cases, especially in this country, where it is so common to travel, or to transact business through agents, or to correspond by letter, from one state to another, it is more just, as well as more convenient, to have regard to the law of the place of the contract, as a uniform rule operating on all contracts of the same kind, and which the contracting parties may be presumed to have in contemplation when making their contracts, than to require them at their peril to know the domicil of those with whom they deal, and to ascertain the law of that domicil, however remote, which in many cases could not be done without such delay as would greatly cripple the power of contracting abroad at all.

As the law of another state can neither operate nor be executed in this state by its own force, but only by the comity of this state, its operation and enforcement here may be restricted by positive prohibition of statute. A state may always by express enactment protect itself from being obliged to enforce in its courts contracts made abroad by its citizens, which are not authorized by its own laws. Under the French code, for instance, which enacts that the laws regulating the status and capacity of persons shall bind French subjects, even when living in a foreign country, a French court cannot enforce a contract made by a Frenchman abroad, which he is incapable of making by the law of France. See Westlake, §§ 399, 400.

It is possible also that in a state where the common law prevailed in full force, by which a married woman was deemed incapable of binding herself by any contract whatever, it might be inferred that such an utter incapacity, lasting throughout the joint lives of husband and wife, must be considered as so fixed by the settled policy of the state, for the protection of its own citizens, that it could not be held by the courts of that state to yield to the law of another state in which she might undertake to contract.

But it is not true at the present day that all civilized states recognize the absolute incapacity of married women to make contracts. The tendency of modern legislation is to enlarge their capacity in this respect, and in many states they have nearly or quite the same powers as if unmarried. In Massachusetts, even at the time of the making of the contract in question, a married woman was vested by statute with a very extensive power to carry on business by herself, and to bind herself by contracts with regard to her own property, business and earnings, and, before the bringing of the present action, the power had been extended so as to include the making of all kinds of contracts, with any person but her husband, as if she were unmarried. There is therefore no reason of public policy which should prevent the maintenance of this action.

Judgment for the plaintiffs.

---

1. A contract may touch a number of jurisdictions. For example, it may be formed in State A but call for performance in State B. Why should the place of formation (which is not always obvious in an era of easy communication between people in different locations) determine the governing law rather than the place of performance or some other jurisdiction to which the contract bears a close relationship?

2. *Milliken v. Pratt* is not about the contract itself so much as it is about the capacity of one of the parties to enter into it. Aren't the commentators who argue that matters of capacity should be governed by the law of the domicile (notwithstanding what law governs the contract itself) correct?

3. The opinion in *Milliken* concludes that the payment of one dollar mentioned in the guaranty contract was not paid and implicitly treats the guaranty contract as a unilateral contract, formed when (and where) the plaintiffs sold goods to Daniel Pratt in reliance on the guaranty. Do you agree with that analysis? If the court found that the dollar had been paid, would that make the guaranty a bilateral contract formed in Massachusetts? Would that mean that Massachusetts law would govern?

4. What if the creditor had been from Massachusetts and Mrs. Milliken had been a Maine domiciliary and the contract was entered into in Massachusetts. Should Massachusetts law apply?

5. The First Restatement of Conflict of Laws put it this way:

§ 332.   Law Governing Validity of Contract.

The law of the place of contracting determines the validity and effect of a promise with respect to

(a) capacity to make the contract:

(b) the necessary form, if any, in which the promise must be made;

(c) the mutual assent or consideration, if any, required to make a promise binding;

(d) any other requirements for making a promise binding;

(e) fraud, illegality, or any other circumstances which make a promise void or voidable;

(f) except as stated in § 358, the nature and extent of the duty for the performance of which a party becomes bound;

(g) the time when and the place where the promise is by its terms to be performed;

(h) the absolute or conditional character of the promise.

§ 358. Law Governing Performance.

The duty for the performance of which a party to a contract is bound will be discharged by compliance with the law of the place of performance of the promise with respect to:

(a) the manner of performance;

(b) the time and locality of performance;

(c) the person or persons by whom or to whom performance shall be made or rendered;

(d) the sufficiency of performance;

(e) excuse for non-performance

6. Contracts, unlike torts, are the product of agreement between the parties. Why not let the parties agree as to what law governs it? Putting aside issues of capacity, is there any reason not to allow parties to choose the governing law directly (rather than manipulating factors about formation and performance to get the law they want)?

C. REAL PROPERTY (IMMOVABLES)

ESTATE OF HANNAN V. GLOVER
523 N.W.2d 672 (Neb. 1994)

FAHRNBRUCH, JUSTICE. . . .

On January 7, 1977, James Hannan, one of five children of the decedent, Janet McClymont Hannan, adopted Glover, his wife's 35-year-old daughter from a previous marriage. On March 13, 1977, Janet Hannan executed her last will and testament in Alexandria, Virginia, her place of residence. In May 1977, James Hannan died of cancer, leaving no children except Glover. On April 2, 1982, Janet Hannan died.

On April 28, 1982, the decedent's will was admitted to probate in the circuit court for the City of Alexandria, Virginia. The will provided for the decedent's residual estate to be divided in equal shares among her surviving children and the "issue" of her deceased children per stirpes. Glover filed a petition asking the court to declare that she was the issue of James Hannan and was entitled to a prescribed share of the decedent's estate.

Ultimately, the Virginia Supreme Court held that the word "issue," absent any indication of the testator's intent to the contrary, was to be given its common-law meaning and that, under Virginia law, issue did not include adopted children. See *Hyman v. Glover*, 348 S.E.2d 269 (1986) (Citation omitted).

In Nebraska, an ancillary probate proceeding was filed by the personal representative in the Phelps County Court, requesting permission to sell the decedent's real property located in Phelps County. The property has been sold by stipulation of the parties. Also by stipulation, Glover's share of the proceeds has been held in escrow pending determination of whether she was entitled, under Nebraska law, to a share of the Nebraska real estate and thus to a share in the proceeds from its sale.

The Phelps County Court found that Nebraska is not required to accept Virginia's definition of the word "issue"; found that under Nebraska law, an adopted child is entitled to the same rights and privileges to inherit property as a natural child; and ordered that Glover receive a 20-percent share of the proceeds of the property, minus the required taxes due and paid. The district court affirmed the order of the county court.

The Court of Appeals reversed the district court. *In re Estate of Hannan*, 2 Neb.App. 636, 513 N.W.2d 339 (1994). The Court of Appeals found that Nebraska law controls the devise of Nebraska real property, but that a cardinal principle of Nebraska law is that the intent of the testator be followed. The Court of Appeals further found that, in making a will, a testator is more likely to subscribe to the domiciliary state's definition of a word than to the definition provided under the law of the situs of the real property. Finally, the Court of Appeals held that although Nebraska has a public policy of treating adopted children equally with natural children, the presumed intent of the testator to disinherit her adopted granddaughter overrides this policy. This court granted Glover's petition for further review. . . .

ANALYSIS

In order to determine whether Glover is entitled to a share of the proceeds from the sale of the decedent's Nebraska real estate, we must determine whether Nebraska law or Virginia law governs the definition of the word "issue" in the decedent's will.

As the Court of Appeals correctly noted, Nebraska "adheres to the rule that the law of the state where real property is situated governs exclusively the right of parties to real property and the methods of its transfer, including devise by will." *In re Estate of Hannan*, 2 Neb.App. at 642–43, 513 N.W.2d at 344.

Although Nebraska does grant reciprocal recognition to the final orders of other states as to the validity or construction of a will pursuant to Neb.Rev.Stat. § 30–2432 (Reissue 1989), Virginia has no such reciprocal statutory provision. In fact, Virginia has indicated that its policy is to apply its own law to the devise of real property located in Virginia. Therefore, we determine that Nebraska law controls Janet Hannan's devise of her real property located in Phelps County, Nebraska.

Under the Nebraska Probate Code, issue of a person is defined as "all his lineal descendants of all generations, with the relationship of parent and child at each generation being determined by the definitions of child and parent contained in this code." Neb.Rev.Stat. § 30–2209(23) (Reissue 1989).

The definition of "child" includes "any individual entitled to take as a child under this code by intestate succession from the parent whose relationship is involved and excludes any person who is only a stepchild, a foster child, a grandchild or any more remote descendant." § 30–2209(3). . . .

Nebraska statutes further provide that an adopted child is the child of an adopting parent, Neb.Rev.Stat. § 30–2309(1) (Reissue 1989), and that adopted persons are included in class gift terminology. Neb.Rev.Stat. § 30–2349 (Reissue 1989).

The cardinal rule concerning a decedent's will is the requirement that the intention of the testator or testatrix shall be given effect, unless the maker of the will attempts to accomplish a purpose or to make a disposition contrary to some rule of law or public policy. [Citations omitted.] To arrive at a testator's or testatrix's intention expressed in a will, a court must examine the decedent's will in its entirety, consider and liberally interpret every provision in a will, employ the generally accepted literal and grammatical meaning of words used in the will, and assume that the maker of the will understood words stated in the will.

Generally, a term of art used in reference to a devise or other testamentary disposition or provision has a technical but clear meaning. . . . When intention is expressed in clear language used in a testator's will, a court must give full force and effect to the testator's intention so expressed. When language in a will is clear and unambiguous, construction of a will is unnecessary and impermissible. (Citations omitted). It is clear that, under Nebraska law, Glover is included in the class gift to issue of the decedent's deceased children.

The Court of Appeals correctly stated that the word "issue" is a term of art. Therefore, because the meaning of the word "issue" is clear and unambiguous as defined by Nebraska statutes, it was unnecessary and impermissible for the Court of Appeals to construe Janet Hannan's will. Rather, it was the duty of that court to give full force and effect to Hannan's intention as expressed by that clear language.

Accordingly, because under Nebraska law Glover is the issue of her adoptive father, James Hannan, the deceased child of the decedent, we hold that Glover is entitled to take her father's proportionate share of the proceeds from the sale of the decedent's real property located in this state.

CONCLUSION

Having held that the definition of the word "issue" is determined by Nebraska law as to the devise of real property located in this state and that Glover is therefore entitled to take as issue of her deceased father pursuant to the terms of Janet Hannan's will, we reverse the decision of the Nebraska Court of Appeals and remand the cause to that court with direction to affirm the judgment of the district court for Phelps County.

REVERSED

———————————

1.   Note that, as a result of this decision and the Virginia decision, Glover will receive nothing from the decedent's Virginia estate but will receive 20% of the value of the land located in Nebraska. Is it likely that the decedent was trying to bring about this result?

2.   Nebraska has a statute providing for the recognition of a final order determining the validity or construction of a will from another state, but the statute did not apply in this case. Here is the statute:

> A final order of a court of another state, which state has an applicable provision of law similar in reciprocal effect to this section, determining testacy, the validity or construction of a will, made in a proceeding involving notice to and an opportunity for contest by all interested persons must be accepted as determinative by the courts of this state if it includes, or is based upon, a finding that the decedent was domiciled at his death in the state where the order was made.

Neb.Rev.St. § 30–2432. Under this statute, Nebraska will recognize another state's order only if the other state has a similar statute. Should a state's decision to apply the law of another state depend on whether the other state would do the same?

3.   Why such heavy reliance on the law of the situs of the property? In the Introductory Note to the subject of the law governing "immovables" in Tentative Draft No. 5 of the Restatement, Second, of Conflict of Laws (April 24, 1959) the drafters set forth the following rationale:

> The term "immovables," as used in the Restatement of this Subject, refers to land and to things that are so attached, or otherwise related, to the land as legally to be regarded a part of it. For three

reasons, it is a firmly established principle that questions involving interests in immovables are governed by the law of the situs. First, land and things attached to the land are within the exclusive control of the state in which they are situated, and the officials of that state are the only ones who can lawfully deal with them physically. Since interests in immovables cannot be affected without the consent of the state of the situs, it is natural that the latter's law should be applied by the courts of other states. The second reason is that immovables are of greatest concern to the state in which they are situated; it is therefore proper that the law of this state should be applied to them. The third reason is to be found in the demands of certainty and convenience. Transactions involving land are of great importance to the parties involved and, in the normal course of events, are not entered into until considerable thought has been given to their possible consequences. This is an area where it is peculiarly important that there be uniformity and predictability of result, and where the law of a single state should govern. This law should be that of the situs for the reasons stated above and also because it is the one with which the parties, their lawyers and title searchers will generally be most familiar.

In the final draft, the reporters softened the language somewhat and said that there may be instances where the situs rule would not apply. Nonetheless, the reasons set forth above are those classically given. Do any of the reasons given support the application of Nebraska law in Estate of Hannon? When we study the policy-based approach to choice-of-law in the later chapters you may want to revisit the situs rule.

HILL V. HILL

262 A.2d 661 (Del. Ch. 1970)

DUFFY, CHANCELLOR.

The action is one to enforce a pre-nuptial agreement which a surviving wife says she honored and her husband did not before he died.

A.

Plaintiff is Sara Gideon Hill, widow of Harry Murdock Hill. Defendants are the residuary legatees and devisees under Mr. Hill's will and the beneficiary of insurance policies on his life: his mother, Anna Mary Hill, his sister, Ruth M. Huhn, and his brother, Thomas Wallace Hill. All defendants have moved to dismiss the complaint on the ground that it fails to state a claim upon which relief can be granted.

Plaintiff alleges that she and Mr. Hill signed a contract on December 30, 1965 in Salisbury, Maryland, where they were married on the following day. He died domiciled in Delaware on October 20, 1967. The agreement was recorded in the Office of the Recorder of Deeds for Sussex County, Delaware, on March 12, 1968.

The agreement recites that the parties respectively own certain property: Mr. Hill owns real property in Seaford, Delaware, stocks, securities and insurance policies upon his life; his intended wife owns two properties in the Borough of Gettysburg, Pennsylvania, one alone and another with her son as joint tenants with right of survivorship. The dispositive parts of the agreement state:

'1.   The intended husband will within thirty days after the marriage by proper deed convey all of his real property to him and the intended wife as tenants by the entireties.

'2.   The intended wife will within thirty days after the marriage takes place by proper deed convey her real estate situated on the South side of Springs Avenue in the Borough of Gettysburg, Pennsylvania, to her and the intended husband as tenants by entireties.

'3.   The intended husband will within thirty days after the marriage takes place transfer all of his stocks and securities, other than United States Savings Bonds, to him and the intended wife as joint tenants with right of survivorship.

'4.   The intended husband will, within thirty days after the marriage takes place have the intended wife named primary beneficiary on all life insurance policies owned by him at the time of the execution of this agreement insuring his life and agrees not to thereafter change the primary beneficiary on such policies during the lifetime of the intended wife. * * * ' . . .

Mr. Hill's probated will directs that his residuary estate, which includes real property at Hearn's Pond (near Seaford), Delaware, be divided into equal parts and distributed to the three defendants. He named his mother as the beneficiary of life insurance.

Plaintiff alleges that she performed all of the obligations required of her under the agreement and that she remained Mr. Hill's wife until his death. She says that Mr. Hill performed several of his obligations but he failed, through oversight, to: (a) execute a deed transferring the Hearn's Pond property to himself and plaintiff as tenants by the entireties, and (b) make plaintiff a beneficiary of all his life insurance.

Mrs. Hill says that she is the equitable owner of the Hearn's Pond property and she claims the proceeds of the insurance. She thus seeks an order requiring defendants to hold their respective interests in those properties in trust for her.

B.

The legal issue on which the parties are at odds is narrow and, as in so many disputes, the result turns, not on which side offers "better" law, but which of equally sound principles is applicable. The inquiry begins with a contract, which is the foundation of plaintiff's claim. That contract, say defendants, if it is enforced here, would affect title to Delaware real estate. For that reason, defendants argue, Delaware law governs and under our law the agreement is a nullity because it does not conform technically to 13 Del.C. § 301, which provides:

> "A man and woman in contemplation of matrimony, by a marriage contract executed in the presence of two witnesses at least ten days before the solemnization of the marriage, may determine what rights each shall have in the other's estate during marriage and after its dissolution by death, and may bar each other of all rights in their respective estates not so secured to them, and any such contract duly acknowledged before any officer authorized to take acknowledgments may be recorded in the deed records in the office of the Recorder in any and all counties of the State."

Are the requirements of this statute applicable to the pre-nuptial agreement made in Maryland and relating to real property in Delaware and Pennsylvania? That is the issue forced by defendants' motion to dismiss and it is crucial because plaintiff tacitly concedes that the agreement was not executed in the presence of two witnesses at least ten days before the date of marriage, and it was not duly acknowledged before an officer authorized to take acknowledgments.

It is well established that the law of the situs of real property determines the effect of actions involving its ownership. Security Trust Co. v. Hanby, 32 Del.Ch. 70, 79 A.2d 807 (1951). Cf. Dick v. Reves, 42 Del.Ch. 187, 206 A.2d 671 (1965).

But the agreement between the Hills can hardly be characterized as a title document or as a document designed to in some way directly affect title to Delaware real estate. It is certainly true that the agreement concerns real estate and that it commits the parties to do something about real estate in two different states. And that points up its true nature, which is this: in contemplation of marriage the Hills promised each other to take certain specified acts as to stock, securities, life insurance—and real estate. That is what the contract said, that is what the parties expected it to accomplish. I therefore find applicable the principles stated in 16 Am.Jur.2d, Conflict of Laws § 15:

> "It has been broadly stated that contracts or executory contracts relating to real property are governed by the law of the jurisdiction or place where the property is located. However, a

distinction is made between contracts directly affecting title to real property, which are to be so construed according to the law of the state where the property is situated, and contracts which while relating to real property, do not directly affect the title to or an interest in the property itself but are purely personal. Agreements of the latter nature are governed by the usual rules of contracts, and will not be influenced by the lex rei sitae."

The same distinction is made by the Restatement, Conflicts [sic] of Laws § 340, which provides:

"The law of the place of contracting determines the validity of a promise to transfer or to convey land."

And see the comments thereto.

Neither the purpose nor the effect of the agreement was to act as an instrument of conveyance. It was simply an agreement whereby two people prior to marriage decided to fix their respective interests in real property, securities and life insurance proceeds. In short, the agreement was a "personal contract" as opposed to one directly affecting real property and under Delaware choice of law rules, the law of the place of making the contract determines whether or not it is enforceable. (Citations omitted). . . .

Defendants not having shown any reason why the agreement is invalid under Maryland law, it follows that their motion to dismiss the complaint must be denied.

———————

1.   Under the logic of this case, the Delaware court is not being asked to determine who has title to Delaware land (a matter concededly governed by Delaware law) but, rather, to determine whether a contract to convey Delaware land was breached and, if so, enforce that contract; thus, the question is what law governs the contract made in Maryland rather than what law governs the ownership of property in Delaware. Could the same logic have been applied in *Glover* to reason that the court was being asked to interpret a will made in Virginia rather than to determine the ownership of Nebraska property?

2.   The question of whether to characterize the issue as grounded in "property" or in "contract" has been around for over one hundred years with cases going both ways. The old chestnut on this issue is *Polson v. Stewart*, 45 N.E. 737 (Mass. 1897). In that case, a husband and a wife domiciled in North Carolina entered into a contract in which the husband would release his dower rights in the wife's land located in Massachusetts. Such a contract was valid under the law of North Carolina but invalid under the law of Massachusetts where husband and wife were not permitted to contract with each other. In an action seeking specific performance of the contract, the Massachusetts court held that it would enforce the contract since it was not a conveyance of land

but merely a personal contract between the parties. Accord: *Selover, Bates & Co. v. Walsh*, 226 U.S. 112 (1912).

D. PERSONAL PROPERTY (MOVABLES)

IN RE JONES' ESTATE
182 N.W. 227 (Iowa 1921)

FAVILLE, J.

The decedent, Evan Jones, was a native of Wales. When he was about 33 years of age, he came to America as an immigrant. This was in 1883. He came over on the same ship with the wife and children of one David P. Jones. At that time, David P. Jones was living in Oskaloosa, Iowa, to which place the decedent went. After the death of David P. Jones, the decedent married his widow, who subsequently died in January, 1914. The decedent, Evan Jones, was a coal miner, an industrious, hard-working, thrifty Welshman, who accumulated a considerable amount of property. In 1896, he was naturalized in the district court of Wapello county, Iowa, and thereafter voted at elections. The reason for his leaving Wales at the time he did was because of bastardy proceedings which had been instituted against him by the mother of the appellant. In 1915, the decedent disposed of his property, which then consisted of two farms and some city real estate. He was advised by his banker to leave the greater part of his money in a bank at Ottumwa until he got to Wales, and did so deposit it. He purchased a draft for about $2,000 and left some $20,000 on deposit in the bank, and also a note and mortgage for collection, and left with the banker the address of a sister in Wales, stating that he intended to live with said sister. He sailed from New York on May 1, 1915, on the ill-fated Lusitania, and was drowned when the boat was sunk by a German submarine on May 7, 1915. The Lusitania was a vessel of the Cunard line, flying the British flag. Thereafter the brothers and sisters of the decedent secured the appointment of an administrator in Wapello county, Iowa. Various proceedings were had, which finally resulted in the trial of the issues in this cause.

I.   The question for our determination in this case is whether or not, under the facts stated, the domicile of the decedent at the time of his death was in Wapello county, Iowa, or in Wales. If his domicile at the time that the Lusitania sank was legally in Wales, then it is conceded by all the parties that, under the laws of the British Empire, the appellant, as his illegitimate child, would have no interest in his estate. On the other hand, if the decedent at said time legally had his domicile in Wapello county,

Iowa, then the property passed to the appellant as his sole heir under the laws of this state.

For the purposes of the present discussion, it may be conceded that the evidence is sufficient to justify a finding that the appellant was the child of the decedent and had been so recognized and declared to such an extent as to satisfy the requirements of Code, § 3385.

It may also be conceded, for present purposes, that it is established by the evidence in the case that the decedent had by acts and declarations evidenced a purpose to leave his home in Iowa permanently and to return to his native country, Wales, for the purpose of living there the remainder of his life.

The question of what constitutes domicile has often been passed upon by the courts, but the cases are so unlike in their facts that precedents to aid us in the determination of this precise question are difficult to find. . . .

It is well settled that every person, under all circumstances and conditions, must have a domicile somewhere. (Citations omitted).

There are different kinds of domiciles recognized by the law. It is generally held that the subject may be divided into three general classes:

(1) Domicile of origin.

(2) Domicile of choice.

(3) Domicile by operation of law.

The "domicile of origin" of every person is the domicile of his parents at the time of his birth. In Prentiss v. Barton, 19 Fed. Cas. 1276, No. 11384, Circuit Justice Marshall said:

> "By the general laws of the civilized world, the domicile of the parents at the time of birth, or what is termed 'the domicile of origin,' constitutes the domicile of an infant, and continues, until abandoned, or until the acquisition of a new domicile, in a different place."

The "domicile of choice" is the place which a person has elected and chosen for himself to displace his previous domicile. (Citations omitted).

"Domicile by operation of law" is that domicile which the law attributes to a person independent of his own intention or action of residence. This results generally from the domestic relations of husband and wife, or parent and child. (Citations omitted).

In the instant case, we have to deal only with the first two kinds of domicile; that is, domicile of origin and domicile of choice. Applying these general definitions to the facts of this case, the domicile of origin of Evan Jones was in Wales, where he was born, and the domicile of choice was Wapello county, Iowa. The question that concerns us is: Where was his domicile for the purpose of descent of personal property on the 7th day of May, 1915, when the Lusitania was sunk off the western coast of the British Isles?

The matter of the determination of any person's domicile arises in different ways and is construed by the courts for a variety of different purposes. Apparent inconsistencies occur in the authorities because of the failure to clearly preserve the distinctions to be made by reason of the purpose for which the determination of one's domicile is being legally ascertained. The question frequently arises where it becomes important to determine the domicile for the purpose of taxation, or for the purpose of attachment, or for the levy of execution, or for the exercising of the privilege of voting, or in determining the statute of limitations, or in ascertaining liability for the support of paupers, and perhaps other purposes. Definitions given in regard to the method of ascertaining the domicile for one purpose are not always applicable in ascertaining the domicile for another purpose. Some of the courts have made the broad assertion that a person can have only one domicile. (Citations omitted). . . .

In the instant case, we are concerned only in the matter of the domicile of the decedent, Evan Jones, as it affects the question of the descent of his personal estate. An examination of the record satisfies us that the evidence is sufficient to amply justify a finding that the said decedent disposed of his property in Wapello county, Iowa, and converted the same into money or securities, and left Wapello county, Iowa, with the present intention of abandoning his domicile there, and without any present intention of returning thereto, and also with the express intention of returning to his native country, Wales, to make his permanent home there. Or, in the language of the books, decedent's intention was to abandon his domicile of choice and return to his domicile of origin. He died in itinere. It is needless for us to cite the vast number of cases announcing the general rule that the acquisition of a new domicile must have been completely perfected, and hence there must have been a concurrence both of the fact of removal and the intent to remain in the new locality before the former domicile can be considered lost. . . .

At the outset, it is obvious that under the circumstances of the instant case the domicile of the decedent at the time of his death must in any event be determined by the assumption of a fiction. All will agree that the decedent did not have a domicile on the Lusitania. In order to determine his domicile, then, one of two fictions must be assumed, either that he retained the Iowa domicile until one was acquired in Wales, or that he acquired a domicile in Wales the instant he abandoned the Iowa domicile and started for Wales, with the intent and purpose of residing there. Which one of these fictions shall we assume for the purpose of determining the disposition of his personal property? This question first came before the courts at an early day, long before our present easy and extensive methods of transportation, and at a time before the present ready movement from one country to another. At that time men left Europe for the Western Continent or elsewhere largely for purposes of adventure or in search of an opportunity for the promotion of commerce. It was at a time before the invention of the steamboat and before the era of the oceanic cable. Men left their native land knowing that they would be gone for long periods of time, and that means of communication with their home land were infrequent, difficult, and slow. The traditions of their native country were strong with these men. In the event of death, while absent, they desired that their property should descend in accordance with the laws of the land of their birth. . . .

These reasons, which were, to an extent at least, historical and patriotic, found early expression in the decisions of the courts on the question of domicile. The general rule was declared to be that a domicile is retained until a new domicile has been actually acquired. At an early time, however, an exception was ingrafted upon this rule to the effect that, for the purposes of succession, a party abandoning a domicile of choice with the intent to return to his domicile of origin regains the latter the instant that the former domicile is abandoned.

It will be observed that this exception involves two elements: First, that the party is seeking to return from a domicile of choice to a domicile of origin; and, second, that the question arises in a case involving succession to an estate. It is apparent that this exception to the general rule grew out of the conditions that we have before suggested and was a recognition of the desire on the part of the English trader in distant lands to have his estate administered according to the laws of the land of his birth. . . .

Perhaps no better case could be found than the instant case to illustrate the effect of the adoption of the exception to the general rule. The decedent in this case had not only acquired a domicile in the United States, but had become a citizen of this country. Under the general rule, if he had abandoned his domicile in Iowa with the intention of acquiring a domicile in Norway or in France, and had been on the ill-fated Lusitania, it would have been universally held that the domicile in Iowa was still retained. No one will dispute that proposition. But, because, although a citizen of the United States, and residing here for many years, he was en route to Wales, the land of his birth, instead of to some other country, it is contended that he acquired a domicile in that country instantly upon abandoning his domicile in Iowa. If some native of Iowa had done exactly what the decedent did, had disposed of his property with the avowed and declared intention of abandoning his domicile in Iowa and of securing one in Wales, and had accompanied Jones on his trip, and had gone down on the same boat, his estate would have been administered according to the laws of the state of Iowa, because he had not yet acquired a new domicile anywhere else, while Jones' estate, under the theory of the English rule, would be administered according to the laws of Wales, because he happened to have been born in that country. If such a rule is to be applied as between different states of the Union, with our freedom of movement between the various states, it would lead to very startling results. The laws of the states differ greatly in regard to descent. There is no logical reason why the rule should not be applied between different states of the Union as readily as between different governments. Under such a doctrine, if applied between the various states of the Union, if a man had been born in the state of New York, and at an early age had removed to Iowa, and had lived in this commonwealth for many years, had voted here and had become familiar with our laws, and should finally decide to remove to New York to live, and should die in itinere, he would be regarded as domiciled in New York. If, however, under identical circumstances, he intended to remove to Massachusetts, he would be regarded as domiciled in Iowa.

What good reason is there why "native allegiance" to the state of New York, where he was born, should be the determining factor which would prevail in such instance? One reason that is persuasive why such a rule should not be adopted is that a person who in these days abandons his domicile of origin and acquires a legal domicile in another jurisdiction, presumably, at least, is familiar with the laws of the jurisdiction of the latter domicile, and there is, to say the least, as strong a presumption that he desires his estate to be administered according to the laws of that jurisdiction as of the jurisdiction of the domicile of origin. While there may have been a good reason for the establishment of the English rule at the time and under the conditions under which it was announced, we do not believe that any good reason exists for the recognition of such a rule under the circumstances disclosed in this case. The general rule that a domicile once legally acquired is retained until a new domicile is secured, and that, in the acquisition of such new domicile, both the fact and the intention must concur, it seems to us is a rule of universal and general application and that there is neither good logic nor substantial reason for the application of an exception to that rule in the case where the party is in itinere toward the domicile of origin. In other words, going back to the original proposition, the fiction is assumed generally that any domicile, either of choice or of origin, is retained until a new domicile has been legally acquired. We see no good reason for changing that rule in the one instance where the descent of property is involved and the party is in itinere to the domicile of origin. We believe that the general rule is the better rule, and that the exception laid down by Story and followed by the English courts should not be recognized either as between the states of the union or between this country and a foreign country, under the facts disclosed in this case.

It therefore follows that the domicile of the decedent was in the state of Iowa until a new domicile had been actually acquired in Wales. No such domicile having been acquired, at the time of his death, his personal estate must be administered according to the laws of Iowa. We think the general rule should be followed, even though the decedent was in itinere to his domicile of origin at the time of his death. We have examined the record and hold that the appellant was legally recognized as the child of the decedent, as required by our statute and the decisions of this court, and is his lawful heir.

It follows that the judgment of the trial court must be, and the same is, reversed.

---

1.   Would it make any difference to you if you learned that all the contestants to Jones' estate were domiciled in Wales?

2.   Why must the court decide the case based on what it calls a "fiction"? Why not examine the facts of the case and decide the case using common sense? Whose law would you apply utilizing the "common sense" rule?

NOTE: JURISDICTION-SELECTING RULES

Critics of the First Restatement choice of law rules have correctly labeled them as "jurisdiction selecting rules" They argue that after identifying the subject matter under consideration (*e.g.* torts, contracts, property) the First Restatement rules point to the law of a given jurisdiction without inquiring about the content of the rules that are in conflict and without looking at the fact pattern that gives rise to the apparent conflict. Thus, all tort actions are governed by the law of the state in which the last act necessary to consummate the tort took place. Does it make sense for one, inexorable rule to govern choice of law for all tort issues and under all fact patterns? In fact, as we will see in the next section many courts seemingly adhering to the mechanical First Restatement rules nonetheless found ways to escape from using them when the courts perceived that the result would be unjust. These "escape devices" were a harbinger of a revolution in choice of law which we will take up at length in the following chapters. Yet, the escape devices are not merely of historical interest. Ten or so states still retain allegiance to the First Restatement rules (and thus may use these escape devices). Furthermore, even the courts of other states occasionally find it necessary or convenient to revert to some of the First Restatement rules.

Office Talk

#1

Neil: Aaron, You seem to be down on all jurisdiction selecting rules, whether for contract, tort, or property. You intimate that these rules are too rigid and should be replaced by more fact-sensitive approaches that take into account the real interests of the states in the context of the particular dispute. But won't fact-sensitive approaches undermine predictability and certainty? I can understand why you might take this "sort everything out after the fact" approach to torts. After all, people typically don't plan to be involved in a tort, so there is comparatively little cost to figuring out what law governs only when a problem arises. But aren't there some advantages to predictable rules, even if they are somewhat arbitrary, for what law governs a consensual transaction? After all, a testator can comply with whatever rules are applicable for a valid will, but needs to know now, rather than after death, which law applies. The same thing applies to contracts—the contracting parties can shape their transaction to meet the governing law, but only if they know what that law is.

Moreover, in the context of voluntary transactions such as contracts, anyone who is hurt by application of jurisdiction-selecting rules usually has no one to blame but himself or herself. After all, most contract law rules relate to matters than can be changed by the parties by agreement. Thus, anyone who wants a result that can be reached by agreement (as opposed to casually assuming that the law will insert a term bringing about that result) could easily have brought about the result by simple drafting.

Aaron: There is something to what you say. But, first of all, the jurisdiction selecting rules are plenty fuzzy. In *Estate of Jones*, the court wrote a long tortured essay as to where the decedent was domiciled. Other courts using the domicile rule could very well find the domicile to be elsewhere. Second, wild horses will not stop courts from reaching results that they believe to be more just. Thus, in *Hill* the court said the issue was the validity of the contract not the transfer of property. In the next chapter, we will see that courts are more than willing to characterize a cause of action in a manner that will get them the result they want. So courts are not going to get off the hook from deciding hard cases. Third, there are cases where one state will disallow distribution even if the testator makes clear his/her wishes. Some states will not allow a husband to deny his wife a given share of property where other states will allow such a devise that gives the testator greater latitude. Finally, it is the law's obligation to deal as fairly as it can with people who could plan their affairs more efficiently but neglect to do so. One size fits all does not work well in the law and certainly not in conflict of laws.

CHAPTER 2

ESCAPING THE RIGIDITY OF FIRST RESTATEMENT RULES

■ ■ ■

A. CHARACTERIZATION

The first step in applying the traditional rules embodied in the First Restatement was to identify the subject under consideration. After all, the rules for torts were different than the rules for contracts. But, how to "name the baby" was not always clear. Was the underlying issue in a dispute one of contract or tort? Was the issue substantive or procedural? And even if it was pretty clear that one label or another was more fitting, what if a court preferred the choice of law rule associated with the other label because it would bring about a result that the court implicitly considered more just? Sorting this all out turns out to be more fun than a barrel of monkeys.

LEVY V. DANIELS' U-DRIVE AUTO RENTING CO., INC.
143 A. 163 (Conn. 1928)

WHEELER, C. J.

The complaint alleged these facts: The defendant, Daniels' U-Drive Auto Renting Company, Incorporated, rented in Hartford to Sack an automobile, which he operated, and in which Levy, the plaintiff, was a passenger. During the time the automobile was rented and operated, the defendant renting company was subject to § 21 of chapter 195 of the Public Acts of Connecticut, 1925, which provides:

> "Any person renting or leasing to another any motor vehicle owned by him shall be liable for any damage to any person or property caused by the operation of such motor vehicle while so rented or leased."

While the plaintiff was a passenger, Sack brought the car to a stop on the main highway at Longmeadow, Mass., and negligently allowed it to stand directly in the path of automobiles proceeding southerly in the same direction his automobile was headed, without giving sufficient warning to automobiles approaching from his rear, and without having a tail light in operation, and when, due to inclement weather, the visibility was reduced to an exceedingly low degree. At this time the defendant Maginn negligently ran into and upon the rear end of the car Sack was operating, and threw plaintiff forcibly forward, causing him serious injuries. The

33

specific acts of Maginn's negligence are set up at length in the complaint; it is not essential at this time to recite them. The plaintiff suffered his severe injuries in consequence of the concurrent negligence of both defendants.

The defendant demurred to the complaint upon several grounds, upon only one of which the trial court rested its decision; namely, that the liability of the defendant must be determined by the law of Massachusetts, which did not impose upon persons renting automobiles any such obligation as the Connecticut act did. . . .

It is the defendant's contention in support of this ground of demurrer that the action set forth in the complaint is one of tort, and, since Massachusetts has no statute like, or substantially like, the Connecticut act, it must be determined by the common law of that state, under which the plaintiff must prove, to prevail, the negligence of the defendant in renting a defective motor vehicle and in failing to disclose the defect. If this were the true theory of the complaint, the conclusion thus reached must have followed. "The locus delicti determined the existence of the cause of action." Orr v. Ahern, 107 Conn. 174, 176, 139 A. 691, 692; Commonwealth Fuel Co. v. McNeil, 103 Conn. 390, 130 A. 794. Under the law of Massachusetts, the plaintiff concededly would have a cause of action against Sack and Maginn for their tortious conduct in the operation of the cars they were driving. The plaintiff concedes the correctness of this. His counsel, however, construe the complaint as one in its nature contractual. The act makes him who rents or leases any motor vehicle to another liable for any damage to any person or property caused by the operation of the motor vehicle while so rented or leased. Liability for "damage caused by the operation of such motor vehicle" means caused by its tortious operation. This was undoubtedly the legislative intent; otherwise the act would be invalid. The plaintiff concedes this to be the true construction of these words, and the defendant acquiesces in this construction.

The complaint alleges a tortious operation of the automobile rented to Sack by the defendant, causing the injuries to the plaintiff as alleged, and constituting an action ex delicto. The statute gives, in terms, the injured person a right of action against the defendant which rented the automobile to Sack, though the injury occurred in Massachusetts. It was a right which the statute gave directly, not derivatively, to the injured person as a consequence of the contract of hiring. The purpose of the statute was not primarily to give the injured person a right of recovery against the tortious operator of the car, but to protect the safety of the traffic upon highways by providing an incentive to him who rented motor vehicles to rent them to competent and careful operators, by making him liable for damage resulting from the tortious operation of the rented vehicles. The common law would not hold the defendant liable upon the facts recited in the complaint for the negligence of Sack in the operation of this automobile. . . .

The rental of motor vehicles to any but competent and careful operators, or to persons of unknown responsibility, would be liable to result in injury to the public upon or near highways, and this imminent danger justified, as a reasonable exercise of the police power, this statute, which requires all who engage in this business to become responsible for any injury inflicted upon the public by the tortious operation of the rented motor vehicle. . . .

The statute made the liability of the person renting motor vehicles a part of every contract of hiring a motor vehicle in Connecticut. A liability ex delicto is created by the law of the place of the delict. (Citations omitted). A liability arising out of a contract depends upon the law of the place of contract, "unless the contract is to be performed or to have its beneficial operation and effect elsewhere, or it is made with reference to the law of another place." (Citations omitted). We will enforce rights of action on contracts arising in other jurisdictions unless these contravene our own law, or our own fundamental and important public policy imperatively requires their nonenforcement. (Citations omitted). It is a general rule, subject to the exceptions we have noted, that rights ex contractu may be enforced anywhere. (Citations omitted).

If the liability of this defendant under this statute is contractual, no question can arise as to the plaintiff's right to enforce this contract, provided the obligation imposed upon this defendant was for the "direct, sole and exclusive benefit" of the plaintiff. The contract was made in Connecticut; at the instant of its making the statute made a part of the contract of hiring the liability of the defendant which the plaintiff seeks to enforce. The law inserted in the contract this provision. The statute did not create the liability; it imposed it in case the defendant voluntarily rented the automobile. Whether the defendant entered into this contract of hiring was his own voluntary act; if he did he must accept the condition upon which the law permitted the making of the contract. The contract was for the "direct, sole, and exclusive benefit" of the plaintiff, who is alleged to have been injured through the tortious operation of the automobile rented by the defendant to Sack. The right of the plaintiff as a beneficiary of this contract to maintain this action is no longer an open question in this state. (Citations omitted). . . .

There is error, the judgment of the superior court is reversed, and the cause remanded to be proceeded with according to law.

––––––––––––

The Connecticut court says that the policy behind the renter's liability rule is to protect safety on the highways by insuring that cars are rented to competent drivers. Does this sound like a contract policy or one based in tort? Under the reasoning of this case, would a Massachusetts rental agency located near the border of Massachusetts and Connecticut that non-negligently rented a car to a Connecticut lessee who then had an accident in Connecticut injuring a Connecticut citizen have its liability be determined by Massachusetts law and, thus, get off the hook?

In its unpublished opinion in *Townsend v. Boclair*, 2007 WL 126933 (Conn. Super. Ct. 2007) a Connecticut Superior Court characterized a case similar to *Levy* as a tort case but still applied the law of the state in which the rental contract was made rather than the law of the place of injury. The plaintiffs, Maine domiciliaries, were injured in a single car accident in Connecticut. The car was rented in Maine by a Maine domiciliary from a rental company doing business in Maine. Maine did not have a renter's liability statute. Connecticut, the place of the accident, had the statute described in the *Levy* case. By this time, however, Connecticut had abandoned First Restatement rules and opted for an analysis of the sort described in the Second Restatement (which we will take up at length in subsequent chapters).

Although renter and lessor liability statutes were enacted in many states, they are all now a matter of history. In 2005, Congress passed a statute abolishing renter and lessor liability unless the lessor was negligent in renting the car. See 49 U.S.C. § 3016 (a) [Graves Amendment]. This statute was upheld as within Congress's power under the Commerce Clause in *Garcia v. Vanguard Car Rental USA, Inc.*, 540 F.3d 1242 (11th Cir. 2008), *cert.* denied, 555 U.S. 1174 (2009). Thus, vicarious liability for the negligence of the driver no longer attaches to lessors on rentals of automobiles. Nonetheless, *Levy* is one of the classic cases demonstrating that a court seeking to avoid the application of the *lex loci* rule for determining the law governing a tort case could get around that rule by characterizing the case in a manner that would get it to a different set of choice of law rules (here contract).

HAUMSCHILD V. CONTINENTAL CASUALTY CO.
95 N.W.2d 814 (Wis. 1959)

CURRIE[1], JUSTICE

This appeal presents a conflict of laws problem with respect to interspousal liability for tort growing out of an automobile accident. Which law controls, that of the state of the forum, the state of the place of wrong, or the state of domicile? Wisconsin is both the state of the forum and of the domicile while California is the state where the alleged wrong was committed. Under Wisconsin law, a wife may sue her husband in tort. Under California law she cannot. (Citations omitted).

This court was first faced with this question in Buckeye v. Buckeye, 234 N.W. 342 (1931). In that case, Wisconsin was the state of the forum and domicile, while Illinois was the state of the place of wrong. It was there held that the law governing the creation and extent of tort liability is that

---

[1] As we will see, the name Currie figures prominently in American conflict of laws. In particular, we will study extensively the pathbreaking views of Professor Brainerd Currie in subsequent chapters. His son, Professor David Currie, is a co-author of one of the leading casebooks in Conflict of Laws. The author of this opinion, however, is neither of those Curries but, rather, Justice George R. Currie of the Supreme Court of Wisconsin.

of the place where the tort was committed, citing Goodrich, Conflict of Laws (1st ed.), p. 188. From this premise, it was further held that interspousal immunity from tort liability necessarily is governed by the law of the place of injury. . . .

The principle enunciated in the Buckeye case and followed in subsequent Wisconsin cases, that the law of the place of wrong controls as to whether one spouse is immune from suit in tort by the other, is the prevailing view in the majority of jurisdictions in this country. However, criticism of the rule of the Buckeye case, by legal writers, some of them recognized authorities in the field of conflict of laws, and recent decisions by the courts of California, New Jersey, and Pennsylvania, have caused us to re-examine the question afresh. . . .

The most comprehensive treatment of the problem that we have discovered is the excellent thirty page article in 15 University of Pittsburgh Law Review 397, entitled, 'Interspousal Liability for Automobile Accidents in the Conflict of Laws: Law and Reason Versus the Restatement,' by Alan W. Ford published in 1954. The article contains a careful analysis of the American cases on the subject commencing with our own Buckeye case. The author's conclusion is stated as follows (pp. 423–424):

> 'The *lex fori* and the *lex loci delicti* rules have already been criticized as inadequate. Between them, these two rules encompass all of the American cases. To find a more desirable alternative we must, therefore, go beyond those cases. The foreign experience briefly discussed above, is a useful starting point. As that experience suggests, there is some logic in separating questions of status and tort, in determining the incidents of the marital relationship by the family law, and the problems of tort by the law of torts. If a conflicts problem is involved, there is no reason why both questions should be determined by the law of torts. Instead, the two questions should remain separate, and problems of status or capacity could be referred, by an appropriate conflicts rule, to the law of the place of the domicile.' . . .

The first case to break the ice and flatly hold that the law of domicile should be applied in determining whether there existed an immunity from suit for tort based upon family relationship is Emery v. Emery, 1955, 45 Cal.2d 421, 289 P.2d 218. In that case two unemancipated minor sisters sued their unemancipated minor brother and their father to recover for injuries sustained in an automobile accident that occurred in the state of Idaho, the complaint alleging wilful misconduct in order to come within the provisions of the Idaho 'guest' statute. All parties were domiciled in California. The opinion by Mr. Justice Traynor recognized that the California court, in passing on the question of whether an unemancipated minor child may sue the parent or an unemancipated brother, had a choice to apply the law of the place of wrong, of the forum, or of the domicile. It was held that the immunity issue was not a question of tort but one of capacity to sue and be sued, and rejected the law of the place of injury as 'both fortuitous and irrelevant.' In deciding whether to apply the law of the forum, or the law of the domicile, the opinion stated this conclusion (289 P.2d at pages 222–223):

> 'Although tort actions between members of the same family will ordinarily be brought in the state of the family domicile, the courts of another state will in some cases be a more convenient forum, and thus the question arises whether the choice of law rule should be expressed in terms of the law of the forum or that of the domicile. We think that disabilities to sue and immunities from suit because of a family relationship are more properly determined by reference to the law of the state of the family domicile. That state has the primary responsibility for establishing and regulating the incidents of the family relationship and it is the only state in which the parties can, by participation in the legislative processes, effect a change in those incidents. Moreover, it is undesirable that the rights, duties, disabilities, and immunities conferred or imposed by the family relationship should constantly change as members of the family cross state boundaries during temporary absences from their home.' . . .

The two reasons most often advanced for the common law rule, that one spouse may not sue the other, are the ancient concept that husband and wife constitute in law but one person, and that to permit such suits will be to foment family discord and strife. The Married Women's Acts of the various states have effectively destroyed the 'one person' concept thereby leaving as the other remaining reason for the immunity the objective of preventing family discord. This is also the justification usually advanced for denying an unemancipated child the capacity to sue a parent, brother or sister. Clearly this policy reason for denying the capacity to sue more properly lies within the sphere of family law, where domicile usually controls the law to be applied, than it does tort law, where the place of injury generally determines the substantive law which will govern. . . .

We are convinced that, from both the standpoint of public policy and logic, the proper solution of the conflict of laws problem, in cases similar to the instant action, is to hold that the law of the domicile is the one that ought to be applied in determining any issue of incapacity to sue based upon family relationship. . . .

FAIRCHILD, JUSTICE (concurring).

I concur in the reversal of the judgment, but do not find it necessary to re-examine settled Wisconsin law in order to do so. A fundamental change in the law of Wisconsin such as the one announced by the majority in this case, which will importantly affect many people, should be made, if at all, in a case where the question is necessarily presented. Both parties assumed that their case would be decided under the principle which is being overturned by the majority, and accordingly, we have not had the benefit of brief or argument upon the validity of the principle.

1. *Solution of this case without overruling previous decisions.* Plaintiff wife alleges a personal injury tort cause of action arising in California against defendant husband. Defendant husband pleads that she has no cause of action because she was his wife. It has been the rule in Wisconsin that the existence or non-existence of immunity because of family relationship is substantive and not merely procedural, and is to be determined by the law of the locus state. The law of California is that the existence or non-existence of immunity is a substantive matter, but that it is an element of the law of status, not of tort. The tort law of California is no more concerned with immunity than is Wisconsin's. Thus it makes no difference under the facts of this case whether we look directly to the law of Wisconsin to determine that immunity is not available as a defense or look to the law of Wisconsin only because California, having no general tort principle as to immunity, classifies immunity as a matter of status . . .

In summary, I would dispose of the present case upon the theory that California law governs the existence of the alleged cause of action and that in California the immunity question can not be decided by resort to the law of torts but rather the law of status. I would leave to a later case the consideration of whether the Wisconsin rule of choice of law as to the defense of family immunity should remain as heretofore or, if it is to be changed, which rule will be best.

I am authorized to state that MR. JUSTICE BROWN concurs in this opinion.

———————

Wasn't Justice Fairchild right in his concurring opinion? If Wisconsin law would allow this cause of action and a California court would also allow it (by referring the matter to the law of Wisconsin), why should any court even consider imposing interspousal immunity? Justice Fairchild thus justified application of Wisconsin law by looking not only at California substantive law but at California's choice of law rules as well. We will later identify this gambit by the fancy term "renvoi." (Does the vested rights view of traditional jurisdiction-selecting rules suggest that courts should utilize renvoi and apply the choice of law rules of the state in which an accident took place since those choice of law rules—whatever they are—are part of the right that was vested there?)

B. SUBSTANCE AND PROCEDURE

The substance/procedure distinction is one that pervades much of the law. It is not unique to choice of law. Early on, Walter Wheeler Cook suggested his view of the proper way to analyze the substance/ procedure distinction in a choice of law setting:

> In determining the legal consequences of certain conduct or events it has seemed reasonable to apply "foreign substantive law" because of some factual connection of the situation with the foreign state; but on the other hand it would obviously be quite inconvenient for the court of the forum, though not unfair to the litigants concerned, to take over all the machinery of the foreign court for the "enforcement," as we say, of the "substantive rights." If we admit that the "substantive" shades off by imperceptible degrees into the "procedural," and that the "line" between them does not "exist," to be discovered merely by logic and analysis, but is rather to be drawn so as best to carry out our purpose, we see that the problem resolves itself substantially into this: How far can the court of the forum go in applying the rules taken from the foreign system of law without unduly hindering or inconveniencing itself?

> Against the inconvenience involved in learning the foreign rule is the fact that so closely are "procedure" and "substance" connected that in many cases a refusal to accept the foreign rule as to a matter falling into the doubtful class will defeat the policy involved in following the foreign substantive law. Clearly a decision on this basis might place the line at a somewhat different point from where it might be drawn when the purpose is that involved in [cases involving other problems, such as the constitutionality of retroactive legislation].

W.W. Cook, *"Substance" and "Procedure" in the Conflict of Laws*, 42 Yale L.J. 333, 343–344 (1933).

Despite Cook's neutral-sounding analysis, the substance/ procedure distinction is often manipulated in order to apply the law of the forum (on the ground that the matter is procedural) rather than the law of another state (which would apply if the matter were substantive). Consider the following case:

VEST V. ST. ALBANS PSYCHIATRIC HOSPITAL, INC.

387 S.E.2d 282 (W.Va. 1989)

NEELY, JUSTICE:

The appellants, Otis and Pauline Vest, citizens of West Virginia, brought this action in the circuit court of Raleigh County, West Virginia, charging the defendant, a Virginia corporation, with medical malpractice occurring in the Commonwealth of Virginia. The action was dismissed because the appellants failed to comply with a notice provision of Virginia's statute on medical malpractice review panels. . . .

The Virginia legislature has established a system of medical malpractice review panels that are available to either party in a potential medical-malpractice lawsuit. *Va.Code*, 8.01–581.1 *et seq.* [1984]. A plaintiff may not bring suit against a "health-care provider" registered in Virginia without first notifying the defendant of the claim and allowing time for the case to be reviewed by a medical review panel. Such panels are convened, case-by-case, by appointment of the Chief Justice of Virginia, at the request of either party. The panel comprises one trial-court judge (as chairman), three impartial Virginia lawyers, and three impartial Virginia doctors. The panel hears evidence and issues a non-binding opinion on the issues of liability and extent of injury. The panel's opinion is admissible as evidence if the matter goes to a full civil trial.

The Circuit Court granted the appellee's motion to dismiss the action, on the ground that the appellants had failed to notify the appellee before filing suit, as required by *Va.Code*, 8.01–581.2(A) [1984]. The appellants seek relief here, on the ground that the notice provisions of the Virginia statute are procedural only, not substantive law, and cannot be applied to bar their action in a West Virginia court.

We now reverse the judgment below, and hold that, in a West Virginia court, a citizen of West Virginia suing a Virginia hospital for injuries sustained in Virginia need not comply with the medical review panel provisions of Virginia law.

I

At first blush, the issue may appear to be a question of "choice of law" or "conflict of laws." In tort cases, West Virginia courts apply the traditional choice-of-law rule, *lex loci delicti*; that is, the substantive rights between the parties are determined by the law of the place of injury. *Paul v. National Life*, 177 W.Va. 427, 352 S.E.2d 550 (1986). There is no dispute that the substantive law to be applied in this case is the law of Virginia. It is just as clear that West Virginia procedure applies in all cases before West Virginia state courts, and a merely procedural rule of Virginia law would be ignored here.

A leading commentator on conflict of laws writes:

> [One] type of rule often called procedural actually is designed to govern access to courts, and necessarily governs access only to courts of the state having the rule. A state can control access to its own courts but it cannot prevent courts of another state, if they have jurisdiction, from proceeding to exercise it. (Citations omitted).

The *Erie* doctrine has forced the federal courts to become adept at distinguishing between the substantive law and the procedural law of their forum states. *Erie Railroad Co. v. Tompkins*, 304 U.S. 64, 58 S.Ct. 817, 82 L.Ed. 1188 (1938). The federal courts of Virginia have held that, for purposes of the *Erie* doctrine, the notice provision of Virginia's medical review panel statute is substantive law. *DiAntonio v. Northampton-Accomack Memorial Hospital*, 628 F.2d 287 (4th Cir.1980). The plaintiff in *DiAntonio*, a New Jersey citizen, filed an action against the defendant, a Virginia hospital, in the federal court of the Eastern District of Virginia. The plaintiff had failed to notify the defendant before filing suit, as required by *Va.Code*, 8.01–581.2 [1977]. The Fourth Circuit held that the action had properly been dismissed, because, for purposes of the *Erie* doctrine, the statute was substantive:

> The Act's notice requirement and provision for panel review at the instance of either party were so "intimately bound up" with the rights and obligations being asserted as to require their application in federal courts under the doctrine of *Erie* Railroad Co. v. Tompkins, [*supra*].

Id. at 290.

We do not in the least disagree with the holding in *DiAntonio*. We part ways with the Fourth Circuit in this case not on the grounds of technical choice-of-law rules, but on the connection among sovereignty, *in personam* jurisdiction, and access to the courts of sister states.

Our Federalism comprises two distinct and complementary strands: The national government's relation to the states, controlled by the Supremacy Clause of the U.S. *Constitution* and, in the *DiAntonio* example, by the *Erie* doctrine; and the relation of the government of one state to the governments of her sister states, controlled by the Full Faith and Credit Clause and the Privileges and Immunities Clause of the U.S. *Constitution*, the principle of comity, and, in this particular case, the doctrine of *in personam* jurisdiction. . . .

The decision of the Virginia legislature to close the doors of its courts to medical-malpractice plaintiffs, unless they notify the defendant before filing suit and give the defendant a chance to have a medical review panel convened, must also close the doors to the federal courts sitting in Virginia, because for that purpose they are both courts of the same sovereign, the Commonwealth of Virginia, and exercise the same personal jurisdiction. Note 4, *supra*.

The courts of West Virginia, on other hand, are never under the sovereignty of the Commonwealth of Virginia. A defendant in a West Virginia state court, over whom this state has personal jurisdiction, is subject to the sovereignty of this state. This state may choose, under principles of comity and the broad limits of the U.S. *Constitution*, to apply in its courts the substantive law of another jurisdiction, in accord with this state's choice-of-law rules. Another state may deny plaintiffs access to its own courts, but may not by that act deny access to the courts of West Virginia. When there is a living cause of action (even though itself a creature of Virginia law), venue is proper in a West Virginia state court, and West Virginia has personal jurisdiction over the defendant, the plaintiff may bring his claim before the state courts of West Virginia and be heard. . . .

II

If a defendant has subjected himself to suit in West Virginia under this state's long-arm statute, and the plaintiff is a resident of West Virginia, we refuse to require the plaintiff to litigate his tort claim first before any tribunal in another state. On the other hand, in consideration of our own public policy and principles of comity, we would not permit Virginia citizens with few contacts in this state to sue Virginia "health care providers" here simply to avoid the review panel procedures required in the Commonwealth of Virginia. . . .

The basic principle in this case is that a state can control access only to its own courts. Nonetheless, the particulars of another state's alternatives to the traditional civil trial are bound to influence this Court's decision to defer to that process or not. Virginia's medical malpractice review process, we conclude, is so complicated and expensive that, once it was in motion, a plaintiff would have little choice but to remain in the Virginia courts.

For the reasons set out above, we reverse the judgment of the Circuit Court of Raleigh County and remand the case for further proceedings consistent with this opinion.

Reversed and Remanded. . . .

BROTHERTON, CHIEF JUSTICE, dissenting:

I must dissent in this case because I disagree with the majority's foray into "creative jurisdiction." I do not quibble with the majority's rather blithe assumption of the existence of West Virginia's personal jurisdiction over the defendant Virginia hospital, since the defendant is licensed to do business in West Virginia. What I do object to is the majority's farcical treatment of Virginia's substantive law.

The majority admits that West Virginia adheres to the *lex loci delicti* theory of conflict of laws, thus applying the substantive law of the state where the injury took place. *Paul v. National Life*, 177 W.Va. 427, 352 S.E.2d 550 (1986). It is undisputed that the alleged injury took place in Radford, Virginia. It is also undisputed that the Fourth Circuit Court of Appeals has held that the Virginia statute requiring a medical review panel be convened to review medical malpractice suits is the *substantive* law of that state. *DiAntonio v. Northampton-Accomack Memorial Hospital*, 628 F.2d 287, 290 (4th Cir. 1980). Consequently, the majority's decision to "part ways" with the Fourth Circuit's finding in *DiAntonio* is nothing short of blatant protectionism of West Virginia residents in direct contravention of the *lex loci delicti* theory of conflict of laws. . . .

The question is not controlling "access to the courts of sister states," as the majority so coyly phrases the issue. It is a question of maintaining the integrity and predictability of the internal laws of the sister state as well as avoiding the dreaded specter of "forum shopping" to obtain the most favorable law. In this case, the plaintiff *voluntarily* availed himself of the benefits of the Commonwealth of Virginia, much as if he was involved in an automobile accident on Virginia roads. It is not only fitting, but legally correct, that he be subjected to the substantive law of the state where the injury occurred.

I would point out the majority's words in *Paul*: "we have long recognized that comity does not require the application of the substantive law of a foreign state when the law contravenes the public policy of this State." 177 W.Va. at 433, 352 S.E.2d at 556. Yet at no point in the *Vest* opinion does the majority actually find that the Virginia statute contravenes any public policy of this State. Their actions, however, do just that. Could it be that the contravened public policy is any law belonging to a foreign state that would affect the rights of a West Virginian to sue an entity in that foreign state? If that is so, then the majority has surreptitiously, but effectively, abrogated our adherence to the *lex loci delicti* theory of conflict of laws so steadfastly affirmed in *Paul*.

I can only speculate that if the situation was reversed, and a Virginia court ignored a similar statute in our State, the majority would be appalled at the disregard for comity between two sister states. In this case, however, the majority essentially proclaims: All ye citizens of this great State who stray from the friendly confines of its boundaries and are injured in a foreign state, return home, cast out your nets, and if in the casting, the net reaches far enough to snare the corporate defendant that caused the injury, reel in the net and we will give to you "the most favored citizen" interpretation of our substantive law. Foreign defendants will know to beware of causing harm to our citizens!

For the above reasons, I respectfully dissent.

———————

Courts have had great difficulty trying to work out the procedure/substance distinction. The issues are endless: statutes of limitation, burdens of proof, privileged testimony, damages, etc. Courts determined to apply their own law have characterized issues as procedural to accomplish their goal. In *Grant v. McAuliffe*, 264 P.2d 944 (Cal. 1953), the illustrious Justice Traynor applied California law to allow a suit by a California plaintiff injured in an auto accident in Arizona by a Californian who died before suit. The law of Arizona, the locus of the accident, provided that a tort action, which had not been commenced prior to the death of the decedent, must be abated. California law permitted such suits even if the suit was filed after the death of the defendant. Traynor characterized the California law as procedural and allowed the action to proceed. The case provided a springboard for Professor Brainerd Currie to write a scathing critique of the *lex loci* rule. See, Currie, Survival of Actions: Adjudication Versus Automation in the Conflict of Laws, 10 Stan. L. Rev. 205 (1958), reprinted in *Selected Essays on the Conflict of Laws* 128 (Duke University Press 1963). We will return to the substance/procedure problem with regard to statutes of limitations in a later chapter.

C. PUBLIC POLICY

As discussed below and in Chapter 4, courts may, in narrow circumstances, decline to apply the law of another jurisdiction because application of that law would violate a fundamental policy of the forum (or, as we will see in the discussion on contracts in Chapter 4, of a third state). But when a forum utilizes this doctrine to apply its own law to the case rather than the law that would otherwise govern by application of the forum's choice of law rules, it often is merely circumventing those rules. As such, the reliance on public policy to decide such a case is nothing more than an escape device not unlike those discussed earlier. In other instances, courts simply refuse to provide a forum for what they consider to be odious causes of action. If a court refuses to hear the case rather than apply the offensive foreign law and the plaintiff has no other jurisdiction in which to bring suit, the result is that the plaintiff's action is effectively barred. Nonetheless, an appeal to the "public policy" doctrine to deny a plaintiff a forum may on rare occasions be justified. As the following case indicates, it will be rare indeed when this door-closing mechanism is found to be warranted.

INTERCONTINENTAL HOTELS CORPORATION (PUERTO RICO) V. GOLDEN

203 N.E.2d 210 (N.Y. 1964)

BURKE, JUDGE

On this appeal by the plaintiff from a judgment dismissing the complaint, the only issue is whether the courts of this State must deny access to a party seeking to enforce obligations validly entered into in the Commonwealth of Puerto Rico and enforcible under Puerto Rican law.

Plaintiff, the owner and operator of a government-licensed gambling casino in Puerto Rico, seeks to recover the sum of $12,000 evidenced by defendant's check and I. O. U.s given in payment of gambling debts incurred in Puerto Rico.

Once again we are faced with the question of when our courts may refuse to enforce a foreign right, though valid where acquired, on the ground that its 'enforcement is contrary to (the public) policy of the forum' (Citations omitted).

Since these gambling debts were validly contracted in Puerto Rico and the Puerto Rican law provides a remedy for their enforcement (United Hotels of Puerto Rico v. Willig, P.R.R. (Oct. 9, 1963)), absent a clear showing that the enforcement of the causes of action here would 'offend(s) our sense of justice or menace(s) the public welfare' (Loucks v. Standard Oil Co., 224 N.Y. 99, 110, 120 N.E. 198, 201), we may not withhold aid. We do not think that public policy forbids us to enforce these contracts.

Substantially all of the commentators agree that foreign-based rights should be enforced unless the judicial enforcement of such a contract would be the approval of a transaction which is inherently vicious, wicked or immoral, and shocking to the prevailing moral sense. (Citations omitted).

Applying this test we find decision in this State involving gambling transactions which put this reasoning into practice. Over 100 years ago this court held in Thatcher v. Morris, 11 N.Y. 437 (1854) that a contract involving lottery tickets if legal and valid without the State would be upheld though illegal in New York. In Harris v. White, 81 N.Y. 532 (1880) suit was permitted for wages earned in out-of-State horse races at a time when horseracing was illegal in the State of New York. In Ormes v. Dauchy, 82 N.Y. 443 (1880) suit was upheld for commissions earned by placing extrastate lottery advertisements in out-of-State newspapers. Thus, aware of the common-law rule which barred the enforcement of gambling contracts and conscious that they were illegal and void in almost all the States of this country, the courts of this State took the position, even in Victorian times, that there was no strong public policy to prevent the enforcement of such contracts according to the law of the place of performance. There is nothing suggested by the respondent which should persuade us that Judge CARDOZO was wrong when he said in Loucks v. Standard Oil Co., 224 N.Y. 99, 111, 120 N.E. 198, 202 (1918), supra: 'The courts are not free to refuse to enforce a foreign right at the pleasure of the judges, to suit the individual notion of expediency or fairness. They do not close their doors, unless help would violate some * * * prevalent conception of good morals'.

It has, however, been urged that suits on gambling debts contracted validity elsewhere are contrary to two public policies of this State, i. e., in this jurisdiction gamblers are outlaws, and all gambling contracts made with them are void. . . .

Public policy is not determinable by mere reference to the laws of the forum alone. Strong public policy is found in prevailing social and moral attitudes of the community. In this sophisticated season the enforcement of the rights of the plaintiff in view of the weight of authority would not be considered repugnant to the 'public policy of this State'. It seems to us that, if we are to apply the strong public policy test to the enforcement of the plaintiff's rights under the gambling laws of the Commonwealth of Puerto Rico, we should measure them by the prevailing social and moral attitudes of the community which is reflected not only in the decisions of our courts in the Victorian era but sharply illustrated in the changing attitudes of the People of the State of New York. The legalization of pari-mutuel betting and the operation of bingo games, as well as a strong movement for legalized off-track betting, indicate that the New York public does not consider authorized gambling a violation of 'some prevalent conception of good morals (or), some deep-rooted tradition of the common weal.' (Loucks v. Standard Oil Co., supra, p. 111, 120 N.E. p. 202.)

The trend in New York State demonstrates an acceptance of licensed gambling transactions as a morally acceptable activity, not objectionable under the prevailing standards of lawful and approved social conduct in a community. Our newspapers quote the odds on horse races, football games, basketball games and print the names of the winners of the Irish Sweepstakes and the New Hampshire lottery. Informed public sentiment in New York is only against unlicensed gambling, which is unsupervised, unregulated by law and which affords no protection to customers and no assurance of fairness or honesty in the operation of the gambling devices.

In the present case there is no indication that the evils of gambling, which New York prohibits and Puerto Rico has licensed, will spill over into our community if these debts are enforced in New York courts. The New York constitutional provisions were adopted with a view toward protecting the family man of meager resources from his own imprudence at the gaming tables. (See Carter and Stone, Proceedings and Debates of the Convention, 567 (Hosford, 1821).)

Puerto Rico has made provision for this kind of imprudence by allowing the court to reduce gambling obligations or even decline to enforce them altogether, if the court in its discretion finds that the losses are '(in an) amount (which) may exceed the customs of a good father of a family.' (Laws of Puerto Rico Ann., tit. 31, s 4774.) This regulation is consistent with New York policy and would be properly considered in any case before a New York court which may be asked to enforce a Puerto Rican gambling debt.

There is nothing immoral per se in the contract before us, but injustice would result if citizens of this State were allowed to retain the benefits of the winnings in a State where such gambling is legal, but to renege if they were losers.

The cases relied on by the respondent miss the mark.

In the case of Mertz v. Mertz, 3 N.E.2d 597 (1936) (parallel citations omitted), Judge LEHMAN, writing for the court, said that 'a disability to sue attached by our law to the person of a wife becomes an anomaly if another state can confer upon a wife, even though residing here, capacity to sue in our courts upon a cause of action arising there' (p. 474, 3 N.E.2d p. 600; emphasis added). As distinguished from the present case, in Mertz the court was faced with this State's interest in the marital status situated here. As a practical matter, all the significant contacts of the case were with New York and the language of the opinion indicates that the court was in reality there making a choice of law decision of the kind that this court today follows under the nominal heading of the 'contacts' doctrine. . . .

We think, therefore, that this case falls within the consistent practice of enforcing rights validly created by the laws of a sister State which do not tend to disturb our local laws or corrupt the public.

Accordingly, the judgment of the Appellate Division should be reversed and the judgment of the Supreme Court, New York County, reinstated, with costs in this court and in the Appellate Division.

DESMOND, CHIEF JUDGE (dissenting).

The court is holding that there is no public policy against the use of a New York court as a collection agency by a gambling house proprietor who is guilty of the social wrong of letting his customers gamble on a charge account basis. This comes as a surprise in a State where the professional gambler has always been treated as an outlaw and a gambling house considered as a criminal nuisance. (Citations omitted). . . .

Plaintiff, a Delaware corporation and operator of a Commonwealth-licensed gambling room or casino in its hotel in Puerto Rico, sued defendant, a New York resident, on a $3,000 check and 13 'I. O. U.s' totaling $9,000. The $12,000 total covered defendant's gambling losses at plaintiff's casino where defendant had been allowed to gamble on credit. The trial court sitting without a jury gave judgment for plaintiff but the Appellate Division, reversing, held that such a loan is not collectible in the courts of New York.

The issue: are our courts open to suits by gambling house proprietors who let their customers run up debts; or do such transactions so offend our concept of good morals that our settled public policy prompts us to reject the suit? Closing our doors to such a lawsuit is in principle and under our decisions and statutes the only possible course. It is not a matter of choice of law as between the Puerto Rican and domestic brands. We refuse the suit not because Puerto Rico's law differs from ours but because we cannot in good conscience use our judicial processes to recognize the gamester's claim by giving him a judgment. (Citations omitted). . . .

In truth, not one but two public policies of ours are offended when we give judgment for plaintiff. First, operating a gambling business (as distinguished from casual betting between individuals) was an indictable public nuisance at common law, has always been held criminal conduct in New York State, and professional gamblers are 'outlaws' in New York. (Citations omitted). Second, from earliest times in this State all gambling contracts and loans for gambling have been void and denied enforcement by the professional gambler even to the extent that the bettor-customer may sue for the amount he lost (Penal Law, s 994; Watts v. Malatesta, supra). As this court said in the Watts case in 1933 (p. 82, 186 N.E. p. 211): 'The reason seems obvious. Curb the professional with his constant offer of temptation coupled with ready opportunity, and you have to a large extent controlled the evil.' It denies both history and logic to hold that despite all these showings of public policy our courts must give this plaintiff judgment. . . .

The judgment should be affirmed, with costs.

DYE, FULD, SCILEPPI and BERGAN, JJ., concur with BURKE, J.

DESMOND, C. J., dissents in an opinion in which VAN VOORHIS, J., concurs.

The *Loucks* case, cited several times by the majority, is the leading case in the area. Courts are loath to recognize a "public policy" exception to application of foreign law (*i.e.*, the law of another jurisdiction, whether it be another U.S. state or another nation) unless the foreign law is highly offensive to the forum. We will examine the practical effect of the public policy doctrine in relation to choice of law in contracts in a later chapter (where we will see that reference is also made to the public policy of other jurisdictions).

The majority opinion in *Intercontinental* notes that even under the law of Puerto Rico, allowances are made if the impact on the gambler's family finances are severe. If such allowances were not incorporated in the law of Puerto Rico, would the New York court still have applied Puerto Rican law (or would the lack of that "safety valve" have led to a conclusion that Puerto Rican law violated a fundamental policy of New York)? What if the result were that gambler's family would have to go on welfare?

For an early commentary on the public policy issue see Paulson and Sovern, *"Public Policy in the Conflict of Laws"*, 56 Colum. L.Rev. 969 (1956) (Public policy used as a tool to apply local law without confronting the difficult choice-of-law issues.

D. RENVOI

We have already made brief mention of renvoi when we discussed the dissenting opinion of Justice Fairchild in the *Haumschild* case *supra*. Here is the issue: When a court in State A applies State A conflict of laws rules to conclude that the law of State B governs a case, should the State A court look only to the substantive law of State B or should it look to State B's conflict of laws doctrines as well and apply the law of the jurisdiction that would be applied by the courts of State B? In other words, if State B's conflict of laws rules would lead a State B court to apply the law of State A, or some other third state, to the case at bar, should the State A court simply apply the "internal" law of State B (as suggested by State A's conflict of laws rules) or should the State A court resolve the case as a State B court would resolve it (and, thus, apply the law that would be applied by a State B court applying State B conflict of laws rules)? Should the State A court at least take into consideration the fact that the foreign jurisdiction would not apply its own law? Renvoi has fascinated scholars because it raises jurisprudential issues of great magnitude. For those interested in the subject see Griswold, *Renvoi Revisited*, 51 Harv. L. Rev. 1165 (1938); Kramer, *Return of the Renvoi*, 66 N.Y.U.L. Rev. 979 (1991).

As a practical matter, American courts generally do not look at the choice of law rules of a foreign jurisdiction when deciding which law governs a case. The First Restatement recognized two exceptions to the general rule rejecting renvoi. Under the first Restatement, questions dealing with title to land and the validity of a decree of divorce were decided as would the state of the situs of land (for title to land) and by the domicile of the parties (in divorce actions). The Second Restatement is a bit vaguer; Section 8(2) recognizes renvoi whenever "the objective of the particular choice-of-law rule is that the forum reach the same result on the very facts involved as would the courts of another state." One example given in Section 8(2) is the validity of transfer of interests to land.

A more extensive discussion of renvoi is delayed until a later chapter, after we have discussed modern approaches to choice of law. Until we get there, you might want to think about whether a forum court should be influenced in its choice of law decision by the choice of law views of the other jurisdiction as to the matter at hand even if the forum court does not automatically defer to those rules by application of renvoi.

CHAPTER 3

THE CHOICE-OF-LAW REVOLUTION

■ ■ ■

A. INTRODUCTION

The jurisdiction-selecting rules we have examined in Chapters 1 and 2 operated blindly without taking into account the policies behind the supposedly conflicting domestic rules. By the middle of the 20th century, however, those rigid jurisdiction-selecting rules, adopted in large part by the First Restatement, came under heavy academic fire by outstanding scholars who recognized that intelligent choice-of-law doctrine required a court to examine the content of the rules in potential conflict as they related to the facts of the case under litigation. The most influential work that toppled the First Restatement rules came from the pen of Professor Brainerd Currie. In a series of articles he demonstrated that in many instances what appeared to be a conflict between the laws of differing jurisdictions simply vanished when one examined the facts of the case and the policies behind the conflicting laws. The First Restatement rules, he contended, often got the wrong result for no good reason. Reading Currie for the first time is like watching a bulldozer attack a mountain and leveling it to the ground. His work has been followed by scholars too numerous to enumerate at this point of our discussion. We shall make reference to some, but not all, of them when we take up the cases. But, first things first. Read what Professor Currie had to say in his classic article *Married Women's Contracts: A Study in Conflict-of-Laws Method*, 25 U. Chi. L. Rev. 227 (1958), reprinted in Brainerd Currie, Selected Essays on Conflict of Laws, Ch. 2 (1963). We apologize for the length of the excerpt, but it is the only way that we can give you the true flavor of Currie's writing.

In 1870 Mrs. Pratt, at her home in Massachusetts, executed a guaranty of her husband's credit in favor of a partnership doing business in Portland, Maine. She delivered the instrument to her husband, who mailed it to the firm in Maine. In reliance on the guaranty, and in response to orders placed by Mr. Pratt, the partnership delivered goods to Mr. Pratt, either in person or by common carrier "for him," Mr. Pratt paying the shipping charges. Upon default, the partners sued Mrs. Pratt in Massachusetts on the guaranty. According to a Maine statute enacted in 1866, a married woman was competent to bind herself by contract as if she

51

were unmarried. According to the law of Massachusetts at the time of the transaction, a married woman could not bind herself by contract as surety or for the accommodation of her husband or of any third person.

Reversing a judgment for the defendant, Mr. Justice Gray, for the Supreme Judicial Court of Massachusetts, announced that "[t]he general rule is that the validity of a contract is to be determined by the law of the state in which it is made. . . ." Treating the instrument executed by Mrs. Pratt as an offer for a unilateral contract, and concluding that the offer was accepted when and where the offeree delivered goods to the buyer or to a carrier for him, which was in Maine, the court concluded that Maine law governed and gave the contract validity. The court specifically rejected, on pragmatic grounds, the suggestion that such a question of capacity to contract should be decided in accordance with the law of the domicile. Finally, having determined that the contract was valid according to the applicable foreign law, it declined to take advantage of a second line of defense for Mrs. Pratt, which was available in the doctrine of local public policy. In this it was fortified by the fact that, after the transaction but before the action had been filed, Massachusetts law had been changed so as to remove the incapacity of married women. . . .

Before we begin our discussion of *Milliken v. Pratt*, I should like to change one of the facts. It is evident from the opinion of the court, and the fact has been duly noted, that the change in the Massachusetts law between the time of the transaction and the filing of the suit had a material influence on the decision. But for that fact, it is possible that the Massachusetts court might have held that the applicable law was that of the married woman's domicile, although that seems doubtful in view of Mr. Justice Gray's clear appreciation of the practical inconvenience of such a rule. More likely, the court, while professing adherence to the principle that the law of the place of making governs, would have invoked local public policy as its justification for not applying the "applicable" law. At any rate, the change in the domestic law of Massachusetts destroyed any conflict of interest between Massachusetts and Maine, and so any real problem of conflict of laws. If we are to proceed with this discussion we must have a problem. I therefore suggest that we delete from our consideration the fact that the Massachusetts law was changed. Indeed, I suggest that we go one step farther. We are not a great deal better off if all we know about the position of Massachusetts is that it retained a rule disabling married women to assume the obligations of suretyship. One of the reasons why we can tolerate a mechanical, deductive system of conflict of laws and the anomalies it produces is that frequently—and this is especially true of common-law rules—the purpose and policy of the rule is obscured by the mists of antiquity, or is obsolete, or simply inconsequential. There still may be no discernible conflict of interest. I should therefore like to assume that, shortly prior to 1870, a bill was introduced in the Massachusetts General Assembly for the enactment of a law similar to that enacted in Maine in

1866, removing the contractual disabilities of married women; that the issue was fully debated; that the proposal was defeated by a decisive though by no means overwhelming majority; and that the explicit reason for its defeat was the only one even remotely intelligible in modern times: that (in the judgment of the majority of the General Assembly) married women as a class are a peculiarly susceptible lot, prone to make improvident promises, especially under the influence of their husbands. We thus assume that by its negative action the General Assembly in effect gave deliberate approval to the existing rule: that no contract whereby any married woman might undertake to assume liability as a surety should subject her to judgment in any court. . . .

Lawgivers, legislative and judicial, are accustomed to speak in terms of unqualified generality. Apart from the imperatives, the words most inevitably found in rules of law are words like "all," "every," "no," "any," and "whoever." In part, perhaps, this propensity is traceable to the fact that there lurks in all of us some vestige of the superstition that laws have an inherent quality of universality, derived from their association with Justice and Right Reason. This, however, might not be taken too seriously, because in a great many cases it is quite obvious that the lawgivers do not mean all that they say. Suppose, for example, that we could buttonhole in the statehouse corridor the personification of the Massachusetts General Assembly and ask, "Now, really, do you mean to say that, if a married woman living in Maine should execute in Maine a guaranty of her husband's obligation to a Maine creditor, a Maine court could not or should not enter judgment on the guaranty against her?" There is no doubt at all what the startled, condescending reply would be: "Certainly not. What Maine courts do in actions between Maine parties arising out of Maine transactions is no affair of mine. Massachusetts problems are more than enough to keep me busy, thank you." . . .

Let us stipulate that in a case like *Milliken v. Pratt* there are just four factors, which may be significant for our purposes:

1. The domicile, or nationality, or residence, or place of business of the creditor;

2. The domicile, or nationality, or residence of the married woman;

3. The place of the transaction, i.e., the place where the contract is made, or possibly the place where it is to be performed;

4. The place where the action is brought. . . .

In such a case as *Milliken v. Pratt*, then, there are four factors of possible significance for the conflict of laws, each of which may be either domestic or foreign (to Massachusetts). There are therefore sixteen possible combinations—sixteen different cases which may arise. One of these is the purely domestic case, and one is purely foreign. That leaves fourteen conflict-of-laws cases. By oversimplifying the problem and making certain rather arbitrary assumptions we have been able to reduce the possibilities to this relatively small range. Even so, the fourteen different conflict-of-laws cases are difficult to visualize. It may be useful to present the whole array. (Table 1).

If we were to place this array before our personification of the Massachusetts General Assembly, asking that he point out just which of the fourteen mixed cases the Massachusetts rule is intended to govern, and why, we should almost certainly meet with impatience and rebuff. Most likely, the reply would be that such questions belong to the realm of conflict of laws, and are for the courts to determine. This does not mean that legislatures, when they are disposed to specify how their laws shall apply to cases involving foreign factors, refrain from doing so out of deference to the courts. It simply means, in this case, that the legislature has not thought about the matter, and does not want to think about it.

Left thus to our own devices, we may inquire what policy can reasonably be attributed to the legislature, and how it can best be effectuated by the courts in their handling of mixed cases. At the outset, it is well to recognize that the legislature can effectively control the result of litigation only in its own courts, so that strictly speaking we might concern ourselves here with only half of the cases. We shall not so confine ourselves, however, because the legislature may desire to control the event of litigation in foreign courts, and the foreign court may, for one reason or another, defer to that desire.

TABLE 1

	FACTORS *					
	1	2	3	4		
	R	R	K	F		
CASE	C	M				
NUMBER		W				
1.	D	D	D	D	All factors domestic	(1)
2.	F	D	D	D		
3.	D	F	D	D	One foreign factor	(4)
4.	D	D	F	D		
5.	D	D	D	F		
6.	F	F	D	D		
7.	D	F	F	D		
8.	D	D	F	F	Two foreign factors	(6)
9.	F	D	D	F		

	1	2	3	4		
10......	F	D	F	D		
11......	D	F	D	F		
12......	F	F	F	D		
13......	F	F	D	F	Three foreign factors	(4)
14......	F	D	F	F		
15......	D	F	F	F		
16......	F	F	F	F	All factors foreign	(1)

     * 1.   Residence of the creditor.

        2.   Residence of the married woman.

        3.   Place of contracting.

        4.   Forum.

It is surely not a difficult matter to formulate the legislative policy in this case. We have in effect already done so in the act of artificial respiration performed on the moribund body of the law concerning the contractual capacity of married women. Massachusetts, in common with all other American states and many foreign countries, believes in freedom of contract, in the security of commercial transactions, in vindicating the reasonable expectations of promises. It also believes, however, that married women constitute a class requiring special protection. It has therefore subordinated its policy of security of transactions to its policy of protecting married women. More specifically, it has subordinated the interests of creditors to the interests of this particular, favored class of debtors. It has felt the influence of pressure groups—banking and commercial interests, feminists, liberals, traditionalists, conservatives. It has weighed competing considerations. Many of the legislators have been persuaded that there should be a change. Yet, although the decision runs counter to the interests of powerful constituents, the legislature decides in favor of protecting married women.

What married women? Why, those with whose welfare Massachusetts is concerned, of course—*i.e.*, Massachusetts married women. In 1866 Maine emancipated (its) married women. Is Massachusetts declaring that decision erroneous, attempting to alter its effect? Certainly not. Given a slightly different configuration of the little causes that determine the outcome of the legislative process, Massachusetts might have decided the same way. Who can say that Maine, or Massachusetts for that matter, was wrong? All that happened was that in each state the legislature weighed competing considerations, with different results. Well, each to his own. Let Maine go feminist and modern; as for Massachusetts, it will stick to the old ways—for Massachusetts women. Never mind, for the time being, exactly what we mean by "Massachusetts" married women—whether citizens, domiciliaries, residents. For the sake of convenience, until we must decide that question, let us say that it is *residence* in Massachusetts which defines the ambit of the state's protective policy. . . .

The way to judge the rule is to see how it operates. . . .

In Case No. 2, application of the domestic law makes good sense. It protects Massachusetts married women, and that without expense to Massachusetts creditors. If the foreign state is Maine, Maine's interest in the security of transactions is defeated. But if one state's policy must yield, should not the court prefer the policy of its own state?

TABLE 2

		Factors			
		1	2	3	4
		R	R	K	F
CASE		C	M		
NUMBER			W		
2.........		F	D	D	D
3.........		D	F	D	D
6.........		F	F	D	D

In Case No. 3, despite the fact that three of the four factors are domestic, application of the domestic law makes no sense whatever. In the context with which we are concerned, it is abundantly clear that there is at stake no policy of Massachusetts relating to the administration of her courts. Sometimes such a policy is involved, and legitimately, as when the state believes that certain types of claims consume the time of courts without adequate social justification, or tend to the corruption of judicial processes. No such considerations are involved here; no one suggests that the Massachusetts rule as to a married woman's capacity is "procedural." The only policies apparently at stake are those which have been suggested. And how does the application of the domestic law in Case No. 3 accord with those policies? (1) It does not advance the interest of Massachusetts in protecting Massachusetts married women, for the defendant is not a resident of Massachusetts. (2) It subverts the interest of Massachusetts in the security of transactions, to the detriment of a Massachusetts creditor. This interest, it should be remembered, was not renounced by the legislative action, but only subordinated to another interest, which is not present in this case. Moreover, suppose that at this point we inquire into the identity of the foreign state, and into the content of its law. The foreign state proves to be Maine, which has emancipated its married women. In that event, application of the Massachusetts law (3) does not advance any interest of Maine in protecting married women and (4) conflicts with

Maine's general policy of security of transactions, although that policy is not directly involved, since the creditor is a Massachusetts resident. In short, application of the domestic rule advances no interest of either state, and clearly subverts an important interest of Massachusetts itself. That is to say, it advances no interest which has yet become apparent. Whether there are higher interests which warrant such apparently irrational behavior remains to be seen.

In Case No. 6, application of the domestic law makes no sense either. Both parties are nonresidents. Massachusetts has no interest in the married woman, and no apparent justification for upsetting the creditor's reasonable expectations. Massachusetts is merely meddling. In so doing, it subverts Maine's legitimate interest in the security of transactions where Maine creditors are concerned, without advancing any state's interest in protecting married women.

In short, of the three cases which Massachusetts has determined to control, and which she can effectively control, the application of Massachusetts law makes sense, in terms of Massachusetts policy, in only one. In the other two, the application of that law advances the interests of neither state, and subverts an interest of one state or the other. This is, indeed, peculiar behavior.

The cases in which Massachusetts had said that Massachusetts law ought to apply, but in which a foreign court will make the decision, are shown in Table 3.

TABLE 3

	Factors			
	1	2	3	4
	R	R	K	F
CASE	C	M		
NUMBER		W		
5.........	D	D	D	F
9.........	F	D	D	F
11.........	D	F	D	F
13.........	F	F	D	F

In Case No. 5 it is reasonable enough for Massachusetts to express the hope that other states will apply Massachusetts law. That is what Massachusetts would do if the case were in her courts (Case No. 1). No other state appears to have any legitimate interest in the matter.

In Case No. 9, also, it is reasonable for Massachusetts to hope that foreign courts will apply Massachusetts law. This is the foreign creditor against the domestic married woman. If the case were in the Massachusetts courts, Massachusetts would rationally apply domestic law (Case No. 2, discussed above). This may be asking a good deal of the foreign state, since now the power factor is reversed and Maine is in position to give preference to its own policy. But Massachusetts has done what it can.

In Case No. 11, the creditor is a resident of Massachusetts and the married woman is a nonresident. If the foreign state is Maine, it is simply irrational for Massachusetts to express the hope that Massachusetts law will be applied. True, if the case were in a Massachusetts court, Massachusetts would so decide (Case No. 3, discussed above); but that decision would be irrational, and this is so for the same reasons.

In Case No. 13, the Massachusetts hope that the foreign court will apply Massachusetts law is presumptuous and downright laughable. Massachusetts has nothing whatever to do with the case except that the contract was "made" there. If the foreign state is Maine, Massachusetts is asking that the state to subvert its own policy, which gives primacy to the security of transactions, even where Maine interests alone are involved. True, if the case were in a Massachusetts court, Massachusetts would so decide (Case No. 6, discussed above); but if such a result would be indefensible in a Massachusetts court, it would be more painfully so in a court of Maine.

In short, the expression by Massachusetts of hope that foreign courts will apply Massachusetts law makes sense, in terms of Massachusetts interests, in only two of the four cases. In the other two, realization of the hope would advance the policy of neither state, and would defeat the policy of one state or the other.

Of the seven cases which Massachusetts has disclaimed an interest in controlling, four are cases which it has de facto power to control, since they are in Massachusetts courts, as shown in Table 4.

TABLE 4

	Factors			
	1	2	3	4
	R	R	K	F
CASE	C	M		
NUMBER		W		
4.........	D	D	F	D
7.........	D	F	F	D
10........	F	D	F	D
12........	F	F	F	D

In Case No. 4, the position taken by Massachusetts seems incredibly perverse. No state other than Massachusetts has any interest in the matter. Yet Massachusetts goes to the trouble of ascertaining and applying foreign law. To what end? The result, if the foreign state is Maine, is to defeat Massachusetts' own preferred policy of protecting its married women, without advancing any policy whatever.

In Case No. 7, where the creditor is domestic and the married woman a nonresident, the application of foreign law, if the foreign state is Maine, results in the furtherance of Massachusetts' subsidiary interest in security of transactions for local creditors without impairing any interest of either state in the protection of married women.

In Case No. 10, application of the law of Maine results in furthering Maine's legitimate interest in security of transactions at the expense of Massachusetts' legitimate interest in the protection of its married women. Let us not condemn such a result hastily. Where the interest of the foreign state is substantial and legitimate, as here, there may well be, among civilized states, reasons for relaxing the uncompromising attitude of selfishness and requiring legitimate local policy to yield. Inquiry into the possible existence of such reasons is deferred for the time being. We should note now, however, that Massachusetts' position in this case is quite inconsistent with its position in Case No. 2, discussed above, where, faced with the identical conflict of interests, Massachusetts reached the conclusion that the foreign policy must yield. If Massachusetts in Case No. 10 is acting upon altruistic or far-sighted considerations which we have not yet discovered, she does not do so consistently.

In Case No. 12, the result of applying foreign law is eminently satisfactory. Maine alone is concerned. Maine would decide the same way if the case were in a Maine court (Case No. 16). Massachusetts has no reason to desire a different result. Maine policy is furthered without impairment of any policy of Massachusetts.

In short, in these four cases where Massachusetts has disclaimed interest and willingly applied foreign law though it had de facto power to do otherwise with less trouble, the result clearly makes sense in terms of Massachusetts' interests in only two cases. In one case Massachusetts' interests are made to yield to those of the foreign state. In the remaining case, Massachusetts' interests are subverted without advancing any foreign interest.

Finally, Table 5 shows the three cases which Massachusetts has disclaimed an interest in controlling, and which it cannot effectively control since they are in foreign courts.

TABLE 5

	Factors			
	1	2	3	4
	R	R	K	F
CASE	C	M		
NUMBER		W		
8.........	D	D	F	F
14.........	F	D	F	F
15.........	D	F	F	F

In Case No. 8, Massachusetts invites Maine to apply Maine law although Maine has no interest in doing so, and although the result is to subvert Massachusetts policy with no advantage to Maine.

In Case No. 14, Massachusetts invites Maine to apply Maine law, preferring the interest of Maine and its creditors to that of Massachusetts and its married women. (Compare Cases Nos. 2 and 10, discussed above.)

In Case No. 15, Massachusetts invites Maine to apply Maine law with the result that Massachusetts' subsidiary interest in security of transactions is advanced without prejudice to any policy for the protection of married women.

In short, the result of the application of foreign law is subversive of Massachusetts' interests in two cases, in neither of which is any interest of the foreign state advanced. In one case the policy of Massachusetts is advanced without detriment to any state's policy.

Summarizing the entire series, we find that application of the law of the place of making has the results shown in Table 6, if we assume (1) that the foreign law is different and (2) that Massachusetts' wishes will be respected by the foreign state.

	TABLE 6				
I	Domestic interest advanced without detriment to foreign interests.	Case No.	5	(DDD)	(3)
		Case No.	7	(DFF)	
		Case No.	15	(DFFF)	
II	Foreign interest advanced without detriment to domestic interests.	Case No.	12	(FFFD)	(1)
III	Domestic interest advanced at expense of foreign interests.	Case No.	2	(FDD)	(2)
		Case No.	9	(FDD)	
IV	Foreign interest advanced at expense of domestic interest.	Case No.	10	(FDF)	(2)
		Case No.	14	(FDFF)	
V	Foreign interest subverted with no advancement of domestic interests.	Case No.	6	(FFD)	(2)
		Case No.	13	(FFDF)	
VI	Domestic interest subverted without advancement of foreign interests.	Case No.	3	(DFD)	(4)
		Case No.	11	(DFD)	
		Case No.	4	(DDF)	
		Case No.	8	(DDF)	

A startling fact shown by this table is that the *largest* group of cases (group VI) consists of those in which application of the rule subverts domestic interest without advancing any interest of the foreign state. Add to this the group in which foreign interests are subverted with no advancement of domestic policy (group V), and we have a total of six of the fourteen cases in which the operation of the rule seems purely perverse. Against this result, note that application of the rule advances domestic interests in only five cases (groups I and III), and in two of these does so at the expense of foreign interests. Note also that the result in the two cases last mentioned is exactly counterbalanced by the fact that in two cases, apparently indistinguishable (group IV), domestic interests are subordinated to foreign. The deference to foreign interests appears to have a certain rhythm, but is without rhyme or reason. . . .

The most forceful affirmative defense that can be made for the traditional method is that it leads to uniformity of result, regardless of the state in which the action is brought. This, given the assumptions of the method, is undeniably true. It is also undeniably true that uniformity of result should be one of the primary objectives of a rational system of conflict of laws. According to the rule that the law of the place of making governs, any given case is decided in the same way irrespective of the state in which the action is brought. That is to say, this is the result if both states (1) characterize the problem in the same way, as one involving the validity of a contract, and (2) apply the rule that the law of the place of making governs (rather than some alternative rule), and (3) locate the connecting factor (the place of making) in the same way, and (4) do not invoke any second-line defenses, such as local public policy. This is a long list of "ifs," and we are well aware that the discipline of the system is not always sufficient to maintain adherence to all of the necessary conditions when the result is perceived to be anomalous. The ideal uniformity of result is, therefore, to some extent illusory. But assume that the necessary conditions are all observed, and the ideal uniformity results. Is the achievement worth the cost at which it was attained? The cost, be it remembered, is that in six of the fourteen possible cases the interests of one state are defeated without advancement of the interests of the other, and that in two additional cases the interests of the forum are made to yield to foreign interests. In only four cases are the interests of one state advanced without impairment of a foreign interest. In two cases the interest of the forum are given preference over foreign interests. This seems an extravagant price to pay for uniformity of result—the more so since the attainment of that goal is in fact problematical. We are moved to recognize again that uniformity of result, while it is a basic and ever-present desideratum in conflict-of-laws cases, is one which should at times be made to yield to stronger considerations. And it may be added that, in the only two cases in which uniformity can be said to be without question an imperative objective (Nos. 5 and 12, in which all factors except the place of action are associated with the same state), uniformity would be attained if the respective states did no more than consult their own legitimate interests. . . .

The fourteen possible conflict-of-laws cases which have been enumerated fall into two classes. The ten cases in the larger class present *no real conflicts problem*. The four cases in the smaller class present real problems, but they are problems which *cannot be solved* by any science or method of conflict-of-laws. Recognition of these blunt facts provides a basis—so far as I can see, the only basis—for progress toward a more satisfactory method of dealing with the cases. . . .

Turning now to Case No. 3 . . ., which involves a true conflict of interest, I can only repeat that no satisfactory solution can possibly be evolved by means of the resources of conflict-of-laws law. . . .

The sensible and clearly constitutional thing for any court to do, confronted with a true conflict of interests, is to apply its own law. In this way it can be sure at least that it is consistently advancing the policy of its own state. It should apply its own law, not because of any notion or pretense that the problem is one relating to procedure, but simply because a court should never apply any other law except when there is a good reason for doing so. That so doing will promote the interests of a foreign state at the expense of the interests of the forum state is not a good reason. Nor is the fact that such deference may lead to a conjectural uniformity of results among the different forums a good reason, when the price for that uniformity is either the indiscriminate impairment of local policy in half of the cases or the consistent yielding of local policy to the policy of a foreign state. . . .

It will be said that this is a "give-it-up" philosophy. Of course it is. A give-it-up attitude is constructive when it appears that the task is impossible of accomplishment with the resources which are available. It would have been constructive if geometricians had given up long before they did the effort to square the circle by means of straight-edge and compass. "The application of analysis to geometry saves effort by showing the direct way to success for soluble problems, and no less by showing certain others to be insoluble. . . . The classic example is the squaring of the circle by an Euclidean construction. For centuries, geometers were convinced that only a little more skill or luck was wanted for success, and no one was then in a position to assert that every conceivable attempt must fail. By the aid of analysis, that assertion is now proved." It would be constructive if legal scholars were to give up the attempt to construct systems for choice of law—an attempt which cannot result in the satisfactory resolution of true conflicts of interest between states, and which is very likely to result in the creation of problems which do not otherwise exist, and which are badly resolved by the system. . . .

In short, Currie essentially argues that choice-of-law problems are of two kinds: false conflicts that are non-problems and true conflicts that cannot be solved by any choice-of-law rule or methodology. When faced with a true conflict, Currie argues that a court should apply its own law furthering its own interest. As we shall see, courts have, by and large, bought into the first part of Currie's thesis but very few have bought into the notion that there is no rational way to resolve true conflicts. For an early critique of Currie, see Hill, *Governmental Interest Analysis and the Conflict of Laws: A Reply to Professor Currie*, 27 U. Chi. L. Rev. 463 (1960).

Office Talk
#2

Neil   Isn't Currie exactly right that Massachusetts' law was intended to protect Massachusetts married women? If Maine wants to emancipate its married women that should be of no concern to Massachusetts.

Aaron   Not so fast, Neil. According to Currie, if a Maine married women contracts in Massachusetts with a Massachusetts resident then it is a false conflict. Massachusetts should be more than happy to have its resident collect from a Maine married woman who is a debtor. I am far from sure that Currie is right. If Massachusetts has a policy of protecting married women from overbearing husbands who force them to guarantee their debts, then why is that policy not relevant when the coercion takes place in Massachusetts? Think of it: the Maine husband is standing next to his wife in Boston and whispers to her "If you know what is good for you, you had better sign the guarantee. I need those goods for my store." Should Massachusetts not have a say about coercion in its own state?

Neil: I hear you loud and clear. But it is one thing to say that Massachusetts *might* have been concerned about the scenario you imagine, or *should* have been concerned about it, while it is another thing to conclude that Massachusetts *was*, indeed, concerned about it. Nonetheless, if we need to resolve the conflict, isn't it better to resolve it in favor of Maine law and enforce the joint policy of enforcing contracts?

Aaron: Neil, you may be right. In fact, I would probably agree. But not because the case is a false conflict. As you say "it may be better to resolve the conflict in favor of Maine law." If the case is a "true conflict" we need to develop a jurisprudence to deal with true conflicts. Currie, however, believes that true conflicts can't be resolved and that the forum should apply its own law.

B. FALSE CONFLICT CASE LAW

The landmark case that formally rejected the *lex loci dilecti* rule for torts, Babcock v. Jackson, 191 N.E.2d 279 (N.Y. 1963) involved a New York plaintiff who was a passenger in a car driven by a New York defendant, who owned, registered and insured the car in New York. They had gone for a weekend trip to Ontario, where, unfortunately, the driver crashed into a stone wall. The plaintiff returned to New York and sued the defendant for negligence. The defendant raised the Ontario "guest statute" which prohibited suits by guests against negligent hosts as a defense. The New York Court of Appeals found that the purpose of the Ontario guest statute was to prevent fraud and collusion between the driver and guest passenger. The court said, "the fraudulent claims intended to be prevented by the statute are those asserted against Ontario defendants and their insurance carriers, not New York defendants and their insurance carriers. Whether New York defendants are imposed upon or their insurers defrauded by a New York plaintiff is scarcely a valid legislative concern of Ontario simply because the accident occurred there, any more than if the accident had happened in some other jurisdiction." *Id.* at 284. In Currie's lexicon this is a "false conflict" case plain and simple.

In the ensuing years, New York courts were confronted with an array of host-guest cases in which the fact patterns were not so clearly aligned with New York as was the case in *Babcock*. Six years later the Court of Appeals tried to straighten out the mess. We set forth Tooker v. Lopez, 249 N.E.2d 394 (N.Y. 1969), not only because of the majority opinion, but also because the rules articulated by Judge Fuld in his concurring opinion are now dominant in New York and have influenced courts in other jurisdictions.

TOOKER V. LOPEZ
249 N.E.2d 394 (N.Y. 1969)

KEATING, JUDGE

On October 16, 1964, Catharina Tooker, a 20-year-old coed at Michigan State University, was killed when the Japanese sports car in which she was a passenger overturned after the driver had lost control of the vehicle while attempting to pass another car. The accident also took the life of the driver of the vehicle, Marcia Lopez, and seriously injured another passenger, Susan Silk. The two girls were classmates of Catharina Tooker at Michigan State University and lived in the same dormitory. They were en route from the university to Detroit, Michigan, to spend the weekend.

Catharina Tooker and Marcia Lopez were both New York domiciliaries. The automobile which Miss Lopez was driving belonged to her father who resided in New York, where the sports car he had given his daughter was registered and insured.

This action for wrongful death was commenced by Oliver P. Tooker, Jr., the father of Catharina Tooker, as the administrator of her estate. The defendant asserted as an affirmative defense the Michigan 'guest statute' (C.L.S., s 257.401 (Stat.Ann.1960, s 9.2101)) which permits recovery by guests only by showing willful misconduct or gross negligence of the driver. The plaintiff moved to dismiss the affirmative defense on the ground that under the governing choice-of-law rules it was New York law rather than Michigan law which applied. The motion was granted by the Special Term Justice who concluded that: 'New York State 'has the greatest concern with the specific issue raised in the litigation' and New York law should apply.' The Appellate Division (Third Department) agreed with 'the cogent argument advanced by Special Term' but felt 'constrained' by the holding in Dym v. Gordon, 16 N.Y.2d 120, 262 N.Y.S.2d 463, 209 N.E.2d 792 (1965) to apply the Michigan guest statute.

We are presented here with a choice-of-law problem which we have had occasion to consider in several cases since our decision in Babcock v. Jackson, 191 N.E.2d 279 (N.Y. 1963) rejected the traditional rule which looked invariably to the law of the place of the wrong. Unfortunately, as we recently had occasion to observe, our decisions subsequent to rejection of the Lex loci delictus rule 'have lacked a precise consistency'. . . .

[The court discussed *Babcock*]

The issue before us, [in *Babcock*] as Judge Fuld pointed out, was 'not whether the defendant offended against a rule of the road prescribed by Ontario for motorists generally or whether he violated some standard of conduct imposed by that jurisdiction, but rather whether the plaintiff, because she was a guest in the defendant's automobile, is barred from recovering damages for a wrong concededly committed.' As to that issue we concluded it was New York which had the only interest. 'New York's policy of requiring a tort-feasor to compensate his guest for injuries caused by his negligence cannot be doubted * * * and our courts have neither reason nor warrant for departing from that policy simply because the accident, solely affecting New York residents and arising out of the operation of a New York based automobile, happened beyond its borders. Per contra, Ontario has no conceivable interest in denying a remedy to a New York guest against his New York host for injuries suffered in Ontario by reason of conduct which was tortious under Ontario law.' (191 N.E.2d p. 284, Supra.)

Babcock v. Jackson (supra) was followed by Dym v. Gordon, 209 N.E.2d 792 (N.Y. 1965). There, the plaintiff and defendant were both New York domiciliaries who were taking courses at the University of Colorado during the summer of 1959. The plaintiff and defendant became acquainted at school and on one occasion, while a passenger in a car driven by the defendant, plaintiff was injured when the automobile collided with another vehicle.

Upon her return to New York, the plaintiff commenced an action to recover for her personal injuries. Again, a 'guest statute' defense, predicated this time on Colorado law, was asserted. The Colorado statute, less severe in its effect than that of Ontario, permitted a guest to recover upon showing of gross negligence. The standard for recovery was apparently intended to lessen the possibility of fraud by requiring the plaintiff to sustain a heavier burden of proof and also may have represented a policy determination that drivers guilty of such reckless conduct be held fully responsible for their conduct. The assertion of the statute as a defense presented a question similar to that in Babcock v. Jackson (supra).

Judge Burke, speaking for the court, articulated a choice-of-law rule which we have had occasion to apply in numerous cases: '(I)t is necessary first to isolate the issue, next to identify the policies embraced in the laws in conflict, and finally to examine the contacts of the respective jurisdictions to ascertain which has a * * * superior interest in having its policy or law applied.' (209 N.E.2d p. 794, Supra.)

In applying the rule to the facts of the case we concluded that the purpose of this guest statute was not only to prevent fraudulent claims against Colorado insurers, but was intended as well to grant injured parties in other cars priority over the 'ungrateful guest' in the assets of the negligent driver. Since the case, in fact, involved another vehicle and injured third parties, we concluded that Colorado, unlike Ontario in Babcock v. Jackson (supra), had an interest in the application of its law. Faced with a true conflict of laws, a closely divided court determined that Colorado law ought to govern since the parties had resided in that State for so prolonged a period of time and there, therefore, seemed no unfairness in subjecting them to the law of Colorado.

The decision in Dym v. Gordon, upon which the Appellate Division relied in the instant case, is clearly distinguishable from the facts here. There is here no third-party 'non-guest' who was injured and there is no question of denying such a party priority in the assets of the negligent defendant. We cannot, however, in candor rest our decision on this basis in light of a subsequent decision which refused to apply the Ontario guest statute in a case indistinguishable from Dym v. Gordon (supra). See Macey v. Rozbicki, 221 N.E.2d 380 (N.Y. 1966).

The primary point of division in Dym v. Gordon (supra) focused not upon the choice-of-law rule quoted earlier (see dissenting opn. of Fuld, J., 16 N.Y.2d pp. 129–130, 262 N.Y.S.2d pp. 470–471, 209 N.E.2d pp. 797–798, Supra), but rather upon the construction placed on the Colorado guest statute which, upon reflection, we conclude was mistaken.

The teleological argument advanced by some (see Cavers, Choice-of-Law Process, p. 298) that the guest statute was intended to assure the priority of injured nonguests in the assets of a negligent host, in addition to the prevention of fraudulent claims, overlooks not only the statutory history but the fact that the statute permits recovery by guests who can establish that the accident was due to the gross negligence of the driver. If the purpose of the statute is to protect the rights of the injured 'non-guest', as opposed to the owner or his insurance carrier, we fail to perceive any rational basis for predicating that protection on the degree of negligence which the guest is able to establish. The only justification for discrimination between injured guests which can withstand logical as well as constitutional scrutiny (citations omitted) is that the legitimate purpose of the statute—prevention of fraudulent claims against local insurers or the protection of local automobile owners—is furthered by increasing the guest's burden of proof. This purpose can never be vindicated when the insurer is a New York carrier and the defendant is sued in the courts of this State. Under such circumstances, the jurisdiction enacting such a guest statute has absolutely no interest in the application of its law.

The failure to come to grips with this problem in Macey v. Rozbicki (supra) resulted in a decision which has confused and clouded the choice-of-law process in New York. There the defendants, Mr. and Mrs. Vincent Rozbicki, who were New York domiciliaries, were spending the summer in their home in Ontario. They invited Mrs. Rozbicki's sister, Miss Jean Macey, to spend a 10-day vacation with them. Miss Macey was injured when an automobile, owned by her brother-in-law and driven by her sister, collided with another vehicle.

The court correctly concluded that New York law governed, but in so doing ignored the rationale of *Babcock* and *Dym* in order to avoid a reconsideration of the construction placed on the guest statute. Thus the court wrote: 'In the present case the relationship of two sisters living permanently in New York was not affected or changed by their temporary meeting together in Canada for a short visit there, especially since the arrangements for that visit had undoubtedly been made in New York State. Every fact in this case was New York related, save only the not particularly significant one that the particular trip on the day of the accident was between two points in Canada.' 221 N.E.2d p. 381, Supra. . . .

Viewed in the light of the foregoing discussion, the instant case is one of the simplest in the choice-of-law area. If the facts are examined in light of the policy considerations which underlie the ostensibly conflicting laws it is clear that New York has the only real interest in whether recovery should be granted and that the application of Michigan law 'would defeat a legitimate interest of the forum State without serving a legitimate interest of any other State' (Intercontinental Planning v. Daystrom, Inc., Supra, p. 385, 300 N.Y.S.2d p. 828, 248 N.E.2d p. 584).

The policy of this State with respect to all those injured in automobile accidents is reflected in the legislative declaration which prefaces New York's compulsory insurance law: 'The legislature is concerned over the rising toll of motor vehicle accidents and the suffering and loss thereby inflicted. The legislature determines that it is a matter of grave concern that motorists shall be financially able to respond in damages for their negligent acts, so that innocent victims of motor vehicle accidents may be recompensed for the injury and financial loss inflicted upon them.' (Vehicle and Traffic Law, Consol.Laws, c. 71, s 310.)

Neither this declaration of policy nor the standard required provisions for an auto liability insurance policy make any distinction between guests, pedestrians or other insured parties.

New York's 'grave concern' in affording recovery for the injuries suffered by Catharina Tooker, a New York domiciliary, and the loss suffered by her family as a result of her wrongful death, is evident merely in stating the policy which our law reflects. On the other hand, Michigan has no interest in whether a New York plaintiff is denied recovery against a New York defendant where the car is insured here. The fact that the deceased guest and driver were in Michigan for an extended period of time is plainly irrelevant. Indeed, the Legislature, in requiring that insurance policies cover liability for injuries regardless of where the accident takes place (Vehicle & Traffic Law, s 311, subd. 4) has evinced commendable concern not only for residents of this State, but residents of other States who may be injured as a result of the activities of New York residents. Under these circumstances, we cannot be concerned with whether Miss Tooker or Miss Lopez were in Michigan for a summer session or for a full college education (see Baade, *Counter-Revolution or Alliance for Progress? Reflections on Reading Cavers, The Choice-of-Law Process*, 46 Texas L. Rev. 141, 168–170).

The argument that the choice of law in tort cases should be governed by the fictional expectation of the parties has been rejected unequivocally by this court. . . . * * * 'Though our nation is divided into fifty-one separate legal systems, our people act most (of) the time as if they lived in a single one. * * * (They suffer from a) chronic failure to take account of differences in state laws'. * * * It is for this reason that '(f)ew speculations are more slippery than assessing the expectations of parties as to the laws applicable to their activities, and especially is this true where the expectations relate to the law of torts.' Cavers, (Choice-of-Law Process), p. (119), 302 * * *).'

Moreover, when the Legislature has chosen to compel an owner of an automobile to provide a fund for recovery for those who will be injured, and thus taken the element of choice and expectation out of the question, it seems unreasonable to look to that factor as a basis for a choice of law. And, even if we were to engage in such fictions as the expectations of the parties, it seems only fair to infer that the owner of the vehicle by purchasing a New York insurance policy which provided for the specific liability 'intended to protect (the) passenger against negligent injury, as well as to secure indemnity for liability, in whatever state an accident might occur'. (Citations omitted).

The dissenting opinion makes much of the fact that it was purely 'adventitious' that Miss Tooker, a temporary resident in Michigan, chose to ride in Miss Lopez's automobile rather than an automobile owned by a Michigan domiciliary. This factor we are told requires the application of Michigan law. Choice-of-law decisions in guest statute cases, the dissent suggests, ought to turn on whether or not it was 'adventitious' that the passenger was in a car registered and insured in New York as opposed to the jurisdiction in which the relationship is seated and has its purpose.

The dissent is, of course, correct that it was 'adventitious' that Miss Tooker was a guest in an automobile registered and insured in New York. For all we know, her decision to go to Michigan State University as opposed to New York University may have been 'adventitious'. Indeed, her decision to go to Detroit on the weekend in question instead of staying on campus and studying may equally have been 'adventitious'. The fact is, however, that Miss Tooker went to Michigan State University; that she decided to go to Detroit on October 16, 1964; that she was a passenger in a vehicle registered and insured in New York; and that as a result of all these 'adventitious' occurrences, she is dead and we have a case to decide. Why we should be concerned with what might have been is unclear. . . .

Applying the choice-of-law rule which we have adopted, it is not an 'implicit consequence' that the Michigan passenger injured along with Miss Lopez should be denied recovery. Under the reasoning adopted here, it is not at all clear that Michigan law would govern. (Citations omitted). We do not, however, find it necessary or desirable to conclusively resolve a question which is not now before us. It suffices to note that any anomaly resulting from the application of Michigan law to bar an action brought by Miss Silk is 'the implicit consequence' of a Federal system which, at a time when we have truly become one nation, permits a citizen of one State to recover for injuries sustained in an automobile accident and denies a citizen of another State the right to recover for injuries sustained in a similar accident. The anomaly does not arise from any choice-of-law rule.

Indeed, the rule advanced by the dissent, unlike the rule we have adopted, will only foster rather than alleviate such anomalies. Thus, suppose in Babcock v. Jackson (supra) the driver of the vehicle had picked up a hitchhiker in Ontario who was injured along with his guest, Miss Babcock. And suppose in Macey v. Rozbicki (supra) Mrs. Rozbicki had invited her next-door neighbor to go with her and her sister to church and both the Ontario guest and Miss Macey were injured. Under the rule advanced by the dissent, Ontario law would clearly apply to govern the right of the 'Ontario' guests since it was purely 'adventitious' that they were in a New York car rather than an Ontario car. On the other hand, the same rule would permit recovery by the 'New York' guests since it was not 'adventitious' that they should have been in a New York vehicle at the time. We agree with the dissent that a rule which fosters such 'lack of consistency' and 'unpredictability' without any compensating features is hardly worthy of adoption or consideration.

Before concluding this opinion we cannot fail to take note of one additional argument raised in the dissenting opinion to the effect that the choice-of-law rule articulated in our recent decisions merely amounts to a rule which will always result in the application of New York law—'a domiciliary conceptualism that rested on a vested right accruing from the fact of domicile'. (Citations omitted). This argument ignores the fact that our decisions since Babcock v. Jackson (supra) have not always resulted in the application of the law of New York and have, indeed, indicated proper recognition and respect for the legitimate concerns of other jurisdictions and the real expectations of the parties. As we recently observed in the course of an opinion in a tort case, '(w)e must recognize that, in addition to the interest in affording the plaintiff full recovery, there may be other more general considerations which should concern 'a justice-dispensing court in a modern American state'. * * * Among other considerations are the 'fairness' of applying our law where a nonresident or even a resident has patterned his conduct upon the law of the jurisdiction in which he was acting * * * as well as the possible interest of a sister State in providing the remedy for injuries sustained as a result of conduct undertaken within its borders'. (Citations omitted). . . .

The order of the Appellate Division should be reversed, with costs, and the order of Special Term reinstated.

FULD, CHIEF JUDGE (concurring).

I join in the court's opinion but, in doing so, I would add these few brief comments. . . .

Babcock and the decisions it heralded place in our hands an instrument not confined to the rare and unusual situation. Rather, they comprise a sound foundation for a set of basic principles which the practicing lawyer, as well as the conflicts scholar, may be able to wield with good results. They have helped us uncover the underlying values and policies which are operative in this area of the law. Now that these values and policies have been revealed, we may proceed to the next stage in the evolution of the law—the formulation of a few rules of general applicability, promising a fair level of predictability. Although no rule may be found or framed to guarantee a satisfying result in every case, we cannot hope to deal justly with the legion of multi-state highway accident cases by regarding each case as one of a kind and unique. We should attempt, as has been suggested, to avoid 'both unreasonable rules and an unruly reasonableness that is destructive of many of the values of law and that loses sight of the need for coordinating a multi-state system'. (Rosenberg, *Two Views on Kell v. Henderson*, 67 Col.L.Rev. 459, 464.)

Without attempting too much, I believe that we may accept the following principles as sound for situations involving guest statutes in conflicts settings:

1. When the guest-passenger and the host-driver are domiciled in the same state, and the car is there registered, the law of that state should control and determine the standard of care which the host owes to his guest.

2. When the driver's conduct occurred in the state of his domicile and that state does not cast him in liability for that conduct, he should not be held liable by reason of the fact that liability would be imposed upon him under the tort law of the state of the victim's domicile. Conversely, when the guest was injured in the state of his own domicile and its law permits recovery, the driver was has come into that state should not—in the absence of special circumstances—be permitted to interpose the law of his state as a defense.

3. In other situations, when the passenger and the driver are domiciled in different states, the rule is necessarily less categorical. Normally, the applicable rule of decision will be that of the state where the accident occurred but not if it can be shown that displacing that normally applicable rule will advance the relevant substantive law purposes without impairing the smooth working of the multi-state system or producing great uncertainty for litigants. (Cf. Restatement, 2d, Conflict of Laws, P.O.D., pt. II, ss 146, 159.)

Guidelines of the sort suggested will not always be easy of application, nor will they furnish guidance to litigants and lower courts in all cases. They are proffered as a beginning, not as an end, to the problems of sound and fair adjudication in the troubled world of the automobile guest statute.

Since, in the case before us, the guest-passenger and the host-driver were both domiciled in this State and the automobile was here registered, we look to New York law to determine the standard of care to be applied between those parties. . . .

BREITEL, JUDGE (dissenting).

Plaintiff's and defendant's deceased daughters were fellow students in residence in pursuit of academic degrees in Michigan State University at Lansing, Michigan. They and a third fellow student, a resident of Michigan, traveled in a sports car automobile provided for the exclusive use of the defendant's deceased daughter by her father in whose name the car was registered and insured. The trip originated in Lansing and was to end in Detroit, Michigan, but was abruptly terminated by the accident, fatal to defendant's daughter, en route to Detroit. The trip was initiated entirely while the young women were in attendance at the school. The sports car had been newly acquired for the defendant's deceased daughter for her use at school in Michigan and was garaged there. The father had driven it once or twice; he had another automobile for his and his wife's use.

Except for the facts that plaintiff and the deceased were New York residents, that defendant's deceased daughter had a New York operator's license, that the registered owner of the car was a New York resident, and that the car was registered and insured in New York, every other facet of the accident was based in Michigan and was as localized as it could be in that State. The students were in residence at the university, were not in sojourn for short courses or interim sessions, or on tour. The trip was intrinsically and exclusively a Michigan trip, concerned only with Michigan places, roads, and conditions. . . .

What the rules, exemplified by Babcock v. Jackson, [and other New York cases] established, and very rightly so, was that when the territory in which the accident occurs is wholly adventitious to the relationship or status among the parties, that factor should not determine the applicable law. In each of these cases the seat and purpose of the relationship was established to be elsewhere than where the accident occurred. It was the place of the accident that could be changed without changing or affecting the other relationships. In short, except in a rather minimal way, the conduct of the parties was not affected by the place where the accident occurred. It was, therefore, adventitious.

The converse occurred in this case. The incidental registration and ownership of the car, and the domicile of these Michigan students, did not influence their conduct or the establishment or nature of the relationship among them. Regardless of these facts they would undoubtedly have entered into the same relationship, made the same trip, and behaved the same way. These facts were, therefore, extrinsic or adventitious.

On this view, Dym v. Gordon, 16 N.Y.2d 120, 262 N.Y.S.2d 463, 209 N.E.2d 792 was soundly decided, and this case, which is even stronger on its intrinsic facts because of the young women's being students in residence, as that term is used in the academic world, should be decided the same way (Cavers, Choice-of-Law Process, pp. 300–304). In the *Dym* case, the parties were summer students at the University of Colorado, enrolled for a six-week course, and it was out of that relationship that the Colorado automobile trip was initiated and was to be concluded. The New York residence of the parties and the New York registration and ownership of the car were adventitious. Change these adventitious facts and it is likely that the same trip with the same people in perhaps the same car would have taken place just the same. . . .

For that matter any monistic attempt to find some one great principle or doctrine to cover all conflicts problems in all fields of law has not been and is not likely to be successful. Certain it is that contacts theory or governmental interests theory, and their several variations all help to explain the several influences effective in reaching results, but no one of them is entitled to recognition as a universal touchstone, yesterday, today, or tomorrow. The efforts of analysts like Currie, Cavers, Reese,

Ehrenzweig, and the Restatement itself, as much as those of the now-disavowed Beale, seek or sought to articulate why the selection between significant and adventitious facts divides them as it does, and to create or discover a viable rationale. The problem has been exacerbated, of course, by the scholar's, and sometimes the Judge's understandable penchant to discover a single embracive principle to cover all cases.

There are truly difficult cases where the division between the significant and adventitious facts is elusive. This case is hardly such a one. . . .

In modern theories in the field of conflicts, the analysts have generally posited, or in fact assumed, as a significant factor the place where the transaction occurred. (Citations omitted). What has happened of course, is that lip service is paid to the factor of place, and promptly ignored thereafter, if the forum prefers its own policy preconceptions and especially if it requires denial of recover to a plaintiff in a tort case. . . .

Intra-mural speculation on the policies of other States has obvious limitations because of restricted information and wisdom. It is difficult enough to interpret the statutes and decisional rules of one's own State. To be sure, there is no total escape from considering the policies of other States. But this necessity should not be extended to produce anomalies of results out of the same accident, with unpredictability, and lack of consistency in determinations. Thus, it is hard to accept the implicit consequence that Miss Silk, the Michigan resident injured in the accident, should not be able to recover in Michigan (and presumably in New York) but a recovery can be had for her deceased fellow-passenger in the very same accident.

If the trend continues uninterruptedly, the shift to a personal law approach in conflicts law, especially in the torts field, will continue apace (see Cavers, Choice-of-Law Process, Supra, pp. 150–156). Apart from the fact that such a development is not logically consistent with Anglo-American jurisprudence, it would create a sharp division between intra-national conflicts rules and extra-national conflicts rules. It is most unlikely that such a development would be recognized elsewhere. Inevitably, the goals of uniformity, let alone predictability, in conflict rules would be frustrated, and the arbitrary results produced by forum selection would be proliferated beyond tolerable limits.

For all of these reasons, I dissent and vote to affirm, and would deny the motion to dismiss the affirmative defense.

Judge Keating believed that, on its facts, *Tooker* was an easy "false conflict" case. Do you agree? If there is to be fraud or collusion between the passenger and the driver to conjure up a story that supports the claim that the defendant was negligent isn't it likely that the collusion will begin in Ontario right after the accident? Is it irrational for Ontario to seek to deter collusion that takes place on its soil? If so, then *Babcock* is not a false conflict case. For a probing analysis of the manner in which Currie identified and negated interests see Lea Brilmayer, *Interest Analysis and the Myth of Legislative Intent*, 78 Mich. L. Rev. 392 (1980). Professor Singer astutely observes that a court utilizing interest analysis to resolve choice-of-law problems will strain to find a false conflict because "otherwise the court will appear to be trampling on the interests of one state or another . . ." Joseph W. Singer, *Facing Real Conflicts*, 24 Cornell Int'l L. J. 197, 219–20 (1991). Another reason for straining to find a false conflict is that once a true conflict is identified, a court must find a way to decide which interest ought to prevail. As we shall see, doing so in a principled fashion is no easy task. If you have any doubt that Professor Singer is right, look at what the New York Court of Appeals did in the *Schultz* case on page 77.

Office Talk
#3

Aaron: The majority opinion puts off the question of how it would resolve the liability to Susan Silk, the Ontario plaintiff injured by the New York driver in Ontario.

Neil: You are right but Judge Fuld's concurring opinion does address the problem. Her liability is covered by his Rule 3 and would dictate that Ontario law would govern.

Aaron: As we shall see later, Judge Fuld's rules were adopted in a later New York case *Neumeier v. Kuehner* and are applicable to many other conflicts—not just host-guest cases. Some states have followed suit.

Neil: It makes sense to me that Ontario law ought to govern an Ontario resident injured in Ontario.

Aaron: Not so fast, Neil. Currie would label the Susan Silk case as an "unprovided for" case. Ontario has no interest because its host-guest rule is designed to protect its insurers from fraud and New York has no interest because it pro-recovery rule is designed to protect New York domiciliaries and there is no New York domiciliary to protect. According to Currie in such a case the forum should apply its own law.

Neil: I guess that New York just does not agree with Currie.

Aaron: My problem is that New York does not agree with itself. In *Tooker*, the New York court said that territoriality should play no role in deciding a choice of law case. The fact that the parties in *Tooker* were in Michigan for several years does not count. Now with regard to Susan Silk territoriality does count. If not, why deny Susan Silk recovery?

Neil: Aaron, that is a nice debating point. Nonetheless, I can see a difference between a stay-at-home plaintiff injured in her own backyard, so to speak, and a case with parties both domiciled in New York who are in Michigan for a prolonged time. The expectations of the parties are far different.

Aaron: Neil, what you are actually saying is that you will be a territorialist when it suits you and consider territorial concerns as legitimate interests, but you won't recognize territorial interests in the *Tooker* setting. At the very least, in my book *Tooker* is a true conflict case.

––––––––––––

The problem raised in our office talk regarding Susan Silk is most interesting. She is a Michigan resident injured in an accident in her own home state. Under Michigan law, she would not recover because Michigan has a guest statute which bars recovery unless the defendant was guilty of gross negligence. New York, the domicile of the defendant, has no host-guest statute. The purpose of the Michigan statute is to prevent collusion and fraud against Michigan insurers. On the other hand, New York law allows recovery for ordinary negligence to allow its domiciliary recovery. Under Currie's version of interest analysis, Ontario has no interest because there is no Michigan insurer to protect from fraud. New York has no interest because Susan Silk is not a New York domiciliary and New York has no interest in granting recovery to her.

Currie would resolve this case by applying forum law (New York) and granting recovery. New York under Fuld's Rule 3 would apply Michigan law. In a later case, *Neumeir v. Kuehner* on a similar fact pattern, New York denied a recovery by applying Fuld's Rule 3.

Professor Robert Sedler, proposes an interesting solution to this problem. He argues that both New York and Michigan have a common policy of compensating persons injured in auto accidents due to the negligence of the driver. Michigan's policy of protecting insurance companies from fraud is not applicable when the car is not registered and insured in Michigan. Since the only state interested in protecting the defendant and the insurer does not do so, we fall back on the common policy to allow the plaintiff (Silk) to recovery. Sedler, *Interstate Accidents and the Unprovided-For Case: Reflections on Neumeier v. Kuehner*, 1 Hofstra L. Rev. 125, 138 (1973); Also see Kramer, *The Myth of the Unprovided-For Case*, 75 Va. L. Rev. 1045 (1989).

Parenthetically, in *Tooker* the driver was killed in the crash. If the purpose of the Michigan guest statute was to protect Michigan insurers from fraud and collusion, if the driver was killed, how can the driver and guest collude?

SCHULTZ V. BOY SCOUTS OF AMERICA, INC.

480 N.E.2d 679 (N.Y. 1985)

SIMONS, JUDGE.

Plaintiffs, Richard E. and Margaret Schultz, instituted this action to recover damages for personal injuries they and their sons, Richard and Christopher, suffered because the boys were sexually abused by defendant Edmund Coakeley and for damages sustained as a result of Christopher's wrongful death after he committed suicide. Coakeley, a brother in the Franciscan order, was the boys' school teacher and leader of their scout troop. Plaintiffs allege that the sexual abuse occurred while Coakeley was acting in those capacities and the causes of action before us on this appeal charge defendants Boy Scouts of America, Inc., and the Brothers of the Poor of St. Francis, Inc. (sued as Franciscan Brothers of the Poor, Inc.), with negligently hiring and supervising him.

Plaintiffs are domiciled in New Jersey and some of the injuries were sustained there. Thus, a choice-of-law issue is presented because New Jersey recognizes the doctrine of charitable immunity and New York does not. Defendants contend New Jersey law governs this litigation. . . . Following the rationale of *Babcock v. Jackson*, 191 N.E.2d 279, and similar cases, we hold that New Jersey law applies and that plaintiffs are precluded from relitigating its effect on the claims they assert.

I

In 1978 plaintiffs were residents of Emerson, New Jersey, where their two sons, Richard, age 13, and Christopher, age 11, attended Assumption School, an institution owned and operated by the Roman Catholic Archdiocese of Newark. By an agreement with the Archdiocese, defendant Brothers of the Poor of St. Francis, Inc., supplied teachers for the school. One of those assigned was Brother Edmund Coakeley, who also served as the scoutmaster of Boy Scout Troop 337, a locally chartered Boy Scout troop sponsored and approved by defendant Boy Scouts of America. Richard and Christopher attended Coakeley's class and were members of his scout troop.

In July 1978 Coakeley took Christopher Schultz to Pine Creek Reservation, a Boy Scout camp located in upstate New York near the Oneida County community of Foresport. . . . The complaint alleges that while at the camp, Coakeley sexually abused Christopher, that he continued to do so when Christopher returned to Assumption School in New Jersey that fall and that he threatened Christopher with harm if he revealed what had occurred. The complaint also alleges that Coakeley sexually abused Richard Schultz and made similar threats to him during a scout trip to Pine Creek Reservation on Memorial Day weekend in 1978. Plaintiffs claim that as a result of Coakeley's acts both boys suffered severe psychological, emotional and mental pain and suffering and that as a result of the distress Coakeley's acts caused, Christopher Schultz committed suicide by ingesting drugs on May 29, 1979. They charge both defendants with negligence in assigning Coakeley to positions of trust where he could molest young boys and in failing to dismiss him despite actual or constructive notice that Coakeley had previously been dismissed from another Boy Scout camp for similar improper conduct. . . .

[D]efendants moved for summary judgment, urging that plaintiffs' claims were barred by New Jersey's charitable immunity statute (N.J.Stat.Ann. § 2A:53A–7). . . . In opposition, plaintiffs contended that under applicable choice-of-law principles, New York should apply its law, not that of New Jersey, and, alternatively, that even if the New Jersey charitable immunity statute applies under choice-of-law rules, the New York courts should refuse to enforce it on public policy grounds. Special Term granted defendants' motions. . . . A divided Appellate Division affirmed.

II

A

The choice-of-law question presented in the action against defendant Boy Scouts of America is whether New York should apply its law in an action involving codomiciliaries of New Jersey when tortious acts were committed in New York. . . . [O]riginally [Boy Scouts] maintained its national headquarters in New Brunswick, New Jersey, but moved to Dallas, Texas, in 1979. New Jersey is considered defendant's domicile because its national headquarters was in that State. (Citations omitted). Its change of domicile after the commission of the wrongs from New Jersey to Texas. . . . provides New York with no greater interest in this action than it would have without the change. . . .

The question presented in the action against defendant Franciscan Brothers is what law should apply when the parties' different domiciles have conflicting charitable immunity rules. The Franciscan order is incorporated in Ohio and it is a domiciliary of that State. (Citations omitted). At the time these causes of action arose Ohio, like New Jersey, recognized charitable immunity. . . . The Ohio rule denied immunity in actions based on negligent hiring and supervision, however . . . whereas New Jersey does not. For this reason, no doubt, defendant Franciscan Brothers does not claim Ohio law governs and the choice is between the law of New York and the law of New Jersey. . . .

B

Historically, choice-of-law conflicts in tort actions have been resolved by applying the law of the place of the wrong. In *Babcock v. Jackson*, 12 N.Y.2d 473, 240 N.Y.S.2d 743, 191 N.E.2d 279, *supra*, we departed from traditional doctrine, however, and refused to invariably apply the rule of *lex loci delicti* to determine the availability of relief for commission of a tort. . . .

The analysis was flexible and to the extent that it may have placed too much emphasis on contact-counting without specifying the relative significance of those contacts, the necessary refinements were added in later decisions of this court. In four of the five subsequent tort cases presenting the same *Babcock*-style fact pattern of common New York domiciliaries and a foreign locus having loss-distribution rules in conflict with those of New York we reached results consistent with *Babcock* and applied New York law. (Citations omitted). . . . In each of the five cases, however, the court rejected the indiscriminate grouping of contacts, which in *Babcock* had been a consideration coequal to interest analysis, because it bore no reasonable relation to the underlying policies of conflicting rules of recovery in tort actions. (Citations omitted). Interest analysis became the relevant analytical approach to choice of law in tort actions in New York. "[T]he law of the jurisdiction having the greatest interest in the litigation will be applied and * * * the [only] facts or contacts which obtain significance in defining State interests are those which relate to the purpose of the particular law in conflict". (Citations omitted). . . .

Thus, under present rules, most of the nondomicile and nonlocus contacts relied on in *Babcock v. Jackson* (*supra*), such as where the guest-host relationship arose and where the journey was to begin and end, are no longer controlling in tort actions involving guest statutes. (Citations omitted). . . .

These decisions also establish that the relative interests of the domicile and locus jurisdictions in having their laws apply will depend on the particular tort issue in conflict in the case. Thus, when the conflicting rules involve the appropriate standards of conduct, rules of the road, for example, the law of the place of the tort "will usually have a predominant, if not exclusive, concern" (citations omitted), because the locus jurisdiction's interests in protecting the reasonable expectations of the parties who relied on it to govern their primary conduct and in the admonitory effect that applying its law will have on similar conduct in the future assume critical importance and outweigh any interests of the common-domicile jurisdiction. (Citations omitted). Conversely, when the jurisdictions' conflicting rules relate to allocating losses that result from admittedly tortious conduct, as they do here, rules such as those limiting damages in wrongful death actions, vicarious liability rules, or immunities from suit, considerations of the State's admonitory interest and party reliance are less important. Under those circumstances, the locus jurisdiction has at best a minimal interest in determining the right of recovery or the extent of the remedy in an action by a foreign domiciliary for injuries resulting from the conduct of a codomiciliary that was tortious under the laws of both jurisdictions. (Citations omitted). Analysis then favors the jurisdiction of common domicile because of its interest in enforcing the decisions of both parties to accept both the benefits and the burdens of identifying with that jurisdiction and to submit themselves to its authority. . . .

As to defendant Boy Scouts, this case is but a slight variation of our *Babcock* line of decisions and differs from them on only two grounds: (1) the issue involved is charitable immunity rather than a guest statute, and (2) it presents a fact pattern which one commentator has characterized as a "reverse" *Babcock* case because New York is the place of the tort rather than the jurisdiction of the parties' common domicile. (Citations omitted).

Although most of our major choice-of-law decisions after *Babcock* involved foreign guest statutes in actions for personal injuries, we have not so limited them, but have applied the *Babcock* reasoning to other tort issues as well. (Citations omitted). Nor is there any logical basis for distinguishing guest statutes from other loss-distributing rules because they all share the characteristic of being post event remedial rules designed to allocate the burden of losses resulting from tortious conduct in which the jurisdiction of the parties' common domicile has a paramount interest. Both plaintiffs and defendant Boy Scouts in this case have chosen to identify themselves in the most concrete form possible, domicile, with a jurisdiction that has weighed the interests of charitable tort-feasors and their victims and decided to retain the defense of charitable immunity. (Citations omitted). . . .

Thus, if this were a straight *Babcock* fact pattern, rather than the reverse, we would have no reason to depart from the first *Neumeier* rule and would apply the law of the parties' common domicile. Because this case presents the first case for our review in which New York is the forum-locus rather than the parties' common domicile, however, we consider the reasons most often advanced for applying the law of the forum-locus and those supporting application of the law of the common domicile.

The three reasons most often urged in support of applying the law of the forum-locus in cases such as this are: (1) to protect medical creditors who provided services to injured parties in the locus State, (2) to prevent injured tort victims from becoming public wards in the locus State and (3) the deterrent effect application of locus law has on future tort-feasors in the locus State. (Citations omitted). The first two reasons share common weaknesses. First, in the abstract, neither reason necessarily requires application of the locus jurisdiction's law, but rather invariably mandates application of the law of the jurisdiction that would either allow recovery or allow the greater recovery. (Citations omitted). They are subject to criticism, therefore, as being biased in favor of recovery. Second, on the facts of this case neither reason is relevant since the record contains no evidence that there are New York medical creditors or that plaintiffs are or will likely become wards of this State. Finally, although it is conceivable that application of New York's law in this case would have some deterrent effect on future tortious conduct in this State, New York's deterrent interest is considerably less because none of the parties is a resident and the rule in conflict is loss-allocating rather than conduct-regulating.

Conversely, there are persuasive reasons for consistently applying the law of the parties' common domicile. First, it significantly reduces forum-shopping opportunities, because the same law will be applied by the common-domicile and locus jurisdictions, the two most likely forums. Second, it rebuts charges that the forum-locus is biased in favor of its own laws and in favor of rules permitting recovery. Third, the concepts of mutuality and reciprocity support consistent application of the common-domicile law. In any given case, one person could be either plaintiff or defendant and one State could be either the parties' common domicile or the locus, and yet the applicable law would not change depending on their status. Finally, it produces a rule that is easy to apply and brings a modicum of predictability and certainty to an area of the law needing both.

As to defendant Franciscan Brothers, this action requires an application of the third of the rules set forth in *Neumeier* because the parties are domiciled in different jurisdictions with conflicting loss-distribution rules and the locus of the tort is New York, a separate jurisdiction. In that situation the law of the place of the tort will normally apply, unless displacing it " 'will advance the relevant substantive law purposes without impairing the smooth working of the multi-state system or producing great uncertainty for litigants' " (Citations omitted). For the same reasons stated in our analysis of the action against defendant Boy Scouts, application of the law of New Jersey in plaintiffs' action against defendant Franciscan Brothers would further that State's interest in enforcing the decision of its domiciliaries to accept the burdens as well as the benefits of that State's loss-distribution tort rules and its interest in promoting the continuation and expansion of defendant's charitable activities in that State. Conversely, although application of New Jersey's law may not affirmatively advance the substantive law purposes of New York, it will not frustrate those interests because New York has no significant interest in applying its own law to this dispute. Finally, application of New Jersey law will enhance "the smooth working of the multi-state system" by actually reducing the incentive for forum shopping and it will provide certainty for the litigants whose only reasonable expectation surely would have been that the law of the jurisdiction where plaintiffs are domiciled and defendant sends its teachers would apply, not the law of New York where the parties had only isolated and infrequent contacts as a result of Coakeley's position as Boy Scout leader. Thus, we conclude that defendant Franciscan Brothers has met its burden of demonstrating that the law of New Jersey, rather than the law of New York, should govern plaintiffs' action against it. . . .

[The Court then found that applying New Jersey charitable immunity does not violate New York public policy.]

Accordingly, the order of the Appellate Division should be affirmed, with costs.

JASEN, JUDGE (dissenting).

I respectfully dissent. In my view, the majority overstates the significance of New Jersey's interests in having its law apply in this case and understates the interests of New York. While I agree with much of the majority's general exposition of the rules governing conflict of laws, nevertheless I believe that its application of these rules to the facts of this case and the resulting analysis are uneven. By casting the issue almost exclusively in terms of New Jersey's law of charitable immunity and the policy purposes represented thereby, the majority preordains its decision that the application of New Jersey law would best serve the interests deemed relevant. A more balanced approach, which recognizes that the conflict in this case involves not only New Jersey's law of charitable immunity but also New York's law of charitable nonimmunity, and which accords a proper analysis and fairer significance to the policies underlying the latter, would dictate a different result. Because New Jersey's interests in having its law of charitable immunity apply are rather attenuated in this case and, by sharp contrast, New York's interests as the "locus-forum" in applying its rule of charitable nonimmunity are overriding—especially in light of the heinous nature of the alleged tortious conduct involved and the repugnancy of immunizing those responsible from liability—it is my view that New York law should govern this case. A brief highlighting of those factors which I believe to be most pertinent illustrates what, in my view, the majority has either understated or overlooked.

New Jersey's interests, denominated by the majority as loss-distribution, are hardly pressing under the circumstances. While it is true that laws providing for charitable immunity typically are intended to serve the purpose of protecting and promoting the charities incorporated within a state's jurisdiction, that function is virtually irrelevant in this case. Presently, neither corporate defendant is a resident of New Jersey. The Brothers of the Poor of St. Francis (the Franciscan Brothers) has at all relevant times been a resident of the State of Ohio, a jurisdiction which recognizes only a limited charitable immunity that does not extend to negligence in the selection and retention of personnel. (Citations omitted). The Boy Scouts of America, although originally incorporated in New Jersey at the time of its alleged tortious conduct, has since relocated in Texas, a State which has wholly rejected charitable immunity. . . .

Consequently, because the majority cannot in actuality rely upon New Jersey's interest in protecting resident charities—into which category neither corporate defendant now falls—the decision today is, in effect, predicated almost exclusively upon the plaintiffs' New Jersey domicile. What emerges from the majority's holding is an entirely untoward rule that nonresident plaintiffs are somehow less entitled to the protections of this State's law while they are within our borders. Besides smacking of arbitrary and injudicious discrimination against guests in this State and before our courts (citations omitted), such a position, without more, has severely limited, if any, validity in resolving conflicts questions. (Citations omitted) This is especially so where, as here, the defendants' contacts with the foreign State are insignificant for the purposes of interest analysis while, at the same time, the parties' contacts with New York are so clear and direct, and the resulting interests of this State so strong.

There can be no question that this State has a paramount interest in preventing and protecting against injurious misconduct within its borders. This interest is particularly vital and compelling where, as here, the tortious misconduct involves sexual abuse and exploitation of children, regardless of the residency of the victims and the tort-feasors. (Citations omitted). . . .

As the majority stresses, a charitable immunity law such as New Jersey's typically serves a loss-distribution purpose reflecting a legislative paternalism toward resident charities. But that is obviously not true with regard to a rule, such as New York's, which denies charitable immunity. . . .

These purposes, to which the majority refuses to accord any significance are preventive, protective and compensatory. Indeed, in *Bing v. Thunig*, 2 N.Y.2d 656, 163 N.Y.S.2d 3, 143 N.E.2d 3, where New York's prior rule of charitable immunity was abolished, this court held that "[i]t is not alone good morals but sound law that individuals and organizations should be just before they are generous, and there is no reason why that should not apply to charitable [institutions] * * * Insistence upon * * * damages for negligent injury serves a two-fold purpose, for it both assures *payment of an obligation to the person injured and gives warning that justice and the law demand exercise of care."* . . .

As previously discussed, there can be little doubt that New York has an interest in insuring that justice be done to nonresidents who have come to this State and suffered serious injuries herein. There is no cogent reason to deem that interest any weaker whether such guests are here for the purpose of conducting business or personal affairs, or, as in this case, have chosen to spend their vacation in New York. Likewise, it cannot be denied that this State has a strong legitimate interest in deterring serious tortious misconduct, including the kind of reprehensible malfeasance that has victimized the nonresident infant plaintiffs in this case. Indeed, this deterrence function of tort law, whether it be in the form of imposing liability or denying immunity, is a substantial interest of the locus state which is almost universally acknowledged by both commentators and the courts to be a prominent factor deserving significant consideration in the resolution of conflicts problems. (Citations omitted). While the majority mentions New York's interest in deterrence, it dismisses that interest in short fashion by referring to the "rule in conflict" as being "loss-allocating rather than conduct-regulating." (Citations omitted). Of course, there is not one but two rules at issue, and the majority's characterization is accurate only with regard to New Jersey's law granting immunity, not with regard to New York's rule denying the same. (Citations omitted). . . .

For all these reasons, I would reverse the order of the Appellate Division, apply the law of New York denying immunity to defendant charities, and permit plaintiffs to proceed on their complaint.

WACHTLER, C.J., and MEYER, KAYE and ALEXANDER, JJ., concur with SIMONS, J. JASEN, J., dissents and votes to reverse in a separate opinion.

———————

Schultz is a false conflict case only if New York has little or no interest in applying its tort law to an organization that negligently allows sex-offenders to come into the state and abuse youngsters to the point that one commits suicide. Is that credible? Yet, the distinction between conduct-regulating and loss-allocating rules is crucial to the manner in which New York resolves choice-of-law problems. Several scholars believe that the distinction is ephemeral. Tort law embodies both deterrence and compensation in its rules. They cannot be surgically separated. See e.g. O'Hara & Ribstein, *From Politics to Efficiency in Choice of Law*, 67 U. Chi. L. Rev. 1151 (2000); Hay & Ellis, *Bridging the Gap Between Rules and Approaches in Tort Choice of Law in the United States: A Survey of Current Case Law*, 27 Int'l Law 369, 382 (1993). But, other scholars see value in the distinction. See e.g. Symeonides, *The Need for a Third Conflicts Restatement*, 75 Ind. L.J. 437, 452–53 (2000); Borchers, *The Return of Territorialism to New York Conflicts Law: Padula v Lilarn Properties Corp*, 58 Alb. L. Rev. 775 (1995). The authors of this casebook are not enamored with the distinction. To say that the abolition of charitable immunity is not conduct-regulating strikes us as silly. The dissent in *Schultz* got it right.

At this stage of the discussion we can make one clear prediction. For states that have abandoned the *lex loci* rule, where the state of the common domicile favors recovery more than the law of the state of conduct and injury, the law of common domicile will govern. Professor Symeonides has surveyed the case law in his *Annual Survey of Choice of Law in the American Courts*, 57 Am. J. Comp. Law 269, 284 (2009) and found that 33 of 35 cases (94%) with this fact pattern applied the law of the common domicile. This is, of course, the *Babcock, Tooker* fact pattern—one that courts have identified as a "false conflict."

Well, how have the courts dealt with the "reverse *Babcock*" fact pattern? In New York the answer is clear. The law of the common domicile governs. In *Edwards v. Erie Coach Lines*, 952 N.E.2d 1033 (N.Y. 2011), a charter bus carrying members of an Ontario women's hockey team collided with the rear end of a tractor-trailer parked on the shoulder of a highway near Geneseo, New York. Three bus passengers and the tractor-trailer's driver died; several bus passengers were seriously injured. The conflict between the law of Ontario and that of New York was substantial. Ontario, the domicile of the bus passenger plaintiff and the bus company limits recovery for non-economic loss (pain and suffering) to the American equivalent of $310,000. New York law does not limit recovery for non-economic loss. The Court of Appeals found that what damages should be awarded an Ontario plaintiff against an Ontario defendant was a loss allocating rule to be governed by the law of the common domicile. We will return to a further discussion of the *Edwards* case when we confront which law should govern a suit against the tractor-trailer driver (a Pennsylvania domiciliary).

In a case that mirrored the fact pattern in *Schultz*, the New Jersey Supreme Court came up with a very different result in *P.V. et. al v. Camp Jaycee*, 962 A.2d 453 (N.J. 2008). In that case, plaintiff, a twenty-one year old female from New Jersey who suffered from Down Syndrome, was sexually abused in Camp Jaycee, a camp that was operated in Pennsylvania by a New Jersey not-for-profit corporation. The complaint alleged negligent supervision of the plaintiff that allowed another camper to sexually abuse the young girl. New Jersey law would not allow recovery based on its doctrine of charitable immunity. Pennsylvania had abolished its charitable immunity doctrine and its law would allow recovery against the camp. In a lengthy opinion, the New Jersey court found that Pennsylvania had the predominant interest in deterring the negligent conduct and that the abolition of charitable immunity provided the correct incentive to reflect that deterrent interest.

We believe that the New Jersey court got it right. But the larger question is whether, in the reverse-*Babcock* fact pattern, the courts are applying the rule of the common domicile. We turn again to Professor Symeonides' survey. *Supra* at 285. He finds that, as of the time of that writing, 26 cases reflected the reverse-*Babcock* fact pattern. Of this cohort, 18 found that the law of the common domicile governed (69%), rather than the law of the place of injury, thus denying the plaintiff the favorable rule of the state of injury.

All in all, common domicile for loss-regulating rules has a powerful impact on choice-of-law. It has a neutral sound to it and has substantial adherents. In the cases (like *Camp Jaycee*) where courts have applied the pro-recovery rule of the state of injury rather than the law of common domicile, the courts have emphasized that the recovery rules have a strong conduct-regulating aspect to them and should be given preference.

It should not be lost on you that, whereas New York treats the *Schultz* facts as presenting a false conflict, New Jersey treats the identical fact pattern in *Camp Jaycee* as a true conflict. Isn't this fun? But, there is more fun to come. Consider the following case, which Brainerd Currie considered to be a "brilliant" resolution of a potentially thorny conflicts problem.

BERNKRANT V. FOWLER
360 P.2d 906 (Cal. 1961)

[Some time before 1954, plaintiffs Louis, Florence and Bernkrant (all Nevada residents) bought a Las Vegas apartment building from John Granrud. In July 1954, the plaintiffs still owed Granrud $36,000.00 (the unpaid balance on the apartments). At the time, Granrud wanted to buy a trailer park and was short on cash. He requested that plaintiffs refinance the debt they owed and come up with about $13,000.00 in cash that would reduce the debt and permit him to buy the trailer park. To entice them to refinance (which cost the plaintiffs about $800 in out-of-pocket expenses) Granrud said that if the plaintiffs would refinance and provide him with the $13,000, he would provide by will that any debt that remained on the purchase price at the time of his death would be cancelled and forgiven.]

TRAYNOR, JUSTICE

. . . .

Granrud died testate on March 4, 1956, a resident of Los Angeles County. His will, dated January 23, 1956, was admitted to probate, and defendant was appointed executrix of his estate. His will made no provision for cancelling the balance of $6,425 due on the note at the time of his death. Plaintiffs have continued to make regular payments of principal and interest to defendant under protest.

Plaintiffs brought this action [against Fowler, the administrator of the estate] to have the note cancelled and discharged and the property reconveyed to them and to recover the amounts paid defendant after Granrud's death. . . .

Subdivision 6 of § 1624 of the Civil Code provides that 'An agreement which by its terms is not to be performed during the lifetime of the promisor, or an agreement to devise or bequeath any property, or to make any provision for any person by will' is 'invalid, unless the same, or some note or memorandum thereof, is in writing, and subscribed by the party to be charged or by his agent.' They contend, however, that only the Nevada statute of frauds is applicable and point out that the Nevada statute has no counterpart to subdivision 6. . . .

We are . . . confronted with a contract that is valid under the law of Nevada but invalid under the California statute of frauds if that statute is applicable. We have no doubt that California's interest in protecting estates being probated here from false claims based on alleged oral contracts to make wills is constitutionally sufficient to justify the Legislature's making our statute of frauds applicable to all such contracts sought to be enforced against such estates. See Rubin v. Irving Trust Co., 305 N.Y. 288, 298, 113 N.E.2d 424; Emery v. Burbank, 163 Mass. 326–329, 39 N.E. 1026, 28 L.R.A. 57. The Legislature, however, is ordinarily concerned with enacting laws to govern purely local transactions, and it has not spelled out the extent to which the statute of frauds is to apply to contract having substantial contacts with another state. Accordingly, we must determine its scope in the light of applicable principles of the law of conflict of laws. See People v. One 1953 Ford Victoria, 48 Cal.2d 595, 598–599, 311 P.2d 480.

In the present case plaintiffs were residents of Nevada, the contract was made in Nevada, and plaintiffs performed it there. If Granrud was a resident of Nevada at the time the contract was made, the California statute of frauds, in the absence of a plain legislative direction to the contrary, could not reasonably be interpreted as applying to the contract even though Granrud subsequently moved to California and died here. See McCabe v. Bagby, 6 Cir., 186 F.2d 546, 550. The basic policy of upholding the expectations of the parties by enforcing contracts valid under the only law apparently applicable would preclude an interpretation of our statute of frauds that would make it apply to and thus invalidate the contract because Granrud moved to California and died here. Such a case would be analogous to People v. One 1953 Ford Victoria, 48 Cal.2d 595, 311 P.2d 480, where we held that a Texas mortgagee of an automobile mortgaged in Texas did not forfeit his interest when the automobile was subsequently used to transport narcotics in California although he had failed to make the character investigation of the mortgagor required by California law. A mortgagee entering into a purely local transaction in another state could not reasonably be expected to take cognizance of the law of all the other jurisdictions where the property might possibly be taken, and accordingly, the California statute requiring an investigation to protect his interest could not reasonably be interpreted to apply to such out of state mortgagees. Another analogy is found in the holding that the statute of frauds did not apply to contracts to make wills entered into before the statute was enacted (Rogers v. Schlotterback, 167 Cal. 35, 45, 138 P. 728). Just as parties to local transactions cannot be expected to take cognizance of the law of other jurisdictions, they cannot be expected to anticipate a change in the local statute of frauds. Protection of rights growing out of valid contracts precludes interpreting the general language of the statute of frauds to destroy such rights whether the possible applicability of the statute arises from the movement of one or more of the parties across state lines or subsequent enactment of the statute. See Currie and Schreter,

Unconstitutional Discrimination in the Conflict of Laws: Privileges and Immunities, 69 Yale L.J. 1323, 1334.

In the present case, however, there is no finding as to where Granrud was domiciled at the time the contract was made. Since he had a bank account in California at that time and died a resident here less than two years later it may be that he was domiciled here when the contract was made. Even if he was, the result should be the same. The contract was made in Nevada and performed by plaintiffs there, and it involved the refinancing of obligations arising from the sale of Nevada land and secured by interests therein. Nevada has a substantial interest in the contract and in protecting the rights of its residents who are parties thereto, and its policy is that the contract is valid and enforcible. California's policy is also to enforce lawful contracts. That policy, however, must be subordinated in the case of any contract that does not meet the requirements of an applicable statute of frauds. In determining whether the contract herein is subject to the California statute of frauds, we must consider both the policy to protect the reasonable expectations of the parties and the policy of the statute of frauds. See Cheatham and Reese, *Choice of the Applicable Law*, 52 Col. L. Rev. 959, 978–980. It is true that if Granrud was domiciled here at the time the contract was made, plaintiffs may have been alerted to the possibility that the California statute of frauds might apply. Since California, however, would have no interest in applying its own statute of frauds unless Granrud remained here until his death, plaintiffs were not bound to know that California's statute might ultimately be invoked against them. Unless they could rely on their own law, they would have to look to the laws of all of the jurisdictions to which Granrud might move regardless of where he was domiciled when the contract was made. We conclude, therefore, that the contract herein does not fall within our statute of frauds. (Citations omitted). Since there is thus no conflict between the law of California and the law of Nevada, we can give effect to the common policy of both states to enforce lawful contracts and sustain Nevada's interest in protecting its residents and their reasonable expectations growing out of a transaction substantially related to that state without subordinating any legitimate interest of this state.

The judgment is reversed.

GIBSON, C. J., and SCHAUER, MCCOMB, PETERS, WHITE and DOOLING, JJ., concur.

––––––––––

Statutes of Frauds deny enforcement to an oral contract to make a will because allegations of such contracts are particularly susceptible to fraud. After all, the decedent is not available to testify that the conversation did not take place or that, even if it did, the terms of the agreement were far different than alleged by the plaintiff. So how does the court blithely conclude that

California (the presumed domicile of the decedent at the time of his death) has no interest in protecting his estate from the possibility of a trumped-up claim? How does Justice Traynor conclude that there is no conflict between the law of California and Nevada? Brainerd Currie believed that Justice Traynor had found a perfect way out. He argued that "no principle dictates that a state exploit every possible conflict, or exert to the outermost limit its constitutional power." A state, in order to avoid a conflict with another state, should read its interest in a "moderate and restrained" fashion. See Brainerd Currie, *The Disinterested Third State*, 28 Law & Contemp. Probs. 754, 757 (1963). Scholars have been more than a little skeptical about Justice Traynor's dubbing *Bernkrant* as a false conflict. See Cavers, *The Changing Choice of Law Process and the Federal Courts,* 28 Law & Contempt Probs. 732, 734 n.9. (1963). Isn't his reasoning a close cousin to what the New York court did in *Schultz*? When faced with a true conflict the way out is to negate your own state's interest and the conflict disappears. Oh, by the way, there was evidence in the case that Granrud used the money from the plaintiffs to buy the trailer park. Should that make a difference?

Office Talk
#4

Aaron: Neil, do you think that the evidence that there really was a contract to forgive any indebtedness that the Bernkrants had at the time of Granrud's death should make a difference in this case? After all, there must have been something in it for the Bernkrants or else why would they have spent $800 in refinancing?

Neil: I don't think so. That relates to whether the Statute of Frauds should prohibit enforcement of a contract that we have some reason to believe really exists, not whether a particular state's Statute of Frauds should apply. Most judges hate the Statute of Frauds because it is used to prevent enforcement of a contract that we have reason to believe exists. After all, if we didn't believe that the contract exists, we wouldn't need a Statute of Frauds to deny enforcement of it. The way the California Statute of Frauds would work in this case, you could have ten bishops and rabbis testifying that there was a contract to make a will and the contract would still not be enforced.

Aaron: Is what you are saying that in a conflicts case dealing with the Statute of Frauds judges ought to seize on any excuse to enforce a contract that they believe actually exists? I can see the judge saying to herself, "in a totally domestic case, I am stuck with this horrible statute, but in a conflicts case I have the maneuvering room to do the right thing."

Neil: No. That kind of thinking would be giving judges in a conflicts case license to choose whatever they think is the better rule of law. A few courts say that but most courts and scholars believe that is unprincipled and so do I.

Aaron: Well, if Justice Traynor was not doing that I don't understand how he concludes that, if Granrud was a California domiciliary at the time of the contract and continued to live in California until the time of his death, California nonetheless had no interest in applying its Statute of Frauds.

Neil: Justice Traynor was doing something very legitimate. He was interpreting the territorial scope of the California statute. He concluded that California's Statute of Frauds does not reach transactions that are so completely centered in Nevada.

Aaron: But, ultimately, Justice Traynor is applying a territorial choice of law rule under the guise of statutory interpretation. By the way, do you believe that people contracting for rights that are to take effect after the death of the promisor should not consider the possibility that the promisor may die domiciled in a state that has a Statute of Frauds?

Neil: Here I probably agree with you. If a lawyer was involved in advising the parties, he/she probably should have insisted that the contract be reduced to writing.

Aaron: That is interesting. Should the case turn on whether the parties were advised by counsel? That would be pretty wild.

C. "TRUE CONFLICT" CASE LAW

When it comes to resolving a conflicts case in which the policies of the two states clash when applied to the facts, courts struggle to articulate a principled way to decide the case. With the exception of a very small number of states that have bought into Brainerd Currie's view that, when each state has a legitimate interest, the forum ought to apply its law, and the few courts that buy into Professor Leflar's view that a court should apply the "better rule of law" in a conflicts case, the majority of courts seem to be weighing competing state interests and deciding which one is more weighty. According to the Restatement (Second) of Conflicts (1971) the state that has the "most significant contacts" wins. Of course, how to determine which contacts are "most significant" is the $64,000 question. The courts utilize different labels to identify their varying approaches. We leave it to you to decide whether there is anything other than interest weighing going on. Instead of setting forth the differing theoretical approaches, we organize the discussion around five different issues. As we go along, we will comment on the various theoretical approaches.

1. CONTRIBUTORY FAULT

As you know from your first year Torts course, most courts have adopted some form of comparative fault and have rejected contributory negligence as a complete bar. Several states, however, still apply the complete bar rule. Furthermore, a sharp division exists between states that apply pure comparative fault and those that apply modified comparative fault. Under the "pure comparative fault" system, a plaintiff who is, for example, 80% at fault can recover 20% of her damages. Under a "modified comparative fault" system a plaintiff whose fault is either equal to or greater than the fault of the defendant (depending on the jurisdiction) is barred from recovery. Thus, there is plenty of opportunity for interstate conflicts. Consider the following two cases.

SINNOTT V. THOMPSON
32 A.3d 351 (Del. 2011)

Before HOLLAND, BERGER and RIDGELY, JUSTICES

HOLLAND, JUSTICE

. . . .

Sinnott and Thompson were students at Campbell University ("Campbell") in Buies Creek, North Carolina. Thompson's primary residence is in Jamaica, New York. Sinnott's primary residence is Georgetown, Delaware. On January 13, 2008, Sinnott and Thompson were drinking alcoholic beverages on Campbell's campus in celebration of Thompson's birthday. Sinnott and Thompson then decided to leave campus to get something to eat. They left in a vehicle owned by Pepper, with Sinnott driving and Thompson riding as a passenger. Thompson knew that Sinnott had been drinking. As they were driving, a North Carolina police officer observed them speeding at over 85 miles per hour. He activated his lights and siren and followed the vehicle. The vehicle crossed the centerline twice, finally entering a ditch. It then became airborne and overturned. Before the vehicle came to rest, Thompson was ejected and landed on the roadway.

Sinnott was arrested for failing to stop for a patrolman's lights and siren, eluding an officer, and failing to stop at a stop sign. He was later charged with being under the influence of alcohol at the time of the accident and subsequently pled guilty to driving while impaired.

As a result of the collision, Thompson sustained a left subdural hematoma and traumatic brain injury, among other injuries. Thompson initially received treatment at Duke University Hospital in North Carolina and later received treatment from multiple healthcare providers in New York.

On November 24, 2009, Thompson filed suit against Sinnott alleging that Sinnott's "negligent, reckless and willful conduct and drinking" resulted in Thompson's injuries. . . . The appellants filed a motion for summary judgment requesting that the Superior Court apply North Carolina's substantive law based on the most significant relationship test. The appellants asserted that under North Carolina law, the doctrine of contributory negligence applied and barred Thompson's claim. Thompson responded by arguing that the "most significant relationship test" required an application of Delaware law, which applies the doctrine of comparative negligence. The Superior Court held that Delaware law applied to Thompson's claims and denied the appellants' motion for summary judgment.

Most Significant Relationship

We review the Superior Court's grant or denial of summary judgment *de novo*. This case presents a choice of law question. When conducting a choice of law analysis, Delaware courts follow the "most significant relationship test" in the *Restatement (Second) of Conflict of Laws* (the "Restatement"). § 145(1) of the Restatement provides that the law of the state that has the most significant relationship to the occurrence and the parties under the principles stated in § 6 is the governing law. § 6(2) provides that the following seven factors are relevant to the choice of law inquiry:

(a) the needs of the interstate and international systems,

(b) the relevant policies of the forum,

(c) the relevant policies of other interested states and the relative interests of those states in the determination of the particular issue,

(d) the protection of justified expectations,

(e) the basic policies underlying the particular field of law,

(f) certainty, predictability and uniformity of result, and

(g) ease in the determination and application of the law to be applied.

§ 145(2) also instructs that when applying the § 6 factors, courts should take into account the following four contacts:

(a) the place where the injury occurred,

(b)   the place where the conduct causing the injury occurred,

(c)   the domicile, residence, nationality, place of incorporation and place of business of the parties, and

(d)   the place where the relationship, if any, between the parties is centered.

The appellants contend that North Carolina law, and not Delaware law, applies to Thompson's claim. They argue that using the four contacts in the Restatement § 145(2), North Carolina has the most significant relationship because the injury occurred in North Carolina, the conduct occurred in North Carolina, Thompson and Sinnott were college students in North Carolina and were in the vehicle because of the contact in North Carolina, and the only relationship between the parties developed in North Carolina.

Thompson argues that Delaware has the predominant interest in regulating the behavior that gave rise to the conduct that led to his injuries. He asserts that the seven factors in the Restatement § 6(2) "most significant relationship test" are based on the quality of the contacts with the parties and not the quantity. Thompson further contends that Delaware's contacts are superior to North Carolina's because Sinnott and Pepper are both Delaware residents, Sinnott is a licensed driver in the state of Delaware, and the vehicle that Sinnott was driving was registered and insured in Delaware. . . .

The appellants . . . contend that *Yoder v. Delmarva Power & Light Co.* is instructive. However, *Yoder* is . . . distinguishable. In that case, the plaintiff was injured at his home in Maryland when a pole he was carrying came into contact with an overhead power line owned and maintained by the defendant, a Delaware corporation. The Superior Court rejected plaintiff's argument that defendant's conduct occurred in Delaware and concluded that the conduct giving rise to the injuries occurred in Maryland. Consequently, the Superior Court applied the law of Maryland, where the plaintiff was injured, to the contributory negligence issue. Notwithstanding, the Superior Court concluded Delaware's policy against a cap on non-economic damages was superior to Maryland's policy, which limited non-economic awards. In consideration of these competing policy interests, the Superior Court concluded Delaware had the most significant relationship to the damages issue and applied Delaware law to that issue.

Delaware Law Applies

The appellants assert that North Carolina's interest in regulating drivers and accidents on its roadways makes North Carolina's interests superior to Delaware's interests. In that regard, we conclude that North Carolina's interests are sufficiently protected by its ability to impose criminal penalties for violating its motor vehicle laws. Adjudicating the civil claims against Sinnott in a Delaware court based on Delaware law does not infringe upon those interests, particularly where, as here, North Carolina's interests in regulating Sinnott's conduct were vindicated when Sinnott pled guilty to driving while impaired.

Thompson brought this action in the State of Delaware and "the interest of the forum state in applying its law and policies to those who seek relief in its courts is paramount." Delaware law reflects a strong public policy against contributory negligence as a complete bar to recovery in negligence actions. Delaware applies the doctrine of comparative negligence and reduces a plaintiff's recovery based on the amount of negligence attributed to the plaintiff. Accordingly, Delaware courts have declined to apply the law of the state where the accident occurred when that law "is clearly repugnant to the settled public policy of [Delaware] the forum."

Sinnott is a Delaware citizen and Delaware has an overriding interest in regulating the conduct of its citizens. Delaware's interests include regulating the conduct of its licensed drivers and the vehicles that it has registered and which are insured under its law. Accordingly, we hold with regard to Thompson's negligence claim against Sinnott, Delaware has the most significant relationship to the occurrence and the parties under the § 6(2) policy factors after taking into consideration the § 145(2) contacts. . . .

Conclusion

The record reflects that Delaware has the most significant relationship to the parties and the occurrence. Therefore, the Delaware doctrine of comparative negligence applies to Thompson's claims against . . . Sinnott. . . . The judgment of the Superior Court is affirmed.

Welcome to the Second Restatement of Conflict of Laws. As we shall see, it is clear as mud. Nonetheless a strong majority of jurisdictions say that they follow the dictates of the Second Restatement. Consider the following questions with regard to *Sinnot*:

(1) Why did the court pay no attention to the law of New York where plaintiff, Thompson, was domiciled? The court would have found that New York has adopted pure comparative fault. Delaware follows modified comparative fault. Under Delaware law, a plaintiff can recover only if the plaintiff's fault was not greater than that of the defendant. If Thompson was less than 50% at fault, under the laws of both New York and Delaware he could recover damages minus his percentage of fault. Since, under those facts, both New York and Delaware would allow the same amount of recovery, would the case now be a false conflict? Is this situation covered by Judge Fuld's Rule 1 that applies the law of the common domicile?

(2)   Delaware professes to have an "overriding interest in regulating the conduct of its citizens." However, the Court notes that North Carolina, by imposing criminal sanctions on Sinnot's conduct, will assure that there is proper deterrence of Sinnot. The real question here is whether North Carolina can speak to the conduct of Thompson by denying him recovery for his conduct in getting into a car with a drunken driver. That Sinnot will be criminally punished does not speak at all to the interest of North Carolina in deterring Thompson's negligent conduct.

(3)   As to the "public policy" argument, wait until you read the next case. Judge Posner does a good job of demolishing the idea that North Carolina's contributory negligence bar is contrary to a fundamental policy of Delaware.

(4)   Does it make sense to say that Delaware saddles its defendants with tough Delaware law wherever they travel? This car ride took place in North Carolina between parties who met in North Carolina and went for a domestic North Carolina trip.

Now for another view of how to deal with this kind of conflict using the identical Restatement sections:

SPINOZZI V. ITT SHERATON CORPORATION
174 F.3d 842 (7th Cir. 1999)

POSNER, CHIEF JUDGE.

Dr. Thomas Spinozzi, a dentist who lives and works in Illinois, and his wife Linda went to Acapulco on vacation. They stayed at a Sheraton hotel. Dr. Spinozzi fell into a maintenance pit on the hotel grounds and was seriously injured. He and his wife (the wife claiming loss of consortium) brought suit in a federal district court in Illinois, under the diversity jurisdiction, against the Mexican corporation that owns the hotel, and three affiliates of that corporation. The suit alleges negligence. It was dismissed on summary judgment. The district judge held that under Illinois conflict of laws principles, which of course bind him in this diversity suit, *Klaxon v. Stentor Electric Mfg. Co.*, 313 U.S. 487, 61 S.Ct. 1020, 85 L.Ed. 1477 (1941), Mexican law governs the substantive issues; and that law, he concluded, bars the plaintiff's claims, mainly because it makes contributory negligence a complete defense to negligence liability and the uncontested facts showed that Dr. Spinozzi had been contributorily negligent. The Spinozzis' appeal challenges both the conflicts ruling-they contend that Illinois rather than Mexican tort law applies-and the ruling that Dr. Spinozzi was contributorily negligent as a matter of law.

The ownership structure of the Sheraton Acapulco Resort is complex, but to simplify the opinion we shall assume, favorably to the plaintiffs, that it is owned and operated by ITT Sheraton Corporation ("Sheraton"), a

Delaware corporation with its principal place of business in Massachusetts, and forget the other defendants. Sheraton advertises its hotels all over the world, including Illinois, and it was in response to an advertisement in Illinois that the Spinozzis decided to stay at the Sheraton Acapulco. In fact, because Mrs. Spinozzi is a travel agent, Sheraton granted the Spinozzis a special rate to induce them to stay at the hotel. The plaintiffs argue that by its promotional activities in Illinois directed particularly to the small group (travel agents and their spouses) to which the Spinozzis belong, Sheraton should be taken to have "caused" in *Illinois* the injury to Dr. Spinozzi. And this injury-causing activity in Illinois, when taken in conjunction with the fact that the plaintiffs are Illinois residents, establishes (the plaintiffs argue) that the preponderance of "contacts" between the plaintiffs and either Illinois or Mexico was with Illinois, and not, as one might suppose from the location of the accident, with Mexico.

Under the *ancien régime* of conflict of laws, this argument would have been a nonstarter. The rule was simple: the law applicable to a tort suit was the law of the place where the tort occurred, more precisely the place where the last act, namely the plaintiff's injury, necessary to make the defendant's careless or otherwise wrongful behavior actually tortious, occurred, *Restatement of Conflicts* §§ 377–378 (1934); 2 Joseph H. Beale, *A Treatise on the Conflict of Laws* § 377.2, pp. 1287–88 (1935), and here that place was Mexico. This and other simple rules of conflict of laws came to seem too rigid, mainly because of such anomalies as suits between citizens of the same state when it was not the state where the accident had occurred. See, e.g., *Babcock v. Jackson*, 12 N.Y.2d 473, 240 N.Y.S.2d 743, 191 N.E.2d 279 (1963). But the search for flexibility led, alas, to standards that were nebulous, such as the "most significant relationship" test of the *Second Restatement* that is orthodox in Illinois. (Citations omitted).

Often, however, the simple old rules can be glimpsed through modernity's fog, though spectrally thinned to presumptions-in the latest lingo, "default rules." For in the absence of unusual circumstances, the highest scorer on the "most significant relationship" test is-the place where the tort occurred. . . . *Restatement (Second) of Conflict of Laws, supra,* § 145 comment e, § 146. For that is the place that has the greatest interest in striking a reasonable balance among safety, cost, and other factors pertinent to the design and administration of a system of tort law. Most people affected whether as victims or as injurers by accidents and other injury-causing events are residents of the jurisdiction in which the event takes place. So if law can be assumed to be generally responsive to the values and preferences of the people who live in the community that formulated the law, the law of the place of the accident can be expected to reflect the values and preferences of the people most likely to be involved in accidents-can be expected, in other words, to be responsive and responsible law, law that internalizes the costs and benefits of the people affected by it.

Only a tiny fraction of hotel guests in Mexico are from Illinois. Illinois residents may want a higher standard of care than the average hotel guest in Mexico, but to supplant Mexican by Illinois tort law would disserve the general welfare because it would mean that Mexican safety standards (insofar as they are influenced by tort suits) were being set by people having little stake in those standards. Of course the plaintiffs do not argue that Illinois tort law should govern *all* accidents in Mexican hotels. They argue for something that is even worse-that each guest be permitted to carry with him the tort law of his state or country, provided that he is staying in a hotel that had advertised there. The domicile of the hotel's owner would be irrelevant. If a French citizen were injured in a hotel in Mexico owned by a German corporation that had advertised in France, the law applicable to his suit against the German corporation would be French law. If in the course of a year citizens of a hundred different countries and U.S. states stayed at the Sheraton Acapulco Resort, Sheraton would be subject to a hundred different bodies of tort law. Inconsistent duties of care might be imposed. *Kuehn v. Childrens Hospital, supra*, 119 F.3d at 1302. A resort might have a system of firewalls that under the law of some states or nations might be considered essential to safety and in others might be considered a safety hazard. Suppose the resort burned down and dozens of injured guests sued: according to the plaintiffs' notion of conflict of laws, each claim would be governed by a different tort regime if each plaintiff was from a different state or country. If the regimes were incompatible, it might be impossible for Sheraton to escape liability to some of the plaintiffs no matter how careful it had been. Negligence would be strict liability.

Uniformity of tort law and consequent avoidance of anomalies cannot, we recognize, be achieved by an interpretation just of Illinois' conflict of law rules. Guests of the Sheraton Acapulco Resort who come from somewhere else and sue in their home court will be governed by the conflict of laws rules applied by that court, which may differ from Illinois'. But there might be general agreement that the law of the place of the injury is presumptively the right law to apply to issues of duty of care, for the reasons that we have suggested. "[A] state may not exercise jurisdiction to prescribe law with respect to a person or activity having connections with another state when the exercise of such jurisdiction is unreasonable." *Restatement (Third) of the Foreign Relations Law of the United States* § 403(1) (1987). It is unreasonable that the Illinois courts should be setting safety standards for hotels in Mexico.

Sheraton could, it is true, include in all its contracts with its guests a forum-selection clause that would require the guest to sue in a jurisdiction in which *lex loci delicti* (the law of the place of the accident) was the default rule. *Id.*, § 421 comment h; *Carnival Cruise Lines, Inc. v. Shute*, 499 U.S. 585, 593, 111 S.Ct. 1522, 113 L.Ed.2d 622 (1991). It might, for that matter, specify the jurisdiction whose tort law would govern in the event of an accident; contractual choice of tort law provisions are generally enforceable. *Chan v. Society Expeditions, Inc.*, 123 F.3d 1287, 1296–98 (9th Cir.1997); *Kuehn v. Childrens Hospital, supra*, 119 F.3d at 1301–02. Sheraton has followed neither course, and this undermines its claim to be concerned with being subjected to the different and even conflicting tort laws of dozens or hundreds of different jurisdictions. *Id.* at 1302. But that cannot be the end of the analysis. There is no rule that there shall be no conflict of laws analysis-that the law of the jurisdiction where the suit is brought (*lex fori*) shall apply-unless the parties could have negotiated a choice of law clause yet failed to do so. So we must forge on.

Whenever a legal claim, whether technically it is a contract claim or a tort claim, arises out of a voluntary relationship between injurer and victim, a court applying the *Second Restatement*'s test should ask what body of law the parties would have expected to govern an accident arising out of that relationship. *Esser v. McIntyre*, 169 Ill.2d 292, 214 Ill.Dec. 693, 661 N.E.2d 1138, 1142 (1996); *Restatement (Second) of Conflict of Laws, supra*, § 6(2)(d) and comment g. (If the simple rules of the *First Restatement* were still in force, they would know!) We doubt that Dr. Spinozzi would have thought he was carrying his domiciliary law with him, like a turtle's house, to every foreign country he visited. To change the zoological metaphor, he would not, eating dinner with a Mexican in Acapulco, feel himself cocooned in Illinois law, like citizens of imperial states in the era of colonialism who were granted extraterritorial privileges in weak or dependent states. Law is largely territorial, and people have at least a vague intuition of this. They may feel safer in foreign hotels owned by American chains, but they do not feel that they are on American soil and governed by American law. . . .

The plaintiffs' backup position is that a defense of contributory negligence is repugnant to the public policy of Illinois, and therefore an Illinois court would not enforce that defense even if it would apply the rest of Mexico's tort law to an accident such as this. States do refuse to enforce foreign law that is particularly obnoxious to them. But obviously the mere fact that foreign and domestic law differ on some point is not enough to invoke the exception. Otherwise in every case of an actual conflict the court of the forum state would choose its own law; there would be no law of conflict of laws.

The danger of the public policy exception is provincialism: an inability to recognize that a different jurisdiction (especially a foreign country) need not be benighted to have a different approach to a particular legal problem. . . .

Some years ago, by decision of its highest court, Illinois joined the accelerating trend toward replacing contributory negligence by comparative negligence, that is, reducing contributory negligence from a complete defense to a partial defense. *Alvis v. Ribar*, 85 Ill.2d 1, 52 Ill.Dec. 23, 421 N.E.2d 886 (1981). But it did not do so because it thought contributory negligence, like polygamous marriage, e.g., *Spencer v. People*, 133 Colo. 196, 292 P.2d 971, 973 (1956); *Ng Suey Hi v. Weedin*, 21 F.2d 801, 802 (9th Cir.1927); *People v. Kay*, 141 Misc. 574, 252 N.Y.S. 518, 524–25 (1931), deeply offensive; it thought it outmoded and inferior to comparative negligence. It did use some strong language, calling it for example "repulsive," 52 Ill.Dec. 23, 421 N.E.2d at 895, but if it had really meant this, it would not have made its decision prospective only, as it did. . . .

We think it unlikely that Illinois would refuse to apply Mexican law in this case. When the rule of *Alvis* came to be codified, 735 ILCS 5/21116(c), the Illinois legislature curtailed it, retaining contributory negligence as a complete bar in all cases in which the victim is found to be more than 50 percent responsible for the accident. In light of this provision it is no surprise that the legislation is notably devoid of the "void as against public policy" language. . . .

It remains only to consider whether the judge was right to grant summary judgment for Sheraton on the issue of Dr. Spinozzi's contributory negligence; and this brings us at last to the facts. It was 10:30 p.m. when the Spinozzis returned to the hotel from dining out with friends only to find that because of a power outage the hotel was in darkness. Their hotel room was stifling because the air conditioning was not operating, so they went out and sat by the hotel's pool, waiting for the lights to come back on. At some distance from the pool was a maintenance pit, 12 to 14 feet deep, shielded by planters. The entrance to the pit was between two of the planters and was guarded by a low gate on the other side of which a spiral staircase led down to the bottom of the pit. Dr. Spinozzi left the garden area to see whether the lights had come back on in the room occupied by his friends. It was pitch dark, yet rather than walking on one of the paths leading from the poolside area to the hotel, Spinozzi walked into the shrubbery that surrounded that area and in a direction that would bring him to a good vantage point for seeing the window of his friends' room. The gate to the maintenance ditch had been left open. Spinozzi walked through the entrance, thinking he was on a path that would bring him near the window, and fell into the pit.

We may assume that the hotel was negligent in leaving the gate open, and perhaps in other respects, like not having emergency lighting that would show the location of the pit to any guest who happened to be wandering in the shrubbery. But the question of contributory negligence is simply whether, had Dr. Spinozzi exercised due care (negligence is an injurer's failure to use due care, contributory negligence a victim's failure to use due care), the accident would have been averted notwithstanding the hotel's negligence. The answer is yes, because Spinozzi acknowledged in his deposition that he couldn't see where he was going because of the dark. A careful person who finds himself in a strange area in a foreign country and can't see the ground in front of him will walk in a slow and gingerly manner to avoid tripping; he will feel his way. Had Dr. Spinozzi done that, he would have felt the ground drop suddenly when he reached the staircase beyond the gate and would have grabbed the rail and saved himself from falling. Having stepped off the pedestrian path into a completely darkened area of shrubbery, he had no reason to suppose the surface ahead of him smooth. He strode on regardless. He might as well have been blindfolded. His negligence came close to, if indeed it did not cross the line into, a conscious assumption of the risk of disaster, a form of aggravated negligence. (Citations omitted). . . .

AFFIRMED

———————

Judge Posner made a similar finding giving little attention to the plaintiff's domicile in *Carris v. Marriott Int'l*, 466 F.3d 558 (7th Cir. 2006) [decided under Illinois conflicts law]. In that case, the plaintiff booked a reservation at a Marriott Hotel in the Bahamas on the Marriott website. The Marriott in the Bahamas, Nassau Marriott Resort, was actually a franchisee of Marriott International. Under Illinois law, plaintiff could recover from Marriott International due to negligence of its franchisee based on apparent authority if the plaintiff was led to believe that the franchisee was actually run by the franchisor. Under Bahamas' law, there is no liability in tort based on apparent authority. Posner made the identical argument that he propounded in *Spinozzi*, saying that to hold otherwise "any hotel that has a website subjects itself to the tort law of every country whose nationals stay at one of the hotels in the chain." *Id*. at 561.

Even where the plaintiff and defendant are domiciled in the same state that allows recovery, where both the conduct and injury take place in a state that absolves the conduct from liability a court will apply the *lex loci delicti*. Thus in *Bertram v. Norden*, 823 N.E.2d 478 (Ohio Ct. App. 2004) two young Ohio domiciliaries who had set out together to do snowmobiling in Michigan collided while snowmobiling in Michigan. Under Ohio law, plaintiff could recover for negligence but Michigan had a statute that provided that all who participate in the sport of snowmobiling "accept the risks associated with that sport." The Ohio court relied on the presumption in favor of the place of injury set forth in the Second Restatement and applied Michigan law. Since Michigan had a statute absolving participants in snowmobiling from liability its interest was predominant. Also see *Brooks v. General Casualty Co. of Wis.*, 2007 WL 4305577 (E.D. Wis. 2007). The premise in all of the above cases is most probably that all the rules of the locus states were conduct-regulating.

The *Spinozzi* opinion is vintage Posner. He pulls no punches. Note that he cites to Restatement, Second, Section 146. It reads:

§ 146.   Personal Injuries

In an action for a personal injury, the local law of the state where the injury occurred determines the rights and liabilities of the parties, unless, with respect to the particular issue, some other state has a more significant relationship under the principles stated in § 6 to the occurrence and the parties, in which event the local law of the other state will be applied.

He also could have cited to Restatement, Section 156:

§ 156. Tortious Character of Conduct

(1) The law selected by application of the rule of § 145 determines whether the actor's conduct was tortious.

(2) The applicable law will usually be the local law of the state where the injury occurred.

Do these sections lead to the conclusion that in the absence of a false conflict the law of the place of injury applies? Apparently Judge Posner thinks so. The Delaware court in *Sinnott* does not appear to agree.

2. DRAM SHOP

Dram shop cases make for wonderful conflict problems. Under dram shop statutes, or similar common law doctrines, commercial establishments that serve liquor to patrons to the point of intoxication are liable for the harm they cause while in the intoxicated state. But not all states make the establishment liable. Consider the possibilities: When the drunk patron leaves the tavern or restaurant, an accident in which a resident of the same state or another state is injured may follow, either in the state in which the patron was served or in another state. The state in which the patron was served may have no dram shop rule or may have a dram shop rule. The injured party may be a resident of a dram shop state or of a state that does not have a dram shop rule. The combinations and permutations are many.

BERNHARD V. HARRAH'S CLUB
546 P.2d 719 (Cal. 1976)

SULLIVAN, JUSTICE.

Plaintiff appeals from a judgment of dismissal entered upon an order sustaining without leave to amend the general demurrer of defendant Harrah's Club to plaintiff's first amended complaint.

Plaintiff's complaint, containing only one count, alleged in substance the following: Defendant Harrah's Club, a Nevada corporation, owned and operated gambling establishments in the State of Nevada in which intoxicating liquors were sold, furnished to the public and given away for consumption on the premises. Defendant advertised for and solicited in California the business of California residents at such establishments knowing and expecting that many California residents would use the public highways in going to and from defendant's drinking and gambling establishments.

On July 24, 1971, Fern and Philip Myers, in response to defendant's advertisements and solicitations, drove from their California residence to defendant's gambling and drinking club in Nevada, where they stayed until the early morning hours of July 25, 1971. During their stay, the Myers were served numerous alcoholic beverages by defendant's employees, progressively reaching a point of obvious intoxication rendering them incapable of safely driving a car. Nonetheless, defendant continued to serve and furnish the Myers alcoholic beverages.

While still in this intoxicated state, the Myers drove their car back to California. Proceeding in a northeasterly direction on Highway 49, near Nevada City, California, the Myers' car, driven negligently by a still intoxicated Fern Myers, drifted across the center line into the lane of oncoming traffic and collided head-on with plaintiff Richard A. Bernhard, a resident of California, who was then driving his motorcycle along said highway. As a result of the collision plaintiff suffered severe injuries. Defendant's sale and furnishing of alcoholic beverages to the Myers, who were intoxicated to the point of being unable to drive safely, was negligent and was the proximate cause of the plaintiff's injuries in the ensuing automobile accident in California for which plaintiff prayed $100,000 in damages.

Defendant filed a general demurrer to the first amended complaint. In essence it was grounded on the following contentions: that Nevada law denies recovery against a tavern keeper by a third person for injuries proximately caused by the former by selling or furnishing alcoholic beverages to an intoxicated patron who inflicts the injuries on the latter; that Nevada law governed since the alleged tort was committed by defendant in Nevada; and that § 25602 of the California Business and Professions Code which established the duty necessary for liability under our decision in Vesely v. Sager (1971) 5 Cal.3d 153, 95 Cal.Rptr. 623, 486 P.2d 151, was inapplicable to a Nevada tavern. The trial court sustained the demurrer without leave to amend and entered a judgment of dismissal. This appeal followed.

We face a problem in the choice of law governing a tort action. As we have made clear on other occasions, we no longer adhere to the rule that the law of the place of the wrong is applicable in a California forum regardless of the issues before the court. Rather we have adopted in its place a rule requiring an analysis of the respective interests of the states involved—the objective of which is 'to determine the law that most appropriately applies to the issue involved.'

The issue involved in the case at bench is the civil liability of defendant tavern keeper to plaintiff, a third person, for injuries allegedly caused by the former by selling and furnishing alcoholic beverages in Nevada to intoxicated patrons who subsequently injured plaintiff in California. Two states are involved: (1) California—the place of plaintiff's residence and

domicile, the place where he was injured, and the forum; and (2) Nevada—
the place of defendant's residence and the place of the wrong.

We observe at the start that the laws of the two states—California and
Nevada—applicable to the issue involved are not identical. California
imposes liability on tavern keepers in this state for conduct such as here
alleged. In Vesely v. Sager, *supra*, 5 Cal.3d 153, 166, 95 Cal.Rptr. 623, 632,
486 P.2d 151, 160, this court rejected the contention that 'civil liability for
tavern keepers should be left to future legislative action. . . . First, liability
has been denied in cases such as the one before us solely because of the
judicially created rule that the furnishing of alcoholic beverages is not the
proximate cause of injuries resulting from intoxication. This rule is
patently unsound and totally inconsistent with the principles of proximate
cause established in other areas of negligence law. . . . Second, the
Legislature has expressed its intention in this area with the adoption of
Evidence Code § 669, and Business and Professions Code § 25602. . . . It is
clear that Business and Professions Code § 25602 (making it a
misdemeanor to sell to an obviously intoxicated person) is a statute to
which this presumption (of negligence, Evidence Code § 669) applies and
that the policy expressed in the statute is to promote the safety of the
people of California. . . .' Nevada on the other hand refuses to impose such
liability. In Hamm v. Carson City Nuggett, Inc. (1969) 85 N.W. 99, 450 P.2d
358, 359, the court held it would create neither common law liability nor
liability based on the criminal statute banning sale of alcoholic beverages
to a person who is drunk, because 'if civil liability is to be imposed, it should
be accomplished by legislative act after appropriate surveys, hearings, and
investigations to ascertain the need for it and the expected consequences
to follow.' . . .

Although California and Nevada, the two 'involved states' have
different laws governing the issue presented in the case at bench, we
encounter a problem in selecting the applicable rule of law only if Both
states have an interest in having their respective laws applied. '(G)enerally
speaking the forum will apply its own rule of decision unless a party
litigant timely invokes the law of a foreign state. In such event he must
demonstrate that the latter rule of decision will further the interest of the
foreign state and therefore that it is an appropriate one for the forum to
apply to the case before it.

Defendant contends that Nevada has a definite interest in having its
rule of decision applied in this case in order to protect its resident tavern
keepers like defendant from being subjected to a civil liability which
Nevada has not imposed either by legislative enactment or decisional law.
It is urged that in Hamm v. Carson City Nuggett, supra, 85 Nev. 99, 450
P.2d 358, 359, the Supreme Court of Nevada clearly delineated the policy
underlying denial of civil liability of tavern keepers who sell to obviously
intoxicated patrons: 'Those opposed to extending liability point out that to

hold otherwise would subject the tavern owner to ruinous exposure every time he poured a drink and would multiply litigation endlessly in a claim-conscious society. Every liquor vendor visited by the patron who became intoxicated would be a likely defendant in subsequent litigation flowing from the patron's wrongful conduct. . . . Judicial restraint is a worthwhile practice when the proposed new doctrine may have implications far beyond the perception of the court asked to declare it. They urge that if civil liability is to be imposed, it should be accomplished by legislative act after appropriate surveys, hearings, and investigations. . . . We prefer this point of view.' Accordingly defendant argues that the Nevada rule of decision is the appropriate one for the forum to apply.

Plaintiff on the other hand points out that California also has an interest in applying its own rule of decision to the case at bench. California imposes on tavern keeper's civil liability to third parties injured by persons to whom the tavern keeper has sold alcoholic beverages when they are obviously intoxicated 'for the purpose of protecting members of the general public from injuries to person and damage to property resulting from the excessive use of intoxicating liquor.' California, it is urged, has a special interest in affording this protection to all California residents injured in California.

Thus, since the case at bench involves a California resident (plaintiff) injured in this state by intoxicated drivers and a Nevada resident tavern keeper (defendant) which served alcoholic beverages to them in Nevada, it is clear that each state has an interest in the application of its respective law of liability and nonliability. . . .

The search for the proper resolution of a true conflicts case, while proceeding within orthodox parameters of governmental interest analysis, has generated much scholarly examination and discussion. The father of the governmental interest approach, Professor Brainerd Currie, originally took the position that in a true conflicts situation the law of the forum should always be applied. (Currie, *Selected Essays on Conflict of Laws* (1963) p. 184.) However, upon further reflection, Currie suggested that when under the governmental interest approach a preliminary analysis reveals an apparent conflict of interest upon the forum's assertion of its own rule of decision, the forum should reexamine its policy to determine if a more restrained interpretation of it is more appropriate. 'To assert a conflict between the interests of the forum and the foreign state is a serious matter; the mere fact that a suggested broad conception of a local interest will conflict with that of a foreign state is a sound reason why the conception should be reexamined, with a view to a more moderate and restrained interpretation both of the policy and of the circumstances in which it must be applied to effectuate the forum's legitimate purpose. . . . An analysis of this kind . . . was brilliantly performed by Justice Traynor in Bernkrant v. Fowler (1961) 55 Cal.2d 588, 12 Cal.Rptr. 266, 360 P.2d

906.' (Currie, *The Disinterested Third State* (1963) 28 Law & Contemp. Prob., pp. 754, 757; see also Sedler in Symposium, *Conflict of Laws Round Table*, supra, 49 Texas L. Rev. 211, at pp. 224–225.) This process of reexamination requires identification of a 'real interest as opposed to a hypothetical interest' on the part of the forum (Sedler, *Value of Principled Preferences*, 49 Texas L. Rev. 224) and can be approached under principles of 'comparative impairment.' (Baxter, *Choice of Law and the Federal System,* supra, 16 Stan. L. Rev. 1–22; Horowitz, *The Law of Choice of Law in California—A Restatement*, supra, 21 U.C.L.A. L. Rev. 719, 748–758.)

Once this preliminary analysis has identified a true conflict of the governmental interests involved as applied to the parties under the particular circumstances of the case, the 'comparative impairment' approach to the resolution of such conflict seeks to determine which state's interest would be more impaired if its policy were subordinated to the policy of the other state. This analysis proceeds on the principle that true conflicts should be resolved by applying the law of the state whose interest would be the more impaired if its law were not applied. Exponents of this process of analysis emphasize that it is very different from a weighing process. The court does not "weight' the conflicting governmental interests in the sense of determining which conflicting law manifested the 'better' or the 'worthier' social policy on the specific issue. An attempted balancing of conflicting state policies in that sense . . . is difficult to justify in the context of a federal system in which, within constitutional limits, states are empowered to mold their policies as they wish. . . . (The process) can accurately be described as . . . accommodation of conflicting state policies, as a problem of allocating domains of law-making power in multi-state contexts—limitations on the reach of state policies as distinguished from evaluating the wisdom of those policies. . . . (E)mphasis is placed on the appropriate scope of conflicting state policies rather than on the 'quality of those policies. . . .' (Horowitz, *The Law of Choice of Law in California—A Restatement*, supra, 21 U.C.L.A. L. Rev. 719, 753; see also Baxter, *Choice of Law and the Federal System*, supra, 16 Stan. L. Rev. 1, 18–19.) However, the true function of this methodology can probably be appreciated only casuistically in its application to an endless variety of choice of law problems. (See, e.g., the hypothetical situations set forth in Baxter, op. cit., pp. 10–17.)

Although the concept and nomenclature of this methodology may have received fuller recognition at a later time, it is noteworthy that the core of its rationale was applied by Justice Traynor in his opinion for this court in People v. One 1953 Ford Victoria (1957) 48 Cal.2d 595, 311 P.2d 480. There in a proceeding to forfeit an automobile for unlawful transportation of narcotics we dealt with the question whether a chattel mortgage of the vehicle given in Texas and, admittedly valid both in that state and this, succumbed to the forfeiture proceedings. The purchaser of the car, having executed a note and chattel mortgage for the unpaid purchase price, without the consent of the mortgagee drove the vehicle to California where he used it to transport marijuana. Applicable California statutes made it clear that they did not contemplate the forfeiture of the interest of an innocent mortgagee, that is a person whose 'interest was created after a reasonable investigation of the moral responsibility, character, and reputation of the purchaser, and without any knowledge that the vehicle was being, or was to be, used for the purpose charged. . . .' Texas had no similar statute; nor had the mortgagee, though proving that the mortgage was bona fide, also proved that he had made the above reasonable investigation of the mortgagor.

It was clear that Texas had an interest in seeing that valid security interests created upon the lawful purchase of automobiles in Texas be enforceable and recognized. California had an interest in controlling the transportation of narcotics. Each interest was at stake in the case, since the chattel mortgage had been validly created in Texas and the car was used to transport narcotics in California. The crucial question confronting the court was whether the 'reasonable investigation' required by statute of a California mortgagee applied to the Texas mortgagee. Employing what was in substance a 'comparative impairment' approach, the court answered the question in the negative. 'It is contended that a holding that the 'reasonable investigation' requirement is not applicable to respondent will subvert the enforcement of California's narcotics laws. We are not persuaded that such dire consequences will ensue. The state may still forfeit the interest of the wrongdoer. It has done so in this case. Moreover, the Legislature has made plain its purpose not to forfeit the interests of innocent mortgagees. It has not made plain that 'reasonable investigation' of the purchaser is such an essential element of innocence that it must be made even by an out-of-state mortgagee although such mortgagee could not reasonably be expected to make such investigation.' (Id. 48 Cal.2d at p. 599, 311 P.2d at p. 482.)

Mindful of the above principles governing our choice of law, we proceed to reexamine the California policy underlying the imposition of civil liability upon tavern keepers. At its broadest limits this policy would afford protection to all persons injured in California by intoxicated persons who have been sold or furnished alcoholic beverages while intoxicated regardless of where such beverages were sold or furnished. Such a broad policy would naturally embrace situations where the intoxicated actor had been provided with liquor by out-of-state tavern keepers. Although the State of Nevada does not impose such Civil liability on its tavern keepers, nevertheless they are subject to Criminal penalties under a statute making it unlawful to sell or give intoxicating liquor to any person who is drunk or known to be an habitual drunkard. (See Nev.Rev.Stats. 202.100; see Hamm v. Carson City Nuggett, Inc., supra, 85 Nev. 99, 450 P.2d 358.)

We need not, and accordingly do not here determine the outer limits to which California's policy should be extended, for it appears clear to us that it must encompass defendant, who as alleged in the complaint, 'advertis(es) for and otherwise solicit(s) in California the business of California residents at defendant HARRAH'S CLUB Nevada drinking and gambling establishments, knowing and expecting said California residents, in response to said advertising and solicitation, to use the public highways of the State of California in going and coming from defendant HARRAH'S CLUB Nevada drinking and gambling establishments.' Defendant by the course of its chosen commercial practice has put itself at the heart of California's regulatory interest, namely to prevent tavern keepers from selling alcoholic beverages to obviously intoxicated persons who are likely to act in California in the intoxicated state. It seems clear that California cannot reasonably effectuate its policy if it does not extend its regulation to include out-of-state tavern keepers such as defendant who regularly and purposely sell intoxicating beverages to California residents in places and under conditions in which it is reasonably certain these residents will return to California and act therein while still in an intoxicated state. California's interest would be very significantly impaired if its policy were not applied to defendant.

Since the act of selling alcoholic beverages to obviously intoxicated persons is already proscribed in Nevada, the application of California's rule of civil liability would not impose an entirely new duty requiring the ability to distinguish between California residents and other patrons. Rather the imposition of such liability involves an increased economic exposure, which, at least for businesses which actively solicit extensive California patronage, is a foreseeable and coverable business expense. Moreover, Nevada's interest in protecting its tavern keepers from civil liability of a boundless and unrestricted nature will not be significantly impaired when as in the instant case liability is imposed only on those tavern keepers who actively solicit California business.

Therefore, upon reexamining the policy underlying California's rule of decision and giving such policy a more restrained interpretation for the purpose of this case pursuant to the principles of the law of choice of law discussed above, we conclude that California has an important and abiding interest in applying its rule of decision to the case at bench, that the policy of this state would be more significantly impaired if such rule were not applied and that the trial court erred in not applying California law.

Defendant argues, however, that even if California law is applied, the demurrer was nonetheless properly sustained because the tavern keeper's duty stated in Vesely v. Sager, supra, 5 Cal.3d 153, 95 Cal.Rptr. 623, 486 P.2d 151, is based on Business and Professions Code § 25602, which is a criminal statute and thus without extraterritorial effect. It is quite true, as defendant argues, that in Vesely we determined 'that civil liability results when a vendor furnishes alcoholic beverages to a customer in violation of Business and Professions Code § 25602 and each of the conditions set forth in Evidence Code § 669, subdivision (a) is established.'

It is also clear, as defendant's argument points out, that since, unlike the California vendor in Vesely, defendant was a Nevada resident which furnished the alcoholic beverage to the Myers in that state, the above California statute had no extraterritorial effect and that civil liability could not be posited on defendant's violation of a California criminal law. We recognize, therefore, that we cannot make the same determination as quoted above with respect to defendant that we made with respect to the defendant vendor in Vesely.

However, our decision in Vesely was much broader than defendant would have it. There, at the very outset of our opinion, we declared that the traditional common law rule denying recovery on the ground that the furnishing of alcoholic beverage is not the proximate cause of the injuries inflicted on a third person by an intoxicated individual 'is patently unsound.' Observing that '(u)ntil fairly recently, it was uniformly held that (such) an action could not be maintained at common law' and reviewing in detail the common law rule we concluded that 'the furnishing of an alcoholic beverage to an intoxicated person may be a proximate cause of injuries inflicted by that individual upon a third person.' We reasoned: 'If such furnishing is a proximate cause, it is so because the consumption, resulting intoxication, and injury-producing conduct are foreseeable intervening causes, or at least the injury-producing conduct is one of the hazards which makes such furnishing negligent.' (Id. 5 Cal.3d at p. 164, 95 Cal.Rptr. at p. 627, 486 P.2d at p. 155.). . . .

In sum, our opinion in Vesely struck down the old common law rule of nonliability constructed on the basis that the consumption, not the sale, of alcoholic beverages was the proximate cause of the injuries inflicted by the intoxicated person. Although we chose to impose liability on the Vesely defendant on the basis of his violating the applicable statute, the clear import of our decision was that there was no bar to civil liability under modern negligence law. Certainly, we said nothing in Vesely indicative of an intention to retain the former rule that an action at common law does not lie. The fact then, that in the case at bench, § 25602 of the Business and Professions Code is not applicable to this defendant in Nevada so as to warrant the imposition of civil liability on the basis of its violation, does not preclude recovery on the basis of negligence apart from the statute. Pertinent here is our observation in Rowland v. Christian (1968): 'It bears repetition that the basic policy of this state set forth by the Legislature in § 1714 of the Civil Code is that everyone is responsible for an injury caused to another by his want of ordinary care or skill in the management of his property.'

The judgment is reversed and the cause is remanded to the trial court with directions to overrule the demurrer and to allow defendant a reasonable time within which to answer.

BOURGEOIS V. VANDERBILT

639 F.Supp.2d 958 (W.D. Ark. 2009), aff'd 417 Fed. Appx. 605 (8th Cir. 2011)

MEMORANDUM OPINION

HARRY F. BARNES, DISTRICT JUDGE . . .

I.   BACKGROUND

Plaintiff is a resident of Baton Rouge, Louisiana. On July 30, 2005, she was employed as a bus driver for Dixieland Tours and Cruises, Inc., also of Baton Rouge, Louisiana. While she was driving Dixieland's bus south on U.S. Highway 71 in Miller County, Arkansas, she was struck by a northbound truck driven by Separate Defendant Douglas Vanderbilt of Texarkana, Texas. Vanderbilt was returning home from a trip to Harrah's, a casino located in Shreveport, Louisiana. Plaintiff was injured in the collision and has alleged damages exceeding $75,000. Vanderbilt was subsequently convicted of a DWI in Arkansas in connection with the accident.

Plaintiff filed a complaint against Vanderbilt, alleging that he was intoxicated at the time of the accident and was operating his vehicle in an unlawful, imprudent, and unsafe manner. In her Amended Complaint, Plaintiff added Harrah's as a defendant, alleging that Harrah's "contributed to and caused Vanderbilt's severe intoxication, failed to stop providing Vanderbilt liquor, enabled Vanderbilt by tendering his auto and keys, and failed to make any effort to stop Vanderbilt from operating his auto in an intoxicated and exhausted condition, given that he had been in [Harrah's] for at least [fourteen] hours drinking liquor and gambling." Harrah's asserts that it is not liable for Plaintiff's injuries and has filed a motion for summary judgment. The summary judgment motion is now before the Court. . . .

III. DISCUSSION

A.   *Choice of Law*

Plaintiff and Harrah's disagree as to whether Louisiana or Arkansas law applies here. It is acknowledged by both parties that the application of Louisiana law to this case would preclude Plaintiff from recovering damages against Harrah's for the alleged "over-serving" of Vanderbilt that lead to the vehicle accident and Plaintiff's injuries. Louisiana anti-dram shop law expressly provides immunity to vendors of alcohol and places responsibility solely upon the individual who consumes the intoxicating beverage:

> "No person . . . nor any agent, servant, or employee of such person who sells or serves intoxicating beverages . . . to a person over the age of the lawful purchase thereof, shall be liable to such person or to any other person . . . for any injury suffered off the premises, including wrongful death and property damage, because of the intoxication of the person to whom the intoxicating beverages were sold or served.".

LA.REV.STAT. ANN. § 9:2800.1(B). However, if Arkansas dram shop law is to be applied, Plaintiff would retain the possibility of recovery due to the absence of immunity for vendors. Damages can be recovered if the plaintiff proves that the vendor "knowingly sold alcoholic beverages to a person who was clearly intoxicated." ARK.CODE ANN. § 3–3–209. . . .

Arkansas courts have moved away from a mechanical application of the *lex loci delicti* rule and have adopted five choice-influencing factors ("Leflar Factors") to determine which state's law should be applied. *Wallis v. Mrs. Smith's Pie Company*, 261 Ark. 622, 550 S.W.2d 453 (1977). The Leflar Factors are as follows: (1) predictability of results; (2) maintenance of interstate and international order; (3) simplification of the judicial task; (4) advancement of the forum's governmental interests; and (5) application of the better rule of law. The court will now examine each factor as it applies to the present case.

First, "predictability of results" addresses the expectation that the decision on a given set of facts should be the same regardless of where the litigation occurs. *Schubert v. Target Stores, Inc.*, 360 Ark. 404, 410, 201 S.W.3d 917 (2005). This factor is primarily aimed at avoiding forum shopping and ensuring uniform results. *Id.* at 410, 201 S.W.3d at 922. A uniform decision in cases such as the present case may not be possible given the non-uniformity of the states' laws in this area. The resolution of this case depends on which state's law applies. Although forum shopping is a concern in some cases, it is not of great concern here where Arkansas and Louisiana both have a connection to this case.

Second, "maintenance of interstate and international order" discourages a forum's "reflexive application of its own law" where another state has a more substantial interest in having its law prevail. John J. Watkins, *A Guide To Choice of Law in Arkansas*, 2005 ARK. L. NOTES 151, 160. This consideration seeks to minimize any potential friction among states that could lead to retaliatory behaviors among courts. *Id.* Here, Louisiana has a more substantial interest in having its law prevail because it has a more significant relationship to the parties in this case, *see Ganey v. Kawasaki Motors Corp.*, 366 Ark. 238, 252, 234 S.W.3d 838, 847 (2006). Plaintiff is a Louisiana citizen, Harrah's is located in Louisiana, and Harrah's alleged negligent conduct occurred in Louisiana.

The third factor, "simplification of the judicial task," encourages courts to consider applying an out-of-state law when it is outcome-determinative and easy to apply. *Schubert*, 360 Ark. at 411, 201 S.W.3d at 922. However, this simplification of the judicial task is not a "paramount consideration," and a certain law should not be applied only for reasons of simplicity or convenience. *Id.*, 201 S.W.3d at 922. Here, this factor favors Louisiana. The applicable Louisiana law places the responsibilities associated with alcohol consumption solely upon the individual who consumes the intoxicating beverage and basically grants tort immunity to alcohol vendors in most circumstances. Thus, Louisiana law is outcome determinative and probably easier to apply than the applicable Arkansas statute, which allows a plaintiff to recover upon showing proof that the alcohol vendor served alcohol to a clearly intoxicated person and that the intoxicated person caused Plaintiff's injuries.

Fourth, "advancement of the forum's governmental interests" examines how a forum state's policies and citizens will be affected by the application of a certain out-of-state law. *Id.* at 411, 201 S.W.3d at 923. In analyzing this factor, the Court examines the contacts to decide the state's interests. *Id.* Here, Arkansas's sole contact is that the accident occurred in Doddridge, Arkansas. Arkansas certainly has an interest in protecting its citizens and others using its roads from the negligent behavior of others. However, Harrah's is a business located in Louisiana, and Plaintiff is a Louisiana resident. The alleged negligent acts and omissions of Harrah's occurred in Louisiana. Arkansas has no interest in regulating Louisiana businesses by applying the ideals and principles of Arkansas dram shop laws to out-of-state business enterprises and injecting these principles into litigation between two Louisiana citizens.

The final factor, "application of a better rule of law," allows the court to determine which law makes "good socio-economic sense for the time when the court speaks" versus a state law that may be unfair and outdated. *Miller v. Pilgrim's Pride Corp.*, 366 F.3d 672, 675 (8th Cir. 2004); John J. Watkins, *A Guide To Choice of Law in Arkansas*, 2005 ARK. L. NOTES 160, 164. Here, it is difficult to determine which law is the better rule of law. The Court cannot say that Arkansas law is better simply because it provides a possible remedy for Plaintiff in this case when Louisiana law does not. Thus, the Court is hesitant to conclude that this fifth factor militates in favor of either Louisiana or Arkansas.

Reviewing the five choice factors as a whole, the Court concludes that Louisiana anti-dram shop law applies to this case. The Court is not persuaded by Plaintiff's argument that Arkansas dram shop law should apply to a Louisiana alcohol vendor and business. . . .

IV. CONCLUSION

For reasons discussed herein and above, the Court finds that Separate Defendant Harrah's Motion for Summary Judgment should be and hereby is **GRANTED**. An order of even date, consistent with this opinion, shall issue.

---

1.   Are you convinced by the "comparative impairment" theory? Why doesn't the application of the California dram shop rule go the very heart of Nevada's tourist industry? Apparently, Nevada does not want bartenders to be nannies telling customers how much to drink. The more they drink the more likely they are to spend money at the gambling tables. It may be terrible public policy, but if one asks whose ox is being gored more heavily (which state's interests are more impaired) isn't there a good case to be made for Nevada law? See Reppy, Eclecticism in Choice of Law: Hybrid Method or Mishmash, 34 Mercer L. Rev. 645 (1983).

2.   How would the California court decide the case if, instead of the accident taking place in California, the accident took place in Nevada and the California plaintiff had just crossed the border into Nevada?

3.   How would California treat the case if the defendant were a tavern ten miles from the border that did not advertise in California, almost all of whose customers were residents of Nevada (although, on occasion, Californians would also patronize the tavern)? See *Blamey v. Brown*, 270 N.W.2d 884 (Minn. 1978). Minnesota applied its law imposing liability to a Wisconsin vendor who sold liquor to a minor. Under Wisconsin law, the vendor was not liable in tort. The Wisconsin vendor was located 15 miles from the Minnesota border and neither advertised in Minnesota nor attempted to attract Minnesota residents to his establishment.

4.   Perhaps the result in Bernhard can be more easily defended by weighing the interests and finding that California cannot look away from such a powerful interest but that "comparative impairment" really favors the application of Nevada law.

5.   In Bourgeois the Arkansas federal court found in favor of Louisiana denying recovery to the plaintiff who was injured in Arkansas (a state that had a dram shop act). The Court applied Professor Leflar's five factor test. Do you think that the court would have decided the same way if it had adopted the "comparative impairment" theory?

6.   Note that in applying the "better law" test, the Louisiana court did not find that Louisiana had the better rule of law. See Borchers, The Choice-of-Law Revolution: An Empirical Study, 49 Wash. & Lee L. Rev. 357 (1992) (courts applying "better rule of law" approach do not necessarily favor local law). But, how does one decide what is the better rule of law? In cases involving issues such as host-guest statutes that may not be hard. Some rules of law are mere historical relics that have been abandoned by a large majority of states. See, *e.g.*, *Milkovich v. Saari*, 203 N.W.2d 408 (Minn. 1973). But in cases where there is a genuine current policy dispute as to a given issue, is a judge to decide a conflicts case based on her own preferences? Minnesota, a state that has adopted the Leflar factors has, in one case, refused to make a choice between

two viable rules based on what a judge might consider the better rule of law. See *Jepson v. General Casualty Co.*, 513 N.W.2d 467 (Minn. 1994); but see *Allstate Ins. Co. v. Hague*, 449 U.S. 302 (1981).

7.   In applying the Leflar factors, the Arkansas court determined that "simplification of the judicial task" favored the application of Louisiana law. The court reasoned that applying Arkansas law was more complicated because under Arkansas law it would be necessary to prove that the alcohol vendor served drinks to a clearly intoxicated person and that the intoxicated person caused plaintiff's injuries. Does it not strike you as odd that a reason for an Arkansas court not to apply Arkansas law is that Arkansas law is more demanding in proof than Louisiana law that lets the alcohol vendor off the hook entirely?

8.   Why didn't the Arkansas court find that the Arkansas dram shop act was the better rule of law?

9.   Did it make any difference that the plaintiff in Bourgeois was a Louisiana resident?

Back to *Bernhard*, is "comparative impairment" a convenient way to justify applying forum law whenever the state has a plausible interest? A recent case indicates that California does not automatically translate comparative impairment into "we win." In *McCann v. Forster Wheeler LLC*, 225 P.3d 516 (Cal. 2010), plaintiff was exposed to asbestos in 1957 in the state of Oklahoma. In 1965, he left Oklahoma and finally settled in California in 1975. In 2005, he was diagnosed with mesothelioma which he claimed was caused by his 1957 exposure to asbestos in Oklahoma. Now to the conflict: Oklahoma had a statute of repose that barred a California plaintiff from suing an out-of-state manufacturer (the asbestos laden boiler to which plaintiff was exposed was manufactured in New York). The action was not barred under California law. The California court held that Oklahoma had an interest in protecting both in-state and out-of-state manufacturers from long tail liability so as to attract them to do business in the state. The interest of California was not so greatly impaired since the defendant's tortious conduct occurred in another state and the plaintiff was a resident of Oklahoma at the time of exposure. But see *Kearney v. Salomon Smith Barney, Inc.*, 137 P.3d 914 (Cal. 2006) (California law prohibiting the recording of conversations without the consent of both parties was in conflict with Georgia's law allowing recording with the consent of one party. California clients of Smith Barney sought an injunction against Smith Barney's Georgia branch from recording conversations without their consent. California held that its interests were more significantly impaired and allowed the injunctive relief).

3.   MEDICAL MALPRACTICE

ELDER V. PERRY COUNTY HOSPITAL
2007 Ky. App. Unpub. LEXIS 253 (2007)

FACTS

. . . This case has a long and convoluted history. This Court issued a previous opinion in this matter that is relevant to the issue presently before us. We cite the following pertinent portion of that earlier opinion as factual background:

> In February 1999, the Elders took their six-year old son Johnathon to [Perry County Memorial] Hospital [referred to along with defendant Perry County Memorial Hospital Foundation as "PCMH"], because he had a fever and nausea.
>
> Although the Elders lived in Hancock County, Kentucky, and PCMH was in Tell City, Indiana, the Elders took Johnathon to PCMH because it was only about three miles from their home. According to the Elders, Dr. Uzoma Nwachukwu, the emergency room physician, failed [to properly] treat Johnathon, causing him to get sicker. Eventually, Johnathon was transported to a hospital in Evansville, Indiana. By then, a bacterial infection had progressed to such a point that the Evansville medical staff was unable to arrest it. Johnathon died. . . .
>
> In 2004, PCMH filed motions to dismiss based on lack of personal jurisdiction. . . .

[The court held that Perry County Hospital had sufficient contacts with Kentucky and could constitutionally assert jurisdiction over it.]

PCMH. . . . argues that Kentucky lacks subject matter jurisdiction in this case because it should be governed by Indiana's Medical Malpractice Act (MMA), which provides caps for damages in medical malpractice lawsuits. Thus, a choice-of-law argument is presented. Kentucky's courts are courts of general jurisdiction. As noted in *Mohler, supra*, torts need not have been committed in Kentucky in order to be litigated in Kentucky. Nonetheless, we shall carefully examine the choice-of-law issue premised upon Indiana's MMA.

PCMH invokes its right to rely upon the protection afforded by the MMA. However, Kentucky courts will apply Kentucky law "whenever it can be justified." *Rutherford v. Goodyear Tire and Rubber Co.*, 943 F.Supp. 789, 792 (W.D.Ky. 1996). In this case, application of Kentucky law can be justified because Kentucky courts do have jurisdiction over cases involving tortious acts committed outside the Commonwealth. See *Mohler, supra*. Moreover, the plaintiffs are residents of Kentucky, and "Kentucky's. . . .

laws . . . are designed primarily to protect its own citizens." *Rutherford* at 792.

Kentucky courts have historically applied Kentucky law if and when they have determined that application of the laws of a sister state would violate Kentucky public policy. In a highly similar case, a Federal Court of the Eastern District of Kentucky applied Kentucky law in a medical malpractice suit in which a Kentucky resident had been injured in a medical procedure performed in Ohio by an Ohio doctor. *Kennedy v. Ziesmann*, 522 F.Supp. 730 (E.D.Ky. 1981). The court found "the most significant factor" in choosing Kentucky law to be that "a Kentucky resident . . . would, if defendant's theory prevails, be subjected to the Ohio medical claim act, which provides for a procedure which is arguably contrary to Kentucky's public policy." *Id*. at 731. § 54 of the Constitution of Kentucky unequivocally provides: "The General Assembly shall have no power to limit the amount to be recovered for injuries resulting in death . . ." Accordingly, since Indiana's MMA directly contradicts Kentucky public policy, application of Kentucky law is appropriate in this case. . . .

[W]e vacate the orders of dismissal and remand this matter to Jefferson Circuit Court.

———————————

Kentucky and Michigan are two states that will apply their own law (*lex fori*) if their courts discern that they have an interest. They adopt Brainerd Currie's theory that when a state has an interest it is obligated to apply its own law. The leading case in Kentucky is *Foster v. Legget*, 484 S.W.2d 827 (Ky. Ct. App. 1972). In that case, the court said "When the court has jurisdiction of the parties its primary responsibility is to follow its own substantive law. The basic law is the law of the forum, which should not be replaced without valid reasons. For a comprehensive analysis of *Foster, see* Twerski, *To Where Does one Attach the Horses*, 61 Ky. L.J. 393 (1973). Also see, *Sexton v. Ryder Truck Rental, Inc.*, 320 N.W.2d 843 (Mich. 1982). For another case applying the law of the domicile of the plaintiff, even though the malpractice took place in another state, see *Rosenthal v. Warren*, 475 F.2d 438 (2nd Cir. 1973) [applying New York conflicts law]. The plaintiff, a New York resident, died in New England Baptist Hospital in Massachusetts after surgery. A malpractice action was brought in New York against the surgeon and the hospital. Under Massachusetts law wrongful death recovery was limited to $50,000. Under New York law there was no such limitation. The court noted that New England Baptist Hospital drew one-third of its patients from out-of-state and eight percent of its patients from New York. The court emphasized New York's strong interest in adequate compensation in wrongful death cases and applied New York law. After *Schultz v. Boy Scouts of America, Inc., supra*, it is unlikely that the New York Court of Appeals would apply New York law to a claim for malpractice that took place in Massachusetts. In *Barkanic v. General*

Admin. of Civil Aviation of the People's Republic of China, 923 F.2d 957, 963 (2nd Cir. 1991) the Second Circuit said that "*Schultz* suggests to us that *Rosenthal* is no longer an accurate interpretation of New York law." Also see, *Feldman v. Acapulco Princess Hotel*, 520 N.Y.S.2d 477, 483 (N.Y. Sup. Ct. 1987).

WARRINER V. STANTON
475 F.3d 497 (3rd Cir. 2007)

FISHER, CIRCUIT JUDGE.

This is an appeal from an order of the District Court for the District of New Jersey granting the defendant's motion for summary judgment in a diversity action. The sole issue presented on appeal is whether the District Court erred in its choice of law analysis. Applying New Jersey's "governmental interest" test, which requires a court to consider the nature and magnitude of each state's interest in having its law govern a particular issue, the District Court concluded Delaware had a stronger interest than New Jersey in seeing its tort statute of limitations applied to the medical malpractice claim in this case. Consequently, it dismissed the plaintiffs' claim as time-barred under the Delaware statute. For the reasons stated below, we will affirm the judgment of the District Court.

I.   Factual and Procedural History

Robert Troy Warriner, Jr., a New Jersey resident, was born in 1989 with a physical deformity called talipes equinovarus, more commonly known as "club foot." This condition was first diagnosed twelve days after Warriner's birth by physician Robert Stanton, a specialist in pediatric orthopedic surgery at the Alfred I. duPont Hospital for Children ("DuPont Children's Hospital") in Wilmington, Delaware. DuPont Children's Hospital is owned by The Nemours Foundation, Inc. ("Nemours"). Over the next several years, between 1989 and 1996, Warriner underwent multiple corrective surgeries performed by Dr. Stanton at DuPont Children's Hospital. Warriner's suit centers on a final surgery performed in December of 1996. That surgery involved a procedure called "bilateral tibia and fibula anterior closing wedge osteotomies," which Warriner's parents believed would allow Warriner to walk independently. The Warriners allege the surgery was "inappropriately designed" and resulted in an overcorrection that further hampered their son's ability to walk. In the aftermath, Warriner has undergone additional surgeries and physical therapy.

In January of 2003, Warriner, by guardians *ad litem*, filed a complaint for medical malpractice in New Jersey state court against Dr. Stanton and his employer, Nemours. Dr. Stanton was dismissed from the case by agreement of the parties. Nemours removed the case to federal court and filed a motion to dismiss on the basis that the case was barred by Delaware's tort statute of limitations. The parties entered into a stipulation of undisputed facts to aid the District Court in determining whether New Jersey's or Delaware's statute of limitations should apply. That stipulation established the following additional facts. In 1995, Dr. Stanton became licensed in New Jersey at the instruction of his employer Nemours in order to facilitate payments from the State of New Jersey for treatment rendered to New Jersey residents. Dr. Stanton continues to be licensed in New Jersey and, in order to maintain his license, he takes continuing education classes each year. Nemours continues to pay Dr. Stanton's annual renewal fees and he last renewed his license in 2003.

In addition, from September 1998 through May 2001, Dr. Stanton worked as a pediatric specialist with a widely publicized new health program opened by Nemours in southern New Jersey. Dr. Stanton was listed in a professional journal in 2001 as an orthopedic specialist available for appointments at the facility. Since 1995, Dr. Stanton has provided medical treatment to nearly two thousand New Jersey residents at the southern New Jersey facility, The Nemours Children's Clinic in Wilmington, and affiliated sites. Dr. Stanton received his medical malpractice insurance from The Nemours Foundation Self-Insurance Trust Fund to cover his medical malpractice liability. That coverage included medical malpractice claims in New Jersey as well as Delaware.

Analyzing the choice of law issue under New Jersey's governmental interest test, the District Court determined that Delaware law was applicable and that, as a result, Warriner's claims were time-barred under Delaware's tort statute of limitations. The District Court reasoned that New Jersey's primary interest in the case arose out of Warriner's New Jersey residence, and that that interest was greatly attenuated because New Jersey had no connection to the events and conduct giving rise to the lawsuit. By contrast, the District Court observed that all of the events and conduct giving rise to the litigation occurred in Delaware, and Delaware had a strong, clearly stated policy interest in protecting its health care providers through its statute of limitations. In addition, it rejected Warriner's argument that New Jersey's statute of limitations and its minor tolling provision should apply because Dr. Stanton retained a New Jersey medical license and was affiliated with a pediatric practice in New Jersey. It observed that Dr. Stanton was not licensed in New Jersey at the time the Warriners began seeing him in Delaware, and he did not see any patients in New Jersey until nearly two years after the alleged negligent surgery in this case. The District Court concluded that Delaware's strong governmental interest in seeing its law applied to torts alleged to have occurred within its borders, committed by physicians practicing within those borders, predominated and granted defendant's motion for summary judgment.

Warriner filed a timely appeal. . . .

III. Discussion

A. New Jersey's Governmental Interest Test

It is well established that in a diversity action, a district court must apply the choice of law rules of the forum state to determine what law will govern the substantive issues of a case. *Klaxon Co. v. Stentor Elec. Mfg. Co.*, 313 U.S. 487, 496, 61 S.Ct. 1020, 85 L.Ed. 1477 (1941). This diversity action was initiated in the United States District Court for the District of New Jersey, so the District Court properly turned to New Jersey's choice of law rules. . . .

Factors drawn from § 145 of the *Restatement (Second) of Conflict of Law* (1971) guide New Jersey courts in applying the governmental interest test in tort cases. *See Fu v. Fu*, 733 A.2d 1133, 1140–41 (1999). (Parallel citations omitted). Those factors are grouped as follows: "(1) the interests of interstate comity; (2) the interests of the parties; (3) the interests underlying the field of tort law; (4) the interests of judicial administration; and (5) the competing interests of the states." *Id.* The most important of those factors in the context of a tort claim is the competing interests of the states. *Id.* at 1141. As discussed by the New Jersey Supreme Court in *Fu*, the initial focus "should be on what policies the legislature or court intended to protect by having that law apply to wholly domestic concerns, and then, whether these concerns will be furthered by applying that law to the multi-state situation." *Id.* . . .

The governmental interest inquiry proceeds in two steps. The first step involves determining whether an actual conflict of law exists between the states involved, *Veazey*, because "where the application of either state's law would yield the same result, no conflict exists to be resolved." *High v. Balun*, 943 F.2d 323, 325 (3d Cir. 1991). In this case, the parties do not dispute that an actual conflict of law exists. The District Court was faced with the election of a statute of limitations from two possible options- Delaware's statute of limitations, under which plaintiff's claim was time-barred, or New Jersey's statute of limitations, under which the claim was not time-barred because of a tolling provision that preserves a minor plaintiff's claim until the minor reaches the age of eighteen. Since there is no question in this case that an actual conflict exists, we devote our analysis to the second element of the governmental interest inquiry which requires that we "identify the governmental policies underlying the law of each state and how those policies are affected by each state's contacts to the litigation and to the parties." *Veazey*, 510 A.2d at 1189.

B. Policy Interests Underlying Each State's Statute of Limitation

Looking at the policies that underlie the respective state statutes of limitation that are in conflict in this case, we find that the District Court correctly identified the relevant policy concerns of both New Jersey and

Delaware. With respect to the New Jersey statute, we have consistently "identified New Jersey's policies in a tort context as consisting primarily of compensation and deterrence." *Schum v. Bailey*, 578 F.2d 493, 496 (3d Cir.1978). In addition, the New Jersey statute of limitations, N.J. Stat. § 2A:14–2, including as it does a minor tolling provision, evinces a desire on the part of New Jersey to protect "minors who are presumably not well-versed in legal matters from the adverse consequences of their inexperience." *LaFage v. Jani.*

We can assume Delaware's statute of limitations, Del.Code Ann. tit. 18, § 6856, shares New Jersey's interest in compensation and deterrence, "[b]ecause every tort rule, to some extent, is designed both to deter and to compensate." *Fu*, 733 A.2d at 1141. However, Delaware's statute was enacted by the Delaware legislature with an additional policy concern in mind, namely concern over a perceived crisis in health care associated with medical malpractice claims. The Delaware Medical Malpractice Act was enacted in 1976 "due to the concern over the law at that time and the rising costs of malpractice liability insurance," and specifically addressed the applicable statute of limitations for medical malpractice claims. *Meekins v. Barnes*, 745 A.2d 893, 895–96 (Del. 2000). The statute of limitations was designed to provide "an atmosphere in which the number of suits and claims of malpractice, as well as the size of judgments and settlements, would be reduced thereby reducing the cost and/or maintaining the availability of medical malpractice insurance for health care providers." *Miller v. Spicer*, 822 F.Supp. 158, 172 (D. Del. 1993). . . .

C.   Relevant Contacts and their Relationship to the Policy Interests of Each State. . . .

In evaluating the contacts in a choice of law context, the New Jersey Supreme Court has adopted the approach taken by the *Restatement (Second) of Conflict of Laws ("Restatement")* (1971). *Fu*, 733 A.2d at 1152 ("Thus, New Jersey now adheres to the method of analysis set forth in *Restatement*. . . ."). § 145(2) of the Restatement sets forth a list of contacts that are the most pertinent to the governmental-interest test: these are (1) the place where the injury occurred; (2) the place where the conduct causing the injury occurred, (3) the domicile, residence, nationality, place of incorporation, and place of business of the parties; and (4) the place where the relationship, if any between the parties is centered. In this case, those contacts as stipulated by the parties are as follows:

1.   Warriner's alleged injury occurred in Delaware.

2.   Dr. Stanton's alleged tortious conduct occurred in Delaware.

3.   Warriner is domiciled in New Jersey; The Nemours foundation is incorporated in Florida with its principal place of business in Wilmington, Delaware.

4.   Warriner's ten-year patient-doctor relationship with Dr.
     Stanton was based at DuPont Children's Hospital in
     Wilmington, Delaware. Dr. Stanton never treated Robert in
     New Jersey.

Apart from those contacts listed in § 145(2), two additional contacts
exist between the parties and the respective states:

5.   Dr. Stanton became licensed in New Jersey in 1995 in order
     to facilitate collection of payments from New Jersey, one year
     prior to the alleged malpractice. He did not see patients in
     New Jersey until two years after the alleged malpractice.

6.   In 1997, the year following the accident, The Nemours
     Foundation entered into a pediatric partnership with
     AtlanticCare in Southern New Jersey. Dr. Stanton was a
     pediatric specialist employed at the partnership from
     September 1998 through May 2001. He was listed in a
     professional staff directory as an orthopedic specialist
     available for appointments in New Jersey.

Examining these respective contacts, we find the District Court did not
err in concluding Delaware law applied. It correctly placed special
emphasis in this case on the fact that all of the contact between Warriner
and Dr. Stanton occurred in Delaware. In personal injury cases, the New
Jersey Supreme Court has counseled that "the place where the injury
occurred is a contact that, as to most issues, plays an important role in the
selection of the state of the applicable law." *Fu*, 733 A.2d at 1142 (quoting
Restatement, § 145 cmt. e). Furthermore, it has explained that "[w]hen both
conduct and injury occur in a single jurisdiction, with only 'rare exceptions,
the local law of the state where conduct and injury occurred will be applied'
to determine an actor's liability." Id. (quoting *Restatement*, § 145 cmt. d).
This general rule is followed because "a state has an obvious interest in
regulating the conduct of persons within its territory and in providing
redress for injuries that occurred there." *Id*. In this case, both the allegedly
tortious conduct and injury occurred in Delaware. In fact, Warriner's entire
treatment history-beginning a mere twelve days after his birth and
extending over nearly a decade-was based in Delaware and undertaken by
a Delaware doctor. Each of these contacts is relevant to Delaware's stated
public policy of providing a finite period of time for medical malpractice
claims to require plaintiffs to file timely claims, particularly when those
injuries occur within the State of Delaware. Most importantly, considering
the interests of interstate comity, it is apparent that the application of New
Jersey's statute of limitations in this case would directly contravene
Delaware's clearly articulated interest in shielding its health care
providers from liability for a claim that, under its own considered
judgment, expressed through its statute of limitations, is unquestionably
stale. *See Erny*, 792 A.2d at 1217 ("When considering the interests of

interstate comity, a court must determine whether application of a competing state's law would frustrate the policies of other interested states.") (quoting *Fu*, 733 A.2d at 1141).

Furthermore, the fact that all the contacts occurring in this case were in Delaware takes on even greater significance considering that they were not fortuitous but rather intentionally initiated by the Warriners themselves. *Id.* ("The place of injury becomes less important where it is simply fortuitous."). Warriner elected to travel to Delaware from 1989 until 1998 for specialized medical treatment and, even after his final surgery with Dr. Stanton in 1996 and the establishment of a Nemours-related facility in New Jersey in 1997, continued to receive medical treatment in Delaware. In the context of a doctor-patient lawsuit, we have observed that "it is only fair that the law of the state to which the patient has voluntarily traveled, and in which the doctor has chosen to [practice], be applied to adjudicate the respective rights, duties, and obligations between the parties." *Blakesley v. Wolford*, 789 F.2d 236, 243 (3d Cir. 1986). In addition, although Warriner was a resident of New Jersey at the time of the alleged malpractice, "citizens do not . . . carry their home state's laws with them wherever they go." *Amoroso v. Burdette Tomlin Memorial Hosp.*, 901 F.Supp. 900, 906 (D.N.J. 1995). Indeed, it is hornbook law that "by entering the state . . . the visitor has exposed himself to the risks of the territory and should not expect to subject persons living there to a financial hazard that their law had not created." *Id.* (quoting D.F. Cavers, *The Choice of Law Process* 146–47 (1965)). . . .

For the reasons stated, we will affirm the judgment of the District Court.

[Dissenting opinion omitted]

---

1.   How do you think the court that decided *Warriner* would have decided the Elder case?

2.   Putting aside the two states that apply lex fori when they find that their state has an interest, it would seem logical that in malpractice cases courts would, as *Warriner* did, apply the law of the state where the malpractice took place. However, in *Kaiser-Georgetown Community Health Plan, Inc. v. Stutsman*, 491 A.2d 502 (D.C. 1985), the court applied the law of the District of Columbia that did not cap damages for malpractice rather than the law of Virginia that capped malpractice damages at $1 million. The plaintiff was a resident of Virginia and the malpractice took place in Virginia. However, the plaintiff was employed as a nurse in the District of Columbia and she subscribed to the Kaiser Health Plan that had health care facilities both in D.C. and Virginia. In a later case, *Groover Christie & Merritt P.C. v. Burke*, 917 A.2d 1110 (D.C. 2007), the court applied the law of Maryland that capped non-economic damages rather than the law of D.C. that did not cap damages.

In the latter case the plaintiff was a resident of Maryland, and the greater part of the malpractice took place in Maryland. Though a faulty medical report had been sent from Maryland to D.C. the court found that the connection with D.C. was relatively insignificant and that Maryland had the greater interest.

Office Talk

#5

Aaron: Let me ask you something Neil. Are caps on damages conduct-regulating or loss allocating?

Neil: I assume that caps are not conduct-regulating. I can hardly imagine a doctor treating a patient with less care because there is a cap of $50,000.00 rather than unlimited liability. But why are you asking that question?

Aaron: Well, I am just trying to understand what conduct-regulating means. When a state enacts a cap, it seeks to protect doctors and hospital from unlimited liability. With the cap in place, it may encourage doctors to come to the state and practice without fear that malpractice insurance coverage will go through the ceiling. Perhaps the cap also discourages doctors from practicing defensive medicine and ordering CAT scans when a simple x-ray will do.

Neil: Aaron, aren't you just making up those interests? Caps are there to protect domestic doctors from paying high premiums and to lower costs of medical care within the state. If the payment is going to come from an out-of-state insurer as it did in the *Stutsman* case (cited in the note after the *Warriner* case), then maybe the cap should not be honored. The *Stutsman* court emphasized that the HMO that covered the plaintiff was a D.C. corporation that provided services in both D.C. and Virginia. D.C. had an interest in making sure that its medical insurers fairly compensated plaintiffs. Also, the court said that the District of Columbia may wish to compensate members of its work force.

Aaron: So you are telling me that a corporation located in a state that insures doctors who practice in another state where the plaintiff is domiciled and where the malpractice occurred are to be treated differently than Virginia insurers? That seems to me to discriminatory.

Neil: I am beginning to distrust this process of making up interests to suit one's feelings on a case by case basis. It is like "what did you have for breakfast?"

Aaron: Gee, Neil that makes me feel good. Maybe I am not alone in the world.

---

4. PRODUCTS LIABILITY

With the abolition of privity and the adoption of strict tort liability in the 1960's, courts experienced a flood of litigation in cases alleging that a defective product caused injury. In the 1980's and 1990's legislatures and courts reacted to the plaintiff-oriented developments by enacting what has come to be known as "tort reform" proposals. Among the reforms were statutes of repose, limiting the liability of non-manufacturers to negligence, caps on damages for non-economic loss (pain and suffering), limitation on or abolition of punitive damages, and adherence to FDA approved warnings as a total bar to recovery in pharmaceutical failure-to-warn cases.

It takes no great imagination to see that product liability cases would provide a hot bed for difficult choice of law problems. A product could be designed in one state, manufactured in another, sold in a third state and cause injury or be imbided in a fourth state and manifest injury in a fifth state. With the advent of interest analysis many states could lay claim to having their law apply. One would have thought with a loosey-goosey system of choice of law that courts would use the occasion to routinely find for the law that favors the plaintiffs. However, Hay, Borchers and Symeonides in their superb treatise, Conflict of Laws § 17.65 (5th ed. 2010) inform us that their research documents that "slightly more than half the cases decided between 1990 and 2003 applied the law that favored the defendant." They further conclude that since the abandonment of *lex loci* the courts have yet to find a substitute set of rules or even an ideological theory to govern products liability conflict cases.

Keeping with the goal of this book to provide students with a taste of choice of law, the cases that follow do just that. It would be impossible to provide a comprehensive treatment on the subject. For those who wish to delve more deeply into this subject we refer you the aforementioned treatise that discusses the great variety of cases at length.

SINGH V. EDWARDS LIFESCIENCES CORP.

210 P.3d 337 (Wash. Ct. App. 2009)

GROSSE, J. . . .

[In this case, Singh, a Washington resident was seriously injured in October 2004 during heart bypass surgery when a heart monitor manufactured by Edwards Lifesciences, a California corporation, malfunctioned caused a catheter to heat up, destroying his heart. The surgery took place at the Providence Everett Medical Center in Washington.]

After the surgery, doctors were unable to restart Singh's burned heart and he was kept alive with a mechanical heart device for 11 weeks. He then received a heart transplant at the University of Washington Medical Center. The drugs taken to prevent rejection of his transplanted heart caused Singh to develop blood cancer. Currently that cancer is in remission but he is expected to continue to have severe medical problems associated with both the cancer and his heart transplant.

Singh filed a products liability claim against Edwards. Providence filed cross-claims against the manufacturer for fraud, violation of the Consumer Protection Act (CPA), and breach of contract. Both parties sought punitive damages under California law. Edwards admitted its liability for compensatory damages to the plaintiff, but contended that Providence shared in that liability.

The evidence presented at trial revealed that Edwards knew there was a flaw in the heart monitor device as early as 1998. The monitor contained rogue software (Layout 6) that could defeat the fail-safe triggers meant to ensure the catheter would not overheat. The Layout 6 software had originally been installed in an earlier model of the heart monitor. The software was subsequently abandoned but never removed. A July 17, 1998 memorandum from Edwards' principal software designer, Glenn Cox, noted the discovery of the bug in the software. At that time, the monitor's crash was associated with a faulty continuous cardiac output cable attached to a monitor with a bug in the software. The solution proposed and eventually undertaken in 2006 was to remove the Layout 6 software. A release of heart monitors in 2000 did not have the software removed. . . .

In June 2006, Edwards recalled the monitor after an extensive investigation by the United States Food and Drug Administration (FDA). Edwards admitted the monitor malfunctioned during Singh's operation. In August 2007, Edwards admitted that Layout 6 was a proximate cause of injury to Singh. . . .

The jury returned a verdict in favor of the Singh family for $31,750,000 and awarded punitive damages under California law. . . . The jury also found that Edwards' conduct was malicious and, under California law, awarded punitive damages in the amount of $8,350,000 to Singh. . . .

ANALYSIS

Choice of Law

In resolving conflict of law tort questions, Washington has abandoned the lex loci delicti rule and follows the *Restatement (Second) of Conflict of Laws'* most significant relationship test. Where a conflict exists, Washington courts decide which law applies by determining which jurisdiction has the most significant relationship to a given issue. The court must evaluate the contacts both quantitatively and qualitatively, based upon the location of the most significant contacts as they relate to the particular issue at hand. The contacts to be evaluated for their relative importance to the issue were set forth in *Johnson v. Spider Staging Corp.*:

(a) the place where the injury occurred,

(b) the place where the conduct causing the injury occurred,

(c) the domicile, residence, nationality, place of incorporation and place of business of the parties, and

(d) the place where the relationship, if any, between the parties is centered.

In *Johnson,* scaffolding designed and manufactured in Washington collapsed in Kansas, causing the death of a Kansas resident. The conflict of law issue was whether Washington's law, which allowed unlimited recovery in wrongful death actions, or Kansas law which imposed a $50,000 ceiling, should apply. In holding that Washington law applied, the *Johnson* court enunciated a two-step analysis to be employed to determine the appropriate choice of law. The court must first evaluate the contacts with each potentially interested state and then if balanced, evaluate the public policies and governmental interests of the concerned states. The court in *Johnson* concluded without further comment that the contacts were evenly balanced. The *Johnson* court also considered the parties' justified expectations. The Washington corporation sold its products in all 50 states, only a few of which had wrongful death limitations. Thus, the manufacturer could not have justifiably relied on the Kansas limitation. Conflict of law analysis in Washington is thus a hybrid of the *Restatement (Second) of Conflict of Laws* and a governmental interest analysis.

Washington courts have held that these same choice of law principles apply to the issue of punitive damages. In *Kammerer v. Western Gear Corp.,* the court permitted a Washington jury to award punitive damages against a Washington corporation, applying California law to a claim based on fraudulent representation. In so holding, the court noted:

California has an interest in deterring fraudulent activities by corporations having a substantial business presence within its borders. Washington has no interest in protecting persons who commit fraud. Western Gear asserts that differences in

Washington and California law governing fraud suggest that Washington has a policy of greater caution in allowing judgments for fraud. Because we do not find any difference, material to this case, in the laws of the two states, we do not find any interest served by application of Washington law. Because Washington has no interests superior to or inconsistent with the interests of California in this controversy, application of the Restatement rule dictates that California law govern the Kammerers' claim for fraud.

The significant factor in *Kammerer* was the jurisdiction in which the bad behavior—fraudulent misrepresentation—occurred.

In *Barr v. Interbay Citizens Bank. . .,* a companion case issued on the same day as *Kammerer,* the Supreme Court rejected the application of Florida's punitive damages because the conduct that warranted the punitive damages occurred in Nevada and Washington. The Florida lender hired agents in Nevada to travel to Washington to repossess George Barr's automobile. Barr sued for conversion, seeking punitive damages under Florida law. The Supreme Court recognized Florida's legitimate interest in imposing punitive damages, but rejected Florida as the state with the most significant relationship:

> The interest in Florida in providing an example for deterrence would not be furthered when the actual conduct and the acts which might warrant punitive damages were restricted to Nevada and Washington.

In *Barr,* the crux of the complaint was not the decision to repossess the car (purchased in Florida) but rather the method used to repossess that car. . . .

Here, Edwards argues that the methodology employed by the trial court to determine that California law applied was incorrect because the sheer number of contacts with Washington warranted application of its law. But if the particular conduct is viewed as it is in *Kammerer, Barr,* . . . the conduct which resulted in the injury occurred in California. Edwards' corporate headquarters are located in California and the defect in the software was discovered in California as early as 1998. And by 2002, the foreseeable heating of the catheter in a surgical setting was known by Edwards and again the decision was made in California not to recall or warn users. . . .

In analyzing which state has the greater governmental policy interest, Edwards contends that it is Washington with its policy that rejects the award of punitive damages unless provided for by statute. Edwards argues that Washington's interest is in permitting full compensation for injured parties and none in permitting a *windfall* for plaintiffs. But, as already noted, Washington courts have allowed punitive damages in other cases.

In *Kammerer,* in particular, the court explicitly stated that Washington has no interest in protecting companies who commit fraud. The conduct that serves as the basis of the punitive damage award here occurred in California and that state has an interest in deterring its corporations from engaging in such fraudulent conduct. . . .

We affirm the trial court.

———————

Is the court correct in saying that Washington has no interest in applying its "no punitive damage" rule? Admittedly, Washington has no defendant to protect, but a decision not to allow punitive damages could be said to have two goals: (1) not providing a windfall to plaintiffs who receive compensatory damages and (2) encouraging defendants to sell products in the state without fear that damages will skyrocket. In the following cases, *Rowe* and *Townsend,* these considerations were of great importance. We do not mean to imply that *Singh* was wrongly decided, but note only that the argument for no punitive damages has legs.

———————

ROWE V. HOFFMAN-LA ROCHE, INC.
917 A.2d 767 (N.J. 2007)

JUDGE LEFELT (temporarily assigned) delivered the opinion of the Court.

Plaintiff Robert Rowe, a Michigan resident, filed a complaint in Essex County against two New Jersey pharmaceutical manufacturers, defendants Hoffmann-La Roche, Inc. and Roche Laboratories, Inc. Rowe alleged that the manufacturers failed to warn adequately about the health risks associated with Accutane, a drug manufactured by defendants and approved in 1982 by the United States Food and Drug Administration (FDA) to treat recalcitrant nodular acne. Under Michigan law, the FDA approval results in a conclusive determination that the health risk warnings issued by defendants regarding the drug were adequate. *Mich. Comp. Laws* § 600.2946(5) (2006). New Jersey law, however, considers the FDA approval to have created only a rebuttable presumption of adequacy. *N.J.S.A.* 2A:58C–4. Thus, plaintiff's suit is viable in New Jersey but precluded in Michigan. After comparing Michigan's and this State's governmental interests in resolving the adequacy-to-warn issue, we conclude that Michigan's interest is paramount and its conclusive presumption applies. . . .

I.

The facts and procedural history pertaining to this dispute are relatively uncomplicated. Hoffmann-La Roche is a New Jersey corporation, and while the record does not reveal Roche Laboratories' state of incorporation, both companies have their principal place of business in Nutley, New Jersey. Hoffman-La Roche manufactures, labels, and packages Accutane in Nutley, and Roche Laboratories markets, sells, and distributes the drug also from Nutley. While some production and marketing efforts occurred outside New Jersey, almost all of the manufacturing and sales activities by the two companies (hereinafter Hoffmann), including Accutane-related communications with the FDA, took place in or emanated from New Jersey.

Robert Rowe has lived in Michigan all of his life. When Rowe was sixteen years old, in February 1997, a Michigan physician prescribed Accutane to treat his recalcitrant acne. A Michigan pharmacist filled Rowe's prescription, and he used the medicine in Michigan for about three months until May 1997. Approximately three months after he discontinued his use of Accutane, in August 1997, Rowe became depressed and contemplated suicide. In September 1997, Rowe was arrested after crashing a car into a house during an apparent suicide attempt. Thereafter, Rowe sought psychiatric treatment in Michigan and Ohio.

In March 2001, Rowe brought suit against Hoffmann in Essex County, New Jersey. He alleged that Accutane caused him to become severely depressed and suicidal and that Hoffmann failed to warn him adequately about these risks. He also claimed Hoffmann did not adequately test Accutane, and that Hoffmann was aware of the drug's potential adverse psychological effects but failed to advise the FDA of those effects.

After denying Rowe's allegations, Hoffmann moved for summary judgment, seeking dismissal of the lawsuit, contending that Michigan law governed. The trial court . . . concluded that between New Jersey and Michigan, Michigan had the strongest governmental interest in applying its statute to the failure-to-warn issue, and dismissed Rowe's complaint. A divided panel of the Appellate Division reversed. *Rowe, supra*, 383 N.J.Super. at 442, 892 A.2d 694.

The Appellate Division majority disagreed with the trial court and held that New Jersey had the strongest interest in applying its law to Rowe's failure-to-warn claim. *Id.* at 466, 892 A.2d 694. The majority recognized that "the cited conduct of [Hoffmann] with respect to the Accutane warning occurred largely in New Jersey." *Id.* at 456, 892 A.2d 694. Relying on this Court's opinion in *Gantes v. Kason Corp.*, 145 N.J. 478, 679 A.2d 106 (1996), the majority recognized and weighed our strong interest in deterring the manufacture of unsafe products within its borders. *Rowe, supra*, 383 N.J.Super. at 458–59, 892 A.2d 694. . . .

II.

Although the Association of Trial Lawyers of America-New Jersey (ATLA) supports the Appellate Division majority's opinion, all of the other amici curiae, Product Liability Advisory Council, Inc., Healthcare Institute of New Jersey, New Jersey Defense Association, and the Pharmaceutical Research and Manufacturers of America, contend the majority erred by applying New Jersey law to this dispute. ATLA and the Healthcare Institute also take conflicting positions regarding the decision's impact on New Jersey's economy. The Product Liability Advisory Council and the New Jersey Defense Association request that this Court take judicial notice of their contention that since 1996, over ninety percent of mass-tort claims against New Jersey pharmaceutical companies in New Jersey courts have been brought by non-New Jersey residents. The Advisory Council and the Defense Association conclude by arguing that "New Jersey's strong interest in discouraging . . . forum shopping and the associated expense that many thousands of out-of-state residents place on this state's courts and its taxpayers should therefore be accorded great weight." . . .

In applying the governmental-interests analysis, two steps are involved. "The first step in the analysis is to determine whether a conflict exists between the laws of the interested states. Any such conflict is to be determined on an issue-by-issue basis." *Veazey v. Doremus*, 103 N.J. 244, 248, 510 A.2d 1187 (1986). If there is no actual conflict, then the choice-of-law question is inconsequential, and the forum state applies its own law to resolve the disputed issue.

If there is an actual conflict, the second step "seeks to determine the interest that each state has in resolving the specific issue in dispute." *Gantes, supra*, 145 N.J. at 485, 679 A.2d 106. The Court must "identify the governmental policies underlying the law of each state" and determine whether "those policies are affected by each state's contacts to the litigation and to the parties." *Veazey, supra*, 103 N.J. at 248, 510 A.2d 1187. We must apply the law of "the state with the greatest interest in governing the particular issue." *Ibid.*

All parties agree that this case presents an actual conflict. Michigan provides:

> In a product liability action against a manufacturer or seller, a product that is a drug is not defective or unreasonably dangerous, and the manufacturer or seller is not liable, if the drug was approved for safety and efficacy by the [FDA], and the drug and its labeling were in compliance with the [FDA]'s approval at the time the drug left the control of the manufacturer or seller.

[*Mich. Comp. Laws* § 600.2946(5).]

In contrast, New Jersey's law provides:

> In any product liability action the manufacturer or seller shall not be liable for harm caused by a failure to warn if the product contains an adequate warning or instruction or, in the case of dangers a manufacturer or seller discovers or reasonably should

discover after the product leaves its control, if the manufacturer or seller provides an adequate warning or instruction. . . .

If the warning or instruction given in connection with a drug or device or food or food additive has been approved or prescribed by the [FDA], a rebuttable presumption shall arise that the warning or instruction is adequate.

[*N.J.S.A.* 2A:58C–4.]

The Michigan statute thus creates a conclusive presumption that the drug is not defective if the drug and its labeling were approved by the FDA, while New Jersey's statute creates a rebuttable presumption that a drug warning is adequate if it was approved by the FDA. *Compare Zammit v. Shire US, Inc.*, 415 F.Supp.2d 760, 764–65 (E.D.Mich.2006) (holding that defendant drug manufacturer was not liable to plaintiff for failure to warn under § 600.2946(5) because drug was approved by the FDA), *with Feldman v. Lederle Labs.*, 125 N.J. 117, 156–57, 592 A.2d 1176 (1991) (recognizing that presumption is only rebuttable, and not conclusive).

Because an actual conflict exists between New Jersey and Michigan on the very issue in dispute—Rowe's failure-to-warn claim against Hoffmann—we must advance to the next step of the governmental interest analysis. That requires that we identify the policies underlying the New Jersey and Michigan statutes and determine whether those policies are affected by the "state[s'] contacts to the litigation and the parties."

IV.

It is in the weighing of each state's interests in deciding the adequacy-of-warning issue that we part company with the Appellate Division majority. In our view, the majority of the panel overvalued New Jersey's interest and undervalued Michigan's.

The New Jersey statute at issue, *N.J.S.A.* 2A:58C–4, was enacted in 1987 as part of the New Jersey Products Liability Act (NJPLA), *N.J.S.A.* 2A:58C–1 to –7, in order to re-balance the law "in favor of manufacturers." William A. Dreier, et al., *N.J. Prods. Liab. & Toxic Torts Law* at 15:4 (2007). "The Legislature intended for the Act to limit the liability of manufacturers so as to 'balance[ ] the interests of the public and the individual with a view towards economic reality.'" *Zaza v. Marquess & Nell, Inc.*, 144 N.J. 34, 47–48, 675 A.2d 620 (1996) (quoting *Shackil v. Lederle Labs.*, 116 N.J. 155, 188, 561 A.2d 511 (1989)). Furthermore, at least in part, the NJPLA was intended "to establish clear rules with respect to specific matters as to which the decisions of the courts in New Jersey have created uncertainty." Senate Judiciary Committee, *Statement to Senate Committee Substitute for S.B.* No. 2805, at 1 (Mar. 23, 1987).

The legislative history of the NJPLA does not specifically address why the Legislature created only a rebuttable presumption of adequacy for FDA approval of prescription drug warnings. Rowe argues, however, that New Jersey has an interest in applying its rebuttable presumption of adequacy here because Hoffmann is a New Jersey company that has manufactured Accutane in New Jersey. Rowe contends his argument is supported by this Court's decision in *Gantes, supra*, 145 N.J. 478, 679 A.2d 106, a contention we now address.

In *Gantes*, the representative of a deceased Georgia resident filed a products liability action against a New Jersey manufacturer in New Jersey. 145 N.J. at 483–84, 679 A.2d 106. The plaintiff alleged that the decedent was killed when a shaker machine, manufactured by the defendant, struck the decedent in the head at the decedent's place of employment in Georgia. *Id.* at 482, 679 A.2d 106. The defendant had manufactured the shaker machine in New Jersey thirteen years before the accident. *Id.* at 481, 679 A.2d 106. Under Georgia law, the plaintiff's lawsuit was barred because Georgia had a statute of repose that prohibited products liability actions being brought more than ten years after the original sale of the product. *Id.* at 485, 679 A.2d 106. New Jersey law, however, contained no statute of repose. Under New Jersey law, the plaintiff was permitted to proceed with the lawsuit because the plaintiff filed suit within New Jersey's two-year statute of limitation. *Ibid.* The issue before the Court was whether the Georgia statute of repose or the New Jersey statute of limitation applied to the products liability action.

This Court held that New Jersey's statute of limitation, not Georgia's statute of repose applied, *id.* at 497–98, 679 A.2d 106, reasoning that New Jersey "has a strong interest in encouraging the manufacture and distribution of safe products . . . [and] deterring the manufacture and distribution of unsafe products." *Id.* at 490, 679 A.2d 106. In *Gantes*, although plaintiff was not a New Jersey resident and the injury did not occur in New Jersey, our strong interest in deterring the manufacture of unsafe products in this State was directly furthered because plaintiff's suit was timely and not otherwise barred. Georgia's interest was not frustrated by the application of our statute of limitations because its statute-of-repose was designed to stabilize Georgia's insurance industry and to keep stale claims out of its courts. *Id.* at 493, 679 A.2d 106.

New Jersey's interest in allowing Rowe's suit to proceed is not as strong as our interest was in *Gantes*. Rowe argues that unlike Michigan's conclusive presumption, our law provides only a rebuttable presumption of adequacy. However, the law does create a presumption of adequacy rather than simply recognizing FDA approval as one factor to be considered in determining the adequacy of the warnings. *See Rowe*, 383 N.J. Super. at 465 n. 8, 892 A.2d 694 (noting that at least nine states either establish a rebuttable presumption of adequacy "or simply allow FDA-approval as a factor to be considered in determining the adequacy of such warning").

The NJPLA impliedly accepts that the presumption of adequacy will not be rebutted in all cases. It accepts FDA regulation as sufficient, at least in part, to deter New Jersey pharmaceutical companies from manufacturing unsafe prescription drugs. The FDA requires that the labeling accompanying a prescription drug "describe serious adverse reactions and potential safety hazards" and that the labeling "be revised to include a warning as soon as there is reasonable evidence of an association of a serious hazard with a drug." 21 *C.F.R.* § 201.00(e). If any labeling "is false or misleading in any particular and was not corrected within a reasonable time," among other enforcement options, the FDA may withdraw approval for the drug. 21 *U.S.C.A.* § 355(e). As this Court has stated, "absent deliberate concealment or nondisclosure of after-acquired knowledge of harmful effects, compliance with FDA standards should be virtually dispositive" of a failure-to-warn claim. *Perez v. Wyeth Labs., Inc.*, 161 N.J. 1, 25, 734 A.2d 1245 (1999).

The Legislature also provides in the NJPLA that FDA approval of prescription drugs conclusively prohibits an award of punitive damages in products liability actions. *See N.J.S.A.* 2A:58C–5. This provision, along with the rebuttable-presumption contained in *N.J.S.A.* 2A:58C–4, cede to FDA regulation some of this State's interest in policing local pharmaceutical manufacturers, thereby reducing New Jersey's interest in applying its law to this case.

The predominant object of the law is not to encourage tort recoveries by plaintiffs, whether New Jersey citizens or not, in order to deter this State's drug manufacturers. On the contrary, the law limits the liability of manufacturers of FDA-approved products by reducing the burden placed on them by product liability litigation. The Legislature carefully balanced the need to protect individuals against the need to protect an industry with a significant relationship to our economy and public health. New Jersey's interest in applying its law to Rowe's failure-to-warn issue, when properly discerned, is not antithetical to Michigan's interest but substantially congruent.

The relevant Michigan statute, *Mich. Comp. Laws* § 600.2946(5), was enacted by the Michigan Legislature in 1996 as part of a comprehensive reform of Michigan's tort law. *Senate Fiscal Agency Bill Analysis to S.B. 344 & H.B. 4508*, at 1 (Jan. 11, 1996). The Michigan Legislature's express purpose was to immunize pharmaceutical companies that market FDA-approved prescription drugs from liability in a products liability suit. *See Mich. Comp. Laws* § 600.2946(5).

Hoffmann additionally argues that Michigan's interest in enacting this law was to make prescription drugs more available to Michigan residents. The Appellate Division majority found this interest to be unsupported by the record. *Rowe, supra,* 383 N.J. Super. at 461, 892 A.2d 694. Contrary to that finding, however, Michigan's interest in making prescription drugs more available to its residents is supported by the legislative history of the law. Commenting on § 600.2946(5), its proponents stated that "[d]rug companies spend large sums of money and expend enormous energy getting approval for their products. Many valuable products never reach the market or are withdrawn because of successful lawsuits (or the threat of future lawsuits) even though there is no medical evidence that they are harmful." *House Legislative Analysis Section to S.B. 344*, at 9 (June 8, 1995). Supporters in the Michigan State Senate recognized that "[c]onsumers . . . suffer when they are denied new products that would increase public safety or improve their quality of life. . . . [P]roduct liability litigation . . . has added substantially to the cost and unavailability of many goods and services." *Senate Fiscal Agency Bill Analysis to S.B. 344 & H.B. 4508*, at 10 (Jan. 1, 1996). . . .

Michigan "was concerned that unlimited liability for drug manufacturers would threaten the financial viability of many enterprises and could add substantially to the cost and unavailability of many drugs." This concern is echoed by others. For example, speaking of vaccines, several commentators have noted that "the prospect of multi-million dollar verdicts instead [of encouraging safer vaccines] induced manufacturers to abandon the vaccine market altogether." W. Kip Viscusi, et al. *The Effect of Products Liability Litigation on Innovation: Deterring Inefficient Pharmaceutical Litigation: An Economic Rationale for the FDA Regulatory Compliance Defense*, 24 Seton Hall L. Rev. 1437, 1470 (1994); *see also Shackil v. Lederle Labs.*, 116 N.J. 155, 181, 561 A.2d 511 (1989) ("The overriding public policy of encouraging the development of necessary drugs is not unfamiliar to products-liability law.").

V.

This case presents a true conflict of laws because both New Jersey and Michigan have interests that would be furthered by applying their respective statutes to Rowe's failure-to-warn claim against Hoffmann. After properly discerning and weighing the respective policies of New Jersey and Michigan, however, we reach a result different from the Appellate Division majority. In this instance, New Jersey's interest is limited and outweighed by Michigan's interest in making more prescription drugs generally available to its citizens.

Furthermore, comity precludes closing our eyes to Michigan's interest. Even if we were to question the effectiveness of the Michigan statute in accomplishing its goal, "it is the forum state's duty to disregard its own substantive preference." *Fu, supra*, 160 N.J. at 130–31, 733 A.2d 1133 (quoting *O'Connor v. Busch Gardens*, 255 N.J. Super. 545, 549, 605 A.2d 773 (App.Div.1992)). The question is not whether Michigan or New Jersey passed the better law; that is a normative judgment best suited for the legislative process. Our inquiry is limited to which state has the greatest interest in applying its law to Rowe's failure-to-warn claim.

To allow a life-long Michigan resident who received an FDA-approved drug in Michigan and alleges injuries sustained in Michigan to by-pass his own state's law and obtain compensation for his injuries in this State's courts completely undercuts Michigan's interests, while overvaluing our true interest in this litigation.

In this instance, where the challenged drug was approved by the FDA and suit was brought by an out-of-state plaintiff who has no cause of action in his home state, this State's interest in ensuring that our corporations are deterred from producing unsafe products—which was determinative in *Gantes* and however weighty in other contexts—is not paramount. Our interest in deterring local manufacturing corporations from providing inadequate product warnings, within the context of an FDA approved drug, must yield to Michigan's interest. . . .

The judgment of the Appellate Division is reversed and the case is remanded to the Law Division for reinstatement of the trial court's order dismissing the lawsuit.

[Dissenting opinion omitted]

———————

1.   Note the fact pattern in Rowe. Plaintiff was a domiciliary of Michigan, which has a rule more favorable to defendants; the defendant pharmaceutical manufacturer was located in New Jersey, which has a rule more favorable to plaintiffs. The court first says that the case presents a true conflict. Later in the opinion, the court seems to say that the rules are "essentially congruent." Which is it? In the next major section, we will confront what Professor Currie called the "unprovided-for" case. Here, for example, the plaintiff comes from a state that has a defendant-protecting rule (but that state has no defendant to protect) and the defendant is from a state with a plaintiff-protecting rule (but that state has no plaintiff to protect). In that instance, Currie says that neither state has an interest and the forum should apply its law as a default. So, is this case a true conflict, a false conflict or an unprovided-for case?

2.   The New Jersey Supreme Court attempts to differentiate the case at bar from an earlier decision, Gantes v. Kason Corp. Do you understand the distinction?

3.   Professor Willis Reese, an early critic of interest analysis, had this to say:

[A] pure interests approach will require a court to decide each case on an ad hoc basis, since the court is required in every case to ascertain the purpose, or purposes, of each of the potentially applicable local law rules in order to determine which of the rules to apply . . . Such a system can be expected to cast an intolerable burden upon the over-worked trial courts. It can also be expected to lead to a constant stream of appeals, since there would usually be a good possibility that the appellate court would find that a given rule embodies a different policy than did the trial court. . . .

Reese, *Chief Judge Fuld and Choice of Law*, 71 Colum. L. Rev. 548, 559 (1971).

> Was Reese's prediction correct? If so, is that a reason to be skeptical of the value of interest analysis, or is it a cost worth bearing to avoid the arbitrariness of the old mechanical jurisdiction-selecting approaches?

Office Talk
#6

Aaron: In *Rowe*, the court wrote that, if there is an actual conflict, the court must identify the governmental policies underlying the law of each state and determine whether those policies are affected by each state's contacts to the litigation and to the parties. So, it seems very important for the court to identify those governmental policies correctly. Yet, this New Jersey court doesn't seem to have done a very good job of identifying the policy behind New Jersey's statute. It is clear that the statute of New Jersey (where the defendant is located) is the pro-plaintiff statute, while the statute of Michigan (where the plaintiff is located) is the pro-defendant statute. But the court somehow seems to conclude that the New Jersey statute is defense-oriented. That's dead wrong.

Neil: You must be referring to the passage on page 132 where the court says "The predominant object of the law is not to encourage tort recoveries by plaintiffs, whether New Jersey citizens or not, in order to deter this State's drug manufacturers. On the contrary, the law limits the liability of manufacturers of FDA-approved products by reducing the burden placed on them by product liability litigation." [Aaron nods.] The first time I read that passage, I thought that it was crazy; after all, the plaintiff is arguing for the application of New Jersey law. How could that be a liability-limiting rule?

Aaron: My point exactly. The court should have examined New Jersey's pro-plaintiff policy to determine how that policy was affected by New Jersey's contacts to the litigation and the parties—just like the court says that it approaches actual conflicts.

Neil: Well, as I said, I thought that it was crazy at first read; but the more I thought about it, the more I concluded that the court is right on target. The New Jersey statute appears to have been enacted to make it *harder* to win a suit against a defendant that manufactured an FDA-approved drug. So, the court should examine it as a pro-defendant liability-limiting statute.

Aaron: But, Neil, in this case New Jersey's statute is the pro-plaintiff statute because it leaves open the possibility of recovery. If you can't see that that is pro-plaintiff, look again at the Michigan statute under which the plaintiff is guaranteed to lose. The court should have treated this as an unprovided-for case. New Jersey, where there is no plaintiff, has a pro-plaintiff statute, and Michigan, where there is no defendant, has a pro-defendant policy. Instead, the court got it exactly backwards.

Neil: I disagree. A legislature that makes life easier for defendants than it was before the legislature changed the law isn't enacting a pro-plaintiff policy merely because other states are even more pro-defendant. New Jersey moved the needle in the direction of the defendants and, to me, that means New Jersey's policy here was to restrict suits against defendants and, thus, it has an interest in applying its statute to protect the local defendant. I am very dubious, however, about the court's conclusion that a purpose of Michigan's statute is to further "Michigan's interest in making prescription drugs more available to its residents."

Aaron: So, you are skeptical about a factual finding of purpose actually made by the court but accept uncritically the claim that the law that the plaintiff wants to apply is pro-defendant?

Neil: Perhaps so, but in modern conflict of laws cases a lot rides on these characterizations of purpose, and you and I both have serious doubts about at least one of the purposes found by the court in this case. If purpose is so indeterminate, how can it serve as an important element of the conflict of laws decision?

————————

    In a fact-pattern similar to *Rowe*, the Illinois Supreme Court reached a similar result. The discussion in the Illinois case is long and somewhat tortured but it is important to see how the court reasoned to its result.

TOWNSEND V. SEARS, ROEBUCK AND COMPANY
879 N.E.2d 893 (Ill. 2007)

JUSTICE FREEMAN delivered the judgment of the court, with opinion:

Plaintiffs, Michelle Townsend, individually and on behalf of her minor son, Jacob, brought a personal injury action in the circuit court of Cook County against defendant, Sears, Roebuck and Company (Sears). A question arose as to whether Illinois or Michigan law would govern the liability and damages issues presented in the case. The circuit court ruled that Illinois law governs these substantive issues, but certified the following question of law for interlocutory appeal pursuant to Supreme Court Rule 308 (155 Ill. 2d R. 308):

> "Whether Illinois or Michigan law applies to a products liability and negligence action where the plaintiff is a resident of Michigan and the injury occurs in Michigan, the product was manufactured in South Carolina, the defendant is a New York corporation domiciled in Illinois, and the conduct complained of, including certain design decisions, investigations of prior similar occurrences, product testing and the decision to distribute nationally in its retail stores occurred in Illinois[.]" . . .

I.   BACKGROUND

Michelle and James Townsend, and their son, Jacob, reside on North Begole Road in Alma, Michigan. Sears is a New York corporation with its principal place of business and corporate headquarters in Cook County, Illinois. In the spring of 2000, James purchased a Sears Craftsman brand riding lawn tractor from a Sears store in Michigan. The lawn tractor was manufactured by Electrolux Home Products, Inc. (EHP), in South Carolina. James bought the 20-horsepower, 42-inch-wide lawn tractor for use around his home. This particular lawn tractor developed a faulty engine. In early 2001, James received an identical riding lawn tractor as a warranty replacement. Through early May 2001, James had operated the tractor three or four times to mow the Townsends' 1.8-acre property.

On the afternoon of May 11, 2001, James returned home from work and began to mow his lawn. At this time, his four children, including 3½-year-old Jacob, were inside their home. As James was mowing, he encountered the 16- by 14-foot rectangular railroad-tie-edged planting plot in his front yard. He attempted to mow around the plot by positioning the left edge of the mower deck as close to the ties as possible. However, the tractor became stuck against one of the ties. James shifted the tractor into reverse, looked over his right shoulder, and released the brake. The tractor struggled to move rearward, taking approximately 20 seconds to move approximately six feet. While backing up, he heard a noise, looked to his right, and saw Jacob's sandal on the lawn. He stopped the tractor, turned around, and saw Jacob behind and under the tractor's rear wheels. James overturned the tractor, picked up Jacob, and rushed him to Gratiot Community Hospital in Alma. Jacob was subsequently treated at Sparrow Hospital in Lansing, Michigan. Jacob's right foot was amputated and his lower right leg was severely injured.

Michelle, individually and on behalf of Jacob, filed a complaint against Sears pleading strict product liability and negligence, premised on defective design and failure to warn. Plaintiffs alleged that Sears "designed, marketed, manufactured, inspected, tested, and sold a Sears Craftsman Lawn Tractor"; that the tractor "was defectively designed, defectively marketed and unreasonably dangerous"; and that the design created such a risk of injury to small children that a reasonably prudent designer and marketer of riding lawn tractors, being fully aware of the risk, would not have put the lawn tractor on the market. Plaintiffs specifically alleged that the tractor lacked a "no-mow-in-reverse" (NMIR) safety feature to prevent back-over injuries. Plaintiff further alleged that Sears had actual knowledge of this specific unreasonably dangerous condition. . . .

Plaintiffs filed a motion to apply Illinois law to the issues of liability and damages. . . . The circuit court identified conflicts between Illinois and Michigan law pertaining to liability and damages. The court employed the choice-of-law analysis of the Restatement (Second) of Conflict of Laws. The circuit court ruled that Illinois law should govern these substantive issues. . . .

B. Identifying the Conflict. . . .

[W]e take this opportunity to stress that a choice-of-law analysis begins by isolating the issue and defining the conflict. A choice-of-law determination is required only when a difference in law will make a difference in the outcome. In the present case, the parties agree that three conflicts exist between Illinois and Michigan law. The first conflict involves liability. Illinois has adopted a rule of strict liability in tort for product design defects. In contrast, Michigan has refused to adopt the doctrine of strict liability, instead imposing a pure negligence standard for product liability actions based on defective design. The difference between the two theories lies in the concept of fault. A real conflict exists because, in a strict liability action, the inability of the defendant to know or prevent the risk is not a defense. However, such a finding would preclude a finding of negligence because the standard of care is established by other manufacturers in the industry.

The second conflict concerns compensatory damages. Illinois currently does not have a statutory cap on compensatory damages for noneconomic injuries. In contrast, Michigan currently imposes caps on noneconomic damages in product liability actions. The third conflict concerns punitive damages. Illinois does not prohibit the recovery of punitive damages in product liability cases when appropriate. Subject to specific statutory exceptions, "it is well established that generally only compensatory damages are available in Michigan and that punitive damages may not be imposed."

C.   Overview: The Second Restatement of Conflict of Laws

A full understanding of current choice-of-law methodology, including its development, is necessary to properly apply it to the above-identified conflicts.

"Traditionally, questions of choice of law have been solved by applying the law of the place of the wrong (*lex loci delicti*), resulting in the rights and liabilities of the parties being determined by the local law of the State where the injury occurred. The doctrine was relatively easy to apply, provided predictability of outcome, and discouraged forum shopping." *Mitchell v. United Asbestos Corp.*, 426 N.E.2d 350 (1981). . . .

"This approach [*lex loci delicti*] was criticized, and eventually in most states abandoned, because it sometimes resulted in the application of the law of a state that had little connection with the events giving rise to the suit."

By the early 1950s, increasing dissatisfaction with the vested-rights-based approach led the American Law Institute to draft a second restatement of conflict of laws. . . .

One scholar has described the Second Restatement as "a document that could not—and cannot—be fairly called a 'restatement' of anything. Instead, it is an amalgamation of different conflict approaches, producing a document of a distinctly normative character." P. Borchers, *Courts and the Second Conflicts Restatement: Some Observations and an Empirical Note*, 56 Md. L. Rev. 1232, 1237 (1997). Indeed, "the Second Restatement is by far the most popular among the modern methodologies, being followed [as of 2004] in 22 states in tort conflicts." E. Scoles, P. Hay, P. Borchers & S. Symeonides, *Conflict of Laws § 2.23*, at 98 (4th ed. 2004). Except with respect to the relatively few areas for which it provides clear rules, the Second Restatement's methodology has three principal features: (1) the policies of section 6; (2) the concept of the "most significant relationship"; and (3) the lists of particularized connecting factors.

"Section 6 is the cornerstone of the entire Restatement." Scoles, *Conflict of Laws* § 2.14, at 59. Section 6 provides as follows:

"(1) A court, subject to constitutional restrictions, will follow a statutory directive of its own state on choice of law.

(2) When there is no such directive, the factors relevant to the choice of the applicable rule of law include

   (a)   the needs of the interstate and international systems,

   (b)   the relevant policies of the forum,

     (c)   the relevant policies of other interested states and the relevant interests of those states in the determination of the particular issue,

     (d)   the protection of justified expectations,

     (e)   the basic policies underlying the particular field of law,

     (f)   certainty, predictability and uniformity of result, and

     (g)   ease in the determination and application of the law to be applied." *Restatement (Second) of Conflict of Laws* § 6, at 10 (1971).

These multiple and diverse principles are not listed in any order of priority, and some of them point in different directions. Thus, in tort cases, for example, these principles, by themselves, do not enable courts to formulate precise choice-of-law rules. *Restatement (Second) of Conflict of Laws* § 6, Comment *c*, at 12–13 (1971); accord Scoles, *Conflict of Laws* § 2.14, at 60. "In some ways, § 6 was a logical response to the perceived flaws of the traditional rules. Critics had identified a variety of concerns that these rules failed to take into account, and § 6 offers a kind of 'laundry list' response that enables the court to consider all of them when appropriate." Cramton, *Conflict of Laws: Cases—Comments—Questions*, at 117.

Another fundamental concept of the Second Restatement's methodology is the concept of the "most significant relationship." "While section 6 enunciates the guiding principles of the choice-of-law process, the most-significant-relationship formula describes the *objective* of that process: to apply the law of the state that, with regard to the particular issue, has the most significant relationship with the parties and the dispute." (Emphasis in original.) Scoles, *Conflict of Laws* § 2.14, at 61. For example, in a tort case, the general principle that a court applies is: "The rights and liabilities of the parties with respect to an issue in tort are determined by the local law of the state which, with respect to that issue, has the most significant relationship to the occurrence and the parties under the principles stated in § 6." *Restatement (Second) of Conflict of Laws* § 145(1), at 414 (1971). One scholar has described section 145 as "nearly as amorphous as section 6." 56 Md. L. Rev. at 1238–39.

Lastly, the Second Restatement provides a list of the factual contacts or connecting factors that the forum court should consider in choosing the applicable law. In a tort case, for example, section 145(2) provides as follows:

"(2) Contacts to be taken into account in applying the principles of § 6 to determine the law applicable to an issue include:

    (a) the place where the injury occurred,

    (b) the place where the conduct causing the injury occurred,

    (c) the domicil, residence, nationality, place of incorporation and place of business of the parties, and

    (d) the place where the relationship, if any, between the parties is centered.

These contacts are to be evaluated according to their relative importance with respect to the particular issue." *Restatement (Second) of Conflict of Laws* § 145(2), at 414 (1971).

In applying the principles of Section 6 to these contacts to determine the state with the most significant relationship, the forum court should consider the relevant policies of all potentially interested states and the relevant interests of those states in the decision of the particular issue. *Restatement (Second) of Conflict of Laws* § 145, Comment *e*, at 419 (1971). "Thus, section 145 is no more definite than § 6, and perhaps even less so. On top of the 'factors' listed in section 6, section 145 adds a generous dollop of territorial and personal contacts." 56 Md. L. Rev. at 1239. . . .

D. Presumption: The Law of the State Where the Injury Occurred

The parties disagree as to the nature and effect of a choice-of-law presumptive rule applicable in this case. The Second Restatement of Conflict of Laws does not abandon rules entirely. "Separate rules are stated for different torts and for different issues in tort. In other words, the identity of the state of the most significant relationship is said to depend upon the nature of the tort and upon the particular issue." *Restatement (Second) of Conflict of Laws*, ch. 7, Topic 1, Introductory Note 2, at 413 (1971); see Scoles, *Conflict of Laws* § 2.14, at 62–63 (discussing presumptive rules). The Second Restatement's introduction is an understatement.

"Once one ventures past section 145, however, the chapter dramatically changes character. Instead of infinitely open-ended sections, the *Second Restatement*, for the most part, articulates reasonably definite rules. To be sure, these succeeding sections contain escape valves that refer to section 6. Many of the rules echo the *First Restatement's* preference for choosing the law of the injury state. Others do not refer to the injury state directly, but choose connecting factors very likely, if not certain, to lead to the application of the law of the injury state. * * * Only a relatively few sections refer solely to the general formula of section 145 without providing some presumptive choice." 56 Md. L. Rev. at 1239–40.

Thus, the *Second Restatement of Conflict of Laws* has been described as "schizophrenic," in that one portion of its split personality consists of general sections such as sections 6 and 145, while the other portion is a set of reasonably definite rules and a preference for territorial solutions, including the injury-state rule for tort cases, endorsed by its predecessor. The general sections embody a free-form approach to choice of law, while the specific sections are quite close to the territorial system embodied by the First Restatement. 56 Md. L. Rev. at 1240.

We agree with the concern that the bench and bar have overemphasized the general sections of the Second Restatement of Conflict of Laws and have undervalued the specific presumptive rules. . . .

"Generally speaking, . . . the Second Restatement contemplates a two-step process in which the court (1) chooses a presumptively applicable law under the appropriate jurisdiction-selecting rule, and (2) tests this choice against the principles of § 6 in light of relevant contacts identified by general provisions like § 145 (torts) and § 188 (contracts)." Crampton, *Conflict of Laws: Cases—Comments—Questions*, at 120. "[M]aking a serious effort to consider the entire *Second Restatement* would improve the quality of judicial decisionmaking. Courts that are willing to follow the narrow rules of the *Second Restatement* would derive vastly more guidance than that which can be gleaned from sections 6, 145 [torts], and 188 [contracts]." 56 Md. L. Rev. at 1247. . . .

Section 146 provides:

"In an action for a personal injury, the local law of the state where the injury occurred determines the rights and liabilities of the parties, unless, with respect to the particular issue, some other state has a more significant relationship under the principles stated in § 6 to the occurrence and the parties, in which event the local law of the other state will be applied." *Restatement (Second) of Conflict of Laws* § 146, at 430 (1971). . . .

We now apply section 146 to the record before us.

Plaintiffs are domiciled and reside in Michigan, and James works in Michigan. Plaintiffs allege that Sears' tortious conduct occurred in Illinois. Comment *e* of section 146, entitled "When conduct and injury occur in different states," addresses this specific situation. "The local law of the state where the personal injury occurred is most likely to be applied when the injured person has a settled relationship to that state, either because he is domiciled or resides there or because he does business there." *Restatement (Second) of Conflict of Laws* § 146, Comment *e*, at 432 (1971). In contrast:

"The state where the *conduct* occurred is even more likely to be the state of most significant relationship * * * when, in addition to the injured person's being domiciled or residing or doing business in the state, the injury occurred in the course of an activity or of a relationship which was centered there." (Emphasis added.) *Restatement (Second) of Conflict of Laws* § 146, Comment *e*, at 432 (1971).

If this guidance were not enough, the comments to section 146 further advise: "The likelihood that some state other than that where the injury occurred is the state of most significant relationship is greater in those *relatively rare* situations where, with respect to the particular issue, the state of injury bears little relation to the occurrence and the parties." (Emphasis added.) *Restatement (Second) of Conflict of Laws* § 146, Comment *c*, at 430–31 (1971).

In this case, Jacob was injured while James was operating the tractor mower in the front yard of their home in Michigan. This activity was centered in plaintiffs' Michigan community. Based on the record before us, a *strong* presumption exists that the law of the place of injury, Michigan, governs the substantive issues herein, unless plaintiffs can demonstrate that Michigan bears little relation to the occurrence and the parties, or put another way, that Illinois has a more significant relationship to the occurrence and the parties with respect to a particular issue.

E.   Another State With a More Significant Relationship. . . .

[B]eginning in 1981, our appellate court has construed sections 6 and 145 of the *Second Restatement of Conflict of Laws* together to describe a three-step process for determining whether a particular contact is significant for choice-of-law purposes: (1) isolate the issue and define the conflict; (2) identify the policies embraced in the conflicting laws; and (3) examine the contacts of the respective states to determine which has a superior connection with the occurrence and thus would have a superior interest in having its policy or law applied. (Citations omitted). . . .

We now consider the section 145 contacts presented in this case. First, the injury occurred in Michigan. As previously discussed, in a personal injury action, this raises a presumption in favor of Michigan law. *Restatement (Second) of Conflict of Laws* § 146 (1971). In the context of a most-significant-relationship analysis, section 145 cautions that situations exist where the place of the injury will not be an important contact, for example, where the place of the injury is fortuitous. *Restatement (Second) of Conflict of Laws* § 145, Comment *e*, at 419 (1971). In this case, however, Michigan has a strong relationship to the occurrence and the parties. Michigan is the place where James purchased the lawn tractor, the place where he used the lawn tractor, and the place where he and the named plaintiffs, his wife Michelle and his son Jacob, are domiciled and reside.

The second contact in section 145 is the place where the conduct causing the injury occurred. According to plaintiffs' theories of the case, Sears committed the allegedly culpable acts in Illinois. The appellate court excluded from its analysis James' alleged conduct contributing to the injury, reasoning that he was not a party. However, Sears pled affirmative defenses alleging contributory negligence on the part of James and Michelle. A court's consideration of injury-causing conduct in a section 145 analysis includes all conduct from any source contributing to the injury. (considering place of contributory negligence). We view this contact as a wash.

The third contact is the domicile, residence, place of incorporation, and place of business of the parties. Here, plaintiffs reside in Michigan and Sears is headquartered in Illinois. We view this contact as a wash. The fourth contact is the place where the relationship, if any, between the parties is centered. In this case, the relationship between plaintiffs and Sears arose from James' purchase of the lawn tractor at a local Sears store doing business in Michigan.

In sum, the first contact favors Michigan; we consider the second and third contacts each a wash; and the fourth contact favors Michigan. Considered alone, these contacts certainly do not override our presumption that Michigan law governs the substantive issues presented in this case. However, we must not merely "count contacts" but, rather, consider them in light of the general principles embodied in section 6. . . .

Considering the policies and interests of Michigan and Illinois, and of the field of tort law, we are unable to conclude that Illinois' relationship to this case is so pivotal as to overcome the presumption that Michigan, as the state where the injury occurred, is the state with the most significant relationship.

1. Liability

The first conflict is between Illinois' strict liability standard and Michigan's negligence standard for product liability actions based on defective design. The appellate court characterized the underlying policy of Illinois' law as essentially pro-consumer and pro-corporate regulation, and characterized the underlying policy of Michigan's law as essentially producer protective. 368 Ill. App. 3d at 908–09. The appellate court concluded: "Illinois has a strong interest in applying its products liability law to regulate culpable conduct occurring within its borders, induce the design of safer products, and deter future misconduct." 368 Ill. App.3d at 910. Reasonable minds may disagree as to the accuracy of the appellate court's characterization of the underlying policy of Michigan's negligence standard—the Supreme Court of Michigan might. In adopting a negligence standard for product liability actions based on defective design, that court viewed a negligence standard as being pro-consumer. First, a negligence standard would reward the careful manufacturer and punish the careless manufacturer. A fault system would produce a greater incentive to design safer products, where the careful and safe design will be rewarded with fewer claims and lower insurance premiums. Second, a verdict for a plaintiff in a design defect case is the equivalent of a determination that an entire product line is defective. *Prentis*, 421 Mich. at 689–90, 365 N.W.2d at 185. Of course, this court long ago expressed disagreement with this view (*Suvada v. White Motor Co.*, 32 Ill. 2d 612, 618–22, 210 N.E.2d 182 (1965)), but that is not the point. "Every state has an interest in compensating its domiciliaries for their injuries. But tort rules which limit liability are entitled to the same consideration when determining choice-of-law issues as rules that impose liability." We trust that characterizations such as "pro-consumer" or "pro-business" will not often appear in future choice-of-law cases.

2. *Compensatory Damages for Noneconomic Injuries*

The next conflict is between the absence of a statutory cap on compensatory damages for noneconomic injuries in Illinois, and the existence of such a cap in Michigan. The appellate court, observing that this court declared a statutory cap unconstitutional in *Best*, 179 Ill. 2d at 384–416, reasoned as follows:

> "We recognize that plaintiffs, as Michigan residents, are not subject to Illinois's constitutional protections and, therefore, Illinois would have little or no interest in protecting plaintiffs from caps on noneconomic damages. Nevertheless, we must also consider that Illinois, as the forum state where the case will be tried, has a very strong interest in its constitutional protection of separation of powers within its borders and, therefore, has a strong interest in protecting against another state's legislative encroachment on the inherent power of its judiciary to determine whether a jury verdict is excessive. Thus, Illinois has a compelling public policy interest in applying Illinois law with respect to caps on noneconomic damages." 368 Ill. App. 3d at 912.

We cannot accept this reasoning. We agree with Sears that enforcement by an Illinois court of the Michigan cap on noneconomic damages does not constitute an encroachment of separation of powers in Illinois. Rather, such enforcement simply applies a Michigan statute against a Michigan resident that has been upheld as constitutional in Michigan.

3. *Punitive Damages*

The last conflict is between the availability of punitive damages in product liability cases when appropriate, in Illinois, and the general unavailability of punitive damages in Michigan. The appellate court observed that the purposes of punitive damages are to punish the defendant and deter future wrongdoing. Based on this unremarkable premise, the appellate court again posited that punitive damages reflect "a corporate regulatory policy," while the disallowance of punitive damages "reflects a corporate protection policy." The appellate court then determined that "Illinois, where the alleged design defects and corporate knowledge of previous accidents occurred, has a definite interest in punishment, deterrence of future wrongdoing, and corporate accountability." 368 Ill. App. 3d at 911, citing *Restatement (Second) of Conflict of Laws* § 146, Comments *c, e,* at 430, 432 (1971). The appellate court concluded:

> "Michigan, the place of plaintiffs' residence and the place of injury, has an interest in assuring that plaintiffs are compensated for their injuries. Nevertheless, where the purpose of disallowing punitive damages is not related to redressing the plaintiffs' injury, once the plaintiffs are made whole by recovery of the compensatory damages to which they are entitled, the interests of Michigan law are satisfied. [Citation.] Accordingly, Illinois, as Sears' principal place of business and the place where the alleged corporate misconduct occurred, has the most significant relationship to the issue of punitive damages."

We disagree.

Again, the purpose of the section 145 analysis is to test our strong presumption that the law of Michigan, where plaintiffs reside and the place of injury, should govern the substantive issues in this case. *Restatement (Second) of Conflict of Laws* § 146, Comment *e,* at 432 (1971). The appellate court's characterization that Michigan "has an interest" in this conflict is an understatement that fails to recognize the strong presumption in favor of applying Michigan law. . . .

Likewise, the passage in comment *e,* to which the appellate court cited, actually states in full:

> "[A]n important factor in determining which is the state of most significant relationship is the purpose sought to be achieved by the rule of tort law involved. If this purpose is to punish the tortfeasor and thus to deter others from following his example, there is better reason to say that the state where the conduct occurred is the state of dominant interest and that its local law should control than if the tort rule is designed primarily to compensate the victim for his injuries * * *. In the latter situation, the state where the injury occurred would seem to have a greater interest than the state of conduct. *This factor must not be over-emphasized.* To some extent, at least, *every* tort rule is designed *both* to deter other wrongdoers and to compensate the injured person. Undoubtedly, the relative weight of these two objectives varies somewhat from rule to rule, but in the case of a given rule it will frequently be difficult to determine which of these objectives is the more important." (Emphases added.) *Restatement (Second) of Conflict of Laws* § 146, Comment e, at 432–33 (1971).

Despite this explicit caution, the appellate court not only undervalued the strong presumption in favor of Michigan law, but overemphasized its perception of the interests Illinois and Michigan have in their different concepts of tort damages.

Illinois certainly has a legitimate interest in the liability to be imposed on Illinois-based defendants under strict liability or negligence principles. However, Michigan has an equally legitimate interest in the remedies to be afforded its residents who suffer such tort injuries. And if the substantive law of these two states looks in different directions, each state would seem to have an equal interest in having its tort rule applied in the determination of the conflicting issues presented in this case. We conclude that a section 145 analysis does not override our strong presumption that the law of Michigan, as the state where plaintiffs reside and where the injury occurred, governs the conflicting issues presented in this case.

In sum, a court begins a choice-of-law analysis in a tort case by ascertaining whether a specific presumptive rule, such as section 146 in a personal injury action, applies to the disputed conflict. Next, if the presumptive rule points to a specific jurisdiction, then the court must test this presumptive choice against the principles embodied in section 6 in light of the relevant contacts identified by the general tort principle in section 145. The presumptive choice controls unless overridden by the section 145 analysis.

III. CONCLUSION

For the foregoing reasons, the judgment of the appellate court and the order of the circuit court of Cook County are vacated, and this cause is remanded to the circuit court for further proceedings consistent with this opinion.

Appellate court judgment vacated; circuit court order vacated; cause remanded.

CHIEF JUSTICE THOMAS and JUSTICES FITZGERALD, GARMAN, and KARMEIER concurred in the judgment and opinion.

JUSTICES KILBRIDE and BURKE took no part in the consideration or decision of this case.

Now that you have seen a fair number of decisions utilizing the Second Restatement do you have a sense as to what role the presumptive rules play in decision-making? For a perceptive analysis see, Borchers, *Courts and the Second Conflicts Restatement: Some Observations and an Empirical Note,* 56 Md. L. Rev. 1232 (1997).

Office Talk
#7

Neil: Aaron, compare the finding on punitive damages in *Singh* with the finding in *Townsend*. In *Singh*, the Washington court found that a Washington plaintiff injured in Washington was entitled to punitive damages from a California manufacturer even though Washington had a strong policy against punitive damages. The interest of California in applying its punitive damages policy against a California manufacturer, whose reckless conduct in not recalling a defective computer program in a heart monitor that was the cause of the destruction of the plaintiff's heart, was paramount. In *Townsend,* on a similar fact pattern, Illinois did not allow recovery for punitive damages against an Illinois manufacturer of a badly designed lawnmower that caused a child's foot to be amputated in Michigan because Michigan did not permit punitive damages.

Aaron: Maybe the difference is that Illinois read its punitive damages policy in a moderate and restrained manner and refused to apply it to a Michigan plaintiff injured in Michigan. Perhaps there are shades of *Bernkrant* buried here.

Neil: Oh, come on Aaron, this is not *Bernkrant* and you know it. If ever there is deterrent policy at work, it is punitive damages. The focus should be on the state of conduct. Yet Illinois does not apply punitive damages because it adopts the Second Restatement's presumption that the law of the state of injury applies.

Aaron: Well, maybe the difference is that Washington is a more interest analysis state and Illinois is wedded to the black letter of the Second Restatement. Illinois talks interest analysis but when push comes to shove it falls back on the presumption that the law of the state of injury applies.

Neil: Maybe you are right. In any event, this illustrates what is perhaps the most important thing about choice of law these days—when you have a conflicts case, the first thing you must do is to carefully analyze the decisions in the forum state and see how the wind blows.

Aaron: But it still is very hard. How is one to know whether Washington courts will analyze the *Singh* fact pattern as a false conflict or an unprovided-for case? Predictability has gone out the window. Unless you have a fully developed body of conflicts cases, all you can do is make interesting arguments. Do you know of any other field of law that is so unpredictable?

Neil: Our casebooks are chock full of cases in which parties took the cases up to the appellate courts because there were good arguments to be made on both sides.

Aaron: Neil, you are only half-right. Cases at the outer edge fill our casebooks. But cases at the core are black letter law. But when someone with an encyclopedic knowledge of cases across the world, such as Professor Symeonides, tells us that no one can predict the outcome in everyday products liability conflicts cases, there is something very wrong.

COSME V. WHITIN MACHINE WORKS, INC.
632 N.E.2d 832 (Mass. 1994)

NOLAN, JUSTICE.

This case presents the sole issue whether Connecticut's statute of repose should apply in the plaintiff's product liability action brought in a court of this Commonwealth. The Superior Court judge granted the defendant's motion for summary judgment, ruling that the Connecticut statute applies to this action and bars the plaintiff's claim for relief. The plaintiff appealed and we granted his application for direct appellate review. We reverse the judgment, and remand this case for further proceedings. The few relevant facts follow.

The plaintiff, Daniel Cosme, at all relevant times was a resident of the Commonwealth, and was employed in Connecticut. On July 21, 1986, while in the course of his employment, he was injured while cleaning a machine at his place of employment. The machine which allegedly caused his injuries is a Whitin full roller card machine. The machine was designed and manufactured in 1939 by the defendant, Whitin Machine Works, Inc. (Whitin), then a Massachusetts corporation with its principal place of business in Massachusetts. The machine was delivered to the plaintiff's place of employment in 1939, and has remained there since.

The plaintiff commenced this action in the Superior Court on March 13, 1987. The plaintiff alleges that his injuries were caused by Whitin's negligent design and manufacture of the machine, failure to warn of the dangerous condition of the machine, and breach of express and implied warranties concerning the machine. . . . Whitin moved the court for summary judgment on the ground that the plaintiff's action is barred by *Conn. Gen. Stat.* § 52–577a (a) (1993), which provides in part that certain products liability action shall not be brought after ten years from the date that the product left the control of the defendant. The judge granted Whitin's motion, and judgment was entered in favor of the defendant. The judge ruled that under Massachusetts choice-of-law rules, the Connecticut statute of repose applies. . . .

The Commonwealth considers statutes of limitations as procedural: "Massachusetts views statutes of limitation as relating to the remedy, and it applies its own law as the law of the forum." We have not determined whether statutes of repose are procedural with respect to choice of law. We have ruled in another context, however, that statutes of repose are distinguishable from statutes of limitation, in that they "completely eliminate[ ] a cause of action,". . . .

In examining conflicts issues using a functional approach, "we have not elected by name any particular choice-of-law doctrine." *Bushkin Assocs., Inc.*, 393 Mass. at 631. Rather, we consider choice-of-law issues "by assessing various choice-influencing considerations," *id.*, including those provided in the *Restatement (Second) of Conflict of Laws* (1971), and those suggested by various commentators. We examine the present issue guided by the Restatement. . . .

[The court cites to §§ 145 and 146 of the Second Restatement.]

We begin by examining the contacts which Connecticut and Massachusetts have with the parties and the occurrence in this case. See *id.* at § 145(2). Connecticut is the place where the injury occurred, and the place of the plaintiff's employment. In addition, the plaintiff, after being injured, received compensation pursuant to Connecticut's compensation statute. Massachusetts is the plaintiff's place of residence, Whitin's principal place of business and former State of incorporation, and the State wherein the alleged conduct causing the plaintiff's injury occurred.

Under § 146, the law of Connecticut—as the "state where the injury occurred"—applies, unless Massachusetts has a "more significant relationship" to the parties and the occurrence under the considerations provided in § 6. We thus examine the various relevant considerations provided in § 6 as they relate to the issue at hand to determine whether Massachusetts has a more significant relationship.

We recognize the basic policies underlying the field of products liability. Generally, providing a cause of action for compensation of individuals injured is the policy behind products liability actions: "[P]ublic policy demands that the burden of accidental injuries caused by products intended for consumption be placed upon those who market them . . . and that the [user] of such products is entitled to the maximum of protection at the hands of someone, and the proper persons to afford it are those who market the products." *Restatement (Second) of Torts* § 402A comment *c* (1965), quoted in *Correia v. Firestone Tire & Rubber Co.*, 388 Mass. 342, 354–355, 446 N.E.2d 1033 (1983). There exists a corresponding policy of holding accountable those whose defective products cause injuries: "Recognizing that the seller is in the best position to ensure product safety, the law of strict liability imposes on the seller a duty to prevent the release of 'any product in a defective condition unreasonably dangerous to the user or consumer,' into the stream of commerce." *Correia, supra* at 355, 446 N.E.2d 1033, quoting *Restatement (Second) of Torts, supra* at § 402A(1).

The Legislature of Connecticut has chosen to limit the products liability cause of action to a period of ten years from the date that the product was released from the possession or control of a party. See *Conn. Gen. Stat.* § 52–577a (a). The courts of Connecticut have recognized that this provision was intended to protect defendants, and presumably the courts of Connecticut, from "stale claims." *See Daily v. New Britain Mach. Co.,* 200 Conn. 562, 583, 512 A.2d 893 (1986). Massachusetts has not limited products liability actions with a statute of repose, and it therefore has illustrated no similar policy of protecting defendants from claims for injuries caused by older products. We examine the relative interests of Connecticut and Massachusetts in applying their policies in the present case.

Connecticut has an obvious interest in having its law apply, as it is the place where the plaintiff's injury occurred. However, Connecticut's interest in protecting defendants from claims concerning older products is not as compelling in the circumstances as it would be if Whitin were a Connecticut business, and Connecticut's corresponding interest in protecting its courts from such claims is obviously not at stake. . . .

Massachusetts has a significant interest in seeing that its resident plaintiff be compensated, and that its resident defendant, Whitin, be held accountable for its conduct, which took place in Massachusetts, and which allegedly caused the plaintiff's injury. "[T]he fact that the domicil and place of business of [the plaintiff and the defendant] are grouped in a single state is an important factor to be considered in determining the state of the applicable law. The state where these contacts are grouped is particularly likely to be the state of the applicable law if either the defendant's conduct or the plaintiff's injury occurred there." *Restatement (Second) of Conflict of Laws, supra* at § 145 comment *e*, at 421. The interests at stake for Massachusetts, because of its relationship to the parties and the conduct causing the plaintiff's alleged injury are greater than those of Connecticut. Clearly, Massachusetts has a dominant interest in seeing its policy enforced. . . .

In sum, Massachusetts has a more significant relationship to the parties and the occurrence than does Connecticut. . . . We reverse the judge's entry of judgment in favor of the defendant, and remand this case for further proceedings.

So ordered.

In *Romani v. Cramer, Inc.,* 992 F.Supp. 74 (D. Mass. 1998), a Massachusetts federal court applying Massachusetts choice of law rules, dealing with the identical conflict between Connecticut's repose statute and the Massachusetts anti-repose rule, found in favor of the defendant and barred the cause of action. In *Romani,* the plaintiff was employed in Connecticut and the injury took place in Connecticut when the back support of his office chair failed causing him to fall and injure his back. The Court distinguished *Cosme* on the ground that the defendant (unlike *Cosme*) was not a Massachusetts corporation but rather was incorporated in Kansas and had its principal place of business there.

The results in products liability choice-of-law cases are so varied that it is difficult to discern a clear pattern. One federal magistrate judge, after surveying the various approaches to resolving the conflicting interests between the state of plaintiff's domicile, the state of manufacture of an allegedly defective automobile, the state of injury, and the state of the automobile's acquisition, stated that the old *lex loci delicti* rule was "less objectionable once it is understood that there is no alternative that will yield a rational and fair result in all cases, and the Restatement [has] . . . kept it as the presumptively correct rule." *Ness v. Ford Motor Co.,* 1993 WL 996164 at *3 (N.D. Ill. 1993) (unpublished). Does this make you want to give up interest analysis and throw in the towel? Consider the following insights from the Hay, Borchers and Symeonides treatise on *Conflict of Laws* (5th ed. 2010):

§ 17.80 A comprehensive survey of product-liability conflicts decided between 1990 and 2005 produced the following findings:[1]

(1)   Choice-of-law methodology plays a less significant role in the courts' choice of the governing law than do other factors, such as the number and pertinence of factual contacts with a given state.

(2)   Although today's products travel great distances, most multi-state product-liability conflicts (88%) involve only two or three states. In a clear plurality of cases (42%), the victim's domicile and injury and the product's acquisition were in the same state. The majority of those cases (79%) applied that state's law, and, in the majority of those cases (76%), that law favored the defendant.

(3)   Most product-liability plaintiffs tend to sue in their home state. They did so in 53% of the cases.[2]

(4)   Forty-one percent of the cases applied the law of a state that had three contacts, and, in 68% of those cases, that law favored the

---

[1]   *See* S. Symeonides, *The American Choice-of-Law Revolution: Past, Present and Future,* 319–38 (2006).

[2]   In 72% of those cases, the plaintiff's home state had a pro-plaintiff law, which the court applied in 68% of the cases.

defendant. Forty-two percent of the cases applied the law of a state that had two contacts and, in 55% of those cases, that law favored the plaintiff. Fifteen percent of the cases applied the law of a state that had only one contact and, in more than half of those cases (52%) that law favored the defendant.

(5) Most cases (88%) applied the law of a state with plaintiff-affiliating contacts (victim's domicile, place of injury, place of product's acquisition), but in more than half of those cases (52%) that law favored the defendant.

(6) The cases of this period do not support the widely-held assumption that, in their choice-of-law decisions, courts favor plaintiffs as a class. Plaintiffs continue to fare better in state courts (where 58% of the cases applied a pro-plaintiff law), while defendants fare slightly better in federal courts (where 51% of the cases applied a pro-defendant law). Overall, however, the percentage of cases that applied a pro-plaintiff law (52%) barely exceeded the percentage of cases that applied a pro-defendant law (48%).

(7) Courts do not unduly favor the domiciliaries of the forum state (plaintiffs or defendants). Only 41% of the cases applied a law that favored the local litigant,[3] *disfavored* the local litigant;[4]

(8) Courts do not unduly favor the law of the forum. Although the cases that applied forum law outnumber the cases that applied foreign law, the margin is relatively narrow—56% to 44%. Moreover, in most the cases that applied forum law, the forum state had significant aggregations of contacts that could justify the application of its law, even if it was not the forum, and regardless of the choice-of-law theory the court followed.

It should be noted that the above findings are based on cases decided during a relatively brief period (1990–2005) and that if one were to add cases decided before and after that period, some of the above percentages might change. For example, the percentage of cases that applied a pro-plaintiff law could be higher in the years before 1990 and lower in the years after 2005. However, it is unlikely that these changes will be significant enough to re-validate some of the assumptions that the above findings dispel, such as the courts unduly favor plaintiffs, or local litigants, or the law of the forum *qua* forum.

§ 17.81   Unlike other tort conflicts, judicial experience in resolving product-liability conflicts is not susceptible to being recast into descriptive choice-of-law rules that would reproduce the results of the case law with sufficient

---

[3] Approximately two-thirds of those cases applied a law that favored a local plaintiff and one-third applied a law that favored a local defendant.

[4] Approximately two-thirds of those cases applied a law that disfavored a local plaintiff, and one-third applied a law that disfavored a local defendant.

accuracy. However, one who wishes to predict the likely choice-of-law outcome of a product-liability conflict may proceed along the following starting assumptions:

(1)   A court's choice of law is more likely to be based on the relative contacts of the involved states rather than on other factors.

(2)   Most courts consider the following contacts as relevant: (a) place of injury; (b) domicile of the injured party; (c) place of the product's acquisition; (d) place of manufacture; and (e) defendant's principal place of business.

(3)   When one state has any three of the above contacts, the court is likely to choose that state's law.

(4)   If two states have two of the above contacts each, a court is likely to choose the law of the state with the plaintiff-affiliating contacts.

(5)   If no state has three contacts, and only one state has two contacts, a court is likely to choose the law of the two-contact state.

The above assumptions would produce the same results as two thirds of the cases decided during the 1990–2005 period.[5] The fact that the results were different in one-third of the actual cases explains why the above are mere assumptions (rather than rules) which can be rebutted by the circumstances of particular cases.

The inherent complexity of products liability conflicts as well as the courts' uneven performance in handling these conflicts raise the question of whether choice-of-law rules for these conflicts are desirable and, if so, whether they are feasible. . . .

———————

And therefore . . .?

5. WORKERS' COMPENSATION

COONEY v. OSGOOD MACHINERY, INC.
612 N.E.2d 277 (N.Y. 1993)

KAYE, CHIEF JUDGE.

The issue on this appeal is whether a Missouri statute barring contribution claims against an employer—which conflicts with New York law permitting such claims—should be given effect in a third-party action pending here. Applying relevant choice of law principles, we conclude that

———————

[5]   *See* S. Symeonides, *The American Choice-of-Law Revolution: Past, Present and Future*, 334 (2006).

the Missouri workers' compensation statute should be given effect, and therefore affirm the dismissal of the third-party complaint seeking contribution against a Missouri employer.

I.

The facts relevant to this appeal are essentially undisputed. In 1957 or 1958, Kling Brothers, Inc. (succeeded in interest by third-party defendant Hill Acme Co.) manufactured a 16-foot wide "Pyramid Form Bending Roll," a machine to shape large pieces of metal. The device was sold in 1958 to a Buffalo company, American Standard Inc., through a New York sales agent, defendant Osgood Machinery, Inc., which assisted American in the setup and initial operation of the machine. American closed its Buffalo plant around 1961, and the history of the bending roll is obscured until 1969, when Crouse Company—which obtained the equipment in some unknown manner—sold the machine to Paul Mueller Co., a Missouri domiciliary.

Mueller installed the bending roll in its Springfield, Missouri, plant and subsequently modified it by adding a foot switch. In October 1978, plaintiff Dennis J. Cooney, a Missouri resident working at the Missouri plant, was injured while cleaning the machine. The machine was running at the time—a piece of wood having been wedged in the foot switch—and Cooney was unable to reach the switch to stop the machine and avoid injury.

In Missouri, Cooney filed for and received workers' compensation benefits. Because under Missouri law an employer providing such benefits "shall be released from all other liability * * * whatsoever, whether to the employee or any other person" (*Mo. Rev. Stat.* § 287.120[1]), he could not additionally sue his employer, Mueller, in tort. Cooney did, however, bring a products liability action against Osgood—the machine's initial sales agent—in Supreme Court, Erie County. (Missouri apparently would not have had personal jurisdiction over Osgood.)

Seeking contribution from parties it deems more culpable in the event it is found liable to Cooney, Osgood brought a third-party action against Mueller, American Standard, and Hill Acme. Mueller invoked the Missouri statute shielding employers from both direct claims by employees and contribution claims by others, and moved for summary judgment dismissing Osgood's third-party complaint. In light of the conflict between the Missouri statute and New York law permitting contribution claims against employers, Supreme Court undertook a choice of law analysis and concluded that New York law should apply. The Appellate Division unanimously reversed and dismissed the third-party complaint as well as all cross claims against Mueller. . . . [582 N.Y.S.2d 873.]. We now affirm.

II.

An inevitable consequence of a mobile society, where people and goods routinely cross State and national borders, is that disputes may implicate the interests of several jurisdictions having conflicting laws. Choice of law principles become relevant, however, only when a State can, consistent with the Full Faith and Credit and Due Process Clauses of the Constitution (*U.S. Const.,* art. IV, § 1; 14th Amend., § 1), choose between the conflicting laws. A State may lack sufficient nexus with a case so that choice of its law is arbitrary or fundamentally unfair (*Phillips Petroleum Co. v. Shutts,* 472 U.S. 797, 818; *Allstate Ins. Co. v. Hague,* 449 U.S. 302). Mueller argues that New York's connection with the case is so tenuous that a decision to apply New York contribution law would be unconstitutional.

In *Hague,* the Supreme Court upheld the Minnesota high court's decision to interpret an automobile insurance policy under Minnesota law instead of under contrary Wisconsin precedent. The policy was issued to a Wisconsin domiciliary, who was a passenger on a motorcycle operated by a Wisconsin resident when he was struck and killed—in Wisconsin—by an automobile driven by another Wisconsin resident. Nevertheless, the Supreme Court plurality found that three contacts with Minnesota, in the aggregate, were sufficient to generate an adequate Minnesota interest in the case: the decedent was employed in Minnesota; his wife, the appointed representative of the estate, subsequently moved to Minnesota; and the insurance company was at all times present and doing business in Minnesota (449 U.S. at 313–319, 101 S.Ct. at 640).

Similarly, New York's contacts with the present case are, in the aggregate, sufficient to satisfy the constitutional threshold. Osgood has alleged that Mueller has a substantial presence in this State, and there is indication in the record that Mueller does business in New York. Additionally, Osgood, which seeks contribution under New York law, is a domiciliary of this State. Finally, Osgood's alleged tortious conduct with respect to the machine arose in New York, where the machine was ordered, operated for several years, and eventually shipped out of State.

We conclude, therefore, that this State has sufficient interest in the litigation so that if we chose to apply New York law on the contribution issue, that decision would not run afoul of the Federal Constitution. Accordingly, we turn to a choice of law analysis. . . .

Of the various, sometimes competing, schools of thought on choice of law, the one that emerged as most satisfactory was "interest analysis," which sought to effect the law of the jurisdiction having the greatest interest in resolving the particular issue. An immediate distinction was drawn between laws that regulate primary conduct (such as standards of care) and those that allocate losses after the tort occurs (such as vicarious liability rules). If conflicting conduct-regulating laws are at issue, the law of the jurisdiction where the tort occurred will generally apply because that jurisdiction has the greatest interest in regulating behavior within its borders. But if competing "postevent remedial rules" are at stake other factors are taken into consideration, chiefly the parties' domiciles. . . .

In *Neumeier v. Kuehner*, 31 N.Y.2d 121, 335 N.Y.S.2d 64, 286 N.E.2d 454, . . . [a] guest statute case, the Court in seeking to return greater predictability and uniformity to the law, adopted a series of three rules that had been proposed by Chief Judge Fuld (*see, Tooker v. Lopez*, 24 N.Y.2d, at 585, 301 N.Y.S.2d 519, 249 N.E.2d 394, [Fuld, Ch. J., concurring]). Although drafted in terms of guest statutes—drivers and passengers— these rules could, in appropriate cases, apply as well to other loss allocation conflicts.

The Neumeier Rules

Under the first *Neumeier* rule, when the driver-host and passenger-guest share a common domicile, that law should control. Indeed, when both parties are from the same jurisdiction, there is often little reason to apply another jurisdiction's loss allocation rules. The domiciliary jurisdiction, which has weighed the competing considerations underlying the loss allocation rule at issue, has the greater "interest in enforcing the decisions of both parties to accept both the benefits and the burdens of identifying with that jurisdiction and to submit themselves to its authority" (*Schultz*, 65 N.Y.2d, at 198). Moreover, this rule reduces opportunities for forum shopping because the same law will apply whether the suit is brought in the locus jurisdiction or in the common domicile, the two most likely forums.

The second *Neumeier* rule addresses "true" conflicts, where the parties are domiciled in different States and the local law favors the respective domiciliary. When plaintiff's State, for example, would allocate the loss to defendant but defendant's State would force plaintiff to bear the loss, a true conflict arises. The rule provides that when the driver's (defendant's) conduct occurred in the State of domicile and that State would not impose liability, the driver should not be exposed to liability under the law of the victim's domicile. Conversely, when the plaintiff-passenger is injured in the place of domicile and would be entitled to recover, the out-of-State driver should generally be unable to interpose the law of his or her domicile to defeat recovery (31 N.Y.2d, at 128, 335 N.Y.S.2d 64, 286 N.E.2d 454). In essence, then, the second *Neumeier* rule adopts a "place of injury" test for true conflict guest statute cases.

Finally, the third *Neumeier* rule, applicable to other split-domicile cases, provides that the usually governing law will be that of the place where the accident occurred, unless " 'displacing that normally applicable rule will advance the relevant substantive law purposes without impairing the smooth working of the multistate system or producing great uncertainty for litigants' " (31 N.Y.2d, at 128). This rule, too, generally uses the place of injury, or locus, as the determining factor.

Assuming that the interest of each State in enforcement of its law is roughly equal—a judgment that, insofar as guest statutes are concerned, is implicit in the second and third *Neumeier* rules—the situs of the tort is appropriate as a "tie breaker" because that is the only State with which both parties have purposefully associated themselves in a significant way (*see*, Korn, *The Choice-of-Law Revolution: A Critique*, 83 Colum. L. Rev. 772, 801 [1983]). Moreover, locus is a neutral factor, rebutting an inference that the forum. State is merely protecting its own domiciliary or favoring its own law. Additionally, the place of injury was the traditional choice of law crucible. . . .

Contribution rules—as involved in the present case—are loss allocating, not conduct regulating. Had conduct regulating been at issue here, our analysis would be greatly simplified, for the traditional rule of *lex loci delicti* almost invariably obtains. Similarly, if the parties shared the same domicile, we would generally apply that jurisdiction's loss distribution law. Instead, our analysis is necessarily more complicated, calling upon us to evaluate the relative interests of jurisdictions with conflicting laws and, if neither can be accommodated without substantially impairing the other, finding some other sound basis for resolving the impasse.

Interest Analysis

The general scheme of workers' compensation acts is that an employer regardless of culpability is required to make specified payments to an injured employee and in exchange, the law immunizes the employer from further liability. Immunity "is part of the *quid pro quo* in which the sacrifices and gains of employees and employers are to some extent put in balance, for, while the employer assumes a new liability without fault, [it] is relieved of the prospect of large damage verdicts" (2A Larsen, *Workmen's Compensation Law* § 65.11 [1993]).

Some States immunize employers only from direct actions by injured workers; others extend protection from third-party contribution actions as well. The Missouri Supreme Court, in rejecting State and Federal constitutional challenges to the Missouri statute at issue here, noted that immunity " 'is the heart and soul of this legislation which has, over the years been of highly significant social and economic benefit to the working [person], the employer and the State.' ". . . .

Missouri's decision to shield employers from contribution claims is thus a policy choice implicating significant State interests: "to deny a person the immunity granted * * * by a work[er]'s compensation statute of a given state would frustrate the efforts of that state to restrict the cost of industrial accidents and to afford a fair basis for predicting what these costs will be." (*Restatement [Second] of Conflict of Laws* § 184, comment *b*, at 547.) Indeed, as the Restatement concluded in a related context, for another State "to subject a person who has been held liable in work[er]'s compensation to further unlimited liability in tort or wrongful death would frustrate the work[er]'s compensation policy of the State in which the award was rendered." (*Restatement [Second] of Conflict of Laws* § 183, comment *c*, at 544.)

Arrayed against Missouri's interest in maintaining the integrity of its workers' compensation scheme is New York's interest in basic fairness to litigants. Under traditional joint and several liability rules, when more than one tortfeasor was responsible for plaintiff's injury, each was potentially liable for the entire judgment, irrespective of relative culpability. Indeed, plaintiff was not even required to sue all the wrongdoers, but could recover the entire judgment from the "deep pocket," who then had no recourse.

In *Dole v. Dow Chem. Co.*, 30 N.Y.2d 143, 148–149, 331 N.Y.S.2d 382, 282 N.E.2d 288 [1972], this Court mitigated the inequity by allowing a defendant that pays more than its fair share of a judgment, as apportioned by the fact finder in terms of relative fault, to recover the difference from a codefendant. The Legislature, also recognizing the desirability of contribution, subsequently codified the *Dole* principles in CPLR article 14 (L. 1974, ch. 742). Stated simply, the "goal of contribution, as announced in *Dole* and applied since, is fairness to tortfeasors who are jointly liable."

Manifestly, the interests of Missouri and New York are irreconcilable in this case. To the extent we allow contribution against Mueller, the policy underlying the Missouri workers' compensation scheme will be offended. Conversely, to the extent Osgood is required to pay more than its equitable share of a judgment, the policy underlying New York's contribution law is affronted. It is evident that one State's interest cannot be accommodated without sacrificing the other's, and thus an appropriate method for choosing between the two must be found.

This is a true conflict in the mold of *Neumeier's* second rule, where the local law of each litigant's domicile favors that party, and the action is pending in one of those jurisdictions. Under that rule, the place of injury governs, which in this case means that contribution is barred. This holding is consistent with the result reached historically, and reflects application of a neutral factor that favors neither the forum's law nor its domiciliaries. Moreover, forum shopping by defendants—who might attempt to invoke CPLR 1403 and bring a separate action for contribution in New York if sued elsewhere—is eliminated.

A primary reason that locus tips the balance, of course, is that ordinarily it is the place with which both parties have voluntarily associated themselves. In this case, there is some validity to Osgood's argument that it did nothing to affiliate itself with Missouri. Indeed, a decade after Osgood's last contact with the bending roll, the machine wound up in Missouri through no effort, or even knowledge, of Osgood. Moreover, the record establishes that Osgood was not in the business of distributing goods nationwide, but limited its activities to New York and parts of Pennsylvania, and thus Osgood may not have reasonably anticipated becoming embroiled in litigation with a Missouri employer.

For this reason, our decision to apply Missouri law rests as well on another factor that should, at times, play a role in choice of law: the protection of reasonable expectations. In view of the unambiguous statutory language barring third-party liability and the Missouri Supreme Court's holding in *Ferriss*, Mueller could hardly have expected to be haled before a New York court to respond in damages for an accident to a Missouri employee at the Missouri plant. By contrast, in ordering its business affairs Osgood could have had no reasonable expectation that contribution would be available in a products liability action arising out of the sale of industrial equipment. Indeed, Osgood's activity in connection with the bending roll occurred in 1958, some 14 years before *Dole* was decided and the principles of full contribution were introduced into our law. Moreover, even under present law, contribution is not foolproof. A defendant, for example, may be unable to obtain jurisdiction over a joint tortfeasor; the joint tortfeasor may be insolvent or defunct (like Kling Bros. here); or defendant's own assets may be insufficient to pay its share of the judgment (*see, Klinger v. Dudley*, 41 N.Y.2d 362, 369, 393 N.Y.S.2d 323, 361 N.E.2d 974).

In sum, we conclude that Missouri law should apply because, although the interests of the respective jurisdictions are irreconcilable, the accident occurred in Missouri, and unavailability of contribution would more closely comport with the reasonable expectations of both parties in conducting their business affairs.

IV.

Finally, we turn to Osgood's contention that New York's public policy precludes application of the Missouri statute in this case. Under the public policy exception, when otherwise applicable foreign law would "violate some fundamental principle of justice, some prevalent conception of good morals, some deep-rooted tradition of the common weal" (*Loucks v. Standard Oil Co.*, 224 N.Y. 99, 111, 120 N.E. 198 [Cardozo, J.]), the court may refuse to enforce it.

As Judge Simons noted in *Schultz*, the public policy exception should be considered only after the court has first determined, under choice of law principles, that the applicable substantive law is not the forum's law (*Schultz*, 65 N.Y.2d, at 202, 491 N.Y.S.2d 90, 480 N.E.2d 679). We have already cleared that hurdle in the present case. Moreover, the exception could apply only when New York's nexus with the case is substantial enough to threaten our public policy (*id.*, at 202–203). While we have yet to explore whether there is a difference between the minimum contacts needed to satisfy the constitutional choice-of-law threshold and those required to implicate the public policy exception, it is unnecessary to do so today; the facts of this case satisfy both standards. Unlike *Schultz*, where New York's nexus was insufficient to implicate our public policy, this case involves a New York domiciliary who may be cast in liability by the effect of foreign law which is contrary to New York law. Accordingly, New York's interest in this case is sufficient to warrant scrutiny under the public policy exception.

Although we have noted that public policy may be found in the State Constitution, statutes and judicial decisions, plainly not every difference between foreign and New York law threatens our public policy. Indeed, if New York statutes or court opinions were routinely read to express fundamental policy, choice of law principles would be meaningless. Courts invariably would be forced to prefer New York law over conflicting foreign law on public policy grounds.

The refusal of courts to enforce foreign law as repugnant to public policy reached its zenith prior to the advent of modern choice of law doctrine. In fact, commentators have opined that in earlier times the public policy rationale really substituted as a choice of law mechanism when the prevailing rigid choice of law rules permitted no flexibility. . . .

The thrust of Osgood's argument is that New York's law permitting contribution is so strong that any encroachment upon the right violates fundamental public policy. In our choice of law analysis, of course, we explicitly considered New York's interest in allowing contribution and concluded that it is significant. Osgood's view, however, is that no abrogation of the right may be tolerated. We disagree.

Certainly, contribution is not a deeply rooted tradition of the common weal, *Loucks*, 224 N.Y. at 111, 120 N.E. 198, having been introduced into our law only relatively recently. Moreover, as noted, availability of contribution is not invariably guaranteed. And while Osgood claims that being forced to pay more than its equitable share of plaintiff's damages is unfair, "public policy is not measured by individual notions of expediency and fairness or by a showing that the foreign law is unreasonable or unwise." In the considered judgment of the Missouri Legislature, employers providing workers' compensation benefits are not amenable to claims for contribution. New York law is to the contrary. But as Judge Cardozo observed: "Our own scheme of legislation may be different. * * * That is not enough to show that public policy forbids us to enforce the foreign right. * * * We are not so provincial as to say that every solution of a problem is wrong because we deal with it otherwise at home." (*Loucks v. Standard Oil Co.*, 224 N.Y. at 110–111, 120 N.E. 198.) Osgood has not sustained its "heavy burden" of proving that the Missouri statute is offensive to our public policy (*Schultz*, 65 N.Y.2d, at 202, 491 N.Y.S.2d 90, 480 N.E.2d 679).

Accordingly, the order of the Appellate Division should be affirmed, with costs.

For interesting commentary on *Cooney*, see Borchers, *New York Choice of Law: Weaving the Tangled Strands*, 57 Alb. L. Rev. 93 (1993); Twerski, *A Sheep In Wolf's Clothing: Territorialism in the Guise of Interest Analysis in Cooney v. Osgood Machinery, Inc.*, 59 Brook. L. Rev. 1351 (1994).

Office Talk
#8

Neil: Judge Kaye wrote a pretty good decision in *Cooney*.

Aaron: She got the right result but I have trouble with some of her reasoning. For example, she says that rules of law with regard to contribution are loss-allocating rather than conduct-regulating. When a state (like Missouri) prohibits contribution against an employer it trades high-profile tort recovery that fosters heavy deterrence against low dollar worker compensation that significantly diminishes the likelihood that the employer will exercise reasonable care. For me that is conduct-regulating.

Neil: I get your point. Nonetheless, employers are rated for worker compensation insurance rates based on the frequency of claims made against them. Thus, Judge Kaye is not all wrong. What else bothers you?

Aaron: Well, Judge Kaye's conclusion that applying New York contribution law would not violate the *Allstate* guidelines is, in my opinion, wrong.

Neil: After *Allstate* it would take a very strange case to violate the due process clause.

Aaron: I share your view. But this case might do it. In *Allstate,* the defendant insurance company wrote insurance for auto accidents in all fifty states. In this case, the fact that the Mueller did some business in New York totally unrelated to the activity for which it is being sued is too attenuated to apply New York law for an injury that took place in Missouri.

Neil: Aaron, if you are right, applying Missouri law against the contribution plaintiff is also unconstitutional, isn't it? Then where are we?

Aaron: Nice point. But there is an answer. By denying recovery, we are not applying Missouri law. If New York law is inapplicable then the contribution plaintiff does not have any law to support its claim.

Neil: Isn't that too cute? It sounds like you are saying that this is a constitutional unprovided-for case. But, when someone makes a claim, doesn't *some* law always govern whether that claim is a winner? New York law would support the contribution plaintiff here. What law, if it is not Missouri, says that the contribution plaintiff loses?

Aaron: Ok. But for a territorialist like me I am not bothered. You apply the law of Missouri as a default. In fact, perhaps the greatest strength of the opinion is that it confirms the territorialist *Neumeier* rules.

MENDEZ V. ATLANTIC PAINTING COMPANY, INC.
936 N.E.2d 1135 (Ill. App. Ct. 2010)

In this case we must decide whether Kentucky law or Illinois law governs a lawsuit arising from the death in Kentucky of an Illinois resident working for an Illinois corporation. Jaime Mendez, an employee of Eagle Painting and Maintenance Co., died while working on a project Eagle undertook as a subcontractor of another Illinois corporation, Atlantic Painting Co. Jaime's widow, Maria Mendez, received workers' compensation under Illinois law. She sued Atlantic in Illinois for negligence. The trial court granted Atlantic's motion for summary judgment, holding that Kentucky's substantive law applied to the lawsuit and that Kentucky's law immunized Atlantic against Maria's lawsuit. Relying on § 184 of the *Restatement (Second) of Conflict of Laws* (1971), we too find that Kentucky's substantive law applies to this cause of action. Accordingly, we affirm the order granting Atlantic's motion for summary judgment.

BACKGROUND

In June 2004, Atlantic and the Commonwealth of Kentucky signed a contract by which Kentucky agreed to pay Atlantic to paint and clean a bridge across the Ohio River. Atlantic then signed a contract, listing Atlantic as contractor and Eagle as subcontractor, with Eagle agreeing to perform part of the painting and cleaning on the bridge. On July 15, 2005, Jaime fell to his death from a platform from which he had painted part of the bridge. An arbitrator awarded Maria workers' compensation benefits of $700 per week for 20 years.

Maria, as administrator of Jaime's estate, sued Atlantic, charging that its negligence caused Jaime's death. Atlantic filed a motion for summary judgment, arguing that Kentucky law applied to the claim, and that the Kentucky's Workers' Compensation Act (Kentucky Act) (*Ky. Rev. Stat. Ann.* § 342. 690 (LexisNexis 2005)), gave Atlantic immunity from Maria's lawsuit. The parties presented depositions concerning the ties between the cause of action and Kentucky and Illinois. All work on the project took place in Kentucky. Eagle's employees all stayed either in Kentucky or across the river in Indiana while they worked on the project. Kentucky police and paramedics responded to the accident. Jaime lived in Illinois with his wife and three children. Atlantic and Eagle both had their principal offices in Illinois, and they signed their contract in Illinois. Most of Eagle's employees who worked on the project resided in Illinois.

The trial court found that Kentucky had more significant contacts with the accident, so Kentucky's substantive law applied to the cause of action. The court held that Atlantic qualified as a contractor and Eagle as a subcontractor under the Kentucky Act and that the Act provided immunity for contractors like Atlantic, whose subcontractors paid a workers' compensation claim for injuries to an employee of the subcontractor. See *Ky. Rev. Stat. Ann.* § 342.690 (LexisNexis 2005). The trial court entered an order that granted Atlantic's motion for summary judgment and Maria appeals. . . .

Whether Kentucky Law Conflicts With Illinois Law. . . .

Both Kentucky law and Illinois law make workers' compensation the employee's exclusive remedy against his employer. (Citations omitted). However, Kentucky law extends this exclusive remedy protection to contractors when an employee of a subcontractor suffers injury. *Ky. Rev. Stat. Ann.* § 342.690(1) (LexisNexis 2005); *General Electric Co. v. Cain,* 236 S.W.3d 579, 585 (Ky. 2007). Some courts call this provision in the Kentucky Act "up-the-ladder" immunity. *See Cain,* 236 S.W.3d at 607. Illinois law offers no such protection to contractors that hire subcontractors. See *Gannon v. Chicago, Milwaukee, St. Paul & Pacific Ry. Co.,* 22 Ill.2d 305, 322, 175 N.E.2d 785 (1961). . . .

Atlantic contracted with Eagle to have Eagle help with painting the bridge. . . . Because Atlantic hired Eagle to perform "work that is customary, usual, or normal" to Atlantic's usual business, Atlantic counts as a contractor and Eagle as a subcontractor for purposes of the Kentucky Act. While Maria could sue Atlantic for negligence under Illinois law, the Kentucky Act makes workers' compensation Maria's sole remedy against Atlantic. *Ky. Rev. Stat. Ann.* § 342.610(2)(b) (LexisNexis 2005). Accordingly, we find that Illinois law conflicts with Kentucky law as applied to this case.

Restatement (Second) of Conflict of Laws § 184

Maria contends that the trial court should have applied Illinois substantive law to this case because Illinois has a more significant relationship with this dispute and, therefore, § 145 of the *Restatement (Second) of Conflict of Laws* requires application of Illinois law. However, we find that § 184 of the Restatement applies more closely to the facts of this case. See *Palmer v. Freightliner, LLC,* 383 Ill. App. 3d 57, 63, 321 Ill. Dec. 644, 889 N.E.2d 1204 (2008) (citing § 184 of the Restatement (Second) of Conflict of Laws as applicable law). § 184 provides:

> "Recovery for tort or wrongful death will not be permitted in any state if the defendant is declared immune from such liability by the workmen's compensation statute of a state under which the defendant is required to provide insurance against the particular risk and under which
>
> (a) the plaintiff has obtained an award for the injury, or
>
> (b) the plaintiff could obtain an award for the injury, if this is the state (1) where the injury occurred, or (2) where employment is principally located, or (3) where the employer supervised the employee's activities from a place of business in the state, or (4) whose local law governs the contract of employment." *Restatement (Second) of Conflict of Laws* § 184 (1971).

The Kentucky Act requires all employers of employees working in Kentucky to compensate their employees for injuries they suffer at work. The Kentucky Act applies to out-of-state employers of employees who reside outside Kentucky. Because Eagle employed Jaime to work on the bridge in Kentucky, Eagle qualifies as an employer subject to the Kentucky Act.

The Kentucky Act further requires all contractors to compensate injured employees of their subcontractors if the subcontractors prove unable to pay the requisite compensation. Thus, the Kentucky Act required Atlantic to provide workers' compensation coverage for any of Eagle's employees injured in Kentucky while working with Eagle for Atlantic. Under the Kentucky Act, Atlantic, like Eagle, was an entity "required to provide insurance against the particular risk" of injury to Eagle's employees, within the meaning of section 184 of the Restatement. *Restatement (Second) of Conflict of Laws* § 184 (1971).

Maria did not obtain an award for the injury under the Kentucky Act; instead, she proceeded under the Illinois Workers' Compensation Act (820 ILCS 305/1 *et seq.* (West 2004)). However, Maria could have obtained an award under the Kentucky Act. See *Bryant,* 758 S.W.2d at 46–47 (Kentucky Act covers out-of-state employee working for out-of-state employer, if injury occurs during work in Kentucky). And the injury here occurred in Kentucky. Therefore, under section 184, "[r]ecovery for tort or wrongful death will not be permitted in any state if the defendant is declared immune from such liability by the workmen's compensation statute" of Kentucky. *Restatement (Second) of Conflict of Laws* § 184 (1971).

Because the Kentucky Act makes Atlantic responsible for providing workers' compensation coverage for employees of its subcontractors, and because the Kentucky Act immunizes Atlantic from lawsuits in tort brought by those employees of subcontractors, Maria's lawsuit for injuries to Jaime must fail. Accordingly, the trial court correctly entered summary judgment in favor of Atlantic.

Restatement (Second) of Conflict of Laws § 145

While we find that section 184 of the Restatement most directly applies to this case, we note that we would reach the same result under section 145 of the Restatement. Section 145 provides that a court deciding a choice-of-law issue should apply the law of the state with "the most significant relationship to the occurrence and the parties." *Restatement (Second) of Conflict of Laws* § 145(1) (1971). In determining which state has the most significant relationship to the case, the court should consider:

"(a) the place where the injury occurred,

(b) the place where the conduct causing the injury occurred,

(c) the domicil, residence, nationality, place of incorporation and place of business of the parties, and

(d) the place where the relationship, if any, between the parties is centered." *Restatement (Second) of Conflict of Laws* § 145(2) (1971).

Section 145 specifies that "[t]hese contacts are to be evaluated according to their relative importance with respect to the particular issue." *Restatement (Second) of Conflict of Laws* § 145(2) (1971).

Here, the injury occurred in Kentucky. Maria alleged that Atlantic caused the injury by failing to erect a proper scaffold, by failing to provide a working safety harness, by negligently inspecting the work site, by failing to supervise the work site properly, and by failing to train Jaime adequately on proper methods for working on an elevated platform. All of the alleged misconduct would have occurred only in Kentucky, except for the training, which could have occurred in either Illinois or Kentucky. Jaime resided in Illinois and Atlantic had its principal place of business in Illinois, where it is incorporated. The relationship between the parties centered in Illinois, because Atlantic negotiated and signed its contract with Eagle, an Illinois corporation, in Illinois, and Eagle hired Jaime, an Illinois resident, in Illinois.

According to our supreme court, "the local law of the State where the injury occurred should determine the rights and liabilities of the parties, unless Illinois has a more significant relationship with the occurrence and with the parties." *Ingersoll v. Klein,* 46 Ill. 2d 42, 45, 262 N.E.2d 593 (1970). Our supreme court adopted a federal court's explanation for this preference:

" '[I]n the absence of unusual circumstances, the highest scorer on the "most significant relationship" test is—the place where the tort occurred. [Citations.] For that is the place that has the greatest interest in striking a reasonable balance among safety, cost, and other factors pertinent to the design and administration of a system of tort law.' " *Townsend,* 227 Ill. 2d at 165, 316 Ill. Dec. 505, 879 N.E.2d 893, quoting *Spinozzi v. ITT Sheraton Corp.,* 174 F.3d 842, 844–45 (7th Cir. 1999).

The preference takes on special significance when the injured person has recovered workers' compensation. "[T]o deny a person the immunity granted him by a workmen's compensation statute of a given state would frustrate the efforts of that state [1] to restrict the cost of industrial accidents and [2] to afford a fair basis for predicting what these costs will be." *Restatement (Second) of Conflict of Laws* § 184, Comment *b* (1971). . . .

CONCLUSION

Illinois's substantive law conflicts with Kentucky's substantive law in this case because Illinois law would permit Maria to proceed with her lawsuit charging Atlantic, the contractor, with negligence, while Kentucky law would bar Maria's lawsuit. Section 184 of the Restatement, which pertains to cases in which workers' compensation insurance covers an injured employee, governs our decision as to which law to apply. Under the Kentucky Act, Atlantic, as a contractor, bore responsibility for providing workers' compensation coverage for its subcontractor's employees, and Maria could have received a workers' compensation award from Kentucky. Therefore, under Section 184, the Kentucky Act immunizes Atlantic against lawsuits to recover for injuries to any of its subcontractors' employees. If this court were to apply Section 145 of the Restatement, we would reach the same result. Kentucky has a substantial interest in ensuring speedy recovery for workers injured in the state and in making liability of employers for work-related injuries both predictable and limited. Kentucky's interests make its contacts with this case more significant than Illinois's contacts. Therefore, we affirm the trial court's order granting Atlantic's motion for summary judgment.

Several cases raise the choice of law issue between states that grant "up the ladder immunity" and those that provide for the right to sue the general contractor. As we have just seen in *Mendez,* the Illinois court favored the law of the state of injury and granted immunity to the general contractor. However, in *Ellis v. Trustmark Builders, Inc.,* 625 F.3d 222 (5th Cir. 2010) (applying Mississippi conflicts law), the court found that the law of the state of the employment relationship governed and permitted the injured employee to sue the general contractor. Courts go both ways on this issue. Isn't this great fun?

That Illinois chose the law of the place of injury was predictable from what we have seen in *Spinozzi* and *Townsend*. But note that the plaintiff, Mendez, and the defendant, Atlantic (general contractor), were both from Illinois. If this case were to take place in a state that followed a common domicile rule for loss-allocating issues, wouldn't they have applied that law to the case? In other words, if a state were not slavishly following the Restatement rules, but using it only as a general guideline, the result might well have been different.

D. THE UNPROVIDED-FOR CASE

ERWIN V. THOMAS
506 P.2d 494 (Or. 1973)

HOLMAN, JUSTICE.

This is an action for damages for loss of consortium alleged to have been suffered when plaintiff's husband was injured in an accident. Plaintiff appealed from a judgment for defendant which was entered after a demurrer was sustained to plaintiff's complaint and plaintiff refused to plead further.

Defendant Thomas, while operating a truck in the state of Washington in the course of his employment for defendant Shepler, is alleged to have negligently injured plaintiff's husband. Defendant Thomas is an Oregon resident and his employer, defendant Shepler, is an Oregon corporation. Plaintiff and her injured husband are residents of Washington. Washington, by court decision, has followed the common law rule that no cause of action exists by a wife for loss of consortium. . . .

The issue is whether Oregon law or Washington law is applicable. It is with some trepidation that a court enters the maze of choice of law in tort cases. No two authorities agree. Until recently, this court was committed to the traditional, arbitrary, and much criticized rule that in tort cases the law of the place of the wrong, Lex loci delicti commissi, governs. However, in the case of *Casey v. Manson Constr. Co.*, 247 Or. 274, 428 P.2d 898 (1967), this court adopted the equally maligned and almost universally criticized 'most significant relationship' approach of *Restatement (Second) Conflict of Laws*.

However, before engaging in the mysteries of the solution of an actual conflict, we must make certain that we have a conflict of consequence which requires a choice. All authorities agree that there is such a thing as a false conflict which requires no choice. However, typically, there is no agreement on what constitutes a false conflict. Professors Cavers, Currie, and Sedler, together with Mr. Justice Traynor, appear to urge that the policy or governmental interest behind the law of each state be examined and that a false or avoidable conflict be considered present if no substantial conflict is found to exist between the states' policies or interests in the particular factual context in which the question arises. On the other hand, Professors Leflar, Rosenberg, and Ehrenzweig see a false conflict as being limited to a situation where the laws of two states are the same or would produce the same results. Where the laws of two states are not the same or would not produce the same results if applied, these latter authorities see the search for and the comparison of the interests of the two states as a means (not necessarily the best or only means) of deciding an actual conflict, not as a means of determining whether a conflict exists.

Where, in the particular factual context, the interests and policies of one state are involved and those of the other are not (or, if they are, they are involved in only a minor way), reason would seem to dictate that the law of the state whose policies and interests are vitally involved should apply; or, if those of neither state are vitally involved, that the law of the forum should apply. It may well be that determining what interests or policies are behind the law of a particular state is far from an exact science and is something about which there can be legitimate disagreement; but, on the other hand, it is the kind of an exercise, for better or for worse, which courts do every day and, therefore, feel secure in doing. If such a claimed conflict can be so disposed of, whether it is called false or not, the disposition certainly seems preferable to wandering off into the jungle with a compass which everyone but its maker says is defective.

Let us examine the interests involved in the present case. Washington has decided that the rights of a married woman whose husband is injured are not sufficiently important to cause the negligent defendant who is responsible for the injury to pay the wife for her loss. It has weighed the matter in favor of protection of defendants. No Washington defendant is going to have to respond for damages in the present case, since the defendant is an Oregonian. Washington has little concern whether other states require non-Washingtonians to respond to such claims. Washington policy cannot be offended if the court of another state affords rights to a Washington woman which Washington does not afford, so long as a Washington defendant is not required to respond. The state of Washington appears to have no material or urgent policy or interest which would be offended by applying Oregon law.

On the other hand, what is Oregon's interest? Oregon, obviously, is protective of the rights of married women and believes that they should be allowed to recover for negligently inflicted loss of consortium. However, it is stretching the imagination more than a trifle to conceive that the Oregon Legislature was concerned about the rights of all the nonresident married women in the nation whose husbands would be injured outside of the state of Oregon. Even if Oregon were so concerned, it would offend no substantial Washington interest.

It is apparent, therefore, that neither state has a vital interest in the outcome of this litigation and there can be no conceivable material conflict of policies or interests if an Oregon court does what comes naturally and applies Oregon law. Professor Currie expresses it thusly:

' * * * The closest approximation to the renvoi problem that will be encountered under the suggested method is the case in which neither state has an interest in the application of its law and policy; in that event, the forum would apply its own law simply on the ground that that is the more convenient disposition * * *.' B. Currie, *Notes on Methods and Objectives in the Conflict of Laws, Selected Essays on the Conflict of Laws* 184 (Footnote omitted) (1963).

An examination of the writings of those scholars who believe that an actual controversy exists in a situation similar to the present indicates, without an exception, they would reach the same result as we do, by either different or partially different reasoning.

The next question is whether our decision in *Casey v. Manson Constr. Co.*, 247 Or. 274, 428 P.2d 898 (1967), is incompatible with our disposition of the present case. In *Casey*, which adopted and applied *Restatement (Second) Conflict of Laws*, an actual conflict existed. An Oregon wife brought a loss of consortium action because of an injury to her husband, also an Oregon resident, which was negligently inflicted in Washington by a Washington resident. We there held that Washington defendants should not be required to accommodate themselves to the law of the state of residence of any traveler whom they might injure in Washington; that under the given circumstances, Washington's interest in the matter, which was protective of Washington defendants, was paramount to Oregon's interest in having its resident recover for her loss; and that Washington's relationship was the more significant and Washington law applied.

Our confidence in any set body of rules as an all-encompassing and readily applicable means of solution to conflict cases is not so great that we desire to undertake the application of such rules except in those situations where the policies and interests of the respective states are in substantial opposition. We see no such conflict here and, therefore, find it unnecessary to resort to any such set of rules. We are little concerned whether we are presented with a false conflict or with an actual conflict capable of solution by resorting to our analysis of the interests and policies of the respective states. Where such policies and interests can be identified with a fair degree of assurance and there appears to be no substantial conflict, we do not believe it is necessary to have recourse in the 'contacts' of Section 145(2) of *Restatement (Second) Conflict of Laws*.

The judgment of the trial court is reversed and the case is remanded for further proceedings.

TONGUE, J., concurs in the result.

BRYSON, JUSTICE (dissenting).

This vehicle accident occurred in the state of Washington. The defendant Shepler, the truck driver, is an Oregon resident and his employer, Shepler Refrigeration, Inc., is an Oregon corporation. Plaintiff and her injured husband are residents of the state of Washington.

The plaintiff brought this action in Oregon to recover damages for loss of consortium. As stated in the majority opinion, Washington, by common law decision, denies the wife a right of action for loss of consortium for injury to her husband. *Ash v. S. S. Mullen, Inc.*, 43 Wash. 2d 345, 261 P.2d 118 (1953). Oregon, by statute, allows such an action. ORS 108.010. This statute establishes that all Oregon wives have the same civil rights as Oregon husbands, including the 'right of action for loss of consortium of her husband.' I fail to see how the Oregon Legislature can do as much for Washington wives.

Regardless of whether we follow the Restatement (. . .) or the law of the place of the wrong, I do not believe we can or should bestow Oregon statutory rights for women on women of the state of Washington. . . .

Obviously the plaintiff could not bring this action in her state, Washington, but the majority opinion holds that by merely stepping over the state boundary into Oregon she is then bestowed with the right given wives who are residents of the state of Oregon, which includes the right of action for loss of consortium of her husband.

There is definitely a conflict in the policy of the states of Washington and Oregon regarding the right to bring an action for loss of consortium.

I would affirm.

Erwin v. Thomas Chart

On the following pages you will find a chart setting forth various ways of assessing interests based on the *Erwin v. Thomas* fact pattern. The following is a brief explanation of each of the examples.

(1)   This is the analysis set forth by Judge Holman. The forum for this litigation is Oregon in each of the four examples. An Oregon defendant negligently injured a Washington resident in Washington. The wife of the Washington resident seeks recovery for loss of consortium. Under Washington law, the wife cannot recover for loss of consortium. Under the law of Oregon, she is entitled to loss of consortium. Judge Holman says that neither state has an interest in the issue of loss of consortium. Oregon, which allows recovery for loss of consortium, does so to favor Oregon spouses. But there is no Oregon spouse to favor. Washington, which denies loss of consortium recovery, does so to favor Washington defendants. But there is no Washington defendant to protect. Judge

Holman thus concludes (like Currie) that Oregon should do what comes naturally and apply Oregon law. After all, Washington's interest in protecting Washington defendants would not be offended since the recovery is not coming off the back of a Washington defendant.

But is Washington's rule there to protect Washington defendants? One of the reasons for denying loss of consortium claims is to avoid duplicative damages. Juries awarding the husband tort damages may well consider the impact on the spouse and thus provide some compensation for those damages. Furthermore, damages (often emotional) have always been suspect in tort law when third parties claim to have suffered derivatively. Thus, Washington's policy may be directed at keeping plaintiffs from achieving double recovery. If so, wouldn't that be better characterized as anti-plaintiff than as defendant protecting. That leads us to a second way of assessing the interests, in paragraph (2).

(2)   If, as set forth above, Washington's policy is anti-plaintiff in that Washington does not want its plaintiffs to recover for loss of consortium, then Washington does have an interest while Oregon, which is seeking to help its plaintiffs, does not. Thus, under this analysis, the case is a false conflict, and the law of Washington ought to apply to deny recovery.

(3)   Can't Oregon's law be viewed not so much as pro-plaintiff but, rather, as a law that seeks to impose the full cost of negligent conduct on defendants? In that case, Oregon has an interest in imposing the full cost of its conduct on the Oregon defendant; on the other hand, if the Washington rule is seen as pro-defendant, there is no Washington defendant to protect. Thus, under this way of looking at things, the case is a false conflict since only Oregon has an interest, and Oregon's rule allowing recovery for loss of consortium should apply.

(4)   If one characterizes Washington's law as anti-plaintiff and Oregon's law as anti-defendant, then Washington does not want its plaintiff-spouse to recover whereas Oregon wants to impose the full cost of that recovery on the Oregon defendant. Both states have an interest, so the case is then a true conflict.

All of this depends on how we characterize the interests. We submit that none of the characterizations described above and summarized in the charts is unfounded.

Erwin v. Thomas

(1)

Washington	Oregon
Place of the accident	Forum
Location of the plaintiff	Location of the defendant
No action for loss of consortium; therefore, defendant-protecting (but no Washington defendant to protect)	Action for loss of consortium; therefore, plaintiff protecting (but no Oregon plaintiff to protect)

Conclusion: Unprovided-for case

(2)

Washington	Oregon
Place of the accident	Forum
Location of the plaintiff	Location of the defendant
No action for loss of consortium; therefore, anti-plaintiff	Action for loss of consortium; therefore, plaintiff-protecting (but no Oregon plaintiff to protect)

Conclusion: False Conflict, only Washington has an interest

(3)

Washington	Oregon
Place of the accident	Forum
Location of the plaintiff	Location of the defendant
No action for loss of consortium; therefore, defendant-protecting, but no Washington defendant to protect	Action for loss of consortium; therefore, anti-defendant

Conclusion: False conflict, only Oregon has an interest

(4)

Washington	Oregon
Place of the accident	Forum
Location of the plaintiff	Location of the defendant
No action for loss of consortium; therefore, anti-plaintiff	Action for loss of consortium; therefore, anti-defendant

Conclusion: True conflict

The Oregon court sought to reconcile its holding with its decision in *Casey v. Manson Construction Co.* In that case, an Oregon wife sought recovery for consortium for negligent conduct in Washington by a Washington defendant who injured her husband. The court said that the case was a true conflict but that Washington defendants need not accommodate themselves to the law of any state from which a traveler may come. Ultimately, this argument is based on the expectations of Washington defendants that the law of their state will apply when they are acting solely within the state. This leaves us with the question of why in *Erwin* the expectation of a Washington plaintiff injured in Washington should not be that its home state law will apply.

The unprovided-for case has been the subject of much discussion among the commentators. See e.g., Ely, *Choice of Law and the State's Interest in Protecting Its Own*, 23 Wm. & Mary L. Rev. 173 (1981); Sedler, *The Government Interest Approach to Choice of Law: An Analysis and Reformulation*, 25 UCLA L. Rev. 181 (1977). Posnak, *Choice-of-Law: A Very Well—Curried Leflar Approach*, 34 Mercer L. Rev. 731 (1983) (resolve unprovided for case, by applying the Leflar "better law" approach.) As we have noted earlier in the notes following *Rowe v. Hoffman La-Roche, supra*, whenever the defendant is domiciled in a state that has a rule favorable to plaintiff, that state (according to Currie) has no interest because it has no domiciliary to protect. Conversely, if the plaintiff is domiciled in a state that has a defendant-protecting law, that state has no interest because it has no defendant to protect. This was the situation in *Neumeier v. Kuehner*, 286 N.E.2d 454 (N.Y. 1972). A New York driver negligently injured an Ontario plaintiff in Ontario. Ontario had a host-guest statute (presumably to protect Ontario insurers against fraud). New York had no host-guest statute (presumably to allow its domiciliaries to collect for injuries caused to them). Ontario had no interest because no Ontario insurer would be defrauded and New York had no interest because it had no New York domiciliary to compensate. The court in *Neumeier* did not follow the Currie solution and apply the law of the forum. Instead, New York, the forum, applied the law of Ontario saying that Ontario law obviously applied to an Ontario citizen injured in Ontario. In short, *Neumeier* cannot be reconciled with *Erwin v. Thomas*. The chart on the preceding page indicates how tricky it is to characterize the interests in these types of cases. Both the *Rowe* and *Townsend* cases (set forth on pages 127 and 137 respectively), treat this kind of fact pattern as a "true conflict". One of the authors of this book has had some very harsh words to say about interest analysis based on the "unprovided-for" case phenomenon. See Twerski, *Neumeier v. Kuehner: Where Are the Emperor's Clothes?*, 1 Hofstra L. Rev. 104, 107–108 (1973):

> In evaluating interests Currie and his academic followers placed tremendous emphasis on the *interest of the domicile state of the parties in granting or denying recovery.* For example, whenever plaintiff hailed from a state granting recovery and defendant was domiciled in a state denying recovery the interest analysis claimed that there was an irreconcilable conflict. After all doesn't the domicile state of one party want him to recover and the domicile state of the other party seek to deny recovery? There was rarely any attempt to view the policies behind these rules in broader perspective. . . .

> In an unprovided for case like *Neumeier* we face a situation where there are no domiciliary interests to protect on the part of the contact states. New York has no domiciliary interests to protect by its pro-compensation rule since the plaintiff is not a New Yorker. Ontario has no domiciliary interests to protect by its anti-compensation rule because the defendant is not an Ontario domiciliary. Thus, the entire structure of interest analysis crumbled. Having defined the interests as domiciliary oriented when you run out of domiciliaries to protect you run out of interests. The emperor indeed stands naked for all to see.

Some Concluding Remarks on Methodology

Having seen the operation of interest analysis in a sampling of tort cases, you can judge for yourself whether this sophisticated approach to choice-of-law presents a sensible approach to resolving the myriad issues that arise daily in the courts. Although the authors remain skeptical as to whether many cases labeled as false conflicts are truly those in which only one state has an interest, we agree that what Currie calls a false conflict should be resolved in the manner he proposes. After all, if only one state has an interest in a case, why shouldn't that state's law govern? Once you get past the classic false conflict situation, however, the courts have not endorsed Currie's view that the forum should apply its own law. Rather, the cases all reflect some sense of weighing interests. Whether one calls it "moderate and restrained interpretation of forum law", comparative impairment, or the Leflar factors, the opinions all come down to weighing which interest is greater. In the case of anachronistic law, Leflar's "better rule of law" approach does pick the winner in spite of what might lead a court to choose otherwise. However, once we get past anachronistic laws (rules that are on their deathbed anyway), Leflar has little to offer in terms of determining the "better law."

That leaves the question of whether interest weighing is preferable to a mechanical *lex loci* rule. Although ten or so jurisdictions still retain their allegiance to First Restatement rules, there is no looking back in the other states. Though the Second Restatement unleashed us from the arbitrary shackles of the First Restatement, it gave us little direction as to how to resolve a choice-of-law problem with our new freedom. Of course, courts can easily sign on to the Second Restatement approach because it allows any result that they may wish to impose. The cases you have read make that rather clear. The New York approach that, absent common domicile, the law of the place of the injury almost always governs in tort cases provides very clear direction for torts (but does not translate readily to other substantive areas of law). If, however, decisions like *Schultz* result from that approach, those who are troubled by *Schultz* might doubt the wisdom of the approach that generated it.

All that anyone can do is to provide you with a good sampling of the cases. It is child's play to take pot shots at the various approaches. For decades conflicts scholars (including Twerski) did just that. Each scholar had an approach that he/she believes did the trick. But, the reality is that post-Currie, who destroyed the old system, no one has come up with a workable alternative. That is a depressing way of concluding this section but it is in our opinion an honest assessment of the situation. The student is urged to look at each state's choice of law decisions and attempt to make some sense out of them.

E. SOME OTHER ISSUES

1. RENVOI

In earlier chapters, we made reference to renvoi. The issue is whether, when a court initially determines which jurisdiction's law will govern, the court should take into account the choice of law rules of that jurisdiction and apply the law that would be applied by the courts of that jurisdiction, as opposed to simply applying the substantive law of that jurisdiction without regard to whether the courts of that jurisdiction would apply their own law.

With some exceptions, the modern trend has been not to apply renvoi and thus the forum generally applies the law of the foreign jurisdiction even if that jurisdiction would not have applied it to the facts before the court.

An interesting question arises under a policy-centered (interest analysis) approach whether the forum state should do its own interest analysis and pay no attention to the choice of law rules of the foreign jurisdiction or whether there are occasions when looking at the choice of law approach of the foreign jurisdiction would provide valuable information that could change the court's views as to the foreign jurisdiction's interest in the matter.

Consider a case that we focused on earlier in this chapter, *Schultz v. Boy Scouts of America, Inc.* You will recall in that case New York applied the law of New Jersey granting charitable immunity from tort liability to a New Jersey corporation rather than the non-immunity law of New York even though the New Jersey corporation had committed a tort in allowing a scoutmaster with a history of sexual abuse to supervise two youngsters and sexually abuse them while they were in a New York summer camp. New York held that since the plaintiffs and the Boy Scouts were all New Jersey domiciliaries that they should be governed by the law of their common domiciliary and thus should be bound by New Jersey's charitable immunity doctrine. You may also recall that in a later case New Jersey faced a similar situation. In *P. V. et. al v. Camp Jaycee* (discussed supra), plaintiff, a twenty-one year old female from New Jersey who suffered from Down's Syndrome was sexually abused in Camp Jaycee, a New Jersey not-for-profit corporation in a camp that was run by that organization in Pennsylvania. New Jersey law would not allow recovery based on its doctrine of charitable immunity. Pennsylvania, (the place where the sexual abuse took place) had abolished its charitable immunity doctrine. The New Jersey court found that Pennsylvania had the dominant interest and that is own interest in protecting charitable organizations from tort suits was of lesser importance.

Isn't there a good argument to be made that if New York were faced with the same issue again it should take into account New Jersey's pronouncement that it views the role of deterrence of sexual abuse to be greater than its policy of charitable immunity? Thus, New York would look to New Jersey's evaluation of its own domestic charitable immunity doctrine and discover that it is not of such great importance. Note, that we would not be looking to how New Jersey resolves choice of law problems but rather New Jersey's choice of law rule informs us as to the strength of New Jersey's domestic interest in its own charitable immunity doctrine.

Professor Von Mehren and Weintraub both believe that when a forum looks to a foreign state's choice of law rule to define that state's domestic interest that it is proper to do so. See Russell J. Weintraub, Commentary on the Conflict of Laws 90 (5th ed. 2006) and Arthur T. Von Mehren, *The Renvoi and its Relation to Various Approaches to the Choice-of-Law Problem*, in XXth Century Comparative and Conflicts Law, 380, 391 (1961). They also both agree that when the foreign state follows jurisdiction selecting (First Restatement) rules that it makes no sense as to how the foreign state would treat the problem before the court. The jurisdiction selecting rules tell us nothing about a state's domestic interests. However, other commentators believe that attention should be paid to the foreign state's choice of law rules even if they are of the old jurisdiction-selecting variety. See Brilmayer, *The Other State's Interests*, 24 Cornell Int'l L.J. 233, 241 (1991); Kramer, *Return of the Renvoi*, 66 N.Y.U. L. Rev. 979, 1005 (1991).

2. DÉPEÇAGE

Consider the following fact pattern, slightly altered from an actual case:

During the summer of 2010, Alan and Beverley Paden rented a bungalow for a two week vacation in a scenic area in Ontario, Canada, about 50 miles from Toronto. They brought with them their three children. All of the Padens are New York state residents and have been coming to this same bungalow colony for their vacation for the past five years. While at the bungalow colony, the Padens made friends with Robert and Fran Turdom and their children who likewise have been regular guests at the same bungalow colony for many years. The Turdoms have lived all their lives in Ontario. The families over the years have become very close. The children treat the bungalows of each other interchangeably. The Turdoms have a dog "Happy"—and the dog is responsible for creating the conflict of laws problem that we are about to encounter.

The Padens have a seven-year old daughter, Betsy. Over the years, Betsy has paid too much attention to "Happy." For reasons known only to "Happy," he didn't much take to Betsy's playfulness with him. Mrs. Turdom warned the entire Paden family and especially Alan and Beverly that Betsy should leave the dog alone especially during mealtimes.

On the morning of August 10, 2010, the Padens were seated at the kitchen table eating breakfast. "Happy" came to the door and Beverley Paden let "Happy" in and the dog settled himself under the kitchen table. Betsy was sitting next to her mother Beverley. Beverley saw Betsy climb off her chair and go onto the floor under the table, presumably to play with the dog. A minute later, Betsy screamed. Unhappily, "Happy" had attacked Betsy and caused serious and permanent facial injuries.

"Happy" had no previous history of attacking or injuring people. Under New York case law (see *Collier v. Zambito*, 807 N.E.2d 254 (N.Y. 2004)), the owner of a dog who has no reason to know of its vicious propensities is not liable for negligence if the dog unexpectedly injures someone. Ontario, on the other hand (or paw), has a strict liability dog bite statute that makes the owner of a dog liable for injuries caused by the dog without regard to any fault on the part of the owner, but mitigates the harshness of strict liability by permitting dog owners to sue for contribution "from any other person in proportion to the degree to which the other person's fault or negligence caused or contributed to the damages." Ont. Rev. Stat. ch. 65.

Shortly after the injury to Betsy, the Padens filed suit on her behalf against the Turdoms in the United States District Court for the Eastern District of New York. The Turdoms, who now faced potential liability for Betsy's injuries, sought to implead Alan and Beverley Paden for contribution. New York law does not permit a nonparent tortfeasor whose negligence has injured a child to recover contribution from a parent based on theory of negligent supervision. *Holodook v. Spencer*, 324 N.E.2d 338 (1974). The Court in *Holodook* based its decision partially on intrafamily immunity but also because requiring contribution from the negligent parent may effectively reduce the child's compensation, given that the typical family is a "single economic unit." The trial judge granted the Padens' summary judgment with respect to liability, based on the Ontario strict liability statute, but, applying New York law, dismissed the Turdoms' third party complaint against Alan and Beverley Paden based on the claim of negligent supervision. Both parties have appealed the trial judge's decision.

This fact pattern raises a fascinating issue. When, if ever, should a court decide one issue based on the law of one jurisdiction and another issue based on the law of a different jurisdiction? In other words, can a court in a conflicts case come up with a result that would not be the result reached by a court in either jurisdiction applying its own domestic law to the case? In the case set forth above, if a court applied New York law to all issues, the owner of the dog would not be liable for the injuries to Betsy. On the other hand, if a court applied Ontario law to all issues, the owner of the dog would be strictly liable for the injuries caused by it but would be entitled to contribution from Betsy's parents. Was the trial judge correct in holding the dog owner's liable (by application of Ontario law) but denying them contribution (by application of New York law)? This phenomenon of picking and choosing the law depending on the issue is known as dépeçage.

For an interesting discussion of dépeçage, see Reese, *Dépeçage: A Common Phenomenon in Choice of Law*, 73 Colum. L. Rev. 58 (1973); Comment, *False Conflicts*, 55 Cal. Rev. 74, 114,13 (1967). Dépeçage is given a thorough going over by Professor Cavers in his classic book, The Choice of Law Process 34–43 (1965). The Cavers book is an outstanding piece of scholarship that is a must-read for any serious student of conflict of laws.

3. SUBSTANCE AND PROCEDURE REVISITED

In Chapter 2, we examined the substance-procedure distinction as an escape device from rigid jurisdiction-selecting rules. At this juncture we look at the problem trying to discern when a forum should apply its own procedural rules. Perhaps the most contentious and oft-litigated "procedural" issue arises with regard to statutes of limitations. Historically, in the United States (but not in much of the rest of the world) statutes of limitation have been treated as procedural for conflict of laws purposes; thus *lex fori* applied. The movement away from the automatic "procedural" characterization has been substantial. Nonetheless, this aspect of conflicts law remains a mess. A good place to start is an early New Jersey case that was instrumental in moving the courts to rethink the issue.

HEAVNER V. UNIROYAL, INC.

305 A.2d 412 (N.J. 1973)

HALL, J.

This product liability case presents . . . important questions concerning the statute of limitations. The . . . choice-of-law question, is whether New Jersey, as the forum state, should apply its limitations statute or that of North Carolina-the state where all the parties are and where the cause of action arose and all preceding incidents occurred. . . .

In the complaint plaintiff Roy Heavner, the purchaser of a truck tire from defendant Pullman which had been manufactured by defendant Uniroyal, sought recovery from both for personal injuries to himself and contemporaneous damage to his vehicle. His wife, plaintiff Rebecca Heavner, sought a Per quod recovery for loss of consortium. All three claims were alleged to have resulted from a defect in the tire, which blew out while Heavner was driving the rig, causing it to crash into an abutment. Each was stated, in separate counts, on the theories of negligence, breach of express and implied warranty, strict liability in tort and strict liability for misrepresentation as to quality by advertising and otherwise. . . .

The facts pertinent to the questions before us are necessarily taken from the complaint and assumed to be true. Plaintiffs were at the time of the accident, and have been since, residents of North Carolina. Defendant Uniroyal is a New Jersey corporation engaged in the manufacture, sale and distribution of truck tires throughout the United States. Defendant Pullman, a Delaware corporation, is a retailer of trailers equipped with Uniroyal truck tires, likewise doing business throughout the nation.

On October 21, 1966, plaintiff Roy Heavner purchased a truck trailer, having the Uniroyal tire in question mounted on one of its wheels, from Pullman in Charlotte, North Carolina. Presumably, the vehicle was registered there. The accident occurred on April 17, 1967 in that state. No suit has ever been instituted in North Carolina. There is agreement that jurisdiction could have been obtained over both defendants in that state and no explanation has been offered why a timely action was not begun there. The present suit was started here on September 25, 1970—more than three years after the accident, but less than four years from the delivery of the tire by Pullman to Heavner.

We take it to be conceded that, at the time of commencement of this suit, the applicable North Carolina statute of limitations had expired and any action was barred in that state. The limitations period there for actions for tortious injuries to the person or chattels and upon contract at the times here involved was three years from the accrual of the cause of action, the latest possible date for which would be the date of the accident. General Statutes of North Carolina ss 1–15(a), 1–52(1), (4) and (5). The Uniform Commercial Code did not become effective in that state until July 1, 1967. (The four-year limitation section specifically provides, 2–725(4), that it shall not apply to causes of action which have accrued before the act becomes effective.) 1 U.L.A.-U.C.C. (master edition), p. xxxvii.

I

Choice of Law as to the Statute of Limitations

It has long been the common law conflicts rule that the statute of limitations is ordinarily a matter of procedure, affecting the remedy and not the right, and is therefore, like other procedural attributes, controlled by the law of the forum rather than that of the state whose law otherwise governs the cause of action. Restatement, Conflict of Laws ss 603, 604 (1934); Restatement, Conflict of Laws 2d s 142 (1971); Leflar, American Conflicts Law s 127 (1968); Goodrich, Conflict of Laws s 85 (4th ed. 1964). New Jersey has consistently followed the rule, although not without some recent criticism. *Marshall v. Geo. M. Brewster & Son, Inc.,* 37 N.J. 176, 180–181, 180 A.2d 129 (1962). It is, of course, judge-made and may be changed judicially, as we have done with respect to the matter of the substantive law to be applied to a foreign cause of action. See *Mellk v. Sarahson,* 49 N.J. 226, 229 A.2d 625 (1967); *Pfau v. Trent Aluminum Co.,* 55 N.J. 511, 263 A.2d 129 (1970). We think reexamination of the rule is in order.

Sound sense and practical reasons dictate that a suit on a foreign cause of action should be processed and tried according to the procedural rules of the forum state. It would be an impossible task for the court of such a state to conform to procedural methods and diversities of the state whose substantive law is to be applied. The determination of that law is a difficult enough burden to impose upon a foreign tribunal.

A statute of limitations is, however, not subject to the same problems as strictly procedural matters. The limitation period of the foreign state can generally be ascertained even more easily and certainly than foreign substantive law. It came to be included in the category of procedure on the theory that the passage of the period destroys only the remedy and not the right and remedy is considered procedural and governed by the law of the forum. Historically, the thesis developed in England more than two centuries ago when English common law judges restricted as much as possible all reference to or reliance upon the law of foreign countries. Goodrich, supra, p. 152. In any event, the rule fitted very neatly into basic principles of early conflicts law which rather arbitrarily compartmentalized the incidents found in a foreign cause of action into fixed characteristics and mechanical rules in the supposed interests of uniformity and certainty, almost regardless of the justice or good sense of the particular situation-an approach recently abandoned in this and many other states, at least with respect to the substantive law to be applied. See Restatement, Conflict of Laws 2d ss 145, 146.

This law-of-the-forum rule as to the applicable period of limitations has been almost universally criticized by legal commentators, especially in recent times when the whole field of conflicts law has been undergoing so much reevaluation by both scholars and American courts. . . .

The fundamental illogic and unsoundness of the rule are well set forth in selected excerpts from these writings. Goodrich says:

> There is little reason for this rule, other than historical * * *. As an original proposition, it could well be urged that, after suit is barred by the law to which reference is made as governing the claims of the parties, the plaintiff's claim, now deprived of its most valuable attribute, should be unenforceable by action elsewhere. * * * (at pp. 152–153)

Dean Leflar puts it this way:

> * * * The historical explanation of these results is a theory that the passage of the period of limitations destroys only the remedy and not the right inherent in a cause of action. Remedy, classified as a procedural matter, is governed by forum law. This theory, as applied to causes of action barred where they arose, does not make very good sense. A right for which the legal remedy is barred is not much of a right. It would have made better logic if the limitations rule of the state whose substantive law is chosen to govern the right were deemed substantive also, so that both the original and the terminal existence of the right would be related to the same body of law. That, however, was not the way the law developed, save for exceptional situations to be mentioned later. The result is that plaintiffs whose claims are barred by the governing substantive law are allowed to shop around for a jurisdiction in which the statute is longer, in the hope of getting service there on the obligor. . . .

General dissatisfaction with the rule has however, found concrete expression in ways other than by outright judicial change. The first of these is the judge-made principle which has developed that the foreign limitations period will be applicable where a statute creating the cause of action bars the right and not merely the remedy. Wrongful death statutes are a common example. Restatement, Conflict of Laws 2d s 143; Leflar, supra, at pp. 305–306. Professor Sedler has characterized this effort in his . . . article: 'The struggles of the courts to determine whether the locus has destroyed the right are amusing, even if the results are inconsistent and the reasoning at times most specious.' (37 N.Y.U. L. Rev. at p. 848)

The other method which has been utilized to counteract the law-of-the-forum rule is the enactment, by about three-quarters of the states, of so-called 'borrowing statutes.' Generally, these statutes either bar the action if it is barred by the state where the defendant, or both of the parties, resided or of the place where the cause of action arose. See Restatement, Conflict of Laws 2d, s 142 comment f. In modern days, they serve a purpose of preventing forum shopping. Although undoubtedly intended to be mechanical and certain in operation, these statutes are exceedingly diverse and complex and may well be said to have created more problems than they have solved. See Vernon, supra (32 Rocky Mt. L. Rev. 287); Ester, supra (15 U. Fla. L. Rev. 33). New Jersey has never had such a statute. But as Professor Sedler points out: 'The absence of a borrowing statute should not prevent application of the statute of the locus; for a policy against forum shopping can be set out by the judiciary as well as the legislature.' (37 N.Y.U. L. Rev. at p. 850)

We are convinced the time has come, for the reasons previously outlined, to discard the mechanical rule that the limitations law of this state must be employed in every suit on a foreign cause of action. We need go no further now than to say that when the cause of action arises in another state, the parties are all present in and amenable to the jurisdiction of that state, New Jersey has no substantial interest in the matter, the substantive law of the foreign state is to be applied, and its limitation period has expired at the time suit is commenced here, New Jersey will hold the suit barred. In essence, we will 'borrow' the limitations law of the foreign state. We presently restrict our conclusion to the factual pattern identical with or akin to that in the case before us, for there may well be situations involving significant interest of this state where it would be inequitable or unjust to apply the concept we here espouse. . . .

[The court dismissed the plaintiff's case based on North Carolina's statute of limitation. The court's discussion on the New Jersey products liability statute of limitations is omitted.]

Several attempts have been made to codify the conflicts rules with regard to statutes of limitations. The Uniform Conflict of Law-Limitations Act (1982) provides that if a state chooses to apply the substantive law of another state that it is to apply that state's limitation period. The American

Law Institute in a 1988 amendment to the Second Restatement proposed the following rule:

§ 142.   Statute of Limitations

Whether a claim will be maintained against the defense of the statute of limitations is determined under the principles stated in § 6. In general, unless the exceptional circumstances of the case make such a result unreasonable:

(1)   The forum will apply its own statute of limitations barring the claim.

(2)   The forum will apply its own statute of limitations permitting the claim unless:

    (a)   maintenance of the claim would serve no substantial interest of the forum; and

    (b)   the claim would be barred under the statute of limitations of a state having a more significant relationship to the parties and the occurrence.

Both proposals have found their adherents in various states. A large number of states still have "borrowing statutes" on the books. They create their own set of problems. Consider the following case.

IN RE JOINT EASTERN AND SOUTHERN DISTRICT ASBESTOS LITIGATION

721 F.Supp. 433 (E.D.N.Y. 1988)

SIFTON, DISTRICT JUDGE.

Defendants in this asbestos-related personal injury and wrongful death case move for summary judgment based on New York's borrowing statute. Because that statute applies only to causes of action that "accrue without the state" and because defendants have not established this to be the case here as a matter of law, the motions are denied.

The facts are in large part undisputed. Plaintiff and her decedent resided in New York from 1962 to 1975, during which time deceased husband worked as an insulator with asbestos products. Plaintiff testified in her deposition, ["He [decedent] would get winded, dizzy, coughing. I would hear a wheezing, you know. . . . I think I noticed it early in the '70's."] *Accrual?* In 1975, plaintiff and her husband moved to Arizona, and in that and other states her husband continued to be exposed to asbestos. In 1979, he was diagnosed in Arizona as having lung cancer and died in 1981. This action would be time-barred under Arizona's statute of limitations, but, unless subject to the borrowing statute, it is timely under New York's revival statute, L.1986 Ch. 682 § 4, *reprinted in* 1 McKinney's Session Laws of New York 1567 (1986).

Because jurisdiction is based on diversity of citizenship, we apply New York law, including New York conflict-of-laws rules. *Klaxon Co. v. Stentor Electric Mfg. Co.* 313 U.S. 487, 61 S.Ct. 1020, 85 L.Ed. 1477 (1941). Under New York conflict rules, New York applies its own statutes of limitations to lawsuits brought within the state regardless of the location of the facts that gave rise to the lawsuit. *Martin v. Julius Dierck Equipment Co.*, 43 N.Y.2d 583, 403 N.Y.S.2d 185, 374 N.E.2d 97 (1978).

The feature of New York's statutes of limitations with which we are concerned here is the so-called borrowing statute, which provides:

> "An action based upon a cause of action accruing without the state cannot be commenced after the expiration of the time limited by the laws of either the state or the place without the state where the cause of action accrued, except that where the cause of action accrued in favor of a resident of the state the time limited by the laws of the state shall apply."

NYCPLR § 202 (McKinney 1972 & Supp.1988). In other words, an Arizona resident, like plaintiff, will be subject to the Arizona statute of limitations if her cause of action accrued outside of New York and if defendants were subject to personal jurisdiction at the time. *Stafford v. International Harvester Co.*, 668 F.2d 142 (2d Cir.1981).

The meaning of "accrued" as used in the borrowing statute differs from its meaning in the context of statutes of limitation generally. For several years, the term has been the subject of considerable conflict-of-laws litigation in New York State and federal courts: should "accrual" be determined according to the traditional "place of injury" test or according to the modern "grouping of contacts" test?

The New York Court of Appeals has not ruled on this question and, indeed, has declined to express its opinion on the issue when presented with an opportunity. *Martin v. Julius Dierck Equipment Co., supra.* Absent such controlling authority, we are required to "estimate" what the New York Court of Appeals would do.

I conclude that the traditional rule applies. The borrowing statute has remained relatively untouched by the conflict-of-laws reform of *Babcock v. Jackson*, 12 N.Y.2d 473 240 N.Y.S.2d 743, 191 N.E.2d 279 (1963), and its progeny. Only one appellate division case has applied the so-called "modern" method to the borrowing statute, *Martin v. Julius Dierck Equipment Co.*, 52 A.D.2d 463, 384 N.Y.S.2d 479 (2d Dep't 1976); yet, the New York Court of Appeals, affirming the case on other grounds, explicitly refrained from endorsing the appellate division's method. *Martin, supra,* 43 N.Y.2d 583, 403 N.Y.S.2d 185, 374 N.E.2d 97.

On the other hand, endorsing the traditional rule in this context are another appellate division case, *Myers v. Dunlop Tire & Rubber Corp.*, 40 A.D.2d 599, 335 N.Y.S.2d 961 (1st Dep't 1972), and a preponderance of the federal authority. *See, e.g., Sack v. Low,* 478 F.2d 360 (2d Cir.1973); *Arneil v. Ramsey,* 550 F.2d 774 (2d Cir.1977); *Bache Halsey Stuart, Inc. v. Namm,* 446 F.Supp. 692 (S.D.N.Y.1978); *Stafford v. International Harvester Co., supra,* 668 F.2d at 150. . . .

> "Nor are we persuaded by arguments characterizing the 'place of injury' rule as 'mechanical.' The New York courts themselves recognized that the scope of *Babcock* is not unlimited.
>
> 'What the *Babcock* case . . . taught and what modern day commentators largely agree is that *lex loci delictus* is unsoundly applied if it is done indiscriminately and without exception. It is still true, however, that *lex loci delictus* is the normal rule.' "
>
> *Arneil, supra,* 550 F.2d at 780, *quoting Neumeier v. Kuehner,* 31 N.Y.2d 121, 131, 335 N.Y.S.2d 64, 286 N.E.2d 454 (1972).

Applying the traditional rule, the "place of injury" is "the state where the last event necessary to make an actor liable for an alleged tort takes place." *Conklin v. Canadian-Colonial Airways, Inc.,* 266 N.Y. 244, 248, 194 N.E. 692 (1935); Restatement (First) of Conflict of Laws § 377.

It seems clear that, where slowly developing personal injury claims such as this one are concerned, this "last event" is the fact of plaintiff's becoming ill. It is becoming ill that supplies the final element of a negligence or strict liability action and entitles plaintiff to sue. The "last event" is not necessarily plaintiff's discovery of his illness; so to hold would be to confuse the beginning of plaintiff's cause of action with the beginning of its end, i.e., with the starting of the statute of limitations. In support of looking to the time and place of illness rather than to discovery, Comments 1 and 2 to § 377 of the Restatement (First) of Conflict of Laws, explains the "last event" as follows:

> "1. Except in the case of harm from poison, when a person sustains bodily harm, the place of wrong is the place where the harmful force takes effect upon the body.
>
> "2. Where a person causes another voluntarily to take a deleterious substance which takes effect within the body, the place of wrong is where the deleterious substance takes effect and not where it is administered."

The illness/discovery distinction comports with the common sense and of the plain meaning of the phrase in question: "place of injury.". . .

Applying this reading of the traditional rules first to the personal injury claim before us, summary judgment must be denied. Decedent Lyon worked as an insulator in New York for some thirteen years, and plaintiff testified that decedent had a tendency to cough and get easily winded in the "early '70's" (while he still lived in New York). In the face of facts such as these, I cannot conclude as a matter of law that decedent became ill after he left New York.

The same analysis governs the wrongful death claim under the traditional rules. "The law of the place where the wrong causing death occurred governs the right of action for death." *Baldwin v. Powell*, 294 N.Y. 130, 132, 61 N.E.2d 412 (1945), *quoting* Restatement (First) of Conflict of Laws § 391. *See also* Comment b to § 391: "It is in the law of the place of wrong (see § 377), and not that of the place where the defendant's conduct occurs or the place of death, which governs the right." Here, too, summary judgment must be denied because the facts present a triable issue as to where the underlying injury occurred.

The traditional rule is often criticized for tending to highlight fortuitous circumstances, but that is not the case here. Plaintiff was exposed to asbestos in New York for thirteen years; it is his having moved away from New York that is fortuitous, and it would be inappropriate for the case to turn on that fact. Indeed, on a more general level, on issues such as the borrowing statute that concern the initial propriety of bringing suit, the place-of-injury rule avoids creating a trap for the unwary. It protects the as-yet unadvised plaintiff's common-sense notion that he can sue under the law of the place he was injured.

Because plaintiff's causes of action did not as a matter of law "accrue without the state," the borrowing statute is not yet applicable, if at all. Accordingly, I do not reach the issue of whether defendants were subject to personal jurisdiction in Arizona.

For the reasons stated above, defendants' motions for summary judgment are denied.

If plaintiff had not started wheezing until he got to Arizona, it would appear that under New York's borrowing statute Arizona's shorter statute of limitations would apply even if the plaintiff had most or all of his exposure to asbestos in New York. Had New York not been bound by the borrowing statute and used interest analysis, it would most probably have applied New York law.

Professor Symeonides, in his Annual Survey of American Conflicts Law, 60 Am. J. of Comparative Law 340 (2012), suggests that American courts follow one of four approaches to statute of limitations conflicts. The first is exemplified by the *Joint Eastern* case, *supra*. Statutes of limitations are treated as procedural and thus apply forum law unless the state has a borrowing statute or some other judicially engrafted exception. Symeonides finds that a majority of states follow this view. A second approach is that espoused by *Heavner v. Uniroyal, supra*. Symeonides reads *Heavner* to say that statutes of limitations are to be analyzed under the same conflict analysis as other issues in the case. We question whether *Heavner* can be read so broadly. However, it seems rather clear from *Gantes v. Kason Corp.* (discussed in *Rowe, supra*) 679 A.2d 106 (N.J. 1996) that New Jersey applies to statute of limitations the same analysis that it applies to any other choice of law issue. Eight states appear to follow this approach. Yet another approach is set forth in the Uniform Conflict of Law-Limitations Act (1982), which treats statutes of limitations as substantive and ties statutes of limitations to the choice of substantive law that otherwise governs the case. Seven states have enacted the Uniform Act. Finally, seven states follow Restatement section 142, *supra,* that ties the resolution of statute of limitation actions to the flexible consideration set forth in section 6. However, note that section 142 presumes that a state will generally apply its shorter statute of limitations and will apply its own longer statute of limitations unless the forum has no substantial interest in doing so and the claim would be barred by the statute of limitations of a state that has a "more significant interest to the parties and the occurrence."

A host of other issues raise the procedural-substantive problem, including burdens of proof, privileged communications, damages, and direct action statutes. For discussion of these issues, see Russell J. Weintraub, Commentary on the Conflict of Laws (5th ed. 2006).

4. STATUTORY SOLUTIONS

Those who are disillusioned with the Second Restatement or the *Neumeier* rules might consider whether a comprehensive choice of law statute might be the solution to the choice of law quagmire. Professor Symeon Symeonides authored a statute that is now the law in Oregon. In an article entitled *Oregon's New Choice of Law Codification for Torts Conflicts: An Exegesis*, 88 Or. L. Rev. 963 (2009), Professor Symeonides describes at great length why he made the choices that are reflected in the statute. We set out below some provisions of the statute. How would the torts cases in this Chapter have been decided if the Oregon statute applied?

CLAIMS GOVERNED BY OREGON LAW

. . . Oregon law governs noncontractual claims in the following actions:

(1) Actions in which, after the events giving rise to the dispute, the parties agree to the application of Oregon law.

(2) Actions in which none of the parties raises the issue of applicability of foreign law.

(3) Actions in which the party or parties who rely on foreign law fail to assist the court in establishing the relevant provisions of foreign law after being requested by the court to do so.

(4) Actions filed against a public body of the State of Oregon, unless the application of Oregon law is waived by a person authorized by Oregon law to make the waiver on behalf of the public body.

(5) Actions against an owner, lessor or possessor of land, buildings or other real property situated in Oregon that seek to recover for, or to prevent, injury on that property and arising out of conduct that occurs in Oregon.

(6) Actions between an employer and an employee who is primarily employed in Oregon that arise out of an injury that occurs in Oregon.

(7) Actions for professional malpractice arising from services rendered entirely in Oregon by personnel licensed to perform those services under Oregon law. [2009 c.451 § 6]

OR. REV. STAT. § 31.872

PRODUCT LIABILITY CIVIL ACTIONS. (1) Notwithstanding ORS 31.875 and 31.878, Oregon law applies to product liability civil actions, as defined in ORS 30.900, if:

(a) The injured person was domiciled in Oregon and the injury occurred in Oregon, or

(b) The injured person was domiciled in Oregon or the injury occurred in Oregon, and the product:

(A) Was manufactured or produced in Oregon; or

(B) Was delivered when new for use or consumption in Oregon.

(2) Subsection (1) of this section does not apply to a product liability civil action if a defendant demonstrates that the use in Oregon of the product that caused the injury could not have been foreseen and that none of the defendant's products of the same type were available in Oregon in the ordinary course of trade at the time of the injury.

(3) If a party demonstrates that the application of the law of a state other than Oregon to a disputed issue is substantially more appropriate under the principles of ORS 31.878, that issue shall be governed by the law of the other state.

(4) All noncontractual claims or issues in product liability civil actions not provided for or not disposed of under this section are governed by the law of the state determined under ORS 31.878 [2009 c. 451 § 7]

OR. REV. STAT. § 31.875

GENERAL RULES. (1) Noncontractual claims between an injured person and the person whose conduct caused the injury are governed by the law of the state designated in this section.

(2)(a) If the injured person and the person whose conduct caused the injury were domiciled in the same state, the law of that state governs. However, the law of the state in which the injurious conduct occurred determines the standard of care by which the conduct is judged. If the injury occurred in a state other than the one in which the conduct occurred, the provisions of subsection (3)(c) of this section apply.

(b) For the purposes of this section, persons domiciled in different states shall be treated as if domiciled in the same state to the extent that laws of those states on the disputed issues would produce the same outcome.

(3) If the injured person and the person whose conduct caused the injury were domiciled in different states and the laws of those states on the disputed issues would produce a different outcome, the law of the state designated in this subsection governs.

(a) If both the injurious conduct and the resulting injury occurred in the same state, the law of that state governs if either the injured person or the person whose conduct caused the injury was domiciled in that state.

(b) If both the injurious conduct and the resulting injury occurred in a state other than the state in which either the injured person or the person whose conduct caused the injury were domiciled, the law of the state of conduct and injury governs. If a party demonstrates that, under the circumstances of the particular case, the application of that law to a disputed issue will not serve the objectives of that law, that issue will be governed by the law selected under ORS 31.878.

(c) If the injurious conduct occurred in one state and the resulting injury in another state, the law of the state of conduct governs. However, the law of the state of injury governs if:

(A) The activities of the person whose conduct caused the injury were such as to make foreseeable the occurrence of injury in that state; and

(B) The injured person formally requests the application of that state's law by a pleading or amended pleading. The request shall be deemed to encompass all claims and issues against that defendant.

(4) If a party demonstrates that application to a disputed issue of the law of a state other than the state designated by subsection (2) or (3) of this § is substantially more appropriate under the principles of ORS 31.878, that issue is governed by the law of the other state. [2009 c.451 § 8]

OR. REV. STAT. § 31.878

GENERAL AND RESIDUAL APPROACH. Except as provided in ORS 31.870, 31.872, 31.875 and 31.885, the rights and liabilities of the parties with regard to disputed issues in a noncontractual claim are governed by the law of the state whose contacts with the parties and the dispute and whose policies on the disputed issues make application of the state's law the most appropriate for those issues. The most appropriate law is determined by:

(1) Identifying the states that have a relevant contact with the dispute, such as the place of the injurious conduct, the place of the resulting injury, the domicile, habitual residence or pertinent place of business of each person, or the place in which the relationship between the parties was centered.

(2) Identifying the policies embodied in the laws of these states on the disputed issues; and

(3) Evaluating the relative strength and pertinence of these policies with due regard to:

(a) The policies of encouraging responsible conduct, deterring injurious conduct and providing adequate remedies for the conduct; and

(b) The needs and policies of the interstate and international systems, including the policy of minimizing adverse effects on strongly held policies of other states. [2009 c.451 § 9]

5. ANOTHER LOOK AT TORT CONFLICTS IN NEW YORK

This chapter contains several New York cases that are not only of great importance in New York but have also had substantial influence on courts throughout the country: *Babcock v. Jackson, Tooker v. Lopez, Schultz v. Boy Scouts of America, Inc., Cooney v. Osgood Machinery, Inc.* The rules set out in *Neumeier v. Kuehner* have been thoroughly discussed in Judge Fuld's concurring opinion in *Tooker v. Lopez.* Here is one more New York case—*Edwards v. Erie Coach Lines.* Although we have already made mention of *Edwards,* we present it now for two reasons: (1) It is the most recent pronouncement of the New York Court of Appeals and (2) it demonstrates the continued dominance of the *Neumeier* rules.

EDWARDS V. ERIE COACH LINES COMPANY
952 N.E.2d 1033 (N.Y. 2011)

READ, J.

Near Geneseo, New York on January 19, 2005 a charter bus carrying members of an Ontario women's hockey team plowed into the rear end of a tractor-trailer parked on the shoulder of the highway. Three bus passengers and the tractor-trailer's driver died; several bus passengers were seriously hurt. We are called upon to decide the choice-of-law issue presented by these six lawsuits, which were brought to recover damages for wrongful death and/or personal injuries.

I.

Nearly a half-century ago, in *Babcock v. Jackson*, 12 N.Y.2d 473, 240 N.Y.S.2d 743, 191 N.E.2d 279 (1963), we abandoned what had long been our choice-of-law rule whereby the law of the place of the tort invariably governed. . . .

To "accommodat[e] the competing interests in tort cases with multi-State contacts," we adopted the "center of gravity" or "grouping of contacts" approach, which gave the "controlling effect to the law of the jurisdiction which, because of its relationship or contact with the occurrence or the parties ha[d] the greatest concern with the specific issue raised in the litigation". . . .

Over time, the "grouping of contacts" approach put into place by *Babcock* evolved into a more explicit "interest analysis." This method of deciding choice-of-law issues "reject[ed] a quantitative grouping of contacts" because "[c]ontacts obtain significance only to the extent that they relate to the policies and purposes sought to be vindicated by the conflicting laws". . . .

We refined our "interest analysis" so as "to assure a greater degree of predictability and uniformity" in *Neumeier v. Kuehner*, 31 N.Y.2d 121, 127, 335 N.Y.S.2d 64, 286 N.E.2d 454 (1972), a case where a domiciliary of Ontario was killed when the automobile in which he was a passenger collided with a train in Ontario. The vehicle was owned and driven by a resident of New York, who was also killed in the accident. The passenger's wife and administratrix, a citizen of Canada and a domiciliary of Ontario, brought an action for wrongful death in New York against the driver's estate and the railway company, both of which interposed affirmative defenses involving the Ontario guest statute. The wife, asserting that the Ontario statute was unavailable, moved to dismiss the affirmative defenses, and Supreme Court denied the motion (63 Misc.2d 766, 313 N.Y.S.2d 468 [1970]). The Appellate Division reversed (37 A.D.2d 70, 322 N.Y.S.2d 867 [1971]), and asked us if its order was properly made. We answered, "No."

Neumeier set up a three-rule framework for resolving choice of law in conflicts settings involving guest statutes, which by definition allocate losses after the tort occurs rather than regulate primary conduct. Under the first *Neumeier* rule, when the driver and passenger are domiciled in the same state, and the vehicle is registered there, the law of their shared jurisdiction controls (31 N.Y.2d at 128, 335 N.Y.S.2d 64, 286 N.E.2d 454).

The second rule addresses the situation where the driver and the passenger are domiciled in different states, and the law of the place where the accident occurred favors its domiciliary. When the driver's conduct occurs in the state where he is domiciled, which would not impose liability that state's law applies. Conversely, if the law of the place where the accident occurred permits the injured passenger to recover, then the driver, "in the absence of special circumstances," may not interpose a conflicting law of his state as a defense (*id.*; *see also Cooney*, 81 N.Y.2d at 73, 595 N.Y.S.2d 919, 612 N.E.2d 277 ["In essence, . . . the second *Neumeier* rule adopts a 'place of injury' test for true conflict guest statute cases"]).

"In other situations, when the passenger and the driver are domiciled in different states, the rule is necessarily less categorical" (31 N.Y.2d at 128, 335 N.Y.S.2d 64, 286 N.E.2d 454). Thus, under the third *Neumeier* rule, the law of the state where the accident occurred governs unless "it can be shown that displacing that normally applicable rule will advance the relevant substantive law purposes without impairing the smooth working of the multi-state system or producing great uncertainty for litigants" (*id.*).

Since the passenger in *Neumeier* was domiciled in Ontario, where the guest statute did not allow recovery, and the driver in New York, the third rule—the law of the place of the tort (i.e., Ontario)—would normally control. We saw no reason to apply the third rule's proviso since the wife "failed to show that [New York's] connection with the controversy was sufficient to justify displacing" lex loci delicti, the law of the place of the wrong. The wife did not show that ignoring Ontario's guest statute in a case "involv[ing] an Ontario-domiciled guest at the expense of a New Yorker . . . further[ed] the substantive law purposes of New York"; and "failure to apply Ontario's law would impair . . . the smooth working of the multi-state system [and] produce great uncertainty for litigants by sanctioning forum shopping and thereby allowing a party to select a forum [countenancing] a larger recovery than [that party's] own domicile" (*id.* [internal quotation marks omitted]).

We have routinely applied the *Neumeier* framework to conflicts in loss-allocation situations not involving guest statutes. . . .

[The court discusses Schultz v. Boy Scouts of America]

II.

The charter bus's driver (Ryan A. Comfort), his employer (Erie Coach Lines Company), and the company that leased the bus (Trentway-Wagar, Inc.) are Ontario domiciliaries, as are (or were) all the injured and deceased passengers. The tractor-trailer driver (Ernest Zeiset) was a Pennsylvania domiciliary, as are his employer (Joseph French, doing business as J & J Trucking) and the companies that hired the trailer (Verdelli Farms, Inc. and VF. Transportation, Inc.). The injured passengers and the representatives of those who died (collectively, plaintiffs) filed multiple wrongful death and personal injury lawsuits in Supreme Court.

These split-domicile lawsuits presented an obvious choice-of-law issue because Ontario caps noneconomic damages where negligence causes catastrophic personal injury, while New York does not cap such damages in a no-fault case involving serious injury. Following extensive discovery, Erie Coach, Trentway and Comfort (collectively, the bus defendants) and J & J Trucking, the administratrix of Zeiset's estate, Verdelli Farms and V.F. Transportation (collectively, the trailer defendants) moved for orders from Supreme Court determining that, under New York's choice-of-law principles, Ontario law applied to "all loss allocation issues" in these cases.

On March 23, 2009, Supreme Court granted both motions, noting that the Supreme Court of Canada had capped noneconomic damages at CDN $100,000 in 1978 dollars, which was then equivalent to U.S. $310,000. In reaching its decisions, the court concluded that "[p]roper analysis" began with *Neumeier*. Citing the third *Neumeier* rule, the judge stated, without elaboration, that "[a]pplying Ontario loss allocation laws [would] not impair the smooth working of the multi-state system, and [would] advance the relevant substantive law purposes of the jurisdiction having the most significant connections to the allocation of loss"; and that Ontario "clearly [had] the predominant interest[ ] in applying its loss allocation laws to its citizens, whereas New York [had] no such interest.". . .

The trial of these cases was bifurcated, and, during the course of the jury trial on liability, the parties reached a settlement of that issue. In the stipulation of settlement, placed on the record on June 17, 2009, the bus defendants agreed to 90% and the trailer defendants to 10% liability. Meanwhile, plaintiffs had appealed Supreme Court's orders determining that Ontario law would govern any award of noneconomic damages to be made at a damages trial. The Appellate Division affirmed. . . .

Here, the Ontario cap controls any award of noneconomic damages against the bus defendants because they share an Ontario domicile with plaintiffs. We described the relevant choice-of-law principle and its rationale in *Cooney*:

"Under the first *Neumeier* rule, when [the plaintiff and the defendant] share a common domicile, that law should control. Indeed, when both parties are from the same jurisdiction, there is often little reason to apply another jurisdiction's loss allocation rules. The domiciliary jurisdiction, which has weighed the competing considerations underlying the loss allocation rule at issue, has the greater 'interest in enforcing the decisions of both parties to accept both the benefits and the burdens of identifying with that jurisdiction and to submit themselves to its authority' . . . Moreover, this rule reduces opportunities for forum shopping because the same law will apply whether the suit is brought in the locus jurisdiction or in the common domicile, the two most likely forums" (81 N.Y.2d at 73, 595 N.Y.S.2d 919, 612 N.E.2d 277, quoting *Schultz*, 65 N.Y.2d at 198, 491 N.Y.S.2d 90, 480 N.E.2d 679).

We had earlier made the same point at least as forcefully in *Schultz*, where we stressed that "the locus jurisdiction has *at best a minimal interest* in determining the right of recovery or the extent of the remedy in an action by a foreign domiciliary for injuries resulting from the conduct of a codomiciliary that was tortious under the laws of both jurisdictions" (65 N.Y.2d at 198, 491 N.Y.S.2d 90, 480 N.E.2d 679 [emphasis added]). . . .

In sum, Ontario has weighed the interests of tortfeasors and their victims in cases of catastrophic personal injury, and has elected to safeguard its domiciliaries from large awards for nonpecuniary damages. In lawsuits brought in New York by Ontario-domiciled plaintiffs against Ontario-domiciled defendants, New York courts should respect Ontario's decision, which differs from but certainly does not offend New York's public policy (*see Schultz*, 65 N.Y.2d at 202, 491 N.Y.S.2d 90, 480 N.E.2d 679 [emphasizing the "heavy burden" borne by a party seeking to show that a foreign law contravenes New York public policy]).

Finally, we look to the third *Neumeier* rule to decide whether the Ontario cap controls with respect to the trailer defendants. Critically, the third rule establishes the place of the tort—here, New York—as the "normally applicable" choice in a conflicts situation such as this one, where the domicile of plaintiffs, the domicile of the trailer defendants and the place of the tort are different. . . .

The trailer defendants contend that *Schultz* controls, meaning that their situation is comparable to that of the Franciscan Brothers, and so the law of New York should not govern, even though the accident occurred there. We do not agree. While New York employs "interest analysis" rather than "grouping of contacts," the number and intensity of contacts is relevant when considering whether to deviate from lex loci delicti under the third *Neumeier* rule i.e., whether even to analyze if displacing this "normally applicable" choice would "advance the relevant substantive law purposes without impairing the smooth working of the multi-state system or producing great uncertainty for litigants" (*Neumeier*, 31 N.Y.2d at 128, 335 N.Y.S.2d 64, 286 N.E.2d 454).

In *Schultz*, New Jersey was the state where the Franciscan Brothers supplied teachers for a New Jersey school, where some of the acts of sexual abuse allegedly took place, where one of the boys committed suicide, where the two boys allegedly suffered from and were treated for psychological injuries, where the Franciscan Brothers were said to have hired and failed to fire the brother. Under these circumstances, there was every reason to evaluate, under the proviso to the third *Neumeier* rule, whether New Jersey law should displace New York law with respect to the negligent hiring and supervision claim asserted against the Franciscan Brothers in the plaintiffs' lawsuit. Here, by contrast, there was no cause to contemplate a jurisdiction other than New York, the place where the conduct causing injuries and the injuries themselves occurred. The trailer defendants did not ask Supreme Court to consider the law of their domicile, Pennsylvania, and they had no contacts whatsoever with Ontario other than the happenstance that plaintiffs and the bus defendants were domiciled there.

Accordingly, the orders in these cases should be modified, without costs, in accordance with this opinion and as so modified, affirmed, and the certified questions answered in the negative.

CIPARICK, J. (dissenting in part).

Because I believe that a single analysis pursuant to *Neumeier v. Kuehner*, 31 N.Y.2d 121, 335 N.Y.S.2d 64, 286 N.E.2d 454 (1972) should be applied where nondomiciliary defendants are jointly and severally liable to nondomiciliary plaintiffs in a tort action arising out of a single incident within the State of New York, and that under such an analysis New York law should apply to all defendants for purposes of uniformity and predictability, I respectfully dissent. . . .

While the facts in *Schultz* lent themselves to a separate analysis for each defendant, the facts in this case do not justify such an analysis. The plaintiffs in *Schultz* alleged that the two defendants, the Boy Scouts of America and the Brothers of the Poor of St. Francis, had each negligently hired and supervised the same sexually abusive employee. The alleged sexual abuse occurred while the plaintiffs' sons were at a Boy Scout camp in New York and continued at a school in New Jersey. The tortious activities in *Schultz* took place over varied periods of time and in different locations. Moreover, there was no relationship between the defendants' actions other than the fact that they employed the same alleged bad actor. Because the torts were distinct acts occurring at different times, it was appropriate for us to perform a separate choice-of-law analysis.

In contrast, in the instant case, the causes of action arise from a single incident in New York—the collision of the bus into the parked tractor-trailer—and the liability of the defendants is interrelated (*see King v. Car Rentals, Inc.*, 29 A.D.3d 205, 213, 813 N.Y.S.2d 448 [2d Dept.2006] ["(b)ecause the liability of all of the defendants here is thus interrelated, the application of the laws of different jurisdictions to the several defendants may lead to unanticipated complications as potentially inconsistent law is applied"]).

Furthermore, a separate *Neumeier* analysis for differently domiciled defendants creates additional unpredictability and lack of uniformity in litigation that arises from a single incident. The purpose of the *Neumeier* rules is to "assure a greater degree of predictability and uniformity, on the basis of our present knowledge and experience". Applying a single

Neumeier analysis to jointly and severally liable defendants and having them subject to the same laws would further the goals of predictability and uniformity. In fact, this case illustrates the potential for grossly inequitable results when different laws are applied to defendants who are jointly and severally liable. Here, during a jury trial on liability, defendants entered into a stipulation whereby they agreed that they are 100% jointly and severally liable to plaintiffs and further agreed to apportion such liability between themselves at 90% to the bus defendants and the remaining 10% to the tractor-trailer defendants. The majority allows for a situation whereby the tractor-trailer defendants may end up paying more than the bus defendants because of the cap applied on noneconomic tort awards by Ontario—a patently absurd result. Therefore, to further the goal of predictability and uniformity, this matter should be analyzed under a single *Neumeier* analysis.

In analyzing this matter under a single *Neumeier* analysis, it is clear that, because plaintiffs and defendants are differently domiciled, the law of the site of the tort—here New York—should apply as set forth in the third *Neumeier* rule. Moreover, the exception to the third *Neumeier* rule does not apply to these facts. . . .

Thus, in determining which forum has the greatest interest in this litigation, it is clear that it is New York. Not only does New York have a strong interest in regulating the conduct of commercial vehicles on its highways, it also has an even stronger interest in having commercial vehicles that use its highways maintain insurance to compensate victims of torts committed by said vehicles. In contrast, Ontario's primary interest in having its law applied and capping nonpecuniary losses is to keep motor vehicle insurance costs low (*see Arnold v. Teno*, [1978] 2 SCR 287 ¶ 109). That interest, however, need not extend to commercial vehicles operating outside of Ontario and subject to the loss-allocation laws of those states.

Finally, because New York is "the only State with which [all] parties have purposefully associated themselves" (*Cooney*, 81 N.Y.2d at 74, 595 N.Y.S.2d 919, 612 N.E.2d 277) and availed themselves of New York highways for profit and tourism, applying New York law is entirely appropriate in this matter.

Accordingly, I would reverse the order of the Appellate Division.

To round out the New York experience in tort cases, we call your attention to *Padula v. Lilarn Properties Corp.*, 644 N.E.2d 1001 (N.Y 1994). In that case, the plaintiff was a New York resident and the defendant was a New York corporation that owned property in Massachusetts. Plaintiff fell from a scaffold while working on a construction project in Massachusetts. Plaintiff brought an action alleging that the owner of the property was strictly liable for violating regulations under the New York Labor Law. The court was forced to confront the issue of whether the New York Labor Law regulations were loss allocating or conduct regulating. If they were loss allocating, the *Neumeier* rules would presumably apply. If, on the other hand, they were conduct regulating, then the law of the place in which the conduct took place would govern. The court held that the laws governing construction were primarily conduct-regulating and that Massachusetts law would therefore govern. Thus, the owner of the building under construction would not be held liable without proof of fault on its part.

The move to a more territorial view of conflicts in New York after *Cooney* and *Padula* is, in the authors' opinion, quite clear. *See also* Borchers, *The Return of Territoriality to New York's Conflicts Law*, 58 Alb. L. Rev. 775 (1996).

---

6.   THE REMNANTS OF LEX LOCI

BAILEY V. COTTRELL, INC.
721 S.E.2d 571 (Ga. Ct. App. 2011)

ADAMS, JUDGE.

In this products liability case, appellants Steve Bailey and Laura Bailey appeal the trial court's order granting summary judgment under Indiana law to Cottrell, Inc. in the Baileys' suit to recover for injuries Steve Bailey sustained when he fell from the top level of a car-hauler/tractor-trailer rig. Because we find that the trial court erred in failing to apply Georgia law to the Baileys' claims, we reverse.

At all pertinent times, the Baileys were residents of Missouri. Cottrell, Inc. is a Georgia corporation engaged in the design, development and manufacture of car hauling equipment. Steve Bailey worked as a driver for a car-hauling company, Jack Cooper Transport ("JCT"), out of Wentzville, Missouri. The accident at issue occurred in Indiana on October 28, 2005, while Steve Bailey was loading pickup trucks onto his assigned car-hauler, a 1998 Cottrell rig owned by JCT. After Bailey loaded an extended-cab pickup truck with a camper top onto an area called the "headramp," which is located on top of the tractor, he stepped out of the pickup to dismount from the headramp's upper level. Steve Bailey, who was wearing work gloves, stuck his right fingers into the top of the doorjamb above the rear door of the pickup, while closing the pickup's driver door with his left hand. As Steve Bailey closed the door, the air from inside the pickup blew against his right hand, dislodging his fingers. Losing his grip, he fell backward onto the parking lot surface below. Steve Bailey asserts that he sustained traumatic injuries in the fall that have left him disabled.

The Baileys allege that the car-hauler Steve Bailey was using was designed, manufactured and sold by Cottrell with inadequate space for maneuvering and with no fall prevention devices, such as safety chains or grab bars on the rig's upper level, despite the fact that Cottrell knew that drivers like Steve Bailey would be required to load and unload automobiles from that area. Cottrell counters that Steve Bailey had knowledge of these supposed defects in the rig, as well as the knowledge of the specific risks of falling, and that he understood, appreciated and assumed these risks. The trial court, applying Indiana law, found that Steve Bailey voluntarily assumed the risk of working on the upper level of the car hauler and granted Cottrell's motion for summary judgment. . . .

1.   The Baileys first argue that the trial court erred in applying Indiana law to their claims. Although the injury occurred in Indiana and the Baileys acknowledge that Georgia generally applies lex loci delecti (the law of the place where the tort was committed), they assert that the trial court should have applied the public policy exception to the general rule. The Baileys contend that Indiana law violates Georgia public policy in two respects: (1) Indiana law does not allow a strict liability claim for a product design defect with a risk-utility test, while Georgia does; and (2) Indiana law, as applied by the trial court, eliminated the voluntariness element for an assumption of risk defense, which they contend contravenes Georgia public policy.

In Georgia, "[u]nder lex loci delicti, tort cases are governed by the substantive law of the state where the tort or wrong occurred—in this case, [Indiana]." (Footnote omitted.) *Bagnell v. Ford Motor Co.,* 297 Ga.App. 835, 836(1), 678 S.E.2d 489 (2009). *See also Dowis v. Mud Slingers,* 279 Ga. 808, 816, 621 S.E.2d 413 (2005) (reaffirming lex loci delicti as the law in Georgia). But as the Baileys correctly note, Georgia recognizes a public policy exception to the rule of lex loci delicti.

> Even if an application [of the rule of lex loci delicti] renders the law of another state applicable, the forum, within constitutional limits, is not required to give the law of another state extra-territorial effect. That is only done as a matter of courtesy or comity, which will not be enforced if the law of the other state contravenes the public policy of the forum. See OCGA § 1–3–9; *Commercial Credit Plan v. Parker,* 152 Ga.App. 409, 263 S.E.2d 220 (1979).

(a) Georgia law recognizes a product liability claim based upon strict liability against "those actively involved in the design, specifications, or formulation of a defective final product or of a defective component part which failed during use of a product and caused injury." (Citation omitted.) *Davenport v. Cummins Alabama, Inc.,* 284 Ga.App. 666, 671(1), 644 S.E.2d 503 (2007). See OCGA § 51–1–11. Indiana law, however, does not recognize a strict liability claim for design defects:

> The Indiana Product Liability Act generally imposes strict liability for physical harm caused by a product in an unreasonably dangerous defective condition. Ind. Code § 34–20–2–1. For actions

based on an alleged product design defect, however, the Act departs from strict liability and specifies a different standard of proof: "(T)he party making the claim must establish that the manufacturer or seller failed to exercise reasonable care under the circumstances in designing the product." Ind.Code § 34–20–2–2. . . .

Although Indiana recognizes strict liability for manufacturing claims, its failure to recognize a strict liability claim for design defects presents a substantive legal difference. A claim of negligence in an Indiana defective design product liability case differs from a strict liability claim in Georgia in that Georgia has specifically adopted the risk-utility test for determining strict liability as to such claims, while the State of Indiana has specifically rejected this test in favor of a common law negligence analysis. . . . This is not a distinction without a difference. The application of the risk-utility test in Georgia allows the factfinder to consider a number of factors, *Banks,* 264 Ga. at 736(1), n. 6, 450 S.E.2d 671, an approach that the Supreme Court of Indiana has rejected. Although the Supreme Court of Georgia recognized in *Banks* that the risk-utility analysis for design defect claims overlaps to a certain extent with a negligence analysis, the Court also stated that "we cannot agree that the use of negligence principles to determine whether the design of a product was 'defective' necessarily obliterates under every conceivable factual scenario the distinction Georgia law has long recognized between negligence and strict liability theories of liability." *Id.* at 735, n. 3, 450 S.E.2d 671. And since *Banks,* this Court has reiterated that Georgia's strict liability law focuses "not on whether the manufacturer negligently failed to use due care but on whether the marketed product was defective" and has "continued to honor" the distinction between negligence and strict liability for design defect claims. . . .

Indiana law and Georgia law are sufficiently dissimilar that applying Indiana law in this case would contravene the public policy of this State as expressed in OCGA § 51–1–11, and the Baileys are entitled to have Georgia law, including Georgia law regarding any defenses to such a claim, e.g., assumption of risk, applied to their claims against Cottrell. . . .

Judgment reversed.

BARNES, P.J., concurs.

BLACKWELL, J., concurs specially.

BLACKWELL, JUDGE, concurring specially.

As to whether Georgia or Indiana law applies, I am unconvinced that the law of the two states is so "radically dissimilar," that public policy compels the application of Georgia law in this case. Under Indiana law, a defective design claim requires an assessment of whether the manufacturer "exercise[d] reasonable care under the circumstances in designing the product." *TRW Vehicle Safety Systems, Inc. v. Moore*, 936 N.E.2d 201, 209(1) (Ind.2010). Under Georgia law, on the other hand, a defective design claim involves an assessment of whether the manufacturer "acted reasonably in choosing a particular product design, given the probability and seriousness of the risk posed by the design, the usefulness of the product in that condition, and the burden on the manufacturer to take the necessary steps to eliminate the risk." *Banks v. ICI Americas, Inc.*, 264 Ga. 732, 734(1), 450 S.E.2d 671 (1994). These standards do not seem "radically dissimilar" to me. Our Supreme Court has cautioned, of course, that the adoption of a reasonableness standard for defective design claims does not "*necessarily* obliterate[ ] under *every conceivable factual scenario* the distinction Georgia law has long recognized between negligence and strict liability theories of liability," *id.* at 735 n. 3 (1), 450 S.E.2d 671, (emphasis supplied), but neither the Baileys nor the majority persuades me that this case is one in which the differences, if any, between the Georgia reasonableness standard and the Indiana reasonableness standard are meaningful ones. At bottom, the conflict-of-laws analysis of the majority seems to rest mostly upon the fact that the Georgia courts sometimes speak of "strict liability" for defective design claims, notwithstanding that the Georgia standard for such claims is one of objective reasonableness. Accordingly, I am unconvinced that public policy requires the application of Georgia law in this case. . . .

———————

Law *is* public policy, so all differences in law from one jurisdiction to another are differences in public policy. But is it the function of the public policy limitation on applying the law of another state to prevent that law's application whenever it reflects a different policy? We think not. What would Judge Cardozo, the author of the *Loucks* opinion discussed at page 223, say about this case?

CHAPTER 4

CONTRACTS

∎ ∎ ∎

A. GOVERNING LAW IN THE ABSENCE OF CHOICE BY THE PARTIES

In Chapter 1, we read *Milliken v. Pratt* as an example of the traditional view of *lex loci contractus* for determining which jurisdiction's law governs a contract. In Chapter 3, we examined Brainerd Currie's critique of *Milliken*, as well as the more general formation of an alternative theory— interest analysis—for determining what law governs a dispute.

But even before the choice-of-law revolution, the traditional view was showing signs of weakness, eventually leading to a different view in a significant number of states as to how to determine the law governing a contract.

AUTEN V. AUTEN
124 N.E.2d 99 (N.Y. 1954)

FULD, JUDGE.

In this action to recover installments allegedly due for support and maintenance under a separation agreement executed in this state in 1933, the wife's complaint has been dismissed on motion for summary judgment, upon the ground that her institution of an action for separation in England constituted a repudiation and a rescission of the agreement under New York law. Determination of the appeal, involving as it does a question of conflict of laws, requires examination of the facts disclosed by the papers before us.

Married in England in 1917, Mr. and Mrs. Auten continued to live there with their two children until 1931. In that year, according to plaintiff, defendant deserted her, came to this country and, in the following year, obtained a Mexican divorce and proceeded to "marry" another woman. Unable to come to terms with the ocean between them, plaintiff made a trip to New York City to see and talk to defendant about adjustment of their differences. The outcome was the separation agreement of June, 1933, upon which the present action is predicated. It obligated the husband to pay to a trustee, for the "account of" the wife, who was to return to England, the sum of $50 a month for the support of herself and the children. In addition, the agreement provided that the parties were to continue to live

203

separate and apart, that neither should sue "in any action relating to their separation" and that the wife should not "cause any complaint to be lodged against * * * (the husband), in any jurisdiction, by reason of the said alleged divorce or remarriage."

Immediately after the agreement was signed, plaintiff returned to England, where she has since lived with her children, and it is alleged by her but disputed by defendant that the latter [the husband] is also domiciled in that country. Be that as it may, defendant failed to live up to his agreement, making but a few payments under it, with the result that plaintiff was left more or less destitute in England with the children. About a year after the agreement had been executed, in August of 1934, plaintiff filed a petition for separation in an English court, charging defendant with adultery. Defendant was served in New York with process in that suit on December 4, 1936, and, in July, 1938, an order was entered requiring defendant to pay alimony *pendente lite*. This English action which, we are told, never proceeded to trial was instituted upon advice of English counsel that it "was the only method" by which she "could collect money" from defendant; it was done, plaintiff expressly declares, to "enable" her "to enforce" the separation agreement, and not with any thought or intention of repudiating it.

The years passed, and in 1947, having realized nothing as a result of the English action and little by reason of the New York separation agreement, plaintiff brought the present suit to recover the sum of $26,564, which represents the amount allegedly due her under the agreement from January 1, 1935 to September 1, 1947.

In his answer, defendant admitted making the agreement, but, by way of a separate defense, one of several, claimed that plaintiff's institution of the separation suit in England operated as a repudiation of the agreement and effected a forfeiture of her right to any payments under it. Following a motion by the wife for summary judgment and a cross motion by the husband for like relief, the court at Special Term granted the husband's cross motion and dismissed the complaint. The Appellate Division affirmed, with leave to the wife, however, to serve an amended complaint, asserting any cause of action which accrued prior to the date of the commencement of the English suit. The ensuing judgment, dismissing all of the wife's claims which accrued subsequent to that date, is a final judgment of modification, and the wife's appeal therefrom is properly before us as of right. (Citations omitted).

Both of the courts below, concluding that New York law was to be applied, held that under such law plaintiff's commencement of the English action and the award of temporary alimony constituted a rescission and repudiation of the separation agreement, requiring dismissal of the complaint. Whether that is the law of this state, or whether something more must be shown to effect a repudiation of the agreement (citation omitted), need not detain us, since in our view it is the law of England, not that of New York which is here controlling.

Choosing the law to be applied to a contractual transaction with elements in different jurisdictions is a matter not free from difficulty. The New York decisions evidence a number of different approaches to the question. (Citation omitted).

Most of the cases rely upon the generally accepted rules that "All matters bearing upon the execution, the interpretation and the validity of contracts * * * are determined by the law of the place where the contract is made", while "all matters connected with its performance * * * are regulated by the law of the place where the contract, by its terms, is to be performed." [See, *e.g.*, Restatement, Conflict of Laws, §§ 332, 358.] What constitutes a breach of the contract and what circumstances excuse a breach are considered matters of performance, governable, within this rule, by the law of the place of performance. [See, *e.g.*, Restatement, Conflict of Laws, § 370.]

Many cases appear to treat these rules as conclusive. Others consider controlling the intention of the parties and treat the general rules merely as presumptions or guideposts, to be considered along with all the other circumstances. (Citations omitted). And still other decisions, including the most recent one in this court, have resorted to a method first employed to rationalize the results achieved by the courts in decided cases (citation omitted), which has come to be called the "center of gravity" or the "grouping of contacts" theory of the conflict of laws. Under this theory, the courts, instead of regarding as conclusive the parties' intention or the place of making or performance, lay emphasis rather upon the law of the place "which has the most significant contacts with the matter in dispute." (Citations omitted).

Although this "grouping of contacts" theory may, perhaps, afford less certainty and predictability than the rigid general rules, the merit of its approach is that it gives to the place "having the most interest in the problem" paramount control over the legal issues arising out of a particular factual context, thus allowing the forum to apply the policy of the jurisdiction "most intimately concerned with the outcome of [the] particular litigation." Moreover, by stressing the significant contacts, it enables the court, not only to reflect the relative interests of the several jurisdictions involved (citation omitted), but also to give effect to the probable intention of the parties and consideration to "whether one rule or the other produces the best practical result." (Citations omitted).

Turning to the case before us, examination of the respective contacts with New York and England compels the conclusion that it is English law which must be applied to determine the impact and effect to be given the wife's institution of the separation suit. It hardly needs stating that it is England which has all the truly significant contacts, while this state's sole nexus with the matter in dispute entirely fortuitous, at that is that it is the place where the agreement was made and where the trustee, to whom the moneys were in the first instance to be paid, had his office. The agreement effected a separation between British subjects, who had been married in England, had children there and lived there as a family for fourteen years. It involved a husband who, according to the papers before us had wilfully deserted and abandoned his wife and children in England and was in the United States, when the agreement was signed, merely on a temporary visa. And it concerned an English wife who came to this country at that time because it was the only way she could see her husband to discuss their differences. The sole purpose of her trip to New York was to get defendant to agree to the support of his family, and she returned to England immediately after the agreement was executed. While the moneys were to be paid through the medium of a New York trustee, such payments were "for account of" the wife and children, who, it was thoroughly understood, were to live in England. The agreement is instinct with that understanding; not only does it speak in terms of English currency in providing for payments to the wife, not only does it recite that the first payment be made to her "immediately before sailing for England," but it specifies that the husband may visit the children "if he should go to England."

In short, then, the agreement determined and fixed the marital responsibilities of an English husband and father and provided for the support and maintenance of the allegedly abandoned wife and children who were to remain in England. It merely substituted the arrangements arrived at by voluntary agreement of the parties for the duties and responsibilities of support that would otherwise attach by English law. There is no question that England has the greatest concern in prescribing and governing those obligations, and in securing to the wife and children essential support and maintenance. And the paramount interest of that country is not affected by the fact that the parties separate and provide for such support by a voluntary agreement. It is still England, as the jurisdiction of marital domicile and the place where the wife and children were to be, that has the greatest concern in defining and regulating the rights and duties existing under that agreement, and, specifically, in determining the circumstances that effect a termination or repudiation of the agreement.

Nor could the parties have expected or believed that any law other than England's would govern the effect of the wife's institution of a separation action. It is most unlikely that the wife could have intended to subject her rights under English law to the law of a jurisdiction several thousand miles distant, with which she had not the slightest familiarity. On the contrary, since it was known that she was returning to England to live both parties necessarily realized that any action which she took, whether in accordance with the agreement or in violation of it, would have to occur in England. If any thought was given to the matter at all, it was that the law of the place where she and the children would be should determine the effect of acts performed by her.

It is, perhaps, not inappropriate to note that, even if we were not to place our emphasis on the law of the place with the most significant contacts, but were instead simply to apply the rule that matters of performance and breach are governed by the law of the place of performance, the same result would follow. Whether or not there was a repudiation, essentially a form of breach (citations omitted), is also the be determined by the law of the place of performance (citations omitted), and that place, so far as the wife's performance is concerned, is England. Whatever she had to do under the agreement "live separate and apart from" her husband, "maintain, educate and support" the children and refrain from bringing "any action relating to (the) separation" was to be done in England. True, the husband's payments were to be made to a New York trustee for forwarding to plaintiff in England, but that is of no consequence in this case. It might be if the question before us involved the manner or effect of payment to the trustee, but that is not the problem; we are here concerned only with the effect of the wife's performance. (Citation omitted).

Since, then, the law of England must be applied, and since, at the very least, an issue exists as to whether the courts of that country treat the commencement of a separation action as a repudiation of an earlier-made separation agreement, summary judgment should not have been granted.[2]

As to defendant's further contention that, in any event, plaintiff's commencement of the English action amounted to a material breach of her covenant not to sue, barring recovery upon the agreement, we need but say that this question, too, must be governed by English law, and for the same reasons already set forth.

The judgment of the Appellate Division and that of Special Term insofar as they dismiss the complaint should be reversed, with costs in all courts, and the matter remitted for further proceedings in accordance with this opinion.

LEWIS, C. J., and CONWAY, DESMOND, DYE, FROESSEL and VAN VOORHIS, JJ., concur.

In *Matter of Allstate Insurance Co. (Stolarz)*, 613 N.E.2d 936 (N.Y. 1993) the Court of Appeals relied heavily on *Auten* in analyzing whether New Jersey law or New York law governed an insurance contract. Kathleen Stolarz and her husband were injured in a two car accident in New York.

---

[2] In point of fact, the English lawyers, whose affidavits have been submitted by plaintiff, unequivocally opine that the institution of a separation suit and the award of alimony pendente lite did not, under the law of England, constitute a repudiation of the separation agreement or bar the present action to recover amounts due under it.

Both were New York residents. The Stolarz car was leased by Kathleen's employer, Blue Cross/Blue Shield of New Jersey. A New Jersey insurance company insured the car under a policy issued to Blue Cross that was written to conform with New Jersey law. The insurer of the second car paid the Stolarzes $20,000, the liability limits of its policy. The policy issued to Blue Cross provided for uninsurance/underinsurance coverage of $35,000, but any amount paid to plaintiffs was to be deducted from that amount. Such a deduction was valid under New Jersey law but not, it was argued, under New York insurance contract law.

Initially, the Court of Appeals ruled that the deduction clause was enforceable as a matter of New York law. The court went on, however, to also conclude that, even if New York law would not enforce the clause, the issue is governed by New Jersey law, which would enforce it. The New York court, applying a grouping of contacts analysis, found that the contract "overwhelmingly centered on New Jersey" and, therefore, validated the deduction as set forth in the policy. Noting that New York applied interest analysis to tort conflicts the court said:

> By contrast [to torts], contract cases often involve only the *private* economic interests of the parties, and analysis of the public policy underlying the conflicting contract laws may be inappropriate to resolution of the dispute. It may even be difficult to identify competing "policies" at stake, because the laws may differ only slightly, and evolve through the incremental process of common-law adjudication as a response to the facts presented.

The court's reliance on *Auten* and the grouping of contacts approach seems to give interest analysis little weight in contract cases. But the court also said that in some contract cases there are significant state interests and when they are present they will be taken into account.

The mode of analysis that emerged from *Auten* and other, similar cases has been quite influential and has been adopted, in substantial part, by the Restatement (Second). Section 188 of the Restatement (Second) provides:

(1) The rights and duties of the parties with respect to an issue in contract are determined by the local law of the state which, with respect to that issue, has the most significant relationship to the transaction and the parties under the principles stated in § 6.

(2) In the absence of an effective choice of law by the parties (see § 187), the contacts to be taken into account in applying the principles of § 6 to determine the law applicable to an issue include:

(a) the place of contracting,

(b) the place of negotiation of the contract,

(c) the place of performance,

(d) the location of the subject matter of the contract, and

(e) the domicile, residence, nationality, place of incorporation and place of business of the parties.

These contacts are to be evaluated according to their relative importance with respect to the particular issue.

(3) If the place of negotiating the contract and the place of performance are in the same state, the local law of this state will usually be applied, except as otherwise provided in §§ 189–199 and 203.

The grouping of contacts set forth in *Auten* and Second Restatement are not identical. Whereas the former appears to count contacts and looks for the "center of gravity," the latter, by its reference to section 6, necessarily involves the evaluation of the contacts to determine whether they trigger state interests. For a sharp critique of the "center of gravity" approach, see Brainerd Currie, *Conflict, Crisis and Confusion in New York*, 1963 Duke L.J. 1, 38 (1963).

Yet, *Auten* and the Second Restatement have not convinced every state of the wisdom of their approaches. Consider the following view expressed by the Supreme Court of Florida (as well as a rejoinder from one justice of that court):

STURIANO V. BROOKS
523 So.2d 1126 (Fla. 1988)

[The Sturianos, lifelong residents of New York, purchased automobile insurance in New York six years prior to the accident that took the life of Vito Sturiano and injured Josephine Sturiano. After obtaining the insurance, the couple moved to Florida each year for the winter months. They did not notify the insurance company of this migration, and the insurance company had no way of knowing that such a move had taken place. Mrs. Sturiano brought an action against the estate of Mr. Suriano, alleging negligence on his part, and sought to recover the amount of his liability from the insurance company. Under Florida law, the insurance contract would allow such recovery, but under New York law, a spouse could not collect on such a claim unless the policy specifically provided for interspousal claims. A lower court certified to the Supreme Court of Florida the question of which states' law applied.]

KOGAN, J. . . .

Under the doctrine of *lex loci contractus*, it is clear that New York law must apply. That rule specifies that the law of the jurisdiction where the contract was executed should control. However, in recent years this doctrine has been criticized and, in several jurisdictions, discarded in favor of the more flexible "significant relationships" test [set out in Restatement (Second) of Conflict of Laws § 188, which the court recited].

* * *

Thus, under the Restatement view, and seemingly the trend of courts around the nation, the place the contract is executed is only one of five factors used in determining which jurisdiction's law should control.

Sturiano argues that in this modern, migratory society, choice of law rules must be flexible to allow courts to apply the laws which best accommodate the parties and the host jurisdiction. She contends that the archaic and inflexible rule of *lex loci contractus* does not address modern issues or problems in the area of conflict of laws. While it is true that *lex loci contractus* is an inflexible rule, we believe that this inflexibility is necessary to ensure stability in contract arrangements. When parties come to terms in an agreement, they do so with the implied acknowledgment that the laws of that jurisdiction will control absent some provision to the contrary. This benefits both parties, not merely an insurance company. The view espoused in the Restatement fails, in our opinion, to adequately provide security to the parties to a contract.

Although *lex loci contractus* is old, it is not yet outdated. The very reason Sturiano gives as support for discarding *lex loci contractus*, namely that we live in a migratory, transitory society, provides support for upholding that doctrine. Parties have a right to know what the agreement they have executed provides. To allow one party to modify the contract simply by moving to another state would substantially restrict the power to enter into valid, binding, and stable contracts. There can be no doubt that the parties to insurance contracts bargained and paid for the provisions in the agreement, including those provisions that apply the statutory law of that state.

We recognize that this Court has discarded the analogous doctrine of *lex loci delicti* with respect to tort actions and limitations of actions. However, we believe that the reasoning controlling those decisions does not apply in the instant case. With tort law, there is no agreement, no foreseen set of rules and statutes which the parties had recognized would control the litigation. In the case of an insurance contract, the parties enter into that contract with the acknowledgment that the laws of that jurisdiction control their actions. In essence, that jurisdiction's laws are incorporated by implication into the agreement. The parties to this contract did not bargain for Florida or any other state's laws to control. We must presume that the parties did bargain for, or at least expected, New York law to apply.

For these reasons, we answer the certified question concerning conflict of laws ["Does the *lex loci contractus* rule govern the rights and liabilities of the parties in determining the applicable law on an issue of insurance coverage?"] in the affirmative, limiting that answer to situations involving automobile insurance policies.

GRIMES, JUSTICE, concurring.

The more I read of it the more I tend to agree with Dean Prosser when he said that "[t]he realm of the conflict of laws is a dismal swamp, filled with quaking quagmires, and inhabited by learned but eccentric professors who theorize about mysterious matters in a strange and incomprehensible jargon. The ordinary court, or lawyer, is quite lost when engulfed and entangled in it."

The rule of *lex loci contractus* has been roundly criticized as mechanistic and unworkable in practice. It has seldom been applied to issues concerning the performance of a contract. While it is true that more states retain *lex loci contractus* than have abandoned it, perhaps this is so only because many of them have not addressed the issue in recent years. The emerging consensus, even in cases involving questions of contract validity, is to apply the most significant relationship test of section 188 of the Restatement (Second) of Conflict of Laws (1971).

In this complex area of law concerning which I claim no expertise, I am inclined toward the recommendations of the American Law Institute. Because contractual disputes arise in such a great variety of settings, rules of broad application cannot do justice to the various interests and expectations involved. While the application of the significant relationship test may be less certain, it reflects a more realistic standard by which a choice of laws may be made. Furthermore, I believe the majority's concern for predictability and the parties' right to know what the agreement provides is adequately taken into account by factors (d) (the protection of justified expectations) and (f) (certainty, predictability and uniformity of result) of section 6 of the Second Restatement which is made applicable to section 188.

I nevertheless agree with the result reached in the instant case because it would come out the same under the Restatement [because of section 193, which provides a special rule for contracts of fire, surety, or casualty[1]].

---

1. Which rule—*lex loci contractus* or the "significant relationships" (or "center of gravity") approach of *Auten* or the Second Restatement—is better for determining which law governs a contract that is the subject of litigation? Note

---

[1] Restatement (Second), Conflict of Laws, § 193 provides: "The validity of a contract of fire, surety or casualty insurance and the rights created thereby are determined by the local law of the state which the parties understood was to be the principal location of the insured risk during the term of the policy, unless with respect to the particular issue, some other state has a more significant relationship under the principles stated in § 6 to the transaction and the parties, in which event the local law of the other state will be applied."

that the "center of gravity" approach is not identical to the rule in the Second Restatement. How do they differ?

2.   Unlike the parties involved in a tort dispute, who tend to debate the applicable law issue only after the injury has occurred, the parties to a contract consider the costs and benefits of their transaction before entering into it. Which rule best serves the needs of parties considering entering into a contract that touches more than one state? If your answer to this question is different than your answer to Question 1, which conflict of laws rule should a state adopt?

As Question 2 suggests, parties to a transaction may have an interest in predictability and certainty as to the law governing their contract that is different than the general societal interest in determining the appropriate law to govern after a dispute arises (and after we know the nature of the dispute). The move away from *lex loci contractus* toward the approach of the Second Restatement is a move away from predictability and certainty. Can the parties to a contract do anything to bring more certainty to the situation? That is the subject of the materials below.

———————

B. DO THE PARTIES TO THE CONTRACT HAVE THE POWER TO CHOOSE THE GOVERNING LAW?

1. INTRODUCTION

Many of the cases in this book concern the determination of which jurisdiction's law governs a tort claim. Quite obviously, contracts are different from torts in many ways. One way that is of particular relevance to conflict of laws is that contracts are planned transactions, requiring the agreement of both parties, while torts are (with the exception of intentional torts) unplanned and are not the product of agreement between the tortfeasor and victim. Inasmuch as the parties to a contract, with relatively few limits, have the "freedom of contract" to choose the bulk of the rules that will govern their relationship, should that power extend to the ability to choose, by agreement, the jurisdiction whose law will govern the contract?

To Professor Joseph H. Beale, the Reporter for the First Restatement of Conflict of Laws, the suggestion that parties should have that power was heretical:

> The fundamental objection to [the suggestion that parties could have the power to choose the law governing their contract] in point of theory is that it involves permission to the parties to do a legislative act. It practically makes a legislative body of any two persons who choose to get together and contract. The adoption of a rule to determine which of several systems of law shall govern a

given transaction is in itself an act of the law. . . . So in the case of the adoption of a law to govern the nature and obligation of a contract, it is entirely possible from the point of view of any one state that the law of that state or of some other state should be applied to the determination of the question; but if the law of that state is not applied, it is a result of the sovereign will of the state which controls the contract. Now, if it is said that this is to be left to the will of the parties to determine, that gives to the parties what is in truth the power of legislation so far as their agreement is concerned. The meaning of the suggestion, in short, is that since the parties can adopt any foreign law at their pleasure to govern their act, that at their will they can free themselves from the power of the law which would otherwise apply to their acts.[2]

Professor Beale's stature as Reporter notwithstanding, the path that the law has taken over the last century is one that increasingly repudiates his views on this subject.

Before we examine this journey from a world in which conflict of laws rules always determine which law governs a contract to one in which the parties have substantial autonomy to choose the governing law, it may be helpful to distinguish a few situations from each other:

1. The parties to a contract for the shipment of goods have insufficient time to bargain and reach agreement with respect to the details of their relationship (*e.g.*, duties, risk of loss, etc.). It is their understanding, however, that the law of Fredonia addresses these issues in some detail and in a manner that is relatively neutral in the sense that it favors neither the customer nor the shipping company. One party suggests taking the rules in effect in Fredonia and writing them into the contract. The other party, however, suggests simply stating in the contract that the duties of the parties thereunder are governed by the law of Fredonia. The first party accepts this suggestion, and the contract is written in accordance with that suggestion. Later, a dispute arises between the parties, and the "default" rules (*i.e.*, the rules that govern unless the parties have provided different rules in their contract) of State A, whose law would govern under the principles studied in part A of this chapter, are different than the rules under the law of Fredonia. Nothing in the law of State A, however, would prevent the parties from agreeing to terms that are identical to those provided by the law of Fredonia.

---

[2]   Joseph H. Beale, *What Law Governs the Validity of a Contract?*, 23 Harv. L. Rev. 260, 260–61 (1910).

2. One party to a transaction claims that it is not binding as a contract (perhaps, for example, because of failure to satisfy a statute of frauds or because the party's agreement was obtained by duress). Under the law of State A, whose law would govern under the principles studied in part A of this chapter, there would be no binding contract, but under the law of State B, which the parties had specified in their written agreement as governing the contract, the contract would be binding.

3. A contract contains a clause that provides for a penalty if either side breaches it. Under the law of State A, whose law would govern under the principles studied in part A of this chapter, the penalty clause would be invalid, but under the law of State B, which the parties had specified in their written agreement as governing the contract, the penalty clause would be enforced.

A conclusion that effect should be given in example 1 to the law chosen by the parties would seem to be relatively uncontroversial. After all, if the parties could simply have written the Fredonian rules into their contract, and the resulting contract would be enforced by State A, why should the answer be different if they did so more tersely by simply stating that Fredonian law governs? Indeed, using the parties' choice of law for this purpose (sometimes referred to as "rules of construction") has been accepted even more readily than the use of party autonomy for determining the governing rules for the purposes set out in the other two examples (sometimes referred to as "rules of validity").

SIEGELMAN V. CUNARD WHITE STAR
221 F.2d 189 (2d Cir. 1955)

HARLAN, CIRCUIT JUDGE.

Plaintiff, in his own right and as administrator of his wife's estate, brings this action to recover for injuries suffered by his wife on the defendant's vessel, the R.M.S. Queen Elizabeth. The action was begun in a New York state court on December 14, 1951, and removed on diversity grounds to the federal district court for the Southern District of New York on January 3, 1952, the requisite jurisdictional amount being present.

On September 9, 1949, the Compass Travel Bureau, Inc., Cunard's New York agent, issued to Mr. and Mrs. Elias Siegelman document describing itself as a 'Contract Ticket.' It was a large sheet of light green paper, about 13 inches long and 11 inches wide. On the back were certain notices to passengers, relating to baggage, time of collection of ticket, location of the company's piers and offices, etc. On the front was printed in black Cunard's promise to provide specified transportation, in this case from New York to Cherbourg, subject to certain exceptions, and to 22 'terms and conditions,' also printed in black. Printed in red in heavier type was a notice directing the attention of passengers to these 'terms and conditions.' . . .

On September 24, 1949, when the Queen Elizabeth had been at sea four days, Mrs. Siegelman was injured. While she was seated in a dining room chair, she and the chair were overthrown. Her chair was alleged to be the only one in the dining room which was not bolted to the floor. Upon returning to New York, the Siegelmans retained an attorney to prosecute their claim against Cunard. On August 31, 1950, after Cunard's doctor had examined Mrs. Siegelman, Cunard offered $800, the approximate amount of medical expenses stated to have been incurred by the plaintiff and his wife, in settlement of the claim. This offer was made to the Siegelmans' lawyer over the telephone by Swaine, a claim agent of Cunard. Noticing that the ticket required suits for bodily injury to be brought within a year of the injury, and that the injury had occurred barely less than a year ago, the lawyer asked Swaine whether it would be necessary to begin suit in order to protect his clients' rights. Swaine is said to have stated that no suit was necessary, that the filing of an action would be futile in view of the prospect of early settlement, and that Cunard's offer would stand open. . . .

On December 14, 1951, this suit was begun, claiming . . . damages for pain and medical expenses, and on behalf of her husband, damages for other medical expenses and for loss of consort. Cunard denied legal responsibility for the accident, and set up as a further defense the plaintiff's failure to bring the action within a year of the date the injury was suffered. . . .

On this appeal appellant asserts that Cunard is barred from using the period of limitation as a defense, because of Swaine's statement that suit was unnecessary. The provisions of the 'Contract Ticket' relevant to the appeal are as follows. . . .

All questions arising on this contract ticket shall be decided according to English Law with reference to which this contract is made.' . . .

Our next question is: under the federal choice-of-law rule, what law governs the issues here? We are not concerned with the law applicable to the accident. Instead, we must decide what law applies to the validity and interpretation of certain provisions of the 'Contract Ticket,' and to the effect of Swaine's conduct upon Cunard's right to resort to the one-year limitation period in the contract.

The ticket stipulated that 'All questions arising on this contract ticket shall be decided according to English Law with reference to which this contract is made.' Considering, as we do, the ticket to be a contract—see *Foster v. Cunard White Star*, 2 Cir., 1941, 121 F.2d 12—the provision that English law should govern must be taken to represent the intention of both parties. Therefore, this provision, if effective under the federal choice-of-law rule, renders English law applicable here, even though, absent the provision, some other law would govern under the applicable federal conflicts rule. (Citation omitted). . . .

Our issue, then, involves two lines of inquiry: (1) What questions did the parties intend to be controlled by English law? and (2) Will the federal conflicts rule give effect to their intention? In pursuing the first inquiry, we must examine more closely the provision of the ticket quoted above.

Three questions as to the scope of this provision arise under its language. First, are questions to be decided by the 'whole' English law, including its conflicts rules, or just by the substantive English law? That is, are questions to be decided according to the law of England, or instead, as an English court might decide them, applying where appropriate the law of some other country?

We think the provision must be read as referring to the substantive law alone, for surely the major purpose of including the provision in the ticket was to assure Cunard of a uniform result in any litigation no matter where the ticket was issued or where the litigation arose, and this result might not obtain if the 'whole' law of England were referred to. Second, does the provision intend that questions of validity of the contract and its provisions, as well as questions of interpretation, are to be governed by English law? The language of the clause, covering 'all question,' indicates that validity as well as interpretation is embraced. Third, is the recital meant to require the application of English law to the question of what conduct may amount to a waiver of its provisions? Although the wording of the clause—relating to questions arising 'on' the contract—may indicate that such a question was not meant to be covered, it appears unnatural to hold that all questions of validity and interpretation were intended to be governed by English law but that this question was not. We therefore consider that the question of what conduct was sufficient to operate as a waiver of the ticket's provisions was also meant to be determined by English law.

We now come to the inquiry as to the extent to which this provision, so construed, is to be given effect in deciding the particular issues before us. Those issues are: (1) Is the one-year limitation period provided in the contract for the bringing of suits valid? (2) Does Swaine's conduct prevent Cunard from using the period as a defense? and (3) How is this matter affected by the clause requiring alterations of the contract to be in writing? It appears not to be contested that the ticket should be treated as a contract and that failure to bring the action within the contract limitation period would be a defense under English law—see *Jones v. Oceanic Steam*

Navigation Co., (1924) 2 K.B. 730, but since the same result would follow under American law—see 46 U.S.C.A. § 183(b); *Scheibel v. Agwilines, Inc.,* 2 Cir., 1946, 156 F.2d 636—we need not decide whether English law is applicable to the first of these issues. As to the second and third issues— where English and American law may differ—in the view which we take of the case, we need really only deal with applicability of English law to the second issue—via., whether Swaine's conduct prevents Cunard from using the one-year limitations provision as a defense—although in light of what we say below we think that English law would clearly control the third issue—viz., the effect of the 'alterations' clause.

As we have said, we construe the contract as establishing the intention of the parties that English law should govern both the interpretation and validity of its terms. And we think it clear that the federal conflicts rule will give effect to the parties' intention that English law is to be applied to the interpretation of the contract. Stipulating the governing law for this purpose is much like stipulating that words of the contract have the meanings given in a particular dictionary. See Cheatham, Goodrich, Griswold, & Reese, Cases on Conflict of Laws 461 (1951). On the other hand, there is much doubt that parties can stipulate the law by which the validity of their contract is to be judged. Beale, Conflict of Laws § 332.2 (1935). To permit parties to stipulate the law which should govern the validity of their agreement would afford them an artificial device for avoiding the policies of the state which would otherwise regulate the permissibility of their agreement. It may also be said that to give effect to the parties' stipulation would permit them to do a legislative act, for they rather than the governing law would be making their agreement into an enforceable obligation. And it may be further argued that since courts have not always been ready to give effect to the parties' stipulation, no real uniformity is achieved by following their wishes. See Beale, op. cit. supra, at page 1085.

Here, of course, the question is neither one of interpretation nor one of validity, but instead involves the circumstances under which parties may be said to have partially rescinded their agreements or to be barred from enforcing them. The question is, however, more closely akin to a question of validity. Nevertheless, we see no harm in letting the parties' intention control. (Citations omitted). Instead of viewing the parties as usurping the legislative function, it seems more realistic to regard them as relieving the courts of the problem of resolving a question of conflict of laws. Their course might be expected to reduce litigation, and is to be commended as much as good draftsmanship which relieves courts of problems of resolving ambiguities. To say that there may be no reduction in litigation because courts may not honor the provision is to reason backwards. A tendency toward certainty in commercial transactions should be encouraged by the courts. Furthermore, in England, where much of the litigation on these contracts might be expected to arise, the parties' stipulation would probably be respected. Vita Food Products, Inc. v. Unus Shipping Co., Ltd., (1939) A.C. 277 (P.C.) (similar provision in bill of lading given effect; construed, however, as referring to England's whole law, including its conflicts rules).

Where the law of the parties' intention has been permitted to govern the validity of contracts, it has often been said (1) that the choice of law must be bona fide, and (2) that the law chosen must be that of a jurisdiction having some relation to the agreement, generally either the place of making or the place of performance. The second of these conditions is obviously satisfied here. The fact that a conflicts question is presented in the absence of a stipulation is some indication that the first condition is also satisfied. Furthermore, there does not appear to be an attempt here to evade American policy. We have no statute indicating a policy contrary to England's on this subject. *Cf.* New York Life Insurance Co. v. Cravens, 1900, 178 U.S. 389, 20 S.Ct. 962, 44 L.Ed. 1116. And there is no suggestion that English law is oppressive to passengers. We regard the primary purpose of making English law govern here as being not to substitute English for American policies, but rather on the one hand, to achieve uniformity of result, which is often hailed as the chief objective of the conflict of laws, and on the other hand, to simplify administration of the contracts in question. Cunard's employees need be trained in only one set of legal rules.

This is not to suggest that English and American policies on this subject are identical. Any difference in law reflects some difference in policy. Consequently, to the extent English and American policies may differ on this question, we would consider that the parties may choose to have the English policies apply. But we express no opinion on what result would follow if we had stronger policies at stake, or if the parties had attempted a feined rather than a genuine solution of the conflicts problem. . . .

Affirmed.

[The dissenting opinion of JUDGE FRANK is omitted.]

---

2. THE MODERN VIEW

By the 1970s, the party autonomy revolution in American conflicts law had become mainstream. Section 187 of the Restatement (Second) of Conflict of Laws provides:

(1) The law of the state chosen by the parties to govern their contractual rights and duties will be applied if the particular issue is one which the parties could have resolved by an explicit provision in their agreement directed to that issue.

(2)   The law of the state chosen by the parties to govern their contractual rights and duties will be applied, even if the particular issue is one which the parties could not have resolved by an explicit provision in their agreement directed to that issue, unless either

(a)   the chosen state has no substantial relationship to the parties or the transaction and there is no other reasonable basis for the parties' choice, or

(b)   application of the law of the chosen state would be contrary to a fundamental policy of a state which has a materially greater interest than the chosen state in the determination of the particular issue and which, under the rule of § 188, would be the state of the applicable law in the absence of an effective choice of law by the parties.

(3)   In the absence of a contrary indication of intention, the reference is to the local law of the state of the chosen law.

[Note that subsection (3) addresses *renvoi*, addressed in Chapter 2 of this book. The point addressed in subsection (2)(b) is covered at page 223 below.]

———————

1.   Which portion of the Restatement provision addresses rules of construction? Which portion addresses rules of validity?

2.   The Restatement provision upholds party autonomy to choose the state whose law governs a contract if the chosen state has a substantial relationship to the parties or the transaction or "there is a reasonable basis for the parties' choice." How would a court go about determining whether such a reasonable basis exists?

———————

3.   STATUTORY APPROACHES

The Uniform Commercial Code

Even before the promulgation of the Restatement, party autonomy had been the subject of statutory developments. Of particular importance, the Uniform Commercial Code, drafted in the 1940s and 1950s and widely enacted in the 1960s, addressed the power of parties to a transaction to choose the law governing it. The UCC provision, originally codified in section 1–105 of the UCC and now codified as Section 1–301, provides in its current form[3] (which is substantively identical to original section 1–105) that[4]:

> Except as otherwise provided in this section, when a transaction bears a reasonable relation to this state and also to another state or nation the parties may agree that the law either of this state or of such other state or nation shall govern their rights and duties.[5]

---

1.   Does the UCC provision address rules of construction?

2.   Is there a difference between the Restatement standard of a "substantial" relationship and the UCC standard of a "reasonable relation"? Does it make a difference that the Restatement refers to the *state's* relationship to the parties or the transaction, while the UCC refers to the *transaction's* relation to the state? Can you describe a situation in which parties to a contract choose the law of a state that does not have a substantial relationship to the parties or the transaction but, nonetheless, the transaction bears a reasonable relation to the state?

Other State Statutes

A few states, by statute, provide for even greater party autonomy than is found under the approach of the Restatement and the Uniform Commercial Code. Consider the following provisions of the Louisiana Civil Code, particularly article 3540:

Louisiana Civil Code

Article 3537. Except as otherwise provided in this Title, an issue of conventional obligations is governed by the law of the state whose policies would be most seriously impaired if its law were not applied to that issue.

That state is determined by evaluating the strength and pertinence of the relevant policies of the involved states in the light of: (1) the pertinent contacts of each state to the parties and the transaction, including the place of negotiation, formation, and performance of the contract, the location of the object of the contract, and the place of domicile, habitual residence, or business of the parties; (2) the nature, type, and purpose of the contract; and (3) the policies referred to in Article 3515, as well as the

---

[3]   Between the original provision and the current text, the sponsors of the Uniform Commercial Code promulgated, and later withdrew, a significant revision that was adopted only by the U.S. Virgin Islands.

[4]   Of course, the UCC conflict of laws provision governs only transactions that are within the scope of the UCC. See UCC § 1–102.

[5]   UCC § 1–301(a)(2008).

policies of facilitating the orderly planning of transactions, of promoting multistate commercial intercourse, and of protecting one party from undue imposition by the other.

Article 3538. A contract is valid as to form if made in conformity with: (1) the law of the state of making; (2) the law of the state of performance to the extent that performance is to be rendered in that state; (3) the law of the state of common domicile or place of business of the parties; or (4) the law governing the substance of the contract under Articles 3537 or 3540.

Nevertheless, when for reasons of public policy the law governing the substance of the contract under Article 3537 requires a certain form, there must be compliance with that form.

Article 3539. A person is capable of contracting if he possesses that capacity under the law of either the state in which he is domiciled at the time of making the contract or the state whose law is applicable to the contract under Article 3537.

Article 3540. All other issues of conventional obligations are governed by the law expressly chosen or clearly relied upon by the parties, except to the extent that law contravenes the public policy of the state whose law would otherwise be applicable under Article 3537.

Some other states provide a similarly broad range of party autonomy, but only in one direction. Consider the following provision of the New York General Obligations Law:

New York General Obligations Law

§ 5–1401.   Choice of law

1.   The parties to any contract, agreement or undertaking, contingent or otherwise, in consideration of, or relating to any obligation arising out of a transaction covering in the aggregate not less than two hundred fifty thousand dollars, including a transaction otherwise covered by subsection one of § 1–105 of the uniform commercial code, may agree that the law of this state shall govern their rights and duties in whole or in part, whether or not such contract, agreement or undertaking bears a reasonable relation to this state. This section shall not apply to any contract, agreement or undertaking (a) for labor or personal services, (b) relating to any transaction for personal, family or household services, or (c) to the extent provided to the contrary in subsection two of section 1–105 of the uniform commercial code.

2.   Nothing contained in this section shall be construed to limit or deny the enforcement of any provision respecting choice of law in any other contract, agreement or undertaking.

§ 5–1402.   Choice of forum

1.   Notwithstanding any act which limits or affects the right of a person to maintain an action or proceeding, including, but not limited to, paragraph (b) of section thirteen hundred fourteen of the business corporation law and subdivision two of section two hundred-b of the banking law, any person may maintain an action or proceeding against a foreign corporation, non-resident, or foreign state where the action or proceeding arises out of or relates to any contract, agreement or undertaking for which a choice of New York law has been made in whole or in part pursuant to section 5–1401 and which (a) is a contract, agreement or undertaking, contingent or otherwise, in consideration of, or relating to any obligation arising out of a transaction covering in the aggregate, not less than one million dollars, and (b) which contains a provision or provisions whereby such foreign corporation or non-resident agrees to submit to the jurisdiction of the courts of this state.

2.   Nothing contained in this section shall be construed to affect the enforcement of any provision respecting choice of forum in any other contract, agreement or undertaking.

---

1. A contract pursuant to which a party in Louisiana is to perform certain services for a party in New York for one million dollars provides that it is governed by the law of Italy. A dispute arising out of that contract results in a lawsuit in a court in Louisiana. Will the Louisiana court apply the law of Italy to the contract? What would happen if the lawsuit were brought in a court in New York?

2. A contract pursuant to which a party in Italy is to perform certain services for another party in Italy for one million Euros provides that it is governed by the law of New York. A dispute arising out of that contract results in a lawsuit in a court in New York. Will the New York court apply the law of New York to the contract? What would happen if the lawsuit were brought in a court in Louisiana?

---

4.   LIMITS ON PARTY AUTONOMY

Inasmuch as the modern approach to party autonomy for the choice of the jurisdiction whose law will govern a contract gives the parties substantial leeway in selecting the applicable law, it is possible (indeed likely) that in many cases litigation concerning a contract will take place in a state other than the state whose law was chosen by the parties. In such a case, the court in that state is put in the position of applying the law of that other state, which may not only be different than the law of the forum state but may even be based on rules that the forum state considered and

SEC. B

DO THE PARTIES TO THE CONTRACT HAVE THE
POWER TO CHOOSE THE GOVERNING LAW?

223

rejected (or adopted and later repealed). This, of course, is the nature of conflict of laws; otherwise conflict of laws would be a very simple course with only one rule—always apply the law of the forum. Moreover, the chosen state may be different from the state whose law would govern in the absence of choice by the parties. That state, too, may have rejected the rule in the selected state. Are there limits on the obligation of a forum to apply law that differs from the forum's law or from the law of the state whose law would govern in the absence of selection of a different state by the parties? The answer is yes, but applying those limits is not always easy.

Recall that the Restatement addresses this issue in section 187, providing that the law of the chosen state need not be applied if "application of the law of the chosen state would be contrary to a fundamental policy of a state which has a materially greater interest than the chosen state in the determination of the particular issue and which . . . would be the state of the applicable law in the absence of an effective choice of law by the parties."

The judiciary has spoken as well. The decision in *Loucks*, set out below, is a classic formulation of the circumstances in which a court may decline enforcement of a right created and existing under the law of a different jurisdiction because application of that law would be inconsistent with domestic policy. While the case is not a contract case, the opinion is frequently cited by courts examining whether the chosen law in a contract should be denied enforcement on the ground that it is inconsistent with public policy:

LOUCKS V. STANDARD OIL CO.
120 N.E. 198 (N.Y. 1918)

CARDOZO, J.

The action is brought to recover damages for injuries resulting in death. The plaintiffs are the administrators of the estate of Everett A. Loucks. Their intestate, while traveling on a highway in the state of Massachusetts, was run down and killed through the negligence of the defendant's servants then engaged in its business. He left a wife and two children, residents of New York. A statute of Massachusetts (R. L. c. 171, § 2, as amended by L. 1907, c. 375) provides that:

> "If a person or corporation by his or its negligence, or by the negligence of his or its agents or servants while engaged in his or its business, causes the death of a person who is in the exercise of due care, and not in his or its employment or service, he or it shall be liable in damages in the sum of not less than $500, nor more than $10,000, to be assessed with reference to the degree of his or its culpability, or * * * that of his or its * * * servants, to be recovered in an action of tort commenced within two years after

the injury which caused the death, by the executor or administrator of the deceased, one-half thereof to the use of the widow and one-half to the use of the children of the deceased, or, if there are no children, the whole to the use of the widow, or, if there is no widow, the whole to the use of the next of kin."

The question is whether a right of action under that statute may be enforced in our courts.

* * *

A foreign statute is not law in this state, but it gives rise to an obligation, which, if transitory, "follows the person and may be enforced wherever the person may be found." (Citations omitted). "No law can exist as such except the law of the land; but * * * it is a principle of every civilized law that vested rights shall be protected." (Citation omitted). The plaintiff owns something, and we help him to get it. (Citations omitted). We do this unless some sound reason of public policy makes it unwise for us to lend our aid. "The law of the forum is material only as setting a limit of policy beyond which such obligations will not be enforced there." (Citation omitted). Sometimes we refuse to act where all the parties are nonresidents. (Citations omitted). That restriction need not detain us; in this case all are residents. If aid is to be withheld here, it must be because the cause of action in its nature offends our sense of justice or menaces the public welfare.

Our own scheme of legislation may be different. We may even have no legislation on the subject. That is not enough to show that public policy forbids us to enforce the foreign right. A right of action is property. If a foreign statute gives the right, the mere fact that we do not give a like right is no reason for refusing to help the plaintiff in getting what belongs to him. We are not so provincial as to say that every solution of a problem is wrong because we deal with it otherwise at home. Similarity of legislation has indeed this importance; its presence shows beyond question that the foreign statute does not offend the local policy. But its absence does not prove the contrary. It is not to be exalted into an indispensable condition. The misleading word 'comity' has been responsible for much of the trouble. It has been fertile in suggesting a discretion unregulated by general principles. Beale, Conflict of Laws, § 71.

The sovereign in its discretion may refuse its aid to the foreign right. (Citations omitted). From this it has been an easy step to the conclusion that a like freedom of choice has been confided to the courts. But that, of course, is a false view. (Citation omitted). The courts are not free to refuse to enforce a foreign right at the pleasure of the judges, to suit the individual notion of expediency or fairness. They do not close their doors, unless help would violate some fundamental principle of justice, some prevalent conception of good morals, some deep-rooted tradition of the common weal.

This test applied, there is nothing in the Massachusetts statute that outrages the public policy of New York. We have a statute which gives a civil remedy where death is caused in our own state. We have thought it so important that we have now imbedded it in the Constitution. (Citation omitted). The fundamental policy is that there shall be some atonement for the wrong. Through the defendant's negligence, a resident of New York has been killed in Massachusetts. He has left a widow and children, who are also residents. The law of Massachusetts gives them a recompense for his death. It cannot be that public policy forbids our courts to help in collecting what belongs to them. We cannot give them the same judgment that our law would give if the wrong had been done here. Very likely we cannot give them as much. But that is no reason for refusing to give them what we can. We shall not make things better by sending them to another state, where the defendant may not be found, and where suit may be impossible. Nor is there anything to shock our sense of justice in the possibility of a punitive recovery. The penalty is not extravagant. It conveys no hint of arbitrary confiscation. (Citation omitted). It varies between moderate limits according to the defendant's guilt. We shall not feel the pricks of conscience, if the offender pays the survivors in proportion to the measure of his offense. . . .

We hold, then, that public policy does not prohibit the assumption of jurisdiction by our courts and that this being so, mere differences of remedy do not count. For many years the courts have been feeling their way in the enforcement of these statutes. A civil remedy for another's death was something strange and new, and it did not find at once the fitting niche, the proper category, in the legal scheme. We need not be surprised, therefore, if some of the things said, as distinguished from those decided, must be rejected to-day. But the truth, of course, is that there is nothing sui generis about these death statutes in their relation to the general body of private international law. We must apply the same rules that are applicable to other torts; and the tendency of those rules to-day is toward a larger comity, if we must cling to the traditional term. (Citation omitted). The fundamental public policy is perceived to be that rights lawfully vested shall be everywhere maintained. At least, that is so among the states of the Union. (Citations omitted). There is a growing conviction that only exceptional circumstances should lead one of the states to refuse to enforce a right acquired in another. The evidences of this tendency are many. One typical instance will suffice. For many years, Massachusetts closed her courts to actions of this order based on foreign statutes. (Citation omitted). She has opened them now, and overruled her earlier decisions. (Citations omitted). The test of similarity has been abandoned there. If it has ever been accepted here, we think it should be abandoned now.

The judgment of the Appellate Division should be reversed, and the order of the Special Term affirmed, with costs in the Appellate Division and in this court.

For a modern application of the "fundamental policy" doctrine to invalidate a choice of law in a contract, see *Feeney v. Dell, Inc.*, 454 Mass. 192, 908 N.E.2d 753 (2009), in which the Supreme Judicial Court of Massachusetts stated: "Because Texas law [chosen by the contract] likely would result in the enforcement of the class action prohibition [contained in the contract], leaving Massachusetts consumers and businesses with small claims without an effective remedy, enforcing the choice-of-law provision would lead to a result contrary to our fundamental policy. For this reason, Massachusetts law applies, and Dell's class action prohibition is unenforceable." *Accord Coady v. Cross Country Bank*, 729 N.W.2d 732 (Wis. Ct. App. 2007), *review denied*, 737 N.W.2d 432 (Wis. 2007).

Similarly, some courts have refused to honor party autonomy when the issue is a non-compete clause. *See DeSantis v. Wackenhut Corp.*, 793 S.W.2d 670 (Tex. 1990) (court held that enforcement of a non-compete covenant as valid under Florida law chosen by the parties violated Texas public policy).

It is interesting to note that one contract issue that could be seen to raise the "public policy" problem—usury—is the subject of its own section in the Restatement (Second) of Conflict of Laws.

§ 203.   Usury

The validity of a contract will be sustained against the charge of usury if it provides for a rate of interest that is permissible in a state to which the contract has a substantial relationship and is not greatly in excess of the rate permitted by the general usury law of the state of the otherwise applicable law under the rule of section 188.

Note, however, that state law with respect to a number of usury issues has been affected by the federal Depositary Institutions Deregulation and Monetary Control Act (Pub. L. 96–221, 94 Stat. 132 (1980)).

NEDLLOYD LINES B.V. ET AL. V. THE SUPERIOR COURT OF SAN MATEO COUNTY
834 P.2d 1148 (1992)

BAXTER, ASSOCIATE JUSTICE . . .

Plaintiff and real party in interest Seawinds Limited (Seawinds) is a shipping company, currently undergoing reorganization under chapter 11 of the United States Bankruptcy Code, whose business consists of the operation of three container ships. Seawinds was incorporated in Hong Kong in late 1982 and has its principal place of business in Redwood City, California. Defendants and petitioners Nedlloyd Lines B.V., Royal Nedlloyd Group N.V., and KNSM Lines B.V. (collectively referred to as

Nedlloyd) are interrelated shipping companies incorporated in the Netherlands with their principal place of business in Rotterdam.

In March 1983, Nedlloyd and other parties (including an Oregon corporation, a Hong Kong corporation, a British corporation, three individual residents of California, and a resident of Singapore) entered into a contract with Seawinds to purchase shares of Seawinds's stock. The contract, which was entitled "Shareholders' Agreement in Respect of Seawinds Limited," stated that its purpose was "to establish [Seawinds] as a joint venture company to carry on a transportation operation." The agreement also provided that Seawinds would carry on the business of the transportation company and that the parties to the agreement would use "means reasonably available" to ensure the business was a success.

The shareholders' agreement between the parties contained the following choice-of-law and forum selection provision: "This agreement shall be governed by and construed in accordance with Hong Kong law and each party hereby irrevocably submits to the non-exclusive jurisdiction and service of process of the Hong Kong courts."

In January 1989, Seawinds sued Nedlloyd, alleging in essence that Nedlloyd breached express and implied obligations under the shareholders' agreement by: "(1) engaging in activities that led to the cancellation of charter hires that were essential to Seawinds' business; (2) attempting to interfere with a proposed joint service agreement between Seawinds and the East Asiatic Company, and delaying its implementation; (3) making and then reneging on commitments to contribute additional capital, thereby dissuading others from dealing with Seawinds, and (4) making false and disparaging statements about Seawinds' business operations and financial condition." Seawinds's original and first amended complaint included causes of action for breach of contract, breach of the implied covenant of good faith and fair dealing (in both contract and tort), and breach of fiduciary duty. This matter comes before us after trial court rulings on demurrers to Seawinds's complaints.

Nedlloyd demurred to Seawinds's original complaint on the grounds that it failed to state causes of action for breach of the implied covenant of good faith and fair dealing (either in contract or in tort) and breach of fiduciary duty. In support of its demurrer, Nedlloyd contended the shareholders' agreement required the application of Hong Kong law to Seawinds's claims. In opposition to the demurrer, Seawinds argued that California law should be applied to its causes of action.

In ruling on Nedlloyd's demurrer, the trial court expressly determined that California law applied to all of Seawinds's causes of action. It sustained the demurrers with leave to amend as to all causes of action, relying on grounds not pertinent to the issues before us. Nedlloyd sought a writ of mandate from the Court of Appeal directing the application of Hong Kong law. After the Court of Appeal summarily denied Nedlloyd's initial writ petition, we granted Nedlloyd's petition for review and transferred the case back to the Court of Appeal with instructions to issue an alternative writ.

After complying with our direction, the Court of Appeal denied Nedlloyd's first writ petition and discharged the alternative writ. In a published opinion, the Court of Appeal upheld the application of California law to Seawinds's claims. We granted Nedlloyd's petition for review. . . .

DISCUSSION

I. *The proper test*

We have not previously considered the enforceability of a contractual choice-of-law provision. We have, however, addressed the closely related issue of the enforceability of a contractual choice-of-forum provision, and we have made clear that, "No satisfying reason of public policy has been suggested why enforcement should be denied a forum selection clause appearing in a contract entered into freely and voluntarily by parties who have negotiated at arm's length." (Citation omitted). . . .

We reaffirm this approach. In determining the enforceability of arm's-length contractual choice-of-law provisions, California courts shall apply the principles set forth in Restatement § 187, which reflect a strong policy favoring enforcement of such provisions.

More specifically, Restatement § 187, subdivision (2) sets forth the following standards: "The law of the state chosen by the parties to govern their contractual rights and duties will be applied, even if the particular issue is one which the parties could not have resolved by an explicit provision in their agreement directed to that issue, unless either [¶] (a) the chosen state has no substantial relationship to the parties or the transaction and there is no other reasonable basis for the parties choice, or [¶] (b) application of the law of the chosen state would be contrary to a fundamental policy of a state which has a materially greater interest than the chosen state in the determination of the particular issue and which, under the rule of § 188, would be the state of the applicable law in the absence of an effective choice of law by the parties."

Briefly restated, the proper approach under Restatement § 187, subdivision (2) is for the court first to determine either: (1) whether the chosen state has a substantial relationship to the parties or their transaction, or (2) whether there is any other reasonable basis for the parties' choice of law. If neither of these tests is met, that is the end of the inquiry, and the court need not enforce the parties' choice of law. If, however, either test is met, the court must next determine whether the chosen state's law is contrary to a *fundamental* policy of California. If there is no such conflict, the court shall enforce the parties' choice of law. If, however, there is a fundamental conflict with California law, the court must then determine whether California has a "materially greater interest

than the chosen state in the determination of the particular issue. . . ."
(Rest., § 187, subd. (2).) If California has a materially greater interest than
the chosen state, the choice of law shall not be enforced, for the obvious
reason that in such circumstance we will decline to enforce a law contrary
to this state's fundamental policy. We now apply the Restatement test to
the facts of this case. . . .

[The court found that the law of Hong Kong had a substantial
relationship to the parties and did not violate California public policy.]

C. *Fiduciary duty cause of action*

1. *Scope of the choice-of-law clause*

Seawinds contends that, whether or not the choice-of-law clause
governs Seawinds's implied covenant claim, Seawinds's fiduciary duty
claim is somehow independent of the shareholders' agreement and
therefore outside the intended scope of the clause. Seawinds thus concludes
California law must be applied to this claim. We disagree.

When two sophisticated, commercial entities agree to a choice-of-law
clause like the one in this case, the most reasonable interpretation of their
actions is that they intended for the clause to apply to all causes of action
arising from or related to their contract. Initially, such an interpretation is
supported by the plain meaning of the language used by the parties. The
choice-of-law clause in the shareholders' agreement provides: "This
agreement shall be *governed by* and construed in accordance with Hong
Kong law and each party hereby irrevocably submits to the non-exclusive
jurisdiction and service of process of the Hong Kong courts." (Italics
added.)[6]

The phrase "governed by" is a broad one signifying a relationship of
absolute direction, control, and restraint. Thus, the clause reflects the
parties' clear contemplation that "the agreement" is to be completely and
absolutely controlled by Hong Kong law. No exceptions are provided. In the
context of this case, the agreement to be controlled by Hong Kong law is a
shareholders' agreement that expressly provides for the purchase of shares
in Seawinds by Nedlloyd and creates the relationship between shareholder
and corporation that gives rise to Seawinds's cause of action. Nedlloyd's
fiduciary duties, if any, arise from—and can exist only because of—the

---

[6]   As we have noted, the choice-of-law clause states: "This agreement shall be governed by
and *construed in accordance with Hong Kong law. . . .*" (Italics added.) The agreement, of course,
includes the choice-of-law clause itself. Thus the question of whether that clause is ambiguous as
to its scope (i.e., whether it includes the fiduciary duty claim) is a question of contract
interpretation that in the normal course should be determined pursuant to Hong Kong law. (*S.A.
Empresa, Etc. v. Boeing Co., supra,* 641 F.2d 746, 751 [interpreting choice-of-law clause pursuant
to law chosen by the parties]; The parties in this case, however, did not request judicial notice of
Hong Kong law on this question of interpretation (Evid.Code, § 452, subd. (f)) or supply us with
evidence of the relevant aspects of that law (Evid.Code, § 453, subd. (b)). The question therefore
becomes one of California law. (*Com'l Ins. Co. of Newark v. Pacific-Peru Const.* (9th Cir.1977) 558
F.2d 948, 952; Rest., § 136, subd. (2), com. h, p. 378.)

shareholders' agreement pursuant to which Seawinds's stock was purchased by Nedlloyd.

In order to control completely the agreement of the parties, Hong Kong law must also govern the stock purchase portion of that agreement and the legal duties created by or emanating from the stock purchase, including any fiduciary duties. If Hong Kong law were not applied to these duties, it would effectively control only part of the agreement, not all of it. Such an interpretation would be inconsistent with the unrestricted character of the choice-of-law clause.

Our conclusion in this regard comports with common sense and commercial reality. When a rational businessperson enters into an agreement establishing a transaction or relationship and provides that disputes arising from the agreement shall be governed by the law of an identified jurisdiction, the logical conclusion is that he or she intended that law to apply to *all* disputes arising out of the transaction or relationship. We seriously doubt that any rational businessperson, attempting to provide by contract for an efficient and businesslike resolution of possible future disputes, would intend that the laws of multiple jurisdictions would apply to a single controversy having its origin in a single, contract-based relationship. Nor do we believe such a person would reasonably desire a protracted litigation battle concerning only the threshold question of what law was to be applied to which asserted claims or issues. Indeed, the manifest purpose of a choice-of-law clause is precisely to avoid such a battle.

Seawinds's view of the problem—which would require extensive litigation of the parties' supposed intentions regarding the choice-of-law clause to the end that the laws of multiple states might be applied to their dispute—is more likely the product of postdispute litigation strategy, not predispute contractual intent. If commercially sophisticated parties (such as those now before us) truly intend the result advocated by Seawinds, they should, in fairness to one another and in the interest of economy in dispute resolution, negotiate and obtain the assent of their fellow parties to explicit contract language specifying what jurisdiction's law applies to what issues. . . .

For the reasons stated above, we hold a valid choice-of-law clause, which provides that a specified body of law "governs" the "agreement" between the parties, encompasses all causes of action arising from or related to that agreement, regardless of how they are characterized, including tortious breaches of duties emanating from the agreement or the legal relationships it creates. . . .

For strategic reasons related to its current dispute with Nedlloyd, Seawinds seeks to create a fiduciary relationship by disregarding the law Seawinds voluntarily agreed to accept as binding—the law of a state that also happens to be Seawinds's own corporate domicile. To allow Seawinds to use California law in this fashion would further no ascertainable fundamental policy of California; indeed, it would undermine California's policy of respecting the choices made by parties to voluntarily negotiated agreements. . . .

LUCAS, C.J., and ARABIAN and GEORGE, JJ., concur.

PANELLI, ASSOCIATE JUSTICE, concurring and dissenting.

I generally concur in the majority opinion's explanation of the standards controlling when a contractual choice-of-law provision will be honored by the courts of this state and with the majority's application of these standards to Seawinds's cause of action for breach of the covenant of good faith and fair dealing. I write separately to express my disagreement with the majority's conclusion, based on the record before us, that the choice-of-law clause in this case governs Seawinds's cause of action for breach of fiduciary duty. In my view, the majority's analysis of the scope of the choice-of-law clause is unsound.

The choice-of-law clause in this case reads in pertinent part: "This agreement shall be governed by and construed in accordance with Hong Kong law. . . ."[7] The majority determines that the scope of the choice-of-law clause, which was incorporated into the first amended complaint by attachment, extends to related, *noncontractual* causes of action, such as Seawinds's breach of fiduciary duty claim. In so doing, the majority opinion adopts the rule that "[w]hen two sophisticated, commercial entities agree to a choice-of-law clause like the one in this case, the most reasonable interpretation of their actions is that they intended for the clause to apply to all causes of action arising from or related to their contract." (Maj. opn., *ante,* at p. 335 of 11 Cal.Rptr.2d, p. 1153 of 834 P.2d.) Without citing any authority, the majority opinion announces a binding rule of contractual interpretation, based solely upon "common sense and commercial reality." (*Id.* at p. 336 of 11 Cal.Rptr.2d, p. 1154 of 834 P.2d.) . . .

In my view, the majority's mistaken construction of the choice-of-law clause is clear when the language used in the present contract is compared, as Nedlloyd urges us to do, with the language construed by this court in *Smith, Valentino & Smith, Inc. v. Superior Court* (1976) 17 Cal.3d 491, 131 Cal.Rptr. 374, 551 P.2d 1206. In that case, this court determined that claims for unfair competition and intentional interference with advantageous business relationships were governed by a choice-of-forum clause as " 'actions or proceedings instituted by . . . [Smith] under this Agreement with respect to any matters arising under *or growing out of this*

---

[7] I agree with the majority that the scope of the choice-of-law clause in this contract is a question that would ordinarily be determined under Hong Kong law. (Maj. opn., *ante,* at p. 336, fn. 7 of 11 Cal.Rptr.2d, p. 1154, fn. 7 of 834 P.2d.) I further agree with the majority that, since the parties neither produced any evidence of Hong Kong law relating to this subject nor requested judicial notice of any such law, we may apply California law to ascertain the scope of the clause. (*Ibid.*)

agreement. . . .' " (*Id.* at p. 497, 131 Cal.Rptr. 374, 551 P.2d 1206, emphasis in the original.) In contrast to the language used by Nedlloyd and Seawinds in their agreement, the contractual language, "arising under or growing out of this agreement," which was used in *Smith,* explicitly shows an intent to embrace related noncontractual claims, as well as contractual claims. Although similar language was readily available to them, the sophisticated parties in the present case did not draft their choice-of-law clause to clearly encompass related noncontractual causes of action. Therefore, on demurrer and in the absence of parol evidence, I cannot fairly construe the contractual language at issue here to be consistent with the interpretation proposed by Nedlloyd and adopted in the majority opinion. To do so would violate the statutory canon of contract interpretation that "[t]he language of a contract is to govern its interpretation, if the language is clear and explicit, and does not involve an absurdity." (Citation omitted). . . .

The concurring opinion notes that under Hong Kong law a shareholder of a company owes no fiduciary duty to that company. Under the law of California the courts have held that majority or controlling shareholders owe a fiduciary duty to minority shareholder and to the company itself.

Given the sharp difference between the majority and dissenting opinions as to the scope of the choice of law clause it behooves parties to draw their choice of law clause as broadly as possible to include all causes of action that will arise from the contract. It is interesting to note that both the majority and dissent agree that the scope of the choice of law clause was to be interpreted under Hong Kong law. However, the plaintiff never proved how Hong Kong law would have interpreted the choice of law clause. It is not clear whether this was the result of poor lawyering or whether Hong Kong law itself was not clear on this issue.

---

5. INTERNATIONAL APPROACHES

With decreasing costs of transportation and communication, it is increasingly the case that the borders that contracts cross are national borders rather than state borders. As a result, the conflict of laws issues posed by those contracts are not choices as between two states of the United States (where, in many cases, the differences between the states' bodies of contract law are relatively minimal differences between substantially similar systems) but, rather, choices between two fundamentally different legal systems. Yet, because of those possibly fundamental differences, the parties to an international contract may be seeking even greater certainty as to the identity of the jurisdiction whose law will govern. Perhaps as a result for this greater need, and desire, for certainty, recent years have seen the development of several international instruments that provide for a great deal of party autonomy for such transactions. Excerpts of three instruments appear below. The first instrument, usually referred to as the "Rome I regulation," is binding among the nations of the EU. The second instrument, usually referred to as the "Mexico City Convention," was promulgated by the Organization of American States (of which the United States is a member state); to date, only two nations, Mexico and Venezuela, have signed and ratified it. The third instrument, a non-binding instrument of the Hague Conference on Private International Law (a global inter-governmental organization of which the United States is one of 75 member states), was awaiting final approval as this book went to press.

Note that while, in the U.S., party autonomy is limited when the law of the chosen state or nation would be "contrary to a fundamental policy," these international instruments contain two limits on the parties' choice of applicable law, one limit relating to "mandatory" provisions of law and the other relating to "public order." Both of those concepts are subsumed under the "fundamental policy" rubric in the United States, but they are quite different. The former, as noted in the Rome I Regulation below deals with situations in which the forum's domestic law is "regarded as crucial by a country for safeguarding its public interests, such as its political, social or economic organization, to such an extent that they are applicable to any situation falling within their scope, irrespective of the law otherwise applicable to the contract." Thus, this concept deals with the importance of the forum's domestic rule, not with the unsuitability of the foreign law. The latter, on the other hand, does focus on the foreign law, declining to apply the foreign law when that law is "manifestly incompatible" with the public policy of the forum.

REGULATION (EC) No 593/2008 OF THE EUROPEAN PARLIAMENT AND OF THE COUNCIL OF 17 JUNE 2008 ON THE LAW APPLICABLE TO CONTRACTUAL OBLIGATIONS

(Rome I)

CHAPTER II

UNIFORM RULES

Article 3

Freedom of choice

1.   A contract shall be governed by the law chosen by the parties. The choice shall be made expressly or clearly demonstrated by the terms of the contract or the circumstances of the case. By their choice the parties can select the law applicable to the whole or to part only of the contract. . . .

Article 9

Overriding mandatory provisions

1.   Overriding mandatory provisions are provisions the respect for which is regarded as crucial by a country for safeguarding its public interests, such as its political, social or economic organization, to such an extent that they are applicable to any situation falling within their scope, irrespective of the law otherwise applicable to the contract under this Regulation.

2.   Nothing in this Regulation shall restrict the application of the overriding mandatory provisions of the law of the forum.

3.   Effect may be given to the overriding mandatory provisions of the law of the country where the obligations arising out of the contract have to be or have been performed, in so far as those overriding mandatory provisions render the performance of the contract unlawful. In considering whether to give effect to those provisions, regard shall be had to their nature and purpose and to the consequences of their application or non-application. . . .

Article 21

Public policy of the forum

The application of a provision of the law of any country specified by this Regulation may be refused only if such application is manifestly incompatible with the public policy (*ordre public*) of the forum.

INTER-AMERICAN CONVENTION ON THE LAW APPLICABLE TO INTERNATIONAL CONTRACTS (1994)

* * *

CHAPTER I

Scope of Application

Article 1

This Convention shall determine the law applicable to international contracts.

It shall be understood that a contract is international if the parties thereto have their habitual residence or establishments in different States Parties or if the contract has objective ties with more than one State Party.

SEC. B

DO THE PARTIES TO THE CONTRACT HAVE THE
POWER TO CHOOSE THE GOVERNING LAW?

235

* * *

CHAPTER 2

Determination of applicable law

Article 7

The contract shall be governed by the law chosen by the parties. The parties' agreement on this selection must be express or, in the event that there is no express agreement, must be evident from the parties' behavior and from the clauses of the contract, considered as a whole. Said selection may relate to the entire contract or to a part of same.

Selection of a certain forum by the parties does not necessarily entail selection of the applicable law. . . .

Article 11

Notwithstanding the provisions of the preceding articles, the provisions of the law of the forum shall necessarily be applied when they are mandatory requirements.

It shall be up to the forum to decide when it applies the mandatory provisions of the law of another State with which the contract has close ties. . . .

CHAPTER 4

Scope of the applicable law. . . .

Article 18

Application of the law designated by this Convention may only be excluded when it is manifestly contrary to the public order of the forum.

DRAFT HAGUE PRINCIPLES ON CHOICE OF LAW IN INTERNATIONAL COMMERCIAL CONTRACTS

(AS APPROVED IN APRIL 2014 BY THE COUNCIL ON GENERAL AFFAIRS AND POLICY SUBJECT TO EDITORIAL FINALIZATION)

* * *

Article 2—Freedom of choice

1. A contract is governed by the law chosen by the parties.

2. The parties may choose—

    (a) the law applicable to the whole contract or to only part of it; and

(b) different laws for different parts of the contract.

3.   The choice may be made or modified at any time. A choice or modification made after the contract has been concluded shall not prejudice its formal validity or the rights of third parties.

4.   No connection is required between the law chosen and the parties or their transaction.

* * *

Article 11—Overriding mandatory rules and public policy (ordre public)

1.   These Principles shall not prevent a court from applying overriding mandatory provisions of the law of the forum which apply irrespective of the law chosen by the parties.

2.   The law of the forum determines when a court may or must apply or take into account overriding mandatory provisions of another law.

3.   A court may exclude application of a provision of the law chosen by the parties only if and to the extent that the result of such application would be manifestly incompatible with fundamental notions of public policy (*ordre public*) of the forum.

4.   The law of the forum determines when a court may or must apply or take into account the public policy (*ordre public*) of a State the law of which would be applicable in the absence of a choice of law.

5.   These Principles shall not prevent an arbitral tribunal from applying or taking into account public policy (*ordre public*), or from applying or taking into account overriding mandatory provisions of a law other than the law chosen by the parties, if the arbitral tribunal is required or entitled to do so.

———————

1.   Are there situations in which the rules stated in any of these international instruments would validate a choice of law by the parties that would not be given effect by the Restatement approach or the UCC?

2.   Should the United States become a party to the Mexico City Convention and be bound by its provisions with respect to international contracts?

———————

6. DESIGNATION OF NON-STATE LAW

Should parties to a contract be able to designate "law" that is not the product of a sovereign state as the law governing their contract? For example, UNIDROIT (The International Institute for the Unification of Private Law), an intergovernmental organization with 63 member states including the United States, has promulgated the "UNIDROIT Principles of International Commercial Contracts." The UNIDROIT Principles are a voluntary set of principles that parties may adopt as part of their contract. Parties to international commercial contracts now frequently incorporate the UNIDROIT Principles into their contracts by reference. Should they be able to go one step further and designate the Principles as the law governing their contract even though the Principles are not "law" in the sense of rules promulgated by a sovereign state?

In the preparation of the Rome I Regulation, the European Parliament considered, but rejected, a proposal to allow designation of such non-state "rules of law." More recently, however, the Hague Conference on Private International Law addressed this topic in the Hague Principles on Choice of Law in International Commercial Contracts. Consider the treatment of "rules of law" in Article 3 of the current draft of the Hague Principles:

Article 3—Rules of law

Under these Principles, the law chosen by the parties may be rules of law that are generally accepted on an international, supranational or regional level as a neutral and balanced set of rules, unless the law of the forum provides otherwise.

———————————

Do you think that parties should be able to designate non-state "rules of law" as the law governing international contracts?

Office Talk

#9

Aaron: It is pretty clear that nowadays parties to a contract can choose which law governs it. But wasn't Professor Beale right? However dissatisfied we may be with conflict of laws rules that determine which law governs a contract, those rules are *law* and allowing the parties to bring about a different result is empowering them to change the law, isn't it?

Neil: Well, at one level you (and Beale) are certainly right, but that ship sailed a long time ago and party autonomy now rules the day.

Aaron: Is that the best defense of party autonomy that you can come up with—that it is too late to argue against it?

Neil: Not at all, but it is nice to ground a debate in reality, and the reality is that every U.S. state recognizes party autonomy and the vast majority of the nations of the world do, too. There are good reasons for this. For one thing, as noted by Judge (later Justice) Harlan in *Siegelman*, "Instead of viewing the parties as usurping the legislative function, it seems more realistic to regard them as relieving the courts of the problem of resolving a question of conflict of laws. Their course might be expected to reduce litigation, and is to be commended as much as good draftsmanship which relieves courts of problems of resolving ambiguities. . . . A tendency toward certainty in commercial transactions should be encouraged by the courts." Moreover, as the Restatement notes in comment *e* to section 187, "Prime objectives of contract law are to protect the justified expectations of the parties and to make it possible for them to foretell with accuracy what will be their rights and liabilities under the contract. These objectives may best be attained in multistate transactions by letting the parties choose the law to govern the validity of the contract and the rights created thereby. In this way, certainty and predictability of result are most likely to be secured."

Aaron: But what if the parties choose truly awful or horribly one-sided law to govern the transaction? After all, in a great many contracts, one side has substantially more bargaining power than the other.

Neil: That's why rules giving effect to party autonomy to choose the governing law are always paired with provisions invoking "fundamental public policy" or the like—to protect against such unpleasant scenarios.

Aaron: But, as you know, those doctrines are used only in extreme cases. I'm still worried that the ability of parties to choose the governing law by "agreement" will often create an opportunity for the stronger party to take advantage of the weaker party.

Neil: That is a legitimate worry that I share, but if the stronger party in a transaction wants to take advantage of the weaker party, aren't there plenty of other things that it can do that are more effective than a choice of law clause? For example, it can charge high prices, offer bad service, insist on one-sided but enforceable contract provisions, cut corners on performance in ways that are too expensive for the weaker party to attack, etc. If we would like to get rid of inequality of bargaining power in business deals, I'm not convinced that conflict of laws doctrines are the place to start.

CHAPTER 5

ESTATES AND TRUSTS

■ ■ ■

A. INTESTATE SUCCESSION

For all the impact of interest analysis on choice of law in tort and contracts, the rules governing devolution of property remain frozen in jurisdiction selecting rules akin to those discussed in Chapter 1. Thus, with regard to intestate succession to land the law of the situs controls as to who takes property upon the death of the decedent and what shares of the land those heirs take. It makes no difference that the decedent and all the heirs are domiciled in one state and the land is located in another; the law of the situs applies. Restatement (Second) of Conflict of Laws § 236 (1971). The late Professor Russell Weintraub gave the following example: Mr. Smith dies intestate owning land in State X. Smith (at the time of his death), his wife, and three minor children all resided in State Y. Under State X intestacy law, the widow takes a one-third interest in the real estate and the other two-thirds goes to the children. Under State Y law, the widow gets one-half interest in the realty and the children get the other half. If interest analysis were to govern, State Y law surely would apply. Russell Weintraub, Commentary on the Conflict of Laws, § 8.7 (2010). It is hard to conjure up an interest for State X in deciding who inherits the property. Yet, the law on this issue is so well established that it is rarely litigated. Cases of sixty and seventy year-old vintage pass for modern authority on this subject.

When it comes to intestate devolution of personal property, however, the almost universal rule is that the law of the decedent's domicile at the time of death governs. Restatement (Second) of Conflict of Laws § 260 (1971). *In re Estate of Jones,* set forth in Chapter 1, is illustrative. In that case, an Iowa court applied Iowa law allowing an illegitimate child to recover the entirety of the decedent's personal property even though the two contestants were Welsh citizens and the decedent was on the way back to Wales, his domicile of origin. Under the law of Wales, the illegitimate child was not entitled to inherit. The Iowa court found that the decedent was domiciled in Iowa at the time of his death. No discussion of competing interests was undertaken. That remains the law to this day.

B. TESTAMENTARY SUCCESSION

Before looking at the differences between testamentary disposition of land and movables it is important to note that states differ as to the formal requisites to make a valid will. Such issues as the number of witnesses, the need to notarize a will, the validity of holographic wills, etc. could present a nightmare when a testator owned land or personal property in many states. Thankfully, that problem has been eliminated in nearly all states. The text of the Uniform Probate Code exemplifies the typical "alternative reference" statute. It provides:

> A written will is valid . . . if its execution complies with the law of execution of the place where the will is executed, or of the law of the place where at the time of execution or at the time of death the testator is domiciled, has a place of abode or is a national.

While the Uniform Probate Code provision relates to the formal requisites of a will, the general rule is that the substantive validity and effect of a will of land is governed by the situs of the land. We have already encountered one such case in Chapter 1. You will recall that in *Estate of Hannon v. Glover* the decedent left property located in both Virginia and Nebraska to her surviving children and to "issue" of her deceased children. One of her deceased children was survived by an adopted child. The decedent was domiciled in Virginia. Under Virginia law an adopted child was not considered issue and would not inherit. Under Nebraska law the adopted child met the definition of "issue" and was entitled to inherit Nebraska land. The Nebraska court applied the situs rule and held that the adopted child inherited his share of the Nebraska land. Scholars have ridiculed the slavish reliance on the situs rule where the situs really has no interest as to who will own the property and all the contestants reside in the domicile of the testator. *See* Peter Hay, Patrick J. Borchers and Symeon C. Symeonides, Handbook on the Conflict of Laws, § 20.6 n.9 (2010). Nonetheless the authors of that treatise conclude that that the "situs rule for realty . . . continues to exert a powerful hold on American courts."

When the issue involves the will of personal property, the law of the decedent's domicile at the time of his death usually governs. In the following case, the domicile rule trumped a very specific clause of the will:

IN RE ESTATE OF CLARK
236 N.E. 2d 152 (N.Y. 1968)

FULD, C.J.

This appeal poses an interesting and important question concerning a widow's right of election to take against her husband's will. More particularly, may her husband, domiciled in a foreign state, by selecting New York law to regulate his testamentary dispositions, cut off or otherwise affect the more favorable right given his widow to elect by the law of their domicile?

In the case before us, Robert V. Clark, Jr., died in October of 1964, domiciled in Virginia, and there his widow continues to reside. His estate, consisting of property in Virginia and in New York, had an aggregate value of more than $23,000,000—the bulk of which consisted of securities on deposit with a New York bank. His will, made in 1962, contained a provision that 'this Will and the testamentary dispositions in it and the trusts set up shall be construed, regulated and determined by the laws of the State of New York.' It devised the Clark residence in Virginia, together with its contents, to the widow and created for her benefit a preresiduary marital deduction trust—under which she would receive the income for life, with a general testamentary power of appointment over the principal of the trust. The residue of the estate, after payment of estate taxes, was placed in trust for the testator's mother. There has been a bi-state administration of the estate. The New York executors are administering the major portion of the estate—consisting, as noted, of securities held in New York during Mr. Clark's lifetime—and the Virginia executors are administering the balance, including the real and tangible personal property located in Virginia.

The testamentary trust for the widow's benefit would satisfy the requirements of section 18 of our Decedent Estate Law, Consol.Laws, c. 13. However, it is conceded that, under the statutes of Virginia, the widow has an absolute and unconditional right to renounce her husband's will and take her intestate share (in the absence of issue, one half) of his estate outright. Timely notice of the widow's election having been given, the New York executors initiated this special proceeding in the Surrogate's Court, pursuant to section 145-a of the New York Surrogate's Court Act. The petition requests a determination denying the widow any right of election on the grounds that the terms of the will barred her from recourse to Virginia law and that, under New York law, the testamentary provisions in her favor were sufficient. The executors contend that, by declaring that his testamentary dispositions should be construed by the laws of New York, the testator meant to bar his widow from exercising her Virginia right of election and that section 47 of the Decedent Estate Law requires that we give effect to his purpose. That section provided, in essence, that, when a nondomiciliary testator recites in his will that he elects that his 'testamentary dispositions' shall be construed and regulated by the laws of New York, 'the validity and effect of Such dispositions shall be determined by such laws.' . . .

The Surrogate upheld the executor's position. On appeal, the Appellate Division reversed, deciding that the widow's right to take in opposition to the will must be determined by the law of the domicile of the parties. Section 47—which relates solely to the decedent's 'testamentary dispositions' and their validity and effect—was inapplicable, the court concluded, because 'the right of a widow to inherit despite the will is not a 'testamentary disposition' in any sense' but is, on the contrary, 'a restriction on the right to make a testamentary disposition.' (Citation omitted).

We thoroughly agree with the Appellate division's construction of the statue and with the conclusion it reached. . . .

A moment's reflection is all that is necessary to establish the difference between statutes which have to do with restrictions placed on the decedent's testamentary power—for instance, to disinherit his spouse or other members of his family—and those which bear on discerning and carrying out the testator's wishes and desires. Section 47 is an example of the latter sort of legislation. Its earliest version simply reflected the traditional choice of law rules, referring dispositions of personal property to the law of the decedent's domicile. It provided that the 'validity and effect * * * of a testamentary disposition' of real property were to be regulated by the law of the situs and those of personalty by the law of the domicile; no exception was made for a case in which the testator might express a contrary intent. . . .

Matter of Crichton, 228 N.E.2d 799, . . . is illustrative. A domiciliary of New York had placed his personal property in a state (Louisiana) which had a very different method of protecting a surviving spouse. In deciding that the law of the domicile ought to be applied, our court noted that Louisiana had no 'interest in protecting and regulating the rights of married persons residing and domiciled in New York.' On the contrary, we declared, 'New York, as the domicile of Martha and Powell Crichton, has not only the dominant interest in the application of its law and policy but the only interest.' . . .

[The court discusses cases dealing with inter vivos trusts.]

While Virginia, as well as New York, has demonstrated concern for surviving spouses, the two states have done so in substantially different ways. A right to the income of a trust, sufficient under our law (Decedent Estate Law, s 18), is by no means the equivalent of taking the principal outright as would be the widow's right upon her election under Virginia law. Whether the widow in the case before us would be adequately provided for under the will or our own law is irrelevant, for the same principles must apply to an estate of $23,000 as to one of $23,000,000, and we reject the notion that New York ought to impose upon its sister states its own views as to the adequacy of a surviving spouse's share.

In sum, Virginia's overwhelming interest in the protection of surviving spouses domiciled their demands that we apply its law to give the widow in this case the right of election provided for her under that law. We find nothing in section 47 of the Decedent Estate Law or in the public policy of New York which would permit a decedent, by a mere expression of intent, to change this result.

The order appealed from should be affirmed, with costs to all parties appearing separately and filing separate briefs payable out of the estate.

BURKE, SCILEPPI, BERGAN, BREITEL and JASEN, JJ., concur.

C. TRUSTS

Before discussing the choice of law rules governing substantive validity of trusts, it is important to note that the formal validity of both testamentary trusts and *inter vivos* trusts may be upheld by the validating law of a number of possible jurisdictions. See Section B, *supra*. Thus, similar to the alternative reference rules for upholding the validity of wills, most states either by statute or common law decision will uphold the validity of a trust with regard to formalities if the trust instrument is executed in accordance with law of the place of execution or the domicile of the testator or settlor of the trust.

1.   TESTAMENTARY TRUSTS

The choice of law rules governing testate succession set forth in the previous section apply to testamentary trusts as well. With regard to trusts involving land, the reference is to the local law of the situs. However, courts seeking to escape law that will substantively invalidate a trust have made use of escape mechanisms of the sort described in Chapter 2 to validate the trust and give effect to the will of the testator. When dealing with the validity of testamentary trusts of movables, the courts have evidenced a willingness to be flexible and to apply the rule that will uphold the validity of the trusts even though it violates the law of the domicile. The following case (though of ancient vintage) is much cited for this proposition.

HOPE V. BREWER
32 N.E. 558 (N.Y. 1892)

Appeal from Supreme Court, general term, first department.

O'BRIEN, J.

The general question presented by this appeal is the validity of the twenty-sixth or residuary clause of the will of Thomas Hope, who died on March 3, 1890, without issue. The will contains numerous bequests to collateral relatives, and to institutions and corporations for charitable purposes. By the residuary clause, all the rest, residue, and remainder of the testator's estate was devised and bequeathed to his executors and their survivors, in trust for the purpose of founding and endowing an infirmary for the care and relief of sick and infirm persons, to be established at the testator's native place of Langholm, in Dumfrieshire, Scotland. The testator directed his executors, as trustees, to promptly take all necessary and proper steps for procuring the incorporation and organization of this infirmary.

* * *

The twenty-sixth or residuary clause of the will, as well as the first codicil, in so far as they relate to the founding and endowment of the infirmary in Scotland, were also changed and modified by this second codicil by substituting the following provision: 'Instead of said institution being founded and endowed by said trustees in the manner therein mentioned, I direct them, as soon after my decease as they can conveniently do so, to realize all the rest, residue, and remainder of my said property and estate so bequeathed to them, and to pay, assign, and make over the whole proceeds thereof, when and as realized, to and in favor of William Elphinstone Malcolm, * * * George Maxwell, * * * and Robert Smellie, residing in Langholm aforesaid, * * * as trustees and in trust, to the end that they may apply the same in founding, endowing, and maintaining an institution for the care or relief of sick or infirm persons to be established and located at Langholm, my native place, * * * and to be called 'The Thomas Hope Hospital.". . .

The plaintiff is the nephew of the testator, and one of the legatees under the will, and he brings this action to set aside as void the disposition of the residuary estate, contained in the twenty-sixth clause and the codicils, on the ground that the several provisions for the establishment of the infirmary or hospital are too indefinite and uncertain in their subjects and objects, and unlawfully suspend the power of alienation of real estate and the absolute ownership of personal property. . . . Reference has * * * been made to the language of the will and codicil, wherein the testator undertook to specify and define the persons who were to be the recipients of his charity or the beneficiaries of the trust. There is no defined beneficiary either named or capable of being ascertained within the rules of law applicable to such cases in order to constitute a valid testamentary trust under the law of this state. The words, 'sick, infirm, or aged persons in reduced circumstances,' within a certain town or parish, or within such other towns and parishes, in a certain county, as the governors of the institution might from time to time select and determine, are entirely too vague and indefinite to satisfy the rule, with respect to the beneficiaries of a trust, which prevails in this state. (Citations omitted). . . .

This brings us to the important question in this case, whether the courts of this state are required in such a case to interpose our own laws with respect to the requisites of a valid testamentary trust in order to defeat the disposition which the testator has made of his property, and which is perfectly valid where he intended the gift to take effect. In the great variety of cases bearing upon the validity of trusts of this character, and in the manifold aspects in which questions growing out of such dispositions of property have arisen and been presented to the courts, it is not, perhaps, surprising that, in some of the opinions of the courts, dicta, expressed in general language, may be found giving support to the plaintiff's contention. But I have not been able to find any well-considered case, in which the question was directly involved, where a gift to a foreign charity in trust, contained in a valid testamentary instrument, has been held void, where there was a trustee competent to take and hold, and the trust was capable of being executed and enforced, according to the law of the place to which the property was to be transmitted under the will of the donor. . . .

Our law with respect to the creation of trusts, the suspension of the power of alienation of real estate, and the absolute ownership of personal, was designed only to regulate the holding of property under our laws and in our state, and a trust intended to take effect in another state, or in a foreign country, would not seem to be within either its letter or spirit. When a citizen of this state, or a person domiciled here, makes a gift of personal estate to foreign trustees for the purpose of a foreign charity, our courts will not interpose our local laws with respect to trusts and accumulations to arrest the disposition made by the owner of his property, but will inquire as to two things: First, whether all the forms and requisites necessary to constitute a valid testamentary instrument, under our law, have been complied with; and, second, whether the foreign trustees are competent to take the gift, for the purposes expressed, and to administer the trust under the law of the country where the gift was to take effect. . . . In this case the testator was unquestionably competent to give, and did make the gift under all the forms and requisites necessary to constitute a valid testamentary disposition. So were the trustees to whom the gift was made, competent to take and administer it, under Scotch law, and the only question is whether we must defeat the gift and frustrate the intentions of the testator because he neglected to observe, in all respects, the rules of our local law with regard to the creation of trusts and perpetuities. . . .

We have examined the cases cited by the learned counsel for the plaintiff in support of his contention. They contain general expressions of the rule that a testamentary disposition of property invalid at the domicile of the owner is invalid everywhere, and, indeed, this rule is stated in some of the cases to which I have referred, and, as a general principle, cannot be questioned. But when it is said that such a disposition is invalid everywhere if invalid at the domicile, the rule refers to some defect in the execution of the instrument, the capacity of the testator, the legal construction of the instrument, the form or object of the disposition, and not to the noncompliance, in framing the terms of the trust, with a local statute or rule of law regulating the holding of property by the citizens of the state or country where the will was made, and which had no extraterritorial force. . . . Our conclusion is that, even if it be assumed that the bequest of the residuary estate to the Scotch trustees, in trust for the purpose of founding and maintaining the hospital, should be held void under our law for the reason that the absolute ownership of personal property is unlawfully suspended, or that the beneficiaries of the trust are not sufficiently specified or defined, still that does not render the disposition invalid, as these objections do not apply to a gift in trust to be administered in Scotland, and perfectly valid there. This result, I think, is in harmony with the general tendency of courts to sustain testamentary dispositions of property when it fairly can be done under the rules of law, and in accordance with principles of enlightened justice. The judgment should therefore be affirmed, with costs to the executors, the foreign trustees, and the plaintiff, payable out of the estate.

---

2. INTER VIVOS TRUSTS

With regard to *inter vivos* trusts of land, the situs rule generally governs the validity of the trust. However, with regard to tangible personal property, the settlor of the trust is pretty much free to transfer personal property (e.g. chattels or securities) and be confident that the trust will be upheld under the law of the situs or the law of the domicile of the seller by the trust. The leading case, again from New York, is illustrative.

HUTCHISON V. ROSS
187 N.E. 65 (N.Y. 1933)

LEHMAN, JUDGE.

John Kenneth Ross, a resident of Montreal, married in Toronto in 1902. In anticipation of their marriage, the parties entered into an antenuptial agreement to regulate their property rights in accordance with the law of Quebec, where they intended to reside. They still do reside there. Under the civil law prevailing in that province, there is community of property between spouses, but the parties to a marriage may by antenuptial agreement provide that each shall continue to have separate property. They may also by such antenuptial agreement provide for gifts or trusts in favor of one or the other. After the marriage, such provisions in an antenuptial agreement may not be abrogated, modified, or enlarged. Neither husband nor wife may transfer to the other, directly or in trust, any substantial part of his or her fortune.

The antenuptial agreement made by Ross and his prospective wife provided that the property of each should be separate, and Ross agreed in addition to provide for the support of his wife and to establish either by deed or will a trust fund of $125,000 for the benefit of his wife and children. Since John Kenneth Ross was at that time a young man without personal fortune, though the only son of a very rich man, his father became a party to the antenuptial agreement and guaranteed a 'donation' of $125,000 binding upon his estate.

The father of John Kenneth Ross died in 1913, leaving an estate of about $10,000,000 to his son. In 1916, during the World War, John Kenneth Ross, the son, decided that a provision of $125,000 for his family was insufficient, and he told his wife that he desired to provide for her more adequately by creating a trust fund of $1,000,000, the income to be paid to his wife for life, and the principal to go to their two children upon her death. One D. M. C. Hogg, a Scotchman learned in the law of Scotland, but perhaps not in the law of Quebec, had been the secretary and adviser of Ross' father. Ross, the son, had continued to employ him in the same capacity. Ross directed Hogg to prepare or have prepared appropriate instruments to transfer to the Equitable Trust Company in the city of New York a fund of $1,000,000, to be held in trust for his wife. Both father and son had kept bank deposits and had securities valued at more than half a million dollars in New York City, in the New York branch of the Bank of Montreal. Ross desired that such securities, with substitutions and additions sufficient to create a fund of $1,000,000, should constitute the corpus of the trust estate.

Hogg, in accordance with what he deemed his instructions, prepared a trust deed or agreement. The trustee was to pay the income to Mrs. Ross during her life and after her death to divide the principal among the children of the marriage her surviving or their issue per stirpes or to make other disposition thereof in accordance with the provisions of the instrument. The instrument was submitted to the trust company for approval. After the trust company had agreed to act as trustee, the instrument was sent to Montreal, where Ross and his wife executed it before the American Consul General. The Equitable Trust Company had not yet signed the indenture, but did so after the indenture was sent to it. Then the Bank of Montreal in New York City, acting as agent for Ross, delivered the securities to the trustee. The trust deed contains a recital that: 'Whereas Mr. Ross has become possessed of ample means and is desirous of making suitable provision for Mrs. Ross in lieu of the provisions in her favor contained in said contract of marriage settlement, and Mrs. Ross is willing to renounce and revoke the provisions of said marriage settlement in her favor and to accept in lieu thereof the provisions for her benefit and support hereinafter contained in this agreement.' Mrs. Ross then expressly revoked all conditions or provisions contained in the contract of marriage and all benefits which might accrue to her under the marriage contract.

For about ten years, the trustee carried out the provisions of the trust indenture. During that time, no one questioned its validity. In 1926, Ross retained a Montreal barrister to draw up a will. He told the barrister of the provision he had already made for his family. The barrister promptly told Ross that the trust indenture was patently invalid under the law of Quebec, and so notified the trustee. By that time, most of the estate which Ross had received from his father had been dissipated. Ross was deeply involved in speculations in oil stocks. He owed large sums to some Baltimore banks. He informed the Baltimore banks that the trust he had created was invalid, and, in consideration of his promise to bring legal proceedings to have the trust set aside and to deliver the trust property to the banks as collateral, they agreed not only to extend the existing loans but to make new loans to Ross. He secured the signatures of his wife and children to written consents to revoke the trust. Ross then began an action to set aside the trust on the ground that it was void at its inception and a second action for the revocation of the trust upon the consent of the interested parties.

After the actions were commenced, a petition in bankruptcy was filed against the plaintiff, and the trustee in bankruptcy was substituted in his place. The defendants in the first action assert that under the law of New York the conveyance is valid and should be enforced here. In the second action they assert that the signatures to the consents to revoke the trust were obtained by misrepresentations and that issue of the settlor's children, born and unborn, have an interest in the trust. Both actions were tried together. They resulted in a judgment in favor of the plaintiff in the first action, and a judgment on the merits in favor of the defendants in the second action. Appropriate findings were made in each action. Upon appeal the Appellate Division reversed the judgment in the first action and upon new findings dismissed the complaint upon the merits. It affirmed the judgment in the second action. . . .

The rules that both the capacity to make a valid conveyance of tangible chattels and securities and the essential validity of such conveyance are determined by the law of the state where the chattel is situated at the time of the conveyance have been generally applied to conveyances inter vivos. They are not generally applied to passage of title by will or the intestacy of a decedent owner. With possible limitations, not relevant to the question here presented (30 N.E. 125), the rule is well established that the essential validity of a testamentary trust must be determined by the law of the decedent's domicile, and the same rule often is applied to trusts established as part of a marriage settlement. The plaintiff urges that the same rule should be applied to a conveyance in trust inter vivos, especially where such trust is established for the benefit of the wife and children of the settlor. . . .

In all the affairs of life there has been a vast increase of mobility. Residence is growing less and less the focal point of existence and its practical effect is steadily diminishing. Men living in one jurisdiction often conduct their affairs in other jurisdictions, and keep their securities there. Trusts are created in business and financial centers by settlors residing elsewhere. A settlor, regardless of residence, cannot establish a trust to be administered here, which offends our public policy. If we hold that a nonresident settlor may also not establish a trust of personal property here that offends the public policy of his domicile, we shackle both the nonresident settlor and the resident trustee.

Our courts have sought whenever possible to sustain the validity even to testamentary trusts to be administered in a jurisdiction other than the domicile of the testator. (Citations omitted). In regard to other conveyances or alienations of personal property situated here, they have steadfastly applied the law of the jurisdiction where the personal property is situated. The maxim that movable personal property follows its owner is restricted to the field within which the state, where that property is found, chooses to apply other laws than its own, and modern conditions have caused a limitation of that field to narrow bounds. That is true in other jurisdictions as well as here. Where a nonresident settlor establishes here a trust of personal property intending that the trust should be governed by the law of this jurisdiction, there is little reason why the courts should defeat his intention by applying the law of another jurisdiction. *Cf.* Dicey on Conflict of Laws (4th Ed.) pp. 591 and 713.

We balance the weight of such considerations against the weight of the dicta in old cases. We may throw in the balance also expressions of public policy by the Legislature of this state. It has provided that: 'Whenever a person being a citizen of the United States, or a citizen or a subject of a foreign country, wherever resident, creates a trust of personal property situated within this state at the time of the creation thereof, and declares in the instrument creating such trust that it shall be construed and regulated by the laws of this state, the validity and effect of such trust shall be determined by such laws.' Personal Property Law (Consol. Laws, c. 41) a 12–a. It is true that the statute was enacted long after the creation of the trust now the subject of this litigation, and the validity of the trust must, probably, be determined by the law as it then existed. The statute does not change retroactively a well-established rule of law. It merely establishes a definite public policy in a field where the rules of law were still fluid and undefined. When the courts are called upon to define these rules even as of an earlier date, they cannot entirely disregard this public policy. (Citation omitted). The Legislature has made simpler the choice between possible rules even if it could not dictate such choice.

It is said that the statute establishes a public policy only where there is an express declaration of intention in the instrument that it shall be construed and regulated by the laws of this state. Here there is no express declaration of intention, but the intention is implied in every act and word of the parties. The statute makes express declaration of intention conclusive, but a construction which would deny effect to intention appearing by implication would be unreasonable. Indeed, since the statute in terms applies even to residents of this state, such construction would be almost impossible. It follows that the validity of a trust of personal property must be determined by the law of this state, when the property is situated here and the parties intended that it should be administered here in accordance with the laws of this state. . . .

In the second action brought to revoke the trust with the alleged written consent of all the interested parties, the plaintiff, indeed, describes the instrument creating the trust only as a 'trust deed.' Interesting questions are raised in that action as to whether unborn or infant parties may not have an interest in the trust. We do not reach those questions, for the courts below have found that the consents which have been signed by the wife and children were obtained by misrepresentation. The trier of the fact, on the evidence produced, might reasonably have refused to make such findings. We cannot say that there is no evidence to sustain them. . . .

The judgment in each action should be affirmed, with costs.

[Dissenting opinion omitted].

––––––––––––––––

Accord: *Shannon v. Irving Trust Co.*, 9 N.E.2d 792 (N.Y. 1937) (trust invalid under New York law, the locus of the trust, but valid under New Jersey law, the domicile of the settlor, held to be valid); *National Shawmut Bank v. Cumming*, 91 N.E.2d 337 (Mass. 1950) (trust valid under Massachusetts law, the locus of the trust but invalid under Vermont law, the domicile of the grantor, held to be valid).

Why should antenuptial agreements be treated differently than elections against the will? *See Estate of Clark, supra.* Aren't both part of the domestic relations law of the domicile?

A discussion of probate and administration of estates is beyond the scope of this book. For an extensive discussion see, Hay, Borchers and Symeonides, Conflict of Laws, Chapter 22 (2010).

CHAPTER 6

FAMILY LAW

■ ■ ■

A. INTRODUCTION

Family law cases involve some of the most personal and heartfelt disputes that the legal system must address. Legal rules governing resolution of those disputes thus pick winners and losers in a context that is often emotionally quite charged. When those rules differ from state to state, so that determination of the prevailing party in a dispute requires deciding which state's law governs, the pressure on the choice of law rules is quite high.

This chapter addresses three frequently-recurring family law issues—adoption, marriage, and legitimacy—from the perspective of choice of law rules. it should be noted that interstate and cross-border problems with respect to these matters raise issues not only issues of choice of law but also issues of jurisdiction and (in the domestic context) full faith and credit. Keeping with the focus of these materials on choice of law, however, the cases below focus on that question.

Keep in mind that family law issues such as adoption, marriage, and legitimacy are questions of status (e.g., "are x and y married?" or "is z the child of x and y?"), but lawsuits are rarely about such abstract questions. Rather, lawsuits are much more often about incidents of that status (e.g., "does y, who claims to be the spouse of x, inherit from x who died intestate?"). Thus, the choice of law questions in the cases below arise, for the most part, in connection with disputes about the incidents of the status issues rather than in the abstract.

It should come as no surprise to you by now that the traditional approach to choice of law for family matters, as exemplified by the first restatement, is more mechanical than the newer approach favored by the second restatement. For each of the subjects addressed below, consider which approach you prefer, taking into account not only fairness and justice in the context of a particular case but also ease of administration and predictability and certainty of results.

B. ADOPTION

Adoption cases, while almost always about the incidents of the status created by adoption, usually revolve around a determination of whether the person in question should be determined to have been adopted by the putative adopted parents. Other times, the dispute is not about the occurrence of the adoption but, rather, about which state's law determines the incidents of that adoption. Which law governs the former question (whether adoption occurred) has traditionally been governed by territorial rules familiar to you from the early chapters in this book. consider the following case.

RAMSEY COUNTY V. YEE LEE

770 N.W.2d 572 (Minn. App. 2009)

OPINION

PETERSON, JUDGE.

In this action to establish child-support under Minn.Stat. § 256.87 (2008), appellant county argues that . . . the district court abused its discretion when it failed to recognize that a Hmong cultural adoption that occurred in Thailand is a legally valid adoption. . . . [b]ecause appellant did not prove that the adoption is valid under the law of Thailand . . . we affirm.

FACTS

Appellant Yer Yang and respondent Yee Lee are Hmong refugees who fled from Laos and lived in a refugee camp in Thailand. They were married in 1993. In July 1999, Yang and Lee took in an infant, Y.P.L., who had been in the care of his grandmother because his mother had died. They obtained a birth certificate from Thai government officials. According to Yang, Lee obtained the birth certificate and Yang was not aware of what Lee told officials, but Yang explained that when a child is born in Thailand, the parents go to the Thai government and let them know that the child is theirs, and a certificate that is like a birth certificate in the United States is issued. Lee claimed that he was not aware of the birth certificate. The birth certificate is written in the Thai language, which Lee can read but Yang cannot. The birth certificate lists "Mee Yang" as the mother and "Yer Lee" as the father, which Yang claims were false names used to avoid arrest by Thai authorities.

There is no dispute that the ceremonies conducted to bring Y.P.L. into Yang's and Lee's family as an adopted child were appropriate within the Hmong culture. According to Yang, the decision to adopt was mutual. Lee claims that he did not agree with the adoption, that Yang paid for the adoption ceremonies by herself, and that he "wasn't happy about it."

On June 29, 2002, Yang and Lee obtained a divorce according to Hmong cultural practices. A divorce decree was issued, which was signed by elders who were members of Lee's family. The divorce decree states that Lee failed to assist Yang with daily household chores and activities. Neither the adoption nor the divorce was ever registered with Thai authorities. Nothing in the record demonstrates that the Thai government was aware of the marriage, the adoption, or the divorce.

After the divorce, Lee maintained contact with Y.P.L. while still in Thailand. According to Yang, Y.P.L. cried because he missed his father and would walk to Lee's house, sometimes staying there for an entire day. Lee remarried and adopted his new wife's two children. He came to the United States in 2004 and settled in Ramsey County. Yang came to the United States with Y.P.L in 2005 and settled in Eau Claire, Wisconsin. Since Yang and Lee have been in the United States, Lee has not attempted to contact Y.P.L.

Yang filed for public assistance provided under Title IV-D of the Social Security Act. Wisconsin requested that Minnesota obtain an order setting ongoing child support from Lee, and appellant Ramsey County filed an action to establish child support under Minn.Stat. § 256.87 (2008) and chapter 518C (2008), the Uniform Interstate Family Support Act. The complaint alleged that Lee is the parent of Y.P.L. and owes a duty to support him. Lee filed a request for a hearing on the grounds that he "disagree[d] with the child support amount."

A child support magistrate (CSM) ordered briefing and held a hearing to determine the effect of the cultural marriage, adoption, and divorce on the duty of Lee to support Y.P.L. and the effect of the birth certificate on his duty to support. At the hearing, Yang testified regarding the adoption, Yang's and Lee's marriage and divorce, and the parent-child relationship that developed between Lee and Y.P.L.

Steven Thao, a Hmong elder and expert on Hmong culture, testified regarding the culture of Hmong refugees in Thailand. Thao testified that, in Hmong culture, a woman would not be able to adopt a child without her husband's consent and that it was common for Hmong refugees in Thailand to use false names to avoid arrest by Thai officials. Thao also testified that in Hmong culture, if the husband is at fault in a divorce, everything, including the children, goes to the wife. Thao testified that he was not familiar with Thai law because Hmong refugees were governed by their own laws, not the laws of Thailand.

Lee testified that he had never seen the birth certificate and pointed out that it listed the father as "Yer Lee" not "Yee Lee." Lee testified that he can read Thai and the document appeared to be official and contained signatures from Thai authorities. He also testified that, in order to adopt a child in Thailand, it is necessary to secure the appropriate document and follow a set of Thai legal procedures. He acknowledged that a Hmong cultural adoption took place but claimed that he did not agree and that Yang took care of all of the expenses for the adoption and rituals.

The CSM filed findings of fact, conclusions of law, and an order requiring Lee to pay ongoing child support and granting Yang a judgment for past child support due in 2007 and 2008. In an attached memorandum, the CSM found "that a parent-child relationship was established that is sufficient to create a duty to support the child." The CSM stated that its determination "is not governed by statute, nor is there a well defined body of case law that mandates the outcome." Instead, the CSM concluded that the duty to support was arrived at from the facts and a desire to promote the well-being of Y.P.L.

Lee sought review by the district court, and the district court concluded that "there is no legal avenue available to obligate [Lee] to pay child support. The cultural adoption is not recognized and any other legal doctrine that would impute legal adoption has never been extended to child support cases." Accordingly, the district court ordered that Lee need not pay child support as ordered by the CSM. This appeal followed.

ISSUES

1.   Did appellant prove that the adoption of Y.P.L. in Thailand is legally valid and, therefore, created a parent-child relationship and a duty of support under Minn.Stat. § 256.87 (2008)?

* * *

ANALYSIS

A Minnesota human-services statute provides, "A parent of a child is liable for the amount of public assistance . . . furnished to and for the benefit of the child, including any assistance furnished for the benefit of the caretaker of the child, which the parent has had the ability to pay." A parent who is found able to reimburse the county for public assistance furnished for a child may also be ordered to make continuing support contributions. The county has the burden of proving its reimbursement claim by a preponderance of the evidence.

I.

"The parent and child relationship between a child and . . . an adoptive parent may be established by proof of adoption." Proving that an adoption occurred in a foreign country is relatively straightforward when there is a decree from a foreign court. "The general rule is that things done in one sovereignty in pursuance of the laws of that sovereignty are regarded as valid and binding everywhere." Consequently, "a foreign country's judicial adoption decree will be recognized by United States courts as producing a legal adoption, subject to the condition that the foreign decree not be repugnant to the laws of the state."

In this case, however, there is no adoption decree from a foreign country because the adoption procedure that was followed did not produce a decree. Appellants do not cite, and we have not found, any authority that requires an adoption decree in all instances to establish proof of adoption, but there must be proof that the applicable requirements for a valid adoption in the foreign jurisdiction have been met. The general rule is that[i]f under the law of the place having jurisdiction there has been a valid adoption, the status arising from that adoption will be recognized elsewhere, provided the status is not contrary to positive law and public policy of the place where its recognition is sought. . . . On the other hand, if under the law governing an attempted adoption, the adoption is invalid because of failure to comply with the provision of the law, no status is created which will be recognized elsewhere.

15A C.J.S. Conflict of Laws § 57 (2002).

Minnesota case law is consistent with the principle that a Minnesota court will recognize a foreign adoption as valid if the adoption was valid under the laws of the jurisdiction where it took place. In the context of a marriage contracted in another state, the Minnesota Supreme Court has adopted the following rule: " 'The validity of a marriage normally is determined by the law of the place where the marriage is contracted. If valid by that law the marriage is valid everywhere unless it violates a strong public policy of the domicile of the parties.' " This court applied this rule in a case involving a marriage contracted in another country in which a husband argued that his marriage, which he entered into in the People's Republic of China, could not be dissolved by a Minnesota court order because it was not a valid marriage. This court determined that because evidence of the marriage had been shown, there was a strong presumption of its legality under Minnesota law. This court held that because the husband "presented no evidence of the requirements for a valid marriage under Chinese law or that the marriage was not contracted legally in China," he "failed to meet his burden of proof to rebut the presumption of a valid marriage," and, therefore, the district court properly recognized the marriage. Id.

Minnesota courts have also recognized the validity of an adoption in a foreign country, even though there was no adoption decree. In Patrick v. N. City Nat'l Bank of Duluth (In re Will of Patrick), the testator's brother, who lived in Scotland in 1915, agreed to adopt a child. The brother treated the child as his son but never undertook any formal adoption proceedings. A dispute arose over whether the son was a "descendent" within the meaning of the testator's will. The court noted that there was no statutory procedure for adoption in Scotland. But the court then went on to find that both statute and judicial opinion have recognized the prior existence of a relationship of "de facto adoption." This has also been characterized as "common law adoption" under Scots law. As early as the 19th century, Scotch courts had recognized the right, in certain circumstances, of those who acquired custody of a child by agreement to retain it, and referred to such parents as having "adopted" the child. In the light of all these considerations it appears that some sort of adoption was known to the law in Scotland at the time of the events involved here.

The court held that because the evidence conclusively proved a de facto adoption recognized in Scotland, it was presumed that the testator intended the son to be included within the meaning of the term "descendant."

These Minnesota cases persuade us that when determining whether an adoption in a foreign country has been proved and there is no adoption decree, a Minnesota court must determine whether the adoption complied with the adoption laws in the country where it occurred. If the adoption met the requirements of the foreign country's law, a Minnesota court should recognize the adoption as valid, provided that the adoption is not repugnant to the laws of Minnesota.

The county, which bears the burden of proving that Lee adopted Y.P.L., argues that the Hmong cultural adoption was valid under the law of Thailand. But the only evidence of Thai law that the county cites is the Conflict of Laws Act B.E. 2481, which was enacted by the King of Thailand, by and with the consent of the House of Representatives, in 1938. Section 35 of the Conflict of Laws Act states:

If the adopter and the adopted have the same nationality, the adoption shall be governed by their law of nationality.

If the adopter and the adopted have different nationalities, the capacity and conditions for adoption shall be governed by the law of nationality of each party. However, the effects of adoption on the adopter and the adopted shall be governed by the law of nationality of the adopter.

Citing section 35, the county argues that because Yang, Lee, and Y.P.L. are Hmong, they are governed by the laws of the Hmong, and under the laws of the Hmong, the cultural adoption of Y.P.L. was valid. But section 6 of the Conflict of Laws Act states:

Whenever the law of nationality is to govern, and a person has two or more nationalities acquired successively, the law of nationality last acquired shall govern.

Whenever the law of nationality is to govern, and a person has two or more nationalities acquired simultaneously, the law of nationality of the country where such person has his domicile shall govern; if such person has his domicile in a country other than any such country, the law of his domicile at the time of the institution of action shall govern; if the domicile of such person is unknown, the law of the country where he has his residence shall govern.

In any cases of conflict as regards the nationality of a person, where one of the nationalities in conflict is Thai, the law of nationality which shall govern is the law of Siam.

As regards a person who has no nationality, the law of his domicile shall govern; if his domicile is unknown, the law of the country where he has his residence shall govern.

Whenever by application of the law of nationality, the local law, the communal law or the religious law, as the case may be, is to apply, such law shall govern.

Even if it is true that under the laws of the Hmong, the cultural adoption of Y.P.L. was valid, the county has not shown that the law of the Hmong governs when determining whether the adoption was valid. The record does not demonstrate whether Yang and Lee, who had both lived in at least two countries when the adoption occurred, had only one nationality. It appears that under the Conflict of Laws Act, this is a relevant fact when determining what law governs. And more importantly, the county has not shown that the Conflict of Laws Act applies at all to our determination whether the cultural adoption of Y.P.L. satisfied the legal requirements for an adoption in Thailand.

The county's assertion that the law of the Hmong governs is not implausible, but it is not supported by any authority that demonstrates that the county has correctly described the law of Thailand. The county did not offer any expert testimony regarding the legal effect of the Conflict of Laws Act and its application to Hmong living in Thailand, and appellant's expert on Hmong culture testified that he had no knowledge of Thai law regarding adoption. Even if the county is correct that the Conflict of Laws Act applies, the language of the act, on its face, suggests that to determine what law applies, more must be known about the facts of the case than that Yang, Lee, and Y.P.L. are all Hmong. Therefore, because the county has neither produced a foreign country's adoption decree for Y.P.L.'s adoption nor demonstrated that the adoption satisfied the legal requirements for an adoption in Thailand, we conclude that the district court correctly determined that the county did not prove that the cultural adoption is recognized in Thailand as valid.

[Appellants also argue that even if the adoption was not valid under the law of Thailand, the district court erred by not extending the doctrine of equitable adoption to this case when Y.P.L. was held out as the couple's son and has no remedy against his natural parents. Appellant argued that Minnesota has recognized the doctrine of equitable adoption in inheritance cases, that other jurisdictions have recognized the doctrine in cultural-adoption cases, and that the unique circumstances of this case justify this court's extending the doctrine to cultural adoptions in child-support cases. The court, however, declined to extend the application of the doctrine to circumstances under which it has not previously been applied.]

DECISION

Because the county did not meet its burden of proving that Lee adopted Y.P.L. under the law of Thailand and because, in Minnesota, the doctrine of equitable adoption has been applied only in inheritance cases, the district court did not err in concluding that Lee need not pay child support as ordered by the CSM.

Affirmed.

---

1.   Application of the traditional choice of law rule for adoption in this case required the Minnesota court to immerse itself in the Thai law of adoption. Is this task within the institutional competence of U.S. courts? Should issues of institutional competence determine what the choice of law rule for adoption should be?

2.   At the time of the lawsuit, Yang, Lee, and Y.P.L. were all in the United States, where financial support of Y.P.L. would be utilized. What interest does Thailand have in this dispute?

C. INCIDENTS OF ADOPTION

According to Section 143 of the First Restatement, "The status of adoption, created by the law of a state having jurisdiction to create it, will be given the same effect in another state as is given by the latter state to the status of adoption when created by its own law." Thus, when a state in which the effect of an alleged adoption is disputed adjudicates such a dispute, a court must make determinations about two separate issues governed by two separate bodies of law. First, was the status of adoption created by a foreign state with jurisdiction to do so? Second, what effect would be given to this adoption if it had been created under the law of this state?" The second question can create some interesting interpretive issues as illustrated by In re Goodwin's Estate.

IN RE GOODWIN'S ESTATE
86 A.2d 88 (Me. 1952)

NULTY, J.

From the bill of exceptions and the agreed statement of facts it appears that Caroline G. Wyman, the appellant, was legally adopted by the natural father and mother of Charles Hinds Goodwin, deceased, in the Commonwealth of Massachusetts in 1887; that at the time of said adoption the adoptive parents were legal residents of and domiciled in said Massachusetts; that after said adoption the deceased (Charles Hinds Goodwin) was born to the foster parents (of Caroline G. Wyman) and at the time of their death the said foster parents were residents of and domiciled in the town of Livermore Falls in the State of Maine. The said deceased (Charles Hinds Goodwin) died intestate on October 12, 1948, in said Livermore Falls leaving a widow, no children, the said Caroline G. Wyman (sister by adoption), and four cousins. It also appears from the record that in the orderly administration of the estate of Charles Hinds Goodwin a petition for distribution was filed in the Probate Court for Androscoggin County and on said petition for distribution the Probate Court ruled that the estate should be distributed one-half to the widow and one-eighth to each of the four cousins. From this decision the said Caroline G. Wyman (adoptive sister) duly appealed to the Superior Court for Androscoggin County, sitting as the Supreme Court of Probate, which ruled that the distribution ordered by the Judge of Probate was correct. From this ruling exceptions were taken and brought forward to this Court.

The real question and the only question for the determination of this court is whether or not the said appellant is entitled to inherit under the laws of descent or distribution one-half of the estate of said Charles Hinds Goodwin as an heir at law of her brother by adoption. This question involves and turns upon the proper construction of the language of Section 38, Chap. 145, R.S.1944, hereinafter set forth relating to the legal effect of adoption. Adoption has been defined as 'a judicial act creating between two persons certain relations, purely civil, of paternity and affiliation.' Black's Law Dictionary, Third Edition; Bouvier's Law Dictionary, Rawle's Third Edition, p. 146. Restatement of the Law of Conflict of Laws, Sec. 142, under Adoption, contains the following comment: 'a. Adoption is the relation of parent and child created by law between persons who are not in fact parent and child.' Under Sec. 143, Comment a, we find the following: 'The status of adoption is not created by the common law of England or of the states of the United States, nor does that law give it any legal effect. Unless there is in the state a statute providing for adoption, no effect will be given in England or a state of the United States to the status of adoption as such.' From the last quotation it will be seen that at common law the appellant would have no claim of inheritance in the estate of her adoptive brother, Charles Hinds Goodwin, deceased. Therefore, if she is entitled to rights of inheritance they must originate by virtue of a statute authorizing the same. See Gatchell v. Curtis, 134 Me. 302, 186 A. 669, 670, wherein we said: 'But the important point to remember is that adoption is unknown to the common law; it exists solely by virtue of statute. We must accordingly look to the various legislative acts to determine the rights of the parties affected by the decree of adoption.'

Sec. 38, Chap. 145, R.S.1944, reads as follows: 'Sec. 38. Legal effect of adoption of child; descent of property. R.S. c. 80, § 38. By such decree the natural parents are divested of all legal rights in respect to such child, and he is freed from all legal obligations of obedience and maintenance in respect to them; and he is, for the custody of the person and right of

obedience and maintenance, to all intents and purposes, the child of his
adopters, with right of inheritance when not otherwise expressly provided
in the decree of adoption, the same as if born to them in lawful wedlock,
except that he shall not inherit property expressly limited to the heirs of
the body of the adopters, nor property from their lineal or collateral kindred
by right of representation; but he shall not be reason of adoption lose his
right to inherit from his natural parents or kindred; and the adoption of a
child made in any other state, according to the laws of that state, shall have
the same force and effect in this state, as to inheritance and all other rights
and duties as it had in the state where made, in case the person adopting
thereafter dies domiciled in this state. If the person adopted dies intestate,
his property acquired by himself or by devise, bequest, gift, or otherwise
before or after such adoption from his adopting parents or from the kindred
of said adopting parents shall be distributed according to the provisions of
chapter 156, the same as if born to said adopting parents in lawful wedlock;
and property received by devise, bequest, gift, or otherwise from his natural
parents or kindred shall be distributed according to the provisions of said
chapter 156 as if no act of adoption had taken place.' (Italics ours.)

It will be noted that this statute makes reference to two classes of
adoptions. One may be termed the domestic or local adoption made under
the laws of the State of Maine. The other, an adoption made outside the
State of Maine. Our court has on several occasions interpreted certain
phases of local adoptions made under the laws of the State of Maine. See
Warren v. Prescott, 84 Me. 483, 24 A. 948, 17 L.R.A. 435, which settled the
proposition that by adoption the adopters could make themselves an heir
but they cannot thus make one for their kindred. See also Gatchell et al. v.
Curtis et al., supra, which case historically reviews the statutes and
amendments of this state with respect to local adoptions. See also the case
of Appeal of Latham, Appellant, 124 Me. 120, 126 A. 626, which holds that
a decree of local adoption entered in accordance with power conferred by
statute fixes the status of the child; it does not settle for all time the child's
right to inherit property. That remains as in the case of all persons subject
to legislative regulation, until it becomes vested by the death of him whose
estate may be subject to administration. Our court said in Gatchell et al. v.
Curtis et al., supra, quoting from Latham, Appellant, supra: 'The rights of
descent flow from the legal status of the parties, and, where the status is
fixed, the law supplies the rules of descent, with reference to the situation
as it existed at the death of the decedent.'

So far as we are aware there has been no construction of that part of
our adoption statute, supra, which reads as follows: 'And the adoption of a
child made in any other state, according to the laws of that state, shall have
the same force and effect in this state, as to inheritance and all other rights
and duties as it had in the state where made, in case the person adopting
thereafter dies domiciled in this state.' This section of the statute
apparently was passed by the Legislature in an attempt to clarify the

matter of foreign adoption before mentioned. That is, adoptions legally made outside of the state of Maine and in accordance with the law of the particular state or territory where the adoption took place. The instant case is such a situation, but it should be borne in mind that we are now speaking not of the rights of descent or inheritance from the adopters but are concerned solely with the question of whether or not an adoptive sister, the appellant in this case, can under our laws of descent or inheritance legally succeed to any interest in the property of the appellant's adoptive brother who was a natural child of the adopters.

We have heretofore pointed out the relationship of parent and child created by adoption and Restatement of the Law of Conflict of Laws, Sec. 143, states: 'The status of adoption, created by the law of a state having jurisdiction to create it, will be given the same effect in another state as is given by the latter state to the status of adoption when created by its own law.'

There is, however, considerable difference between the status of adoption, that is, the relationship of parent and child, and the right or capacity of the adopted child to inherit because under our decisions the right of inheritance applicable to local adoptions does not arise until the death of a decedent while the status of adoption becomes effective at the date of the decree of adoption. In 73 A.L.R. 964 under the Annotation entitled Conflict of Laws as to Adoption as Affecting Descent and Distribution of Decedent's Estate, and in 154 A.L.R. 1179 under the same title, and in the Annotation in 18 A.L.R.2d 960 under the title What Law, in Point of Time, Governs as to Inheritance from or through Adoptive Parent will be found many cases wherein the views of various courts of last resort of the United States are set forth and commented upon. Some courts take the view that the law creating the status of adoption is controlling. Others take the view that the law of the place where the property is situated or the law of decedent's domicile controls extent or fact of right of inheritance when in conflict with law creating the status. It does not seem to us that anything would be gained by citing these authorities or considering them in detail, but it seems to be the general rule that usually the status acquired by adoption in one state will be recognized in another and the right of the child to inherit will be given effect as to property located in the latter state and that right to inherit in a state other than that of his adoption will be determined by the law of the state creating the adoption, but it is only the adoption status with its incidental rights, if any, as to inheritance that will follow him to and be recognized in the state where the property is located or situated entitling him to inherit it if and to the extent that the law of the latter state allows a child there adopted to inherit; but the question whether an adopted child (irrespective of where he is adopted) can inherit and the extent of such right of inheritance, will be determined, not by the law of the state where the adoption took place, but by the law of the state where the property is located, or by the law of the domicile of the decedent, as the case may be, so that the fact that an adopted child can inherit under the law of the state of his adoption will not enable a child adopted in one state to inherit property in another state, under the laws of which an adopted child, even if adopted in the state, cannot inherit or can inherit only to a limited extent.

1 Am.Jur. Sec. 63, Page 662, states:

'The right of an adopted child to inherit as an heir of the relatives or descendants of the adoptive parents depends entirely upon statutory or constitutional provisions. And while these statutes, though similar, have not received a uniform construction, yet it is the general view that there is not conferred upon the child a right to inherit from the lineal or collateral kindred of the adoptive parent unless the language of the statutes is clearly to that effect.

'Adoption statutes, as well as matters of procedure leading up to adoption, should be liberally construed to carry out the beneficient purposes of the adoption institution and to protect the adopted child in the rights and privileges coming to it as a result of the adoption. But it does not follow that an adoption statute should be liberally construed to divert from its natural course the descent of property left by those who are not parties to the adoption proceedings. Consanguinity is so fundamental in statutes of descents and distributions that it may only be ignored by construction when courts are forced so to do either by the terms of express statute or by inexorable implication. To prescribe a course of descent which will take property of deceased persons out of the current of their blood, the legislature must use explicit and unmistakable language.'

An examination of the statute in question, namely, Sec. 38, discloses that domestic or local adopted children do not take from lineal or collateral kindred of the adoptive parents by right of representation, in fact, adopted children are specifically denied that right. It therefore follows that if the Legislature had intended to make any exception to a foreign adoption, it should have added explicit words to that effect. It appears to this court that the Legislature by the adoption act simply intended to say that if the foreign law of adoption gave the adopted child capacity to inherit from its adoptive parents the State of Maine would give a like right of inheritance from the adoptive parents provided such adoptive parents died domiciled in Maine. In other words, it is our opinion that that language referring to the person adopting dying domiciled in this state has no bearing on the question before us which is as we have stated before, whether or not the appellant, the adoptive sister of the decedent, is entitled to inherit from her adoptive brother. As we said above, if the adoption of the appellant had taken place under the laws of the State of Maine, she clearly would not have been entitled to receive anything from her adoptive brother's estate.

It is a well known fact that distribution of personal property in this state is governed by the rules of descent in force in this state at the date of death of the decedent, and we are unable to gather any legislative intent from the language used in said Section 38 which in any way would permit a foreign adoptee to take a greater share in a decedent's estate than a domestic or local adoption and we have before pointed out that the appellant, had she been legally adopted under the laws of Maine, would have been specifically excluded from taking any property from her adoptive brother. Thus we cannot believe that the appellant in this case is entitled to share in the estate of her adoptive brother. If the Legislature had intended such a course of descent which would take property of deceased persons out of the current of their blood, the Legislature should have used explicit and unmistakable language.

The mandate will be

Exceptions overruled. Case remanded.

---

1.   The rule in *In re Goodwin's Estate* is also adopted by the Second Restatement. See Restatement (Second) § 290. The rule is not followed everywhere, however. For a contrary view, see *Slattery v. Hartford-Connecticut Trust Co.*, 161 A. 79 (Conn. 1932)

2.   The majority rule creates a dépeçage of sorts, with the existence of adoption being decided by the law of one state and the effect of adoption being decided by the law of a different state. Do you agree that those two issues should be governed by the law of different states? Can the effect of this dépeçage be to resolve the matter disputed in a lawsuit in a way that neither state would have resolved it by applying only its own law?

D. MARRIAGE

In a mobile society, people who have been married (or claim to have been married) in one state often find themselves in another state in which the existence of that marriage is challenged, usually in the context of a dispute as to the incidents of marriage. Accordingly, when rules as to validity of a marriage differ from state to state, resolution of the choice of law question is critical.

The traditional rule in this area, still followed in the bulk of states, was set out in Sections 121 and 122 of the First Restatement. Section 121 provided that (subject to special rules for remarriage after divorce and for polygamous, incestuous, and "abhorrent" marriages) "a marriage is valid everywhere if the requirements of the marriage law of the state where the contract of marriage takes place are complied with." The converse was provided in Section 122: "A marriage is invalid everywhere if any mandatory requirement of the marriage law of the state in which the marriage is celebrated is not complied with."

The traditional rule has come under significant pressure, however, from both the more flexible concepts of the Second Restatement and from cases that confront changing definitions of marriage in some, but not all, states. Consider the following cases:

MCPEEK V. MCCARDLE
888 N.E.2d 171 (Ind. 2008)

RUCKER, J.

Summary

The question raised in this opinion is whether a marriage solemnized in another state in violation of that state's law may be recognized as valid in this state if the marriage complies with this state's law. The answer is yes.

Facts and Procedural History

As a result of her first husband's death, Edwina VanTyle became the sole owner of the family farm located in Ohio County and Switzerland County, Indiana. On June 30, 1994, armed with a marriage license obtained from the clerk of the circuit court in Ohio County, Indiana, Edwina and Charles McCardle, both residents of Indiana, traveled across state lines and were ostensibly married in the state of Ohio. The Reverend Donald S. Campbell performed the wedding ceremony and filled out the marriage certificate. Although Rev. Campbell was apparently authorized by his church to solemnize marriages in the state of Ohio, no marriage license was issued by the state of Ohio. Further, no ceremony took place in the state of Indiana. On July 1, 1994, the clerk of the circuit court in Ohio County, Indiana filed and recorded the marriage license and certificate. Shortly thereafter, in August 1994, Edwina executed a warranty deed transferring ownership of the farm to Charles McCardle and herself as husband and wife.

On July 26, 2004, Edwina died intestate. In December 2004, Edwina's two daughters and one son from her first marriage—Emma McPeek, Brenda Allen, and Caroll VanTyle (referred to collectively as "McPeek")—filed a complaint for declaratory judgment. In the complaint McPeek contended that the marriage between her mother and McCardle was void, and therefore she and her siblings were the proper owners of one-half the farm, which had been in the family for three generations.

Discussion

McPeek argues that her mother's marriage to McCardle is void because it was solemnized in the state of Ohio without the benefit of an Ohio marriage license in violation of Ohio Revised Code section 3101.05.

Unless strong public policy exceptions require otherwise, the law of the place where a marriage occurs generally determines the validity of a marriage. As a corollary, the general rule of law is that a marriage valid where it is performed is valid everywhere. Loughran v. Loughran, 292 U.S. 216, 223 (1934). The converse of this proposition is equally well settled: a marriage void where it is performed is void everywhere.

McPeek insists that her mother's Ohio marriage to McCardle is void. More specifically, according to McPeek, "[b]ecause the McCardle union which took place in Ohio did not meet the legal requirements for a lawful marriage to exist under Ohio law, Indiana must give Full Faith and Credit to the Ohio law and recognize that a lawful marriage did not occur and that their relationship was nothing more than a void common law marriage."

[The Indiana Supreme Court then reviewed Ohio case law and concluded that Ohio law appeared to be that the marriage was not void but, rather, voidable and thus "although defective, was nonetheless valid from its inception under the laws of Ohio and remained so at least until Edwina's death because the parties did not seek dissolution." But the court added a note of caution as an introduction to an alternative basis for its holding: "We acknowledge however that Ohio's court of last resort has not spoken on this subject in fifty years. And the latest reported decision by its intermediate Appellate Court occurred over thirty years ago. We are therefore hesitant to ground the resolution of this case solely on what may or may not be the current law of our sister state. We thus advance an alternative ground as well:"]

Not all jurisdictions adhere to the general rule that the law of the place where the marriage occurs determines the validity of the marriage. The Restatement (Second) Conflict of Laws § 283(1) (1971) advises, "The validity of a marriage will be determined by the local law of the state which, with respect to the particular issue, has the most significant relationship to the spouses and the marriage. . . ." And following the Restatement's guidance several jurisdictions have determined that even if invalid where solemnized, a marriage can be recognized as valid under the law of the forum state. See e.g., Donlann v. Macgurn, 55 P.3d 74, 77–79 (Ariz. App.2002) (Applying Arizona law to recognize an invalid marriage under the law of Mexico, the court declared that a marriage invalid under the law where the ceremony occurred was valid in Arizona if it would have been valid had the ceremony been performed in Arizona.); Matter of Estate of Murnion, 686 P.2d 893, 898–99 (Mont. 1984) (Applying Montana law, the court recognized a marriage which was invalid in the state of Washington because Washington retained no interest in the case.); In re Estate of Shippy, 678 P.2d 848, 851–52 (Wash. App. 1984) (Applying Washington law, the court recognized as valid a marriage that was invalid in the state of Alaska and declared that, although the validity of a marriage is generally governed by the law of the state where it is contracted, the state of Washington had a dominant interest in the validity of the decedent's marriage because decedent and wife were domiciled in Washington, decedent's property was located in Washington, and probate proceedings were pending there.). See also John C. Williams, Recognition by Forum State of Marriage Which, Although Invalid Where Contracted, Would Have Been Valid if Contracted Within Forum State, 82 A.L.R.3d 1240, 1978 WL 42963 (1978) (collecting cases).

We think the foregoing authorities express the better view as applied to this case. Before and after their marriage, Indiana was the domiciliary of both McCardle and Edwina, and both owned real and personal property in the state of Indiana. It appears that the only contact the parties had with Ohio is that the ceremony was conducted in that state. In essence any interest Ohio may have in the McCardles' marriage is overcome by the more substantial interest this state has in recognizing the marriage of the parties who, after all, obviously anticipated that their marriage would be valid. See Restatement § 283 cmt. i (noting that the basic policy underlying the rule recognizing a marriage even where invalid where contracted is "protection of the justified expectations of the parties").

Accordingly, we measure the McCardles' marriage against Indiana's solemnization provisions. Before two people may marry in Indiana they must negotiate a multi-step process. The parties must first obtain a marriage license from the clerk of the circuit court of either person's county of residence. The marriage license issued by the circuit court is the legal authority for an authorized person to marry the betrothed couple. The parties must then present the marriage license to a person who is authorized to solemnize marriages. Marriages may be solemnized by, among others, a member of the clergy of a religious organization. The person solemnizing the marriage must complete a marriage certificate and file the certificate and license with the clerk of the circuit court that issued the license; the clerk must then record the certificate and license.

It is undisputed that Edwina and McCardle complied with the requisite statutes in obtaining and filing their Indiana marriage license and certificate of marriage with the clerk of the Ohio County Circuit Court. And there was no evidence presented to the trial court, and no argument made on appeal, that the couple were married in Ohio with the intent of evading the laws of this state. We conclude that where, as here, a couple has complied with Indiana's statutory requirements regarding marriage licenses, certificates, and solemnization, such that the marriage would have been valid if solemnized in this state, we will recognize the marriage as valid even if the marriage ceremony took place in another state and did not comply with that state's law or public policy.

---

1.   One advantage of the traditional rule is that its results are generally predictable and certain. Does that advantage outweigh the factors found convincing by the court in McPeek?

2.   McPeek involved only two states. In a mobile society, however, it is not uncommon for couples to relocate frequently. As a result, under the McPeek court's reasoning and the Second Restatement rule, couldn't a peripatetic couple find itself married when in some states and unmarried when in others?

LEWIS V. NEW YORK STATE DEPARTMENT OF CIVIL SERVICE

872 N.Y.S.2d 578 (N.Y. App. Div. 3d Dep't 2009)

ROSE, J.

When defendant Department of Civil Service announced that it would recognize the parties to a same-sex marriage as spouses if their marriage were valid in the jurisdiction where it was solemnized, thereby allowing such spouses of state employees access to the benefits provided under the New York State Health Insurance Program, plaintiffs commenced this action as individual taxpayers seeking a declaration that the Department's recognition of such marriages is illegal, unconstitutional and results in the unlawful disbursement of public funds. Defendants then moved for dismissal of the complaint, and plaintiffs cross-moved for summary judgment on their claims. Bound by the holding that New York's marriage recognition rule requires the recognition of out-of-state same-sex marriages in Martinez v. County of Monroe, 50 A.D.3d 189, 850 N.Y.S.2d 740 [4th Dept. 2008], Supreme Court denied plaintiffs' cross motion and, after searching the record, granted summary judgment to defendants. Plaintiffs now appeal, arguing that the marriage recognition rule does not apply or, if it does, such marriages fall within an exception to the rule. Unpersuaded, we affirm Supreme Court's order.

While the type of marriage involved here is relatively novel, there are longstanding rules of law that have guided our courts in determining whether persons validly married elsewhere will be considered married in New York. Rooted ultimately in principles of comity and choice of law that give controlling effect to the laws of other jurisdictions unless they "would do violence to some strong public policy of this [s]tate" [citing, inter alia, Restatement, Second, of Conflict of Laws § 6], the well-settled marriage recognition rule "recognizes as valid a marriage considered valid in the place where celebrated" and the courts of New York must follow that rule unless the out-of-state marriage falls within one of its two exceptions. The first exception occurs where there is a "New York statute expressing clearly the Legislature's intent to regulate within this [s]tate marriages of its domiciliaries solemnized abroad." Such a statute must convey, in express terms, a legislative intent to void a marriage legally entered into in another jurisdiction. The second exception to the marriage recognition rule occurs in cases where an aspect of the out-of-state marriage is abhorrent to New

York public policy, such as incest or polygamy. This exception has been invoked to preclude recognition of an out-of-state polygamous marriage, an out-of-state incestuous marriage, and an out-of-state marriage where one party was under the age of consent.

Our courts have narrowly construed these two exceptions, applying the marriage recognition rule to recognize a wide variety of out-of-state marriages that would not qualify as marriages if they had been solemnized in New York. These include the second marriage of a divorced spouse even though such remarriage was expressly precluded at the time in New York by the former Domestic Relations Law, a marriage solemnized in Rhode Island that would be considered incestuous in New York, but was not found to be offensive "to a degree regarded generally with abhorrence," common-law marriages that are valid in other states but could not be entered into in New York, marriages of persons younger than the legal age of consent to marriage in New York, and marriages by proxy that could not occur in New York.

Given our longstanding application of the marriage recognition rule to determine whether out-of-state marriages not meeting our own definition of a marriage will, nevertheless, be recognized in New York, we must reject plaintiffs' initial contention that the rule can have no application here. Specifically, plaintiffs argue that the rule does not apply because same-sex marriages valid in the jurisdiction where solemnized are not "marriages," as that term is defined in New York. In every case in which the rule has been applied, however, the out-of-state marriage failed to meet New York's definition of a marriage in some respect. Also, while the Court of Appeals has held that the Domestic Relations Law limits marriages solemnized in New York to persons of the opposite sex and stated that any revision of the statute specifying who can be validly married here "rests with our elected representatives," it did not hold that same-sex marriages solemnized elsewhere would not be defined as marriages here, and it observed that the Legislature could rationally choose to permit same-sex couples to marry in New York. In addition, we note that the Supreme Courts of our neighboring states of Connecticut and Massachusetts have defined marriage in their states to include the marriage of same-sex couples. Thus, regardless of how we define marriage in New York, we must apply the marriage recognition rule to determine whether we will recognize same-sex out-of-state marriages for the purpose of according their parties spousal benefits.

Plaintiffs argue in the alternative that such marriages fall within one of the rule's two exceptions. Clearly, however, the rule's first exception is inapplicable because no New York statute expressly precludes recognition of a same-sex marriage solemnized elsewhere. While the Court of Appeals has held that the provisions of the Domestic Relations Law limit marriages solemnized in New York to opposite-sex couples, the Court did not go further and read those statutes as invalidating such marriages solemnized in other jurisdictions.

As for the second exception precluding recognition of an incestuous or polygamous marriage, we note that an out-of-state same-sex marriage would not fall within that preclusion unless the same-sex spouses were closely related or were more than two in number, situations not under consideration here. Nonetheless, since this exception is rooted in the idea that some marriages are abhorrent to New York public policy, we must consider plaintiffs' argument that same-sex marriages should come within this exception because they are as abhorrent to public policy as incest and polygamy. New York's public policy, however, cannot be said to abhor the recognition of out-of-state same-sex marriages.

The Court of Appeals has defined New York's "public policy" as "the law of the [s]tate, whether found in the Constitution, the statutes or judicial records." Unlike a majority of the states, and despite having had the opportunity to do so, New York has not taken the controversial step of enacting legislation to deny full faith and credit to out-of-state same-sex marriages as permitted under the federal Defense of Marriage Act. In addition, although the N.Y. Constitution does not compel recognition of same-sex marriages solemnized in New York, there is no New York court precedent holding that a New York statute or judicial decision precludes recognition of out-of-state same-sex marriages. To the contrary, several courts have recognized such marriages. Furthermore, as the Court of Appeals has twice cautioned us, where the Domestic Relations Law does not expressly declare void a certain type of marriage validly solemnized outside of New York, the statute should not be extended by judicial construction. Nor does our holding restrict the Legislature's ability to preclude recognition of out-of-state same-sex marriages in the future since the marriage recognition rule already admits of exceptions based upon statutory enactments. Accordingly, we conclude that the marriage recognition rule is applicable here and warrants dismissal of plaintiffs' first cause of action alleging an unlawful disbursement of public funds.

In the years since the decision in Lewis, there have been significant developments in the law governing same-sex marriages. Since 2009, many states, including New York, have legalized same-sex marriages, a key portion of the federal Defense of Marriage Act was found unconstitutional by the Supreme Court of the United States, and litigation as to whether states that do not recognize same sex marriage must recognize such marriages that take place elsewhere abounds.

Restatement (Second) of Conflict of Laws

Section 283: Validity of Marriage

(1) The validity of a marriage will be determined by the local law of the state which, with respect to the particular issue, has the most significant relationship to the spouses and the marriage under the principles stated in § 6.

(2) A marriage which satisfies the requirements of the state where the marriage was contracted will everywhere be recognized as valid unless it violates the strong public policy of another state which had the most significant relationship to the spouses and the marriage at the time of the marriage.

Comment b:

. . . Parties enter into marriage with forethought. To the extent that they think about the matter, they would usually expect that the validity of their marriage would be determined by the local law of the state where it was contracted. In situations where the parties did not give advance thought to the question of which should be the state of the applicable law, or where their intentions in this regard cannot be ascertained, it may at least be said that they expected the marriage to be valid.

The need for protecting the expectations of the parties gives importance in turn to the values of certainty, predictability and uniformity of result. For unless these values are attained, the expectations of the parties are likely to be disappointed.

Protection of the justified expectations of the parties by choice-of-law rules in the field of marriage is supported both by those factors in Subsection (2) of § 6 which are directed to the furtherance of the needs of the parties and by those factors which are directed to implementation of the basic policy underlying the particular field of law. Protection of the justified expectations of the parties is a basic policy underlying the field of marriage.

––––––––––––

1.   Why are the justified expectations of the parties relevant when those expectations support a finding that the parties are married but not as relevant under the Restatement rule when the parties purport to wed in a state that does not recognize their marriage? If the parties know that their marriage is not valid where it purported to occur, should an "expectations" test result in a conclusion that the marriage is not valid elsewhere?

2.   Is the "strong public policy" test of Restatement (Second) Section 283(b) justiciable as a practical matter? If the state with the most significant relationship to the spouses and the marriage at the time of marriage does not recognize the marriage, how can a court determine which decisions not to recognize reflect a strong public policy and which decisions reflect a weaker policy? On what basis, for example, could a court conclude that a state's decision not to allow same-sex marriages does not reflect a strong public policy but that the same state's decision to exclude polygamous marriages does reflect such a policy?

E. LEGITIMACY

SMITH V. SMITH
1994 WL 149445 (Minn. Ct. App. 1994)

PETERSON, JUDGE.

On appeal from a marital dissolution decree, Kim Smith challenges the award of physical custody of T.L.S. to respondent Roger Smith arguing that Roger Smith is not the child's biological father. She also argues that the district court's findings were not supported by the evidence and that the district court made no findings regarding T.L.S. We affirm.

FACTS

The parties were married in 1984 in Vancouver, Washington. Before marrying, they lived together for eight years. While they lived together, two children were born. T.L.S., the second of these two children, was born in 1983. Four children were born during the marriage. Respondent has had physical custody of all six children since 1991, when appellant began having mental health problems.

Appellant first alleged that respondent was not the father of T.L.S. during her testimony at the dissolution hearing. She stated that respondent was aware that he was not T.L.S.'s father, but they decided not to disclose this to anyone. She also stated that they decided respondent would be known as the father. The record shows respondent was named as the father on T.L.S.'s birth certificate.

The trial court found that appellant took overdoses of pills in two suicide attempts in 1991 and that the children witnessed these suicide attempts. The trial court also found that appellant's mental health was greatly improved at the time of the dissolution hearing. The trial court found that respondent admitted he once had a drug addiction problem, but that there was no evidence that respondent is currently involved with drugs in any manner.

Appellant alleged that respondent mistreated the children, but the trial court found that extensive investigations by Roseau County Social Services revealed no evidence of maltreatment by respondent.

In making its custody determination, the trial court considered the custody study prepared by Roseau County Social Services, but stated that it was most impressed by the testimony of appellant's mother, who testified that granting physical custody to respondent would be in the best interests of the children. The trial court also found that the children had lived for

more than a year in a stable and satisfactory environment with respondent
and that it is desirable that these conditions be maintained.

DECISION

Appellant argues that respondent cannot be granted custody of T.L.S.
because respondent is not the child's biological father. See Minn.Stat.
§ 257.541, subd. 1 (1992) (biological mother of child neither conceived nor
born during marriage has sole custody of child until paternity is
established).

Paternity is an issue in every dissolution action involving children. A
child's status of legitimacy or illegitimacy generally is determined by the
law under which the child was born. 10 Am.Jur.2d Bastards § 9 (1963).
T.L.S. was born in Oregon. Before applying a choice-of-law analysis, the
court first must determine whether the application of one law instead of
another will produce a different result.

Under Minnesota law, respondent is presumed to be the biological
father of T.L.S. because he married appellant, the biological mother, and,
with his consent, respondent was named as the father on the child's birth
certificate. Under Oregon law, paternity may be established by the
marriage of the parents of a child after the birth of the child, but the Oregon
statute "does not serve to create any presumption that a man marrying a
woman having had a child out of wedlock is the father of that child." It is
necessary to apply a choice-of-law analysis because the law of Oregon will
produce a different result than the law of Minnesota.

Whether a child is legitimate is determined by the local law of the state
which, with respect to the particular issue, has the most significant
relationship to the child and the parent under the principles stated in § 6.
Restatement (Second) of Conflict of Laws § 287(1) (1969).

Restatement (Second) of Conflict of Laws § 6 lists seven factors
relevant to the choice of the applicable rule of law. Among these seven
factors are four of the five factors set forth in Milkovich v. Saari, 203
N.W.2d 408 (Minn. 1973) to be applied to resolve a choice-of-law issue. The
five factors set forth in Milkovich are: (1) predictability of result; (2)
maintenance of interstate and international order; (3) simplification of the
judicial task; (4) advancement of the forum's governmental interest; and
(5) application of the better rule of law. Applying these factors to the facts
of this case we find that Minnesota law should be applied.

(1) Predictability of results: This factor should be given little weight in
    this case since it "relates to consensual transactions where people
    should know in advance what law will govern their act." When T.L.S.
    was born, the parties were not married. They did not plan to move to
    Minnesota years later and dissolve their marriage. Furthermore,
    appellant testified that she and respondent "chose not to disclose that
    [respondent was not the father of T.L.S.] to none of our children and

nobody else and that he would be known as the father." To the extent that the parties anticipated any legal consequences of this decision, it was reasonable to predict that a parent and child relationship would be established.

(2) Maintenance of interstate and international order:

[U]nder this heading no more is called for than that the court apply the law of no state which does not have substantial connection with the total facts and the particular issue being litigated.

The parties and the child reside in Minnesota. This is a substantial connection to Minnesota.

(3) Simplification of the judicial process: The courts of this state are capable of administering the laws of another forum, but the unique facts of this case present a procedural complication. "The limitation of time within which an action may be brought relates to the remedy and is governed by the law of the forum." In re Estate of Daniel, 294 N.W. 465, 469 (Minn. 1940). If we apply Oregon substantive law, paternity is not established on the facts before us because there is no applicable presumption of paternity, which means that paternity would have to be established in an action. But, the procedural law of Minnesota does not allow the action to be brought. See Minn.Stat. § 257.57, subd. 1(b) (1992) (where presumption of paternity exists because man married mother after child's birth and, with man's consent, he is named as father on birth certificate, mother may bring an action for purpose of declaring the nonexistence of father and child relationship no later than three years after child's birth).

(4) Advancement of the forum's governmental interests: The purposes of the Parentage Act are to impose a duty on a father to support his child, to ensure that the mother does not bear the full financial responsibility for a child, and to protect the public by preventing a child from becoming a public charge. All of these purposes are served by applying the presumption under Minn.Stat. § 257.55, subd. 1(c) that respondent is the biological father of T.L.S. This furthers "the clear statutory purpose of promoting legitimacy." The statute also reflects a governmental interest in preventing evidence of paternity from being concealed by requiring that the nonexistence of the father and child relationship presumed under Minn.Stat. § 257.55, subd. 1(c) be established early in a child's life.

(5) Application of the better rule of law: This factor does not apply unless the other factors "leave the choice of law uncertain." We conclude that the first four factors clearly resolve the choice-of-law issue in favor of applying Minnesota law and this factor does not apply.

Under Minnesota law, respondent is presumed to be the biological father of T.L.S. Appellant did not bring an action for the purpose of establishing the nonexistence of the father and child relationship presumed under Minn.Stat. § 257.55, subd. 1(c) during the three-year limitations period and may not now bring such an action. Respondent may obtain custody in the dissolution proceeding because the presumption that he is the biological father of T.L.S. has not been rebutted. Minn.Stat. § 257.541, subd. 2(b) (1992). Determination of custody is governed by Minn.Stat. § 518.17 (1992).

[The court went on to affirm the trial court's decision, under Minnesota law, to award physical custody of T.L.S. to respondent Roger Smith.]

Section 137 of the First Restatement provided that "The status of legitimacy is created by the law of the domicil of the parent whose relationship to the child is in question." Would Smith have been decided differently under the First Restatement?

CHAPTER 7

CONSTITUTIONAL CONTROL OF CHOICE OF LAW

■ ■ ■

A. DUE PROCESS AND FULL FAITH AND CREDIT

It is rather clear that, if a lawsuit involved only Pennsylvania actors and events that took place entirely in Pennsylvania with no connection whatsoever to California, but the court decided to apply the law of California to the case, the adversely affected party could successfully claim that the court deprived that party of "due process of law" under the Fifth or Fourteenth Amendment to the United States Constitution. But, short of such extreme hypotheticals, the role of courts in finding constitutional limits on choice of law has been modest. As we shall see in the ensuing cases, in the past three decades the court has steadfastly declined to conclude that the Constitution mandates (or prohibits) any of the choice of law approaches that we have studied. That was not always so. Early on, the Court seemed to give constitutional status to First Restatement rules.

In *New York Life Ins. Co. v. Dodge*, 246 U.S. 357 (1918), a Missouri resident bought a life insurance policy from a New York insurance company at its office in Missouri. The insured sought to borrow money against the cash surrender value of the policy and mailed an application for the loan to the company office in New York. The application was accepted by return mail from New York. The insured defaulted on the loan. Under the terms of the loan agreement and under New York law, the insurance company cancelled the policy and applied its reserve value to pay off the loan. When the insured died, his widow sought to recover on the policy. Under Missouri law, New York Life was not entitled to cancel the policy. The Missouri court ordered New York Life to pay the face value of the policy to the widow. The Supreme Court, however, held that the loan contract was consummated in New York and New York law applied, saying that "to hold otherwise would permit destruction of the right—often of great value—freely to borrow money upon a policy from the issuing company at is home office, and would moreover, sanction the impairment of that liberty of contract guaranteed to all by the Fourteenth Amendment." In a stinging dissent, Justice Brandeis said the following:

> Even if the rules ordinarily applied in determining the place of a
> contract required this court to hold, as a matter of general law,
> that the loan agreement was made in New York, it would not

necessarily follow that the Missouri statute was unconstitutional, because it prohibited giving effect in part to the loan agreement. . . . The test of constitutionality to be applied here is that commonly applied when the validity of a statute limiting the right of contract is questioned, namely: Is the subject-matter within the reasonable scope of regulation? Is the end legitimate? Are the means appropriate to the end sought to be obtained? If so, the act must be sustained, unless the court is satisfied that it is clearly an arbitrary and unnecessary interference with the right of the individual to his personal liberty. Here the subject is insurance; a subject long recognized as being within the sphere of regulation of contracts. The specific end to be attained was the protection of the net value of insurance policies by prohibiting provisions for forfeiture; an incident of the insurance contract long recognized as requiring regulation. The means adopted was to prescribe the limits within which the parties might agree to dispose of the net value of the policy otherwise than by commutation into extended insurance; a means commonly adopted in nonforfeiture laws, only the specific limitation in question being unusual. The insurance policy sought to be protected was a contract made within the state, between a citizen of the state and a foreign corporation also resident or present there. The protection was to be afforded while the parties so remained subject to the jurisdiction of the state. . . . The statute does not invalidate any part of the loan; it leaves intact the ordinary remedies for collecting debts. The statute merely prohibits satisfying a part of the debt out of the reserve in a manner deemed by the legislature destructive of the protection devised against forfeiture. . . .

Under today's interest analysis, the *Dodge* decision seems comical. Missouri clearly had an interest in protecting its insured for an insurance policy issued in the state to protect the insured against forfeiture of the entire policy, so applying Missouri law would seem to be fully in accord with modern choice of law theory, and hardly a violation of the due process clause. Yet, two other cases—*Home Insurance Co. v. Dick*, 281 U.S. 397 (1930) and *Hartford Acc. & Indemnity Co. v. Delta Pine Land Co.*, 292 U.S. 143 (1934)—seemed to reinforce the view that the due process clause was in lock step with First Restatement rules.

The due process clauses of the Fifth and Fourteenth Amendments are not the only relevant constitutional provisions. The "Full Faith and Credit" clause of the Constitution also provides a potential source of authority (in interstate cases but not, for the most part, in international matters) in deciding which state's law should apply when those laws are in conflict. Article IV, Section 1 of the Constitution provides:

Full faith and credit shall be given in each state to the public acts, records, and judicial proceedings of every other state. And the Congress may be general laws prescribe the manner in which such acts, records, and proceedings shall be proved, and the effect thereof.

In *Alaska Packers Assoc. v. Industrial Acc. Comm'n*, 294 U.S. 532 (1935), a resident of California (Palma) entered into an employment contract in California in which the employer agreed to transport him to Alaska during the salmon canning season and return him to California where he was to be paid for his work. The contract provided that the parties had elected to be bound by the Alaska Workmen's Compensation law. Palma was injured in Alaska and upon his return sought compensation under the California Workmen's Compensation law. The California Workmen's Compensation Act provided that "The Commission shall have jurisdiction over all controversies arising out of injuries suffered with the territorial limits of this state in those cases where the injured employee is a resident of this state at the time of the injury and the contract of hire was made in this state. . . ." California granted Palma an award (presumably greater than would have been awarded in Alaska) and the California Supreme Court refused to set aside the award. The employer appealed to the Supreme Court of the United States.

Interestingly, the Supreme Court easily rejected the appellant's due process argument, finding that California had a rational basis for applying its law to a California resident who entered into the employment contract in California. (What happened to *lex loci delicti*?) The Court then went on to discuss whether California had violated the full faith and credit clause by not giving recognition to the Alaska statute. The Court said that "A rigid and literal enforcement of the full faith and credit clause, without regard to the statute of the forum, would lead to the absurd result that, wherever conflict arises, the statute of each state must be enforced in the courts of the other, but cannot be on its own." For Alaska law to prevail, the employer must show "that of the conflicting interests involved those of the foreign state are superior to those of the forum." California had a legitimate concern in providing compensation for a California resident who was temporarily working in Alaska and would return to California. "The interest of Alaska is not shown to be superior to that of California."

Several years later, in *Pacific Employers Ins. Co. v. Industrial Acc. Comm'n*, 306 U.S. 493 (1939), the Court was confronted with the flip side of the *Alaska Packers* case. This time, a Massachusetts resident regularly employed in Massachusetts was sent to California for temporary assignment. He was injured in California and sought compensation under the California Workmen's Compensation Act. The Court held that California (the state of injury) was entitled to apply its law and grant the employee an award. There was no talk of which state's interests were superior. California had a legitimate interest in applying its law to an injury that occurred in its state.

This very short summary of the history of the due process and the full faith and credit clause will offend scholars who have written voluminously on the subject. For those who are interested in delving further into the history see, Robert H. Jackson, *Full Faith and Credit—The Lawyer's Clause of the Constitution*, 45 Colum. L. Rev. 1 (1945); Laycock, *Equal Citizens of Equal and Territorial States: The Constitutional Foundations of Choice of Law*, 92 Colum. L. Rev. 249 (1992); Roosevelt, *The Myth of Choice of Law; Rethinking Conflicts*, 97 Mich. L. Rev. 2448 (1999).

All the gut-wrenching discussion of the respective roles of the due process and full faith and credit clauses came to a screeching halt with the following landmark decisions by the Supreme Court:

ALLSTATE INSURANCE COMPANY V. HAGUE
449 U.S. 302 (1981)

JUSTICE BRENNAN announced the judgment of the Court and delivered an opinion, in which JUSTICE WHITE, JUSTICE MARSHALL, and JUSTICE BLACKMUN joined.

This Court granted certiorari to determine whether the Due Process Clause of the Fourteenth Amendment or the Full Faith and Credit Clause of Art. IV, § 1 of the United States Constitution bars the Minnesota Supreme Court's choice of substantive Minnesota law to govern the effect of a provision in an insurance policy issued to respondent's decedent. (Citation omitted).

I

Respondent's late husband, Ralph Hague, died of injuries suffered when a motorcycle on which he was a passenger was struck from behind by an automobile. The accident occurred in Pierce County, Wis., which is immediately across the Minnesota border from Red Wing, Minn. The operators of both vehicles were Wisconsin residents, as was the decedent, who, at the time of the accident, resided with respondent in Hager City, Wis., which is one and one-half miles from Red Wing. Mr. Hague had been employed in Red Wing for the 15 years immediately preceding his death and had commuted daily from Wisconsin to his place of employment.

Neither the operator of the motorcycle nor the operator of the automobile carried valid insurance. However, the decedent held a policy issued by petitioner Allstate Insurance Co. covering three automobiles owned by him and containing an uninsured motorist clause insuring him against loss incurred from accidents with uninsured motorists. The uninsured motorist coverage was limited to $15,000 for each automobile.

After the accident, but prior to the initiation of this lawsuit, respondent moved to Red Wing. Subsequently, she married a Minnesota resident and established residence with her new husband in Savage, Minn. At approximately the same time, a Minnesota Registrar of Probate appointed respondent personal representative of her deceased husband's estate. Following her appointment, she brought this action in Minnesota District Court seeking a declaration under Minnesota law that the $15,000 uninsured motorist coverage on each of her late husband's three automobiles could be "stacked" to provide total coverage of $45,000. Petitioner defended on the ground that whether the three uninsured motorist coverages could be stacked should be determined by Wisconsin law, since the insurance policy was delivered in Wisconsin, the accident occurred in Wisconsin, and all persons involved were Wisconsin residents at the time of the accident.

The Minnesota District Court disagreed. Interpreting Wisconsin law to disallow stacking, the court concluded that Minnesota's choice-of-law rules required the application of Minnesota law permitting stacking. The court refused to apply Wisconsin law as "inimical to the public policy of Minnesota" and granted summary judgment for respondent.

The Minnesota Supreme Court, sitting en banc, affirmed the District Court. The court, also interpreting Wisconsin law to prohibit stacking, applied Minnesota law after analyzing the relevant Minnesota contacts and interests within the analytical framework developed by Professor Leflar. *See* Leflar, *Choice-Influencing Considerations in Conflicts Law*, 41 N.Y.U.L.Rev. 267 (1966). The state court, therefore, examined the conflict-of-laws issue in terms of (1) predictability of result, (2) maintenance of interstate order, (3) simplification of the judicial task, (4) advancement of the forum's governmental interests, and (5) application of the better rule of law. Although stating that the Minnesota contacts might not be, "in themselves, sufficient to mandate application of [Minnesota] law," . . . the court concluded that the fifth factor—application of the better rule of law— favored selection of Minnesota law. The court emphasized that a majority of States allow stacking and that legal decisions allowing stacking "are fairly recent and well considered in light of current uses of automobiles." In addition, the court found the Minnesota rule superior to Wisconsin's "because it requires the cost of accidents with uninsured motorists to be spread more broadly through insurance premiums than does the Wisconsin rule." Finally, after rehearing en banc, the court buttressed its initial opinion by indicating "that contracts of insurance on motor vehicles are in a class by themselves" since an insurance company "knows the automobile is a movable item which will be driven from state to state." 289 N.W.2d, at 50 (1979). From this premise the court concluded that application of Minnesota law was "not so arbitrary and unreasonable as to violate due process." (Citation omitted).

II

It is not for this Court to say whether the choice-of-law analysis suggested by Professor Leflar is to be preferred or whether we would make the same choice-of-law decision if sitting as the Minnesota Supreme Court. Our sole function is to determine whether the Minnesota Supreme Court's choice of its own substantive law in this case exceeded federal constitutional limitations. Implicit in this inquiry is the recognition, long accepted by this Court, that a set of facts giving rise to a lawsuit, or a particular issue within a lawsuit, may justify, in constitutional terms, application of the law of more than one jurisdiction. As a result, the forum State may have to select one law from among the laws of several jurisdictions having some contact with the controversy.

In deciding constitutional choice-of-law questions, whether under the Due Process Clause or the Full Faith and Credit Clause, this Court has traditionally examined the contacts of the State, whose law was applied, with the parties and with the occurrence or transaction giving rise to the litigation. In order to ensure that the choice of law is neither arbitrary nor fundamentally unfair, the Court has invalidated the choice of law of a State which has had no significant contact or significant aggregation of contacts, creating state interests, with the parties and the occurrence or transaction.

Two instructive examples of such invalidation are *Home Ins. Co. v. Dick*, 281 U.S. 397 (1930), and *John Hancock Mutual Life Ins. Co. v. Yates*, 299 U.S. 178 (1936). In both cases, the selection of forum law rested exclusively on the presence of one nonsignificant forum contact.

Home Ins. Co. v. Dick involved interpretation of an insurance policy which had been issued in Mexico, by a Mexican insurer, to a Mexican citizen, covering a Mexican risk. The policy was subsequently assigned to Mr. Dick, who was domiciled in Mexico and "physically present and acting in Mexico," although he remained a nominal, permanent resident of Texas. The policy restricted coverage to losses occurring in certain Mexican waters and, indeed the loss occurred in those waters. Dick brought suit in Texas against a New York reinsurer. Neither the Mexican insurer nor the New York reinsurer had any connection to Texas. The Court held that application of Texas law to void the insurance contract's limitation-of-actions clause violated due process.

The relationship of the forum State to the parties and the transaction was similarly attenuated in *John Hancock Mutual Life Ins. Co. v. Yates*. There, the insurer, a Massachusetts corporation, issued a contract of insurance on the life of a New York resident. The contract was applied for, issued, and delivered in New York where the insured and his spouse resided. After the insured died in New York, his spouse moved to Georgia and brought suit on the policy in Georgia. Under Georgia law, the jury was permitted to take into account oral modifications when deciding whether an insurance policy application contained material misrepresentations.

Under New York law, however, such misrepresentations were to be evaluated solely on the basis of the written application. The Georgia court applied Georgia law. This Court reversed finding application of Georgia law to be unconstitutional.

Dick and *Yates* stand for the proposition that if a State has only an insignificant contact with the parties and the occurrence or transaction, application of its law is unconstitutional. *Dick* concluded that nominal residence—standing alone—was inadequate; *Yates* held that a postoccurrence change of residence to the forum State—standing alone— was insufficient to justify application of forum law. Although instructive as extreme examples of selection of forum law, neither *Dick* nor *Yates* governs this case. For in contrast to those decisions, here the Minnesota contacts with the parties and the occurrence are obviously significant. . . .

The lesson from *Dick* and *Yates*, which found insufficient forum contacts to apply forum law, . . . is that for a State's substantive law to be selected in a constitutionally permissible manner, that State must have a significant contact or significant aggregation of contacts, creating state interests, such that choice of its law is neither arbitrary nor fundamentally unfair. Application of this principle to the facts of this case persuades us that the Minnesota Supreme Court's choice of its own law did not offend the Federal Constitution.

III

Minnesota has three contacts with the parties and the occurrence giving rise to the litigation. In the aggregate, these contacts permit selection by the Minnesota Supreme Court of Minnesota law allowing the stacking of Mr. Hague's uninsured motorist coverages.

First, and for our purposes a very important contact, Mr. Hague was a member of Minnesota's work force, having been employed by a Red Wing, Minn., enterprise for the 15 years preceding his death. While employment status may implicate a state interest less substantial than does resident status, that interest is nevertheless important. The State of employment has police power responsibilities towards the nonresident employee that are analogous, if somewhat less profound, than towards residents. Thus, such employees use state services and amenities and may call upon state facilities in appropriate circumstances.

In addition, Mr. Hague commuted to work in Minnesota, . . . and was presumably covered by his uninsured motorist coverage during the commute. The State's interest in its commuting nonresident employees reflects a state concern for the safety and well-being of its work force and the concomitant effect on Minnesota employers.

That Mr. Hague was not killed while commuting to work or while in Minnesota does not dictate a different result. To hold that the Minnesota Supreme Court's choice of Minnesota law violated the Constitution for that reason would require too narrow a view of Minnesota's relationship with the parties and the occurrence giving rise to the litigation. An automobile accident need not occur within a particular jurisdiction for that jurisdiction to be connected to the occurrence. Similarly, the occurrence of a crash fatal to a Minnesota employee in another State is a Minnesota contact. If Mr. Hague had only been injured and missed work for a few weeks the effect on the Minnesota employer would have been palpable and Minnesota's interest in having its employee made whole would be evident. Mr. Hague's death affects Minnesota's interest still more acutely, even though Mr. Hague will not return to the Minnesota work force. Minnesota's work force is surely affected by the level of protection the State extends to it, either directly or indirectly. Vindication of the rights of the estate of a Minnesota employee, therefore, is an important state concern. . . .

Second, Allstate was at all times present and doing business in Minnesota. By virtue of its presence, Allstate can hardly claim unfamiliarity with the laws of the host jurisdiction and surprise that the state courts might apply forum law to litigation in which the company is involved. "Particularly since the company was licensed to do business in [the forum], it must have known it might be sued there, and that [the forum] courts would feel bound by [forum] law." (Citation omitted). Moreover, Allstate's presence in Minnesota gave Minnesota an interest in regulating the company's insurance obligations insofar as they affected both a Minnesota resident and court-appointed representative—respondent—and a longstanding member of Minnesota's work force—Mr. Hague.

Third, respondent became a Minnesota resident prior to institution of this litigation. The stipulated facts reveal that she first settled in Red Wing, Minn., the town in which her late husband had worked. She subsequently moved to Savage, Minn., after marrying a Minnesota resident who operated an automobile service station in Bloomington, Minn. Her move to Savage occurred "almost concurrently," with the initiation of the instant case. There is no suggestion that Mrs. Hague moved to Minnesota in anticipation of this litigation or for the purpose of finding a legal climate especially hospitable to her claim. The stipulated facts, sparse as they are, negate any such inference.

While *John Hancock Mutual Life Ins. Co. v. Yates*, 299 U.S. 178 (1936), held that a postoccurrence change of residence to the forum State was insufficient in and of itself to confer power on the forum State to choose its law, that case did not hold that such a change of residence was irrelevant. Here, of course, respondent's bona fide residence in Minnesota was not the sole contact Minnesota had with this litigation. And in connection with her residence in Minnesota, respondent was appointed personal representative of Mr. Hague's estate by the Registrar of Probate for the County of Goodhue, Minn. Respondent's residence and subsequent appointment in

Minnesota as personal representative of her late husband's estate constitute a Minnesota contact which gives Minnesota an interest in respondent's recovery, an interest which the court below identified as full compensation for "resident accident victims" to keep them "off welfare rolls" and able "to meet financial obligations." (Citation omitted).

In sum, Minnesota had a significant aggregation of contacts with the parties and the occurrence, creating state interests, such that application of its law was neither arbitrary nor fundamentally unfair. Accordingly, the choice of Minnesota law by the Minnesota Supreme Court did not violate the Due Process Clause or the Full Faith and Credit Clause.

Affirmed.

JUSTICE STEWART took no part in the consideration or decision of this case.

JUSTICE STEVENS, concurring in the judgment.

As I view this unusual case—in which neither precedent nor constitutional language provides sure guidance—two separate questions must be answered. First, does the Full Faith and Credit Clause *require* Minnesota, the forum State, to apply Wisconsin law? Second, does the Due Process Clause of the Fourteenth Amendment *prevent* Minnesota from applying its own law? The first inquiry implicates the federal interest in ensuring that Minnesota respect the sovereignty of the State of Wisconsin; the second implicates the litigants' interests in a fair adjudication of their rights.

I realize that both this Court's analysis of choice-of-law questions and scholarly criticism of those decisions have treated these two inquiries as though they were indistinguishable. Nevertheless, I am persuaded that the two constitutional provisions protect different interests and that proper analysis requires separate consideration of each.

I

The Full Faith and Credit Clause is one of several provisions in the Federal Constitution designed to transform the several States from independent sovereignties into a single, unified Nation. The Full Faith and Credit Clause implements this design by directing that a State, when acting as the forum for litigation having multistate aspects or implications, respect the legitimate interests of other States and avoid infringement upon their sovereignty. The Clause does not, however, rigidly require the forum State to apply foreign law whenever another State has a valid interest in the litigation. (Citations omitted). On the contrary, in view of the fact that the forum State is also a sovereign in its own right, in appropriate cases it may attach paramount importance to its own legitimate interests. Accordingly, the fact that a choice-of-law decision may be unsound as a matter of conflicts law does not necessarily implicate the federal concerns embodied in the Full Faith and Credit Clause. Rather in my opinion, the Clause should not invalidate a state court's choice of forum law unless that choice threatens the federal interest in national unity by unjustifiably infringing upon the legitimate interests of another State.

In this case, I think the Minnesota courts' decision to apply Minnesota law was plainly unsound as a matter of normal conflicts law. Both the execution of the insurance contract and the accident giving rise to the litigation took place in Wisconsin. Moreover, when both of those events occurred the plaintiff, the decedent, and the operators of both vehicles were all residents of Wisconsin. Nevertheless, I do not believe that any threat to national unity or Wisconsin's sovereignty ensues from allowing the substantive question presented by this case to be determined by the law of another State.

The question on the merits is one of interpreting the meaning of the insurance contract. Neither the contract itself, nor anything else in the record, reflects any express understanding of the parties with respect to what law would be applied or with respect to whether the separate uninsured motorist coverage for each of the decedent's three cars could be "stacked." Since the policy provided coverage for accidents that might occur in other States, it was obvious to the parties at the time of contracting that it might give rise to the application of the law of States other than Wisconsin. Therefore, while Wisconsin may have an interest in ensuring that contracts formed in Wisconsin in reliance upon Wisconsin law are interpreted in accordance with that law, that interest is not implicated in this case.

Petitioner has failed to establish that Minnesota's refusal to apply Wisconsin law poses any direct or indirect threat to Wisconsin's sovereignty. In the absence of any such threat, I find it unnecessary to evaluate the forum State's interest in the litigation in order to reach the conclusion that the Full Faith and Credit Clause does not require the Minnesota courts to apply Wisconsin law to the question of contract interpretation presented in this case.

II

It may be assumed that a choice-of-law decision would violate the Due Process Clause if it were totally arbitrary or if it were fundamentally unfair to either litigant. I question whether a judge's decision to apply the law of his own State could ever be described as wholly irrational. For judges are presumably familiar with their own state law and may find it difficult and time consuming to discover and apply correctly the law of another State. The forum State's interest in the fair and efficient administration of justice is therefore sufficient, in my judgment, to attach a presumption of validity to a forum State's decision to apply its own law to a dispute over which it has jurisdiction.

The forum State's interest in the efficient operation of its judicial system is clearly not sufficient, however, to justify the application of a rule of law that is fundamentally unfair to one of the litigants. Arguably, a litigant could demonstrate such unfairness in a variety of ways. Concern about the fairness of the forum's choice of its own rule might arise if that rule favored residents over nonresidents, if it represented a dramatic departure from the rule that obtains in most American jurisdictions, or if the rule itself was unfair on its face or as applied.

The application of an otherwise acceptable rule of law may result in unfairness to the litigants if, in engaging in the activity which is the subject of the litigation, they could not reasonably have anticipated that their actions would later be judged by this rule of law. A choice-of-law decision that frustrates the justifiable expectations of the parties can be fundamentally unfair. This desire to prevent unfair surprise to litigant has been the central concern in this Court's review of choice-of-law decisions under the Due Process Clause.

Neither the "stacking" rule itself, nor Minnesota's application of that rule to these litigants, raises any serious question of fairness. As the plurality observes, "[s]tacking was the rule in most States at the time the policy was issued." *Ante*, at 642, n. 22. Moreover, the rule is consistent with the economics of a contractual relationship in which the policyholder paid three separate premiums for insurance coverage for three automobiles, including a separate premium for each uninsured motorist coverage. Nor am I persuaded that the decision of the Minnesota courts to apply the "stacking" rule in this case can be said to violate due process because that decision frustrates the reasonable expectations of the contracting parties. . . .

In this case, no express indication of the parties' expectations is available. The insurance policy provided coverage for accidents throughout the United States; thus, at the time of contracting, the parties certainly could have anticipated that the law of States other than Wisconsin would govern particular claims arising under the policy. By virtue of doing business in Minnesota, Allstate was aware that it could be sued in the Minnesota courts; Allstate also presumably was aware that Minnesota law, as well as the law of most States, permitted "stacking." Nothing in the record requires that a different inference be drawn. Therefore, the decision of the Minnesota courts to apply the law of the forum in this case does not frustrate the reasonable expectations of the contracting parties, and I can find no fundamental unfairness in that decision requiring the attention of this Court.

In terms of fundamental fairness, it seems to me that two factors relied upon by the plurality—the plaintiff's postaccident move to Minnesota and the decedent's Minnesota employment—are either irrelevant to or possibly even tend to undermine the plurality's conclusion. When the expectations of the parties at the time of contracting are the central due process concern, as they are in this case, an unanticipated post-accident occurrence is clearly irrelevant for due process purposes. The fact that the plaintiff became a resident of the forum State after the accident surely cannot justify a ruling in her favor that would not be made if the plaintiff were a nonresident. Similarly, while the fact that the decedent regularly drove into Minnesota might be relevant to the expectations of the contracting parties, the fact that he did so because he was employed in Minnesota adds nothing to the due process analysis. The choice-of-law decision of the Minnesota courts is consistent with due process because it does not result in unfairness to either litigant, not because Minnesota now has an interest in the plaintiff as resident or formerly had an interest in the decedent as employee.

III

Although I regard the Minnesota courts' decision to apply forum law as unsound as a matter of conflicts law, and there is little in this record other than the presumption in favor of the forum's own law to support that decision, I concur in the plurality's judgment. It is not this Court's function to establish and impose upon state courts a federal choice-of-law rule, nor is it our function to ensure that state courts correctly apply whatever choice-of-law rules they have themselves adopted. Our authority may be exercised in the choice-of-law area only to prevent a violation of the Full Faith and Credit or the Due Process Clause. For the reasons stated above, I find no such violation in this case.

JUSTICE POWELL, with whom THE CHIEF JUSTICE and JUSTICE REHNQUIST join, dissenting.

My disagreement with the plurality is narrow. I accept with few reservations Part II of the plurality opinion, which sets forth the basic principles that guide us in reviewing state choice-of-law decisions under the Constitution. The Court should invalidate a forum State's decision to apply its own law only when there are no significant contacts between the State and the litigation. This modest check on state power is mandated by the Due Process Clause of the Fourteenth Amendment and the Full Faith and Credit Clause of Art. IV, § 1. I do not believe, however, that the plurality adequately analyzes the policies such review must serve. In consequence, it has found significant what appear to me to be trivial contacts between the forum State and the litigation. . . .

First, the contacts between the forum State and the litigation should not be so "slight and casual" that it would be fundamentally unfair to a litigant for the forum to apply its own State's law. (Citation omitted). . . .

Second, the forum State must have a legitimate interest in the outcome of the litigation before it. (Citation omitted). . . .

II. . . .

I do not believe, however, that Minnesota had sufficient contacts with the "persons and events" in this litigation to apply its rule permitting stacking. I would agree that no reasonable expectations of the parties were frustrated. The risk insured by petitioner was not geographically limited. (Citation omitted). The close proximity of Hager City, Wis., to Minnesota, and the fact that Hague commuted daily to Red Wing, Minn., for many years should have led the insurer to realize that there was a reasonable probability that the risk would materialize in Minnesota. Under our precedents, it is plain that Minnesota could have applied its own law to an accident occurring within its borders. . . . The fact that the accident did not, in fact, occur in Minnesota is not controlling because the expectations of the litigants *before* the cause of action accrues provide the pertinent perspective.

The more doubtful question in this case is whether application of Minnesota's substantive law reasonably furthers a legitimate state interest. The plurality attempts to give substance to the tenuous contacts between Minnesota and this litigation. Upon examination, however, these contacts are either trivial or irrelevant to the furthering of any public policy in Minnesota.

First, the postaccident residence of the plaintiff-beneficiary is constitutionally irrelevant to the choice-of-law question. *John Hancock Mut. Life Ins. Co. v. Yates, supra.* The plurality today insists that *Yates* only held that a postoccurrence move to the forum State could not "in and of itself" confer power on the forum to apply its own law, but did not establish that such a change of residence was irrelevant. What the *Yates* Court held, however, was that "there was no occurrence, *nothing* done, to which the law of Georgia could apply." 299 U.S., at 182, 57 S.Ct. at 131, (emphasis added). Any possible ambiguity in the Court's view of the significance of a postoccurrence change of residence is dispelled by *Home Ins. Co. v. Dick, supra*, cited by the *Yates* Court, where it was held squarely that Dick's postaccident move to the forum State was "without significance."

This rule is sound. If a plaintiff could choose the substantive rules to be applied to an action by moving to a hospitable forum, the invitation to forum shopping would be irresistible. Moreover, it would permit the defendant's reasonable expectations at the time the cause of action accrues to be frustrated, because it would permit the choice-of-law question to turn on a postaccrual circumstance. Finally, postaccrual residence has nothing to do with facts to which the forum State proposes to apply its rule; it is unrelated to the substantive legal issues presented by the litigation.

Second, the plurality finds it significant that the insurer does business in the forum State. The State does have a legitimate interest in regulating the practices of such an insurer. But this argument proves too much. The insurer here does business in all 50 States. The forum State has no interest in regulating that conduct of the insurer unrelated to property, persons, or contracts executed within the forum State. (Citation omitted). The plurality recognizes this flaw and attempts to bolster the significance of the local presence of the insurer by combining it with the other factors deemed significant: the presence of the plaintiff and the fact that the deceased worked in the forum State. This merely restates the basic question in the case.

Third, the plurality emphasizes particularly that the insured worked in the forum State. The fact that the insured was a nonresident employee in the forum State provides a significant contact for the furtherance of some local policies. The insured's place of employment is not, however, significant in this case. Neither the nature of the insurance policy, the events related to the accident, nor the immediate question of stacking coverage is in any way affected or implicated by the insured's employment status. The plurality's opinion is understandably vague in explaining how trebling the benefits to be paid to the estate of a nonresident employee furthers any substantial state interest relating to employment. Minnesota does not wish its workers to die in automobile accidents, but permitting stacking will not further this interest. The substantive issue here is solely one of compensation, and whether the compensation provided by this policy is increased or not will have no relation to the State's employment policies or police power.

Neither taken separately nor in the aggregate do the contacts asserted by the plurality today indicate that Minnesota's application of its substantive rule in this case will further any legitimate state interest. The plurality focuses only on physical contacts *vel non*, and in doing so pays scant attention to the more fundamental reasons why our precedents require reasonable policy-related contacts in choice-of-law cases. Therefore, I dissent.

———————————

Office Talk
#10

Neil: I must say that I found Justice Stevens's concurring opinion in *Allstate* very interesting. He says two things of note. First, he concludes that there is no violation of the Full Faith and Credit clause in this case. Second, as I noted above, he questions whether the decision of a judge to apply the law of his own state could ever be described as "wholly irrational." I have problems with the second statement (since it leads to the conclusion that a state never violates the due process clause by applying its own law, no matter how ephemeral the contacts with that state) but as to full faith and credit he is probably right. I don't see how there is a threat to Wisconsin sovereignty by the application of Minnesota law. As Justice Stevens points out, this was an automobile insurance policy designed to provide coverage in all states.

Aaron: I am concerned with the Full Faith and Credit clause and believe that this was an assault on Wisconsin sovereignty. Here is my reasoning. The majority in *Allstate* identified several Minnesota interests. They said that Minnesota had an interest in the well-being of Minnesota employees and an interest in Mrs. Hague, who became a Minnesota domiciliary after the accident. Putting to one side whether these stated interests were pure baloney (I think they were), there is something very wrong with the court's reasoning. What if Hague, instead of being employed in Minnesota, had a widowed mother who lived in Minnesota and the Mr. Hague called her five days of every week to check on her health. Assume further that Mr. Hague wrote a will leaving his entire estate to his mother. Would the presence of Mr. Hague's mother in Minnesota, which had no other connection to the dispute, justify application of Minnesota law? Is there anything that, in a federal union, can be characterized as a purely local transaction? Is it sufficient that something I do in New York may have some effect on someone in California? If your answer is yes, then almost every transaction or occurrence, no matter how local, can be held to create a potential conflicts case in which application of the law of a different state is allowable. After all, if Hague is not allowed to stack insurance policies his mother will be deprived of $30,000. Assume she is now living on welfare in Minnesota; she certainly has an interest in becoming solvent and off the welfare roles, and the result of the lawsuit about her son's accident impacts that interest. But using that as a justification for applying Minnesota law makes no sense. In short, I believe that conflicts law must recognize that there is something called a "local transaction" that does not lose its character as such merely because another state may have an interest in a different result. For me that amounts to an assault on the sovereignty of a sister state.

Neil: I hear your argument but you are barking up the wrong tree. *Allstate* won't go away. The case remains unchallenged after thirty years. Time to get off your soap box.

Aaron: One last word. Even if *Allstate*-like cases don't violate the Constitution (big C), should not the considerations I set forth

> be considered as constitution-like (small c) questions and lead
> a court away from far-fetched results.

Neil: I don't get you. Just about everyone (except the Minnesota
        Supreme Court) agrees that application of Minnesota law was
        unwise. I don't see where Big C or small c makes any
        difference.

PHILLIPS PETROLEUM COMPANY V. SHUTTS
472 U.S. 797 (1985)

JUSTICE REHNQUIST delivered the opinion of the Court.

Petitioner is a Delaware corporation which has its principal place of
business in Oklahoma. During the 1970's it produced or purchased natural
gas from leased land located in 11 different States, and sold most of the gas
in interstate commerce. Respondents are some 28,000 of the royalty owners
possessing rights to the leases from which petitioner produced the gas; they
reside in all 50 States, the District of Columbia, and several foreign
countries. Respondents brought a class action against petitioner in the
Kansas state court, seeking to recover interest on royalty payments, which
had been delayed by petitioner. They recovered judgment in the trial court,
and the Supreme Court of Kansas affirmed the judgment over petitioner's
contentions that the Due Process Clause of the Fourteenth Amendment
prevented Kansas from adjudicating the claims of all the respondents, and
that the Due Process Clause and the Full Faith and Credit Clause of Article
IV of the Constitution prohibited the application of Kansas law to all of the
transactions between petitioner and respondents. (Citation omitted). We
granted certiorari to consider these claims. (Citation omitted). . . .

Because petitioner sold the gas to its customers in interstate
commerce, it was required to secure approval for price increases from what
was then the Federal Power Commission, and is now the Federal Energy
Regulatory Commission. Under its regulations the Federal Power
Commission permitted petitioner to propose and collect tentative higher
gas prices, subject to final approval by the Commission. If the Commission
eventually denied petitioner's proposed price increase or reduced the
proposed increase, petitioner would have to refund to its customers the
difference between the approved price and the higher price charged, plus
interest at a rate set by statute. *See* 18 CFR § 154.102 (1984).

Although petitioner received higher gas prices pending review by the
Commission, petitioner suspended any increase in royalties paid to the
royalty owners because the higher price could be subject to recoupment by
petitioner's customers. . . .

Respondents Irl Shutts, Robert Anderson, and Betty Anderson filed suit against petitioner in Kansas state court, seeking interest payments on their suspended royalties which petitioner had possessed pending the Commission's approval of the price increases. Shutts is a resident of Kansas, and the Andersons live in Oklahoma. Shutts and the Andersons own gas leases in Oklahoma and Texas. Over petitioner's objection the Kansas trial court granted respondents' motion to certify the suit as a class action under Kansas law. Kan.Stat.Ann. § 60–223 et seq. (1983). The class as certified was comprised of 33,000 royalty owners who had royalties suspended by petitioner. The average claim of each royalty owner for interest on the suspended royalties was $100. . . .

[The court upheld the certification of the class.]

III

The Kansas courts applied Kansas contract and Kansas equity law to every claim in this case, notwithstanding that over 99% of the gas leases and some 97% of the plaintiffs in the case had no apparent connection to the State of Kansas except for this lawsuit. Petitioner protested that the Kansas courts should apply the laws of the States where the leases were located, or at least apply Texas and Oklahoma law because so many of the leases came from those States. The Kansas courts disregarded this contention and found petitioner liable for interest on the suspended royalties as a matter of Kansas law, and set the interest rates under Kansas equity principles.

Petitioner contends that total application of Kansas substantive law violated the constitutional limitations on choice of law mandated by the Due Process Clause of the Fourteenth Amendment and the Full Faith and Credit Clause of Article IV, § 1. . . .

Petitioner claims that Kansas law conflicts with that of a number of States connected to this litigation, especially Texas and Oklahoma. These putative conflicts range from the direct to the tangential, and may be addressed by the Supreme Court of Kansas on remand under the correct constitutional standard. . . .

The conflicts on the applicable interest rates, alone-which we do not think can be labeled "false conflicts" without a more thoroughgoing treatment than was accorded them by the Supreme Court of Kansas-certainly amounted to millions of dollars in liability. We think that the Supreme Court of Kansas erred in deciding on the basis that it did that the application of its laws to all claims would be constitutional.

Four Terms ago we addressed a similar situation in *Allstate Ins. Co. v. Hague.* In that case we were confronted with two conflicting rules of state insurance law. Minnesota permitted the "stacking" of separate uninsured motorist policies while Wisconsin did not. Although the decedent lived in Wisconsin, took out insurance policies and was killed there, he was employed in Minnesota, and after his death his widow moved to Minnesota for reasons unrelated to the litigation, and was appointed personal representative of his estate. She filed suit in Minnesota courts, which applied the Minnesota stacking rule.

The plurality in *Allstate* noted that a particular set of facts giving rise to litigation could justify, constitutionally, the application of more than one jurisdiction's laws. The plurality recognized, however, that the Due Process Clause and the Full Faith and Credit Clause provided modest restrictions on the application of forum law. These restrictions required "that for a State's substantive law to be selected in a constitutionally permissible manner, that State must have a significant contact or significant aggregation of contacts, creating state interests, such that choice of its law is neither arbitrary nor fundamentally unfair." (Citation omitted). The dissenting Justices were in substantial agreement with this principle. The dissent stressed that the Due Process Clause prohibited the application of law which was only casually or slightly related to the litigation, while the Full Faith and Credit Clause required the forum to respect the laws and judgments of other States, subject to the forum's own interests in furthering its public policy.

The Supreme Court of Kansas in its opinion in this case expressed the view that by reason of the fact that it was adjudicating a nationwide class action, it had much greater latitude in applying its own law to the transactions in question than might otherwise be the case:

> "The general rule is that the law of the forum applies unless it is expressly shown that a different law governs, and in case of doubt, the law of the forum is preferred. . . . Where a state court determines it has jurisdiction over a nationwide class action and procedural due process guarantees of notice and adequate representation are present, we believe the law of the forum should be applied unless compelling reasons exist for applying a different law. . . . Compelling reasons do not exist to require this court to look to other state laws to determine the rights of the parties involved in this lawsuit." . . .

We think that this is something of a "bootstrap" argument. The Kansas class-action statute, like those of most other jurisdictions, requires that there be "common issues of law or fact." But while a State may, for the reasons we have previously stated, assume jurisdiction over the claims of plaintiffs whose principal contacts are with other States, it may not use this assumption of jurisdiction as an added weight in the scale when considering the permissible constitutional limits on choice of substantive law. It may not take a transaction with little or no relationship to the forum and apply the law of the forum in order to satisfy the procedural requirement that there be a "common question of law." The issue of personal jurisdiction over plaintiffs in a class action is entirely distinct from the question of the constitutional limitations on choice of law; the latter calculus is not altered by the fact that it may be more difficult or more burdensome to comply with the constitutional limitations because of the large number of transactions which the State proposes to adjudicate and which have little connection with the forum.

Kansas must have a "significant contact or significant aggregation of contacts" to the claims asserted by each member of the plaintiff class, contacts "creating state interests," in order to ensure that the choice of Kansas law is not arbitrary or unfair. Given Kansas' lack of "interest" in claims unrelated to that State, and the substantive conflict with jurisdictions such as Texas, we conclude that application of Kansas law to every claim in this case is sufficiently arbitrary and unfair as to exceed constitutional limits.

When considering fairness in this context, an important element is the expectation of the parties. *See Allstate, supra*, 449 U.S., at 333, 101 S.Ct., at 650 (opinion of POWELL, J.). There is no indication that when the leases involving land and royalty owners outside of Kansas were executed, the parties had any idea that Kansas law would control. Neither the Due Process Clause nor the Full Faith and Credit Clause requires Kansas "to substitute for its own [laws], applicable to persons and events within it, the conflicting statute of another state," but Kansas "may not abrogate the rights of parties beyond its borders having no relation to anything done or to be done within them."

Here the Supreme Court of Kansas took the view that in a nationwide class action where procedural due process guarantees of notice and adequate representation were met, "the law of the forum should be applied unless compelling reasons exist for applying a different law." Whatever practical reasons may have commended this rule to the Supreme Court of Kansas, for the reasons already stated we do not believe that it is consistent with the decisions of this Court. We make no effort to determine for ourselves which law must apply to the various transactions involved in this lawsuit, and we reaffirm our observation in *Allstate* that in many situations a state court may be free to apply one of several choices of law. But the constitutional limitations laid down in cases such as *Allstate and Home Ins. Co. v. Dick, supra*, must be respected even in a nationwide class action.

We therefore affirm the judgment of the Supreme Court of Kansas insofar as it upheld the jurisdiction of the Kansas courts over the plaintiff class members in this case, and reverse its judgment insofar as it held that Kansas law was applicable to all of the transactions which it sought to adjudicate. We remand the case to that court for further proceedings not inconsistent with this opinion.

It is so ordered.

[JUSTICE STEVENS opinion concurring in part and dissenting in part is omitted.]

———————

Hague was greeted with disdain by most scholars (including Twerski). *See Symposium: Choice of Law Theory After Allstate Insurance Co. v. Hague*, 10 Hofstra L. Rev. 1 (1981). Also *see* Brilmayer, *Legitimate Interests in Multistate Problems: As Between State and Federal Law*, 79 Mich. L. Rev. 1315 (1981). Professor Brilmayer argues that if a state simply declares that it has an interest when no such interest is reflected in its domestic law, then it may be making an unconstitutional choice of law since *Hague* demands that in order to meet due process demands that a state have an interest. Professor Brilmayer argues that when a state, in fact, has a domestic interest it is not the business of the court to second guess the *sufficiency* of the interest. But if a state merely makes up an interest so that it can control choice of law, the court has a right to challenge the *existence* of such an interest at the domestic level. Thus, she argues that there was no evidence in *Hague* that at the domestic level that Minnesota's policy for stacking insurance coverage had any relationship to employment in the state. In short, the employment interest vis-à-vis stacking was a myth concocted to effect an otherwise unconstitutional choice of law. For comment on Professor Brilmayer's argument see, Aaron D. Twerski, *On Territoriality and Sovereignty: System Shock and Constitutional Choice of Law*, 10 Hofstra L. Rev. 149, 164–168 (1981). For other perspectives, *see* James Martin, *Personal Jurisdiction and Choice of Law*, 78 Mich. L. Rev. 872, 886–888 (1980); and Louise Weinberg, *Choice of Law and Minimal Scrutiny*, 49 U. Chi. L. Rev. 440 (1982).

Although the Supreme Court in *Phillips* held that Kansas could not apply its substantive law to cases which did not meet the minimalist test set forth in *Hague*, in a later case, *Sun Oil v. Wortman*, 486 U.S. 717 (1988) arising out of the same set of facts as *Phillips*, the Court held that Kansas could apply its five-year statute of limitations to all cases in the class (far longer than any of the other states). The grounds for allowing the application of forum law was that statutes of limitations have traditionally been characterized as procedural, and a state is free to apply its procedural law to cases litigated before it.

By the way, it is now clear that the due process clause and the full faith and credit clause are identical when it comes to determining whether a state's determination of which state's law to apply meets constitutional demands.

———————

Office Talk

#11

Aaron: Neil, if I understand your position, you believe that post-*Allstate v. Hague* there is almost no case that you can fathom that would violate the due process clause.

Neil: You overstate my position somewhat. In *Shutts*, the Supreme Court held that Kansas could not apply Kansas law to oil and gas leases that had no contact whatsoever with Kansas. But short of no contact whatsoever, I think you have stated my position accurately. Let me make it clear that I think that *Allstate* was wrongly decided but, now that it is on the books, I don't see much place for constitutional control of choice of law. If Minnesota can apply its law to a set of facts that all occurred in Wisconsin, then almost everything goes. Indeed, Justice Stevens essentially admitted as much in his concurrence, where he wrote "I question whether a judge's decision to apply the law of his own State could ever be described as wholly irrational." Let me tell you a story. When I was a neophyte law professor, a colleague and I wrote an article about the upcoming *Allstate v. Hague* case in a publication known as *Supreme Court Preview*. Part of our job was to present as neutrally as possible the argument on both sides. We had a devil of a time trying to come up with arguments in favor of Minnesota applying its own law, and we were shocked when the Court upheld the decision of the Minnesota Supreme Court. Later, a different colleague of ours wrote a letter to Justice Powell (who dissented in *Allstate*) expressing his chagrin at the court's decision and told Justice Powell that we had had a hard time coming up with arguments on Minnesota's side. Justice Powell wrote back indicating that he, too, had had a hard time with that task.

Aaron: Maybe you are right. But, think back to the *Cooney* case. You will remember that, in that case, New York applied the law of Missouri to the question of whether a Missouri defendant who had almost no contact with New York could be sued for contribution under New York law when Missouri immunized Missouri employers from contribution suits. Judge Kaye said that there was no constitutional impediment to New York applying its pro-contribution law. I believe that Judge Kaye was wrong and that Cooney is even more far-fetched than *Allstate*. In *Allstate*, the defendant was a national corporation doing lots of auto insurance business in all states including Minnesota. The plaintiff (the decedent, actually) traveled back

and forth daily between Wisconsin and Minnesota. In *Cooney,*
the Missouri defendant did some business in New York but not
related in any way to the machine in question. That the
contribution plaintiff was from New York did not involve the
Missouri defendant whatsoever into New York. *Cooney* is a far
cry from *Allstate.* I find it hard to see how one can apply New
York law to a Missouri defendant who did nothing in New York
vis-a-vis the transaction under consideration.

Neil: I think that you misperceive my position. I'm not saying that
there *should* be no Constitutional limitations on choice of law.
Rather, I am saying that, after *Allstate,* it appears that there
are no limitations. Do you think that the Supreme Court,
without repudiating *Allstate,* would conclude that the
application of New York law in *Cooney* was unconstitutional?
Or do you agree with my observation as to the current state of
the law but don't like it?

B. CHOICE OF LAW IN FEDERAL DIVERSITY CASES

The discussion that follows assumes that you have covered *Erie* and its
progeny in your first year civil procedure course. The question here is
whether *Erie* requires a federal court in a diversity case to apply not only
the substantive law of the state in which it sits but its choice of law rules
as well.

KLAXON CO. v. STENTOR ELECTRIC MFG. CO., INC.
313 U.S. 487 (1941)

MR. JUSTICE REED delivered the opinion of the Court.

The principal question in this case is whether in diversity cases the
federal courts must follow conflict of laws rules prevailing in the states in
which they sit. . . .

In 1918 respondent, a New York corporation, transferred its entire
business to petitioner, a Delaware corporation. Petitioner contracted to use
its best efforts to further the manufacture and sale of certain patented
devices covered by the agreement, and respondent was to have a share of
petitioner's profits. The agreement was executed in New York, the assets
were transferred there, and petitioner began performance there although
later it moved its operations to other states. Respondent was voluntarily
dissolved under New York law in 1919. Ten years later it instituted this
action in the United States District Court for the District of Delaware,

alleging that petitioner had failed to perform its agreement to use its best efforts. Jurisdiction rested on diversity of citizenship. In 1939 respondent recovered a jury verdict of $100,000, upon which judgment was entered. Respondent then moved to correct the judgment by adding interest at the rate of six percent from June 1, 1929, the date the action had been brought. The basis of the motion was the provision in section 480 of the New York Civil Practice Act directing that in contract actions interest be added to the principal sum 'whether theretofore liquidated or unliquidated.' The District Court granted the motion, taking the view that the rights of the parties were governed by New York law and that under New York law the addition of such interest was mandatory. 30 F.Supp. 425, 431. The Circuit Court of Appeals affirmed, and we granted certiorari, limited to the question whether § 480 of the New York Civil Practice Act is applicable to an action in the federal court in Delaware.

The Circuit Court of Appeals was of the view that under New York law the right to interest before verdict under section 480 went to the substance of the obligation, and that proper construction of the contract in suit fixed New York as the place of performance. It then concluded that § 480 was applicable to the case because 'it is clear by what we think is undoubtedly the better view of the law that the rules for ascertaining the measure of damages are not a matter of procedure at all, but are matters of substance which should be settled by reference to the law of the appropriate state according to the type of case being tried in the forum. The measure of damages for breach of a contract is determined by the law of the place of performance; Restatement, Conflict of Laws s 413.' The court referred also to section 418 of the Restatement, which makes interest part of the damages to be determined by the law of the place of performance. Application of the New York statute apparently followed from the court's independent determination of the 'better view' without regard to Delaware law, for no Delaware decision or statute was cited or discussed.

We are of opinion that the prohibition declared in Erie Railroad v. Tompkins, against such independent determinations by the federal courts extends to the field of conflict of laws. The conflict of laws rules to be applied by the federal court in Delaware must conform to those prevailing in Delaware's state courts. Otherwise the accident of diversity of citizenship would constantly disturb equal administration of justice in coordinate state and federal courts sitting side by side. *See* Erie Railroad v. Tompkins, supra, 304 U.S. at 74–77. Any other ruling would do violence to the principle of uniformity within a state upon which the Tompkins decision is based. Whatever lack of uniformity this may produce between federal courts in different states is attributable to our federal system, which leaves to a state, within the limits permitted by the Constitution, the right to pursue local policies diverging from those of its neighbors. It is not for the federal courts to thwart such local policies by enforcing an independent 'general law' of conflict of laws. Subject only to review by this

Court on any federal question that may arise, Delaware is free to determine whether a given matter is to be governed by the law of the forum or some other law. This Court's views are not the decisive factor in determining the applicable conflicts rule. And the proper function of the Delaware federal court is to ascertain what the state law is, not what it ought to be. . . .

Accordingly, the judgment is reversed and the case remanded to the Circuit Court of Appeals for decision in conformity with the law of Delaware.

Reversed and remanded.

———————

Scholars have debated whether *Klaxon* was a wise decision. Some believe that allowing federal courts to develop federal choice of law rules would have led to a more unbiased system since federal courts are in a unique position to balance conflicting interests between states. But, given what you now know about interest analysis, it is likely that the circuit courts would have developed differing choice of law rules. Any hope that the Supreme Court of the United States would have straightened things out by developing an overarching federal choice of law scheme is unrealistic. That *Klaxon* still governs is not in question. *See Day & Zimmerman v. Challoner*, 423 U.S. 3 (1975). For an extensive discussion of the *Klaxon* doctrine *see* Hay, Borchers, and Symeonides, Conflict of Laws §§ 336 et seq. (5th ed. 2010).

There are yet several additional cases that have to be addressed. They arise from transfer of venue under 28 U.S.C. 1404(a). Under *Van Dusen v. Barrack*, 376 U.S. 612 (1964), when a defendant seeks transfer to a federal court in a different state, the law of the transferor jurisdiction governs. An interesting twist to this problem arose in *Ferens v. John Deere Co.*, 494 U.S. 516 (1990), but in this case the plaintiff sought the transfer. Plaintiff was injured in a farm accident in Pennsylvania and filed suit against Deere in Mississippi federal court so that he could take advantage of Mississippi's six-year statute of limitations (the Pennsylvania statute of limitation had already run). Plaintiff then transferred the case to Pennsylvania. Since Mississippi would have applied its longer statute of limitations, the court held that the law of the transferor jurisdiction governed and Pennsylvania now had to apply that law and allow the suit to go forward. The case drew a strong dissent from Justice Scalia. The real culprit in this story is *Sun Oil v. Wortman*, *supra*, which gave free reign to any state that has jurisdiction to apply its longer statute of limitations even if it has no interest in otherwise applying its law to the case.

INDEX

References are to Pages

DÉPEÇAGE
Issue-based choices of law, 178, 265

DIVERSITY JURISDICTION
See Federal Diversity Cases, this index

DOMESTIC RELATIONS
See Family Law, this index

DOMICILE FACTORS
Common domicile, law of, 84
Conceptualism, domiciliary, 71
Guest statute cases, 72
Kinds of domicile, 25, 53
Modern approaches to conflicts, 53
Native allegiance, 28
Traditional approach to domicile
    determinations, 24

DRAM SHOP CASES
Comparative impairment theory, 112
Governmental interest analysis, 104
Public policy factors, 103
True conflicts, 101 et seq.

DUE PROCESS RIGHTS
    Generally, 277
Allstate guidelines
        Generally, 162, 297
        USSC decision, 280
Arbitrary choices of law, 282, 286
First Restatement, 278
Fundamentally unfair choices of law, 282,
    286
Governmental interests, 296
Nexus requirements, 156
Significant contacts, 294
Workers' compensation, 279

EMPLOYEE LIABILITY CASES
    See also Workers' Compensation
        Cases, this index
Conduct-regulating and loss-allocating
    rules distinguished, 197
Traditional approaches to conflicts, 3

ERIE DOCTRINE
        Generally, 298
        See also Federal Diversity Cases, this
            index
Federalism principle, 42
Substance/procedure distinction, 41

ESTATES LAW
        Generally, 241 et seq.
Adoptions, 16, 260
Formal requirements of wills, 242
Issue, adopted child as, 16
Spousal rights, 244
Testamentary trusts, 243, 245
Uniform Probate Code, 242

EXPECTATION OF THE PARTIES
Contract law, 295
Tort law, 69

EXTRA-NATIONAL CONFLICTS
See International Conflicts of Law, this
    index

FAIRNESS
Fundamentally unfair choices of law, due
    process implications, 282, 286
Modern approaches to conflicts, 71
Traditional approaches to conflicts, 46

FALSE CONFLICTS
        Generally, 64 et seq.
Charitable immunity cases, 77
Guest statute cases, 65
Statutes of frauds, 86
True conflicts distinguished
        Generally, 62
        Charitable immunity cases, 86
        Constitutional issues, 293
        Judicial preferences, 75
Unprovided-for cases, 168 et seq.

FAMILY LAW
Estates, spousal rights, 244
Full faith and credit, 253, 267, 271
Interspousal liability, 36
Issue, adopted child as, 16
Modern approaches to conflicts, 253 et seq.
Prenuptial agreements, 20, 248
Status questions underlying disputes, 253

FEDERAL DIVERSITY CASES
Conflict of law rules of forum state, 298
Federal choice of law rules, 300
Statutes of limitation
        Generally, 300
        Borrowing statutes, 184
Venue transfer issues, 300

FEDERALISM
Choice of law rules impacting, 1
Erie Doctrine and, 42
Full Faith and Credit Clause mandate, 42
Implicit consequences of Federal system,
    70
Privileges and Immunities Clause
    mandate, 42

FELLOW SERVANT RULE
Origin and development, 8
Traditional conflict-of-law approaches, 3

FIRST RESTATEMENT
        See also Traditional Approaches to
            Conflicts, this index
Characterization Problems, this index
Criticisms, 51
Due process rights, 278
Legitimacy laws, 276 et seq.
Place of contracting, 15
Place of the wrong, 9
Renvoi, 50
Second Restatement approach compared,
    98

PRIVILEGES AND IMMUNITIES CLAUSE
Federalism principle, 42

PROCEDURAL QUESTIONS
See Substance/Procedure Distinction, this index

PRODUCTS LIABILITY CASES
Contact factors, 140
Governmental interests, 125
Lex loci delicti, 198
Significant relationship test, 140
Statutes of repose, 149
True conflicts, 123 et seq.

PROTECTIONISM
Traditional approaches to conflicts, 44

PROVINCIALISM
Public policy factors as leading to, 98

PUBLIC POLICY
Generally, 45 et seq.
Comity contrasted, 225
Comity conflicts, 44
Comparative fault cases, 95, 98
Conflicting vs similar policies, 200
Dram shop cases, 103
Gambling laws, 45
Guest statute cases, 68
Law selection clause conflicts, 214
Marriage laws, 265, 269
Medical malpractice cases, 43, 115
Provincialism concerns, 98
Purpose, 45
Sources of public policy, 46, 161
Strong public policy, 272
Trust law, 251
Workers' compensation cases, 160

PUNITIVE DAMAGES
True conflicts, 145

REAL CONFLICTS
See True Conflicts, this index

REAL PROPERTY LAW
Contract law and, characterization problems, 23
Estates, 241 et seq.
Intestate succession, 241
Law of the situs, 241
Testamentary succession, 242
Traditional approaches to conflicts, 16
Trusts, 245 et seq.

REASONABLE EXPECTATIONS
Workers' compensation cases, 160

RECIPROCITY STATUTES
Generally, 19

RENVOI
First Restatement, 50
Modern approaches to conflicts, 176

Traditional approaches to conflicts, 39, 49

RESTATEMENTS
First Restatement, this index
Second Restatement, this index

SECOND RESTATEMENT
Generally, 94
See also Modern Approaches to Conflicts, this index
Contacts analysis, 95, 119
Criticisms, 139
First Restatement approach compared, 98
Grouping of contacts analysis, 209
Law selection contract clauses, 218
Marriage laws, 272
Significant relationship test, 92, 125
Usurious contracts, 226

SIGNIFICANT CONTACTS ANALYSIS
Due process rights, 294
Full faith and credit, 294
True conflicts, 90

SIGNIFICANT FACTORS
Adventitious factors distinguished, 73
Table, modern conflicts-of-law approaches, 53

SIGNIFICANT RELATIONSHIPS
Comparative fault, 92
Default rules, 96
Products liability cases, 140
Second Restatement, 92, 125
Spousal immunity cases, 209
Workers' compensation cases, 165

SPOUSAL IMMUNITY CASES
Significant relationships test, 209

STATUTES OF FRAUDS
False conflicts, 86

STATUTES OF LIMITATION
Borrowing statutes, 184
Federal diversity cases, 300
Substance/procedure distinction, 180

STATUTES OF REPOSE
Products liability cases, 149

STATUTORY CONFLICTS SOLUTIONS
Generally, 188
Comity, statutory restrictions, 14
Law selection clauses, statutory approaches, 219
Uniform Commercial Code, 219
Uniform Probate Code, 242

SUBSTANCE/PROCEDURE DISTINCTION
Generally, 39 et seq.
Access to court rules, 41
Erie Doctrine, 41
Law selection clauses, 216